STRATEGIC
FAILURE

How President Obama's Drone Warfare,
Defense Cuts, and Military Amateurism
Have Imperiled America

MARK MOYAR

Threshold Editions
New York   London   Toronto   Sydney   New Delhi

Threshold Editions
A Division of Simon & Schuster, Inc.
1230 Avenue of the Americas
New York, NY 10020

First Threshold Editions hardcover edition June 2015

THRESHOLD EDITIONS and colophon are trademarks of Simon & Schuster, Inc.

For information about special discounts for bulk purchases, please contact Simon & Schuster Special Sales at 1-866-506-1949 or business@simonandschuster.com.

The Simon & Schuster Speakers Bureau can bring authors to your live event. For more information or to book an event, contact the Simon & Schuster Speakers Bureau at 1-866-248-3049 or visit our website at www.simonspeakers.com.

Manufactured in the United States of America

10 9 8 7 6 5 4 3 2 1

Library of Congress Cataloging-in-Publication Data

Moyar, Mark, 1971–
    Strategic failure : how President Obama's military amateurism has imperiled America / Mark Moyar.
        pages cm
    Includes bibliographical references and index.
    1. Obama, Barack—Military leadership.   2. United States—Military policy—Evaluation.   3. United States—Military policy—History—21st century.   4. National security—United States.   5. United States—Defenses.   6. Downsizing of organizations—United States—History—21st century.   7. United States—Armed Forces—Appropriations and expenditures.   8. World politics—21st century.   9. Strategy. I. Title.
    E908.3.M69   2015
    355'.033573—dc23
                                                                                    2014044053
ISBN 978-1-4767-1324-3
ISBN 978-1-4767-1327-4 (ebook)

To the men and women working on behalf
of the U.S. government around the world

CONTENTS

Preface ix

1 A Man of Change 1

2 The Strategy of Team Obama 15

3 The Afghanistan Debate 32

4 Slashing the Budget 48

5 Lightening the Footprints 60

6 Military Footprints Matter 76

7 COIN Can Work 97

8 Half a COIN Doesn't Work 113

9 Hard Power Crosses Borders 127

10 Drones Are Not Enough 154

11 Allies Are Unreliable 174

12 Bigger Is Better 195

13 Not So Smart Power 222

14 Dangerous Nations 247

15 Reclaiming Military Power 271

16 Rallying the Public 287

Epilogue 293

Acknowledgments 317

Notes 319

Index 367

PREFACE

When work began on this book, in the middle of 2012, pundits of all stripes were declaring Barack Obama to be unusually strong on national security. Admirers, of whom Obama still had a great many, hailed the President for obliterating the long-standing perception that Democrats were second best to Republicans when it came to national defense. Given the stagnation of the economy and the unpopularity of Obama's signature health care legislation, the conventional wisdom held that Obama's foreign policy record constituted the greatest single asset of his reelection campaign.

Daniel Klaidman of *Newsweek*, for instance, could be heard opining that two generations had elapsed since "a Democratic president has been as strong on national security as Barack Obama."[1] In an article for the *American Conservative*, Michael Desch credited Obama with "exorcising George McGovern," the presidential nominee whose antiwar platform had saddled Democrats with the "soft-on-defense" label since 1972.[2] George Packer, one of the nation's most distinguished journalists, was predicting that if Obama lost the election, "he'll be remembered most for his foreign-policy achievements," and if Obama were reelected, "he'll have a chance of being a great foreign-policy President."[3]

Aside from the Republican base, most Americans held Obama's national security record in similarly high regard during 2012. Obama's public approval rating on national security hovered near 50 percent throughout the year, with the disapproval rating roughly 10 percentage points lower. Although national security was not the decisive factor in Obama's electoral victory of November 2012—that distinction went to the tearing down of challenger Mitt Romney by Obama and others— these perceptions certainly helped him on election day.

It was my conviction in 2012, as it is now, that the widespread acclaim of Obama's foreign policy was undeserved. During his first term, Obama had been ineffective in promoting U.S. interests abroad, and his actions were increasing the risks to the American people. Consequently, one of this book's initial objectives was to persuade Americans that the glossy veneer on Obama's national security record masked corrosion blisters that were in danger of rusting through.

During the more than two years required to write the book, opinion on Obama and his national security policies experienced a remarkable reversal, comparable in magnitude to the change in opinion on Jimmy Carter during 1979 and 1980. The leading cause was the rusting through of international problems that Obama had created or exacerbated. Most spectacular among the catastrophes were the killing of the U.S. ambassador at Benghazi, the territorial conquests of the Islamic State of Iraq and Syria (ISIS), and the Russian invasion of Ukraine. Democratic congressmen, centrist pundits, and even some of Obama's former cabinet officials started bemoaning the President's weakness in the international arena. The President's approval numbers on national security fell below his disapproval numbers in the middle of 2013, and by the fall, the approval figure had plunged below 35 percent, while the percentage of Americans disapproving approached 55. Among American military personnel, Obama's approval rating fell from its peak of 35 percent to just 15 percent in late 2014, while his disapproval rating reached 55 percent.[4]

Thus did world events conspire to steal some of the book's originally scheduled thunder. Disabusing Americans of an undue admiration for President Obama's policies, however, was never the sole objective of this book. Indeed, my concern was less with any one individual than with policies that were leading the nation and the world toward disaster. Most of what follows should still be of intense interest to Americans, for several reasons.

For one, the innumerable news stories and cable TV debates on the biggest overseas catastrophes have disseminated only snippets of each catastrophic event to the American public. This book fills in the missing sections, and corrects segments of the media-driven narrative that are inaccurate or misleading. It also explains which elements of the story are truly important, and which are unworthy of endless repetition by television's talking heads. The analysis reveals that the flaws in current policies are broader and deeper than most Americans know, and that they reflect misguided assumptions that are not peculiar to Obama but are shared by the leading pretenders to the next Democratic presidential nomination—Obama's vice president, Joe Biden, and his first secretary of state, Hillary Clinton.

For another, the risks that Obama's policies have created go well beyond the few countries that have figured prominently in the news. Every continent in the world has been affected. This book takes the reader from the remote peaks of North Waziristan and the fishing cities of Somalia to the contested waters of the Scarborough Shoal and the drug-smuggling routes of Central America.

Third of all, this book shows that the deterioration of America's strategic position did not commence in Obama's second term, as public opinion polls and political punditry would suggest, but instead began as soon as Obama took office in January 2009. The strategic decline accelerated in 2011, as White House insiders increasingly took charge of national security policy and the defense budget sustained its first big cuts. Some of the poor choices and resultant setbacks were concealed in the first term because of luck, which among other things thwarted several attacks on the U.S. homeland, or because of the time lag between the making of a decision in Washington, D.C., and the playing out of events in the affected countries. Other deficiencies were hidden from view by the inattention of the mainstream media, which had a tendency to avert its eyes from Obama's early failings. The nation's tardiness in perceiving Obama's shortcomings should serve as a cautionary note for all those who would withhold criticism or unflattering information on account of a politician's ideology or identity. Obama's poor performance in his first term should advise voters against paying more heed to a politician's campaign rhetoric than his voting record, and against expecting that someone with no national security experience and no executive experience can handle the demands of the U.S. presidency.

Fourth, this book demonstrates that Obama subordinated U.S. national security to his own political interests with alarming frequency. While it would be naïve to expect elected politicians to wipe all political calculations from their minds when determining policies, the deployment of American troops into war for reasons of political self-interest should no more be condoned than the misuse of public funds for partisan purposes. Americans deserve a president who will not jeopardize the lives of America's sons and daughters in order to pick up a few thousand votes in swing states, and they deserve to be notified when the President commits such an offense.

Finally, the book's last chapter draws upon the lessons of Obama's presidency to identify a better way for U.S. national security in the twenty-first century. It calls for the U.S. government to reassert proactive global leadership, reverse cuts to defense spending, and reinvigorate American public support for the military. The ultimate objective of these changes is not to invade every hostile country or to remake the whole world in America's image, but rather to protect the United States and maintain the international stability upon which its prosperity depends. This positive vision, it is hoped, will be of value in the debate over national security during the presidential campaign of 2016, and in the U.S. decisions on national security strategy and defense spending after 2016.

I

A MAN OF CHANGE

Hand in hand, the President and First Lady strode toward the center of Hradçany Square through a cloud of rapturous applause that overwhelmed the Czech symphony wafting from the loudspeakers. Youth predominated among the crowd, and Americans among the youth, to the dismay of a blogger from the *Economist* who had shown up to ask Czechs their opinions of the new American president. The official cameras had been positioned to capture Prague's medieval castle in the background, adding Old World gravitas to the excitement generated by the New World couple.

Barack and Michelle Obama circled the podium for sixty seconds, their faces beaming with the joy of people who had been in the White House for only a few months. As the First Lady took her seat, the President's mouth opened into a wide grin that revealed two rows of large, gleaming, and perfectly white teeth. With the rectangular gray boards of his trademark teleprompters on his flanks like oversized rearview mirrors, Obama thanked the crowd and launched into the usual pleasantries.

Obama had come to Prague to deliver his first speech on nuclear weapons, a subject that had long been dear to him. During the presidential race against Senator John McCain, Obama had convinced quite a few people of high reputation that he was a foreign policy realist, cognizant that interests and force ruled international affairs. Yet he aimed the opening salvos of his Prague speech at the views of realists, including the view that nuclear weapons had become a permanent fixture on the global landscape, and the view that nuclear deterrence preserved peace. "If we believe that the spread of nuclear weapons is inevitable," Obama said, "then in some way we are admitting to ourselves that the use of nuclear weapons is inevitable."

Peace, Obama continued, could be achieved not through military strength, but through international cooperation on disarmament. "When we fail to pursue peace, then it stays forever beyond our grasp," Obama intoned. "We know the path when we choose fear over hope. To denounce or shrug off a call for cooperation is an easy but also a cowardly thing to do. That's how wars begin. That's where human progress ends."

Peace-minded people needed to come together to drown out the siren songs of those counseling war. "I know that a call to arms can stir the souls of men and women more than a call to lay them down. But that is why the voices for peace and progress must be raised together."

· · ·

Among journalists, bloggers, talk show hosts, and other political junkies, Obama's Prague speech rekindled interest in an article he had written in college, twenty-six years earlier, on student opposition to nuclear weapons and the military. Near the end of his senior year at Columbia, Obama had decided to write about student activism for the campus publication *Sundial.* At the time, left-wing political activists were struggling to stay above water at America's universities, including Ivy League schools like Columbia where they had flourished in years past. The United States was in a conservative mood, having recoiled at the radical excesses of the late 1960s and early 1970s, which had been centered on university campuses. With the end of the draft and the Vietnam War, student organizers had been deprived of issues that could easily rouse the passions of their classmates, whether they be passions of idealism or self-preservation.

In comparison with their predecessors of the late 1960s and early 1970s, the Ivy League students of 1983 were more focused on traditional college activities. They were far more likely to go to class, drink beer, or frolic with members of the opposite sex than to attend political rallies or drive to Washington to picket members of Congress. Among the politically minded, of whom there still existed a considerable number, some had figured out that more could be gained by advancing within the once-despised "system," by getting good grades and good jobs, than by shouting slogans on the sidewalk.

Disconcerting quietude could be found even at Columbia, which had been rattled by some of the fiercest of the protests against the Vietnam War. Fifteen years earlier, student radicals had occupied five university buildings in opposition to a university administration that they considered to be too supportive of the U.S. government and its war in Vietnam. They held on to the buildings for a week, sustaining themselves on fried chicken that their supporters tossed into the windows. It took an army of New York City policemen wielding clubs and tear gas to evict them.

In March 1983, the student body was "tame if not apathetic," in the words of Obama biographer David Maraniss.[1] Obama went to interview campus organizers at Earl Hall, once the bustling nerve center of the 1968 student protests, which was now a sorry shell of its former self, like a California mining town fifteen years after the Gold Rush. The two campus organizations that young Obama was covering in his article, Arms Race Alternatives and Students Against Militarism, were both struggling to attract members beyond the single digits. Rob Kahn, a member of Students Against Militarism whom Obama would quote in his article, remembered thinking at the time, "This is a group of fifteen people that meets once a week and doesn't do much." In his view, the earnest student journalist with the unusual name took the group more seriously than it deserved.[2]

"By organizing and educating the Columbia community," Obama wrote in his *Sundial* article, the campus activists were laying "the foundation for future mobilization against the relentless, often silent spread of militarism in the country." He observed that "by adding their energy and effort in order to enhance the possibility of a decent world, they may help deprive us of a spectacular experience—that of war. But then, there are some things we shouldn't have to live through in order to want to avoid the experience."

Obama's only reservation about the two campus groups was that they did not go far enough. By concentrating on freezing nuclear weapons, the members of Arms Race Alternatives were not tackling the larger problem of the military itself. "The narrow focus of the Freeze movement, as well as academic discussion of first versus second strike capabilities, suit the military-industrial interests, as they continue adding to their billion-dollar erector sets," Obama lamented. One of the leaders of Arms Race Alternatives, Mark Bigelow, told Obama that the "narrow focus" on nuclear arms control reflected a recognition that abolishing the military entirely was excessively ambitious for the time being. "We do focus primarily on catastrophic weapons," Bigelow explained. "Look, we say, here's the worst part, let's work on that. You're not going to get rid of the military in the near future, so let's at least work on this."

As is customary for articles in college publications, Obama's *Sundial* reportage disappeared soon after it was published. It evaded journalists and opposition researchers during the 2008 election, before mysteriously showing up on the Internet in January 2009. As soon as it came to light, Republicans pounced on its contents as evidence of Obama's misguided views on national security. Obama's own aides did not dismiss the article as the high-minded musings of an immature college student, as might have been expected, but instead described the opinions expressed therein as "deeply felt and lasting," according to author James Mann.[3]

It would be the only early marker of Obama's views on war and the military. Although numerous books have been written about Barack Obama already, including Obama's two pre-presidential memoirs, the evidence on his views of the military between 1983 and 2001 is surprisingly thin. Obama chose to keep quiet on the subject, at least outside of conversations with friends and family. For nearly twenty years, Obama wrote nothing about national security and said nothing that was recorded by others.

His resurfacing came in the aftermath of the September 11, 2001, attacks, when he decided to pen an op-ed on the cataclysm in the *Hyde Park Herald*. A small community newspaper, the *Herald* served a few affluent neighborhoods in the otherwise poverty-stricken south side of Chicago, where Obama was then living as an Illinois state senator. For the Obama of 2001, the devastation of 9/11 did not provoke anger at the terrorists, as it did for so many other Americans. The attack was most significant to him because of what it said about global poverty and America's neglect of it. Terrorism, wrote State Senator Obama, "grows from a climate of poverty and ignorance, helplessness and despair." America needed "to devote far more attention to the monumental task of raising the hopes and prospects of embittered children across the globe—children not just in the Middle East, but also in Africa, Asia, Latin America, Eastern Europe, and within our own shores."[4]

Over the course of the next year, Obama's position on terrorism underwent a dramatic shift. When he appeared at an antiwar rally at Chicago's Federal Plaza on October 2, 2002, Obama began by saying, "After September 11, after witnessing the carnage and destruction, the dust and the tears, I supported this administration's pledge to hunt down and root out those who would slaughter innocents in the name of intolerance, and I would willingly take up arms myself to prevent such tragedy from happening again." Speaking against the backdrop of a fifty-three-foot pink flamingo sculpted by Alexander Calder, Obama told the crowd, "I don't oppose all wars. What I am opposed to is a dumb war. What I am opposed to is a rash war. What I am opposed to is the cynical attempt by Richard Perle and Paul Wolfowitz and other armchair, weekend warriors in this administration to shove their own ideological agendas down our throats, irrespective of the costs in lives lost and in hardships borne. What I am opposed to is the attempt by political hacks like Karl Rove to distract us from a rise in the uninsured, a rise in the poverty rate, a drop in the median income, to distract us from corporate scandals and a stock market that has just gone through the worst month since the Great Depression."[5]

Obama never said why he shifted from decrying 9/11 as proof of America's neglect of global poverty to invoking 9/11 as the cause of a personal desire to take up arms against the perpetrators, in accord with the strategy of the George W. Bush administration. One might surmise that his mind was changed by the discovery that the 9/11 hijackers were neither poor nor ignorant, and were instead uncompromising ideologues who could be stopped only by force. Yet other passages in his speech at the Federal Plaza indicate that he had not abandoned his belief that poverty and ignorance accounted for terrorism. "You want a fight, President Bush?" Obama jeered. "Let's fight to make sure our so-called allies in the Middle East, the Saudis and the Egyptians, stop oppressing their own people, and suppressing dissent, and tolerating corruption and inequality, and mismanaging their economies so that their youth grow up without education, without prospects, without hope, the ready recruits of terrorist cells."

The most plausible reason for Obama's change in position between 2001 and 2002 was a political calculation that it would boost his chances of winning a higher office. In the spring of 2002, Obama had begun exploring the possibility of a run for the U.S. Senate in 2004, and in August 2002 he had brought on a high-powered political consultant by the name of David Axelrod. Raised in Manhattan, Axelrod had studied the political craft while on the staff of the *Chicago Tribune* and then had started his consultancy, Axelrod and Associates, in 1985. By 2002, Axelrod's list of successful clients included the mayors of many of America's major cities. As the *Economist* observed, one of Axelrod's specialties was "packaging black candidates for white voters." Axelrod believed that "the candidate is the message," and "the important thing is to tell a positive story about the candidate rather than to muddy the narrative with lots of talk about policy details."[6]

Axelrod presumably explained to his new client that anyone unwilling to offer some tough talk on terrorism would be incapable of obtaining the votes required for national office. The American voting public had no appetite for left-wing theories that blamed American inattention to poverty for suicide airplane attacks that killed thousands of Americans. Supporting America's intervention in Afghanistan would violate some of Obama's long-held principles, but if Obama were unwilling to abandon principles for the sake of gaining votes, he would have to join the countless others whose commitment to principles ensured that they would never win election to high office. As Axelrod must have told

Obama, politicians can employ many rhetorical means to justify a major shift on an issue so that they do not appear to be unprincipled and instead come across even more favorably. The candidate could be said to have displayed open-mindedness by "reconsidering the issue in light of new developments." The candidate would be a "pragmatist who dealt with each situation on its own merits" rather than "employing simplistic, cookie-cutter solutions."

The new Obama messaging strategy on national security would prove to be a winning one. In the coming years, Obama raked in political points with liberals by pointing out that he had opposed the Iraq War when other leading Democrats had backed it, and at the same time he avoided accusations of weakness on national security by espousing support for the American cause in Afghanistan, which was more popular than Iraq since Afghanistan had sheltered the masterminds of the 9/11 attacks. This national security narrative would be critical in Obama's race for the presidency in 2008.

During his first years in the U.S. Senate, Obama devoted little of his time to national security affairs and had little to say about events overseas, which would give political opponents few opportunities later to fault him for taking the wrong position on specific issues. He became chair of the Senate Foreign Relations Subcommittee on European Affairs in early 2007, but by then he was making a run for the White House, which he used as an excuse to neglect the committee work. During his tenure as chair of the subcommittee, he did not hold a single policy hearing, a fact that rival Hillary Clinton would repeatedly point out in the Democratic primary.

With the start of presidential campaigning, though, Obama had no choice but to start talking about national security. In keeping with Axelrod's messaging doctrine, he provided few policy details and instead concentrated on the story of his support for the "good war" in Afghanistan and his opposition to the "dumb war" in Iraq, employing the latter to bash George W. Bush and distinguish himself from Democratic contenders who had voted in favor of the Iraq War. He vowed to send additional U.S. forces to Afghanistan. As both Obama's admirers and detractors agree, Obama's hawkish position on Afghanistan was driven by a desire to show swing voters that he could be tough on national security, not by a strong conviction about the strategic importance of Afghanistan or dissatisfaction with the current U.S. approach in that country.[7]

While Obama's other foreign policy proposals were few in number, they did foretell some of the major changes Obama was to implement. Candidate Obama vowed to take unilateral action against high-level terrorists in Pakistan if the Pakistani government did not act. He promised to double spending on foreign aid for development and governance in order to reduce poverty and "roll back the tide of hopelessness that gives rise to hate."[8]

Although the strategy of repeating his Afghanistan-and-Iraq narrative limited Obama's risk exposure, even so simple a strategy was destined to trip up a candidate whose inexperience left him ill-prepared to address sensitive political and military issues. On February 11, 2007, the day he announced his candidacy for the presidency, Obama went out of his way to slam the Iraq War, which at that time was considered a lost cause by many Democrats. At a campaign rally on the campus of Iowa State University, Obama declared, "We ended up launching a war that should have never been authorized and should have never been waged— and to which we now have spent $400 billion and have seen over 3,000 lives of the bravest young Americans wasted."

Had the media given the remark more attention, Obama's diminution of the sacrifices of American troops might have sunk his campaign before it left the harbor. Fortunately for Obama, however, most of the major news outlets were starstruck by the young senator, and this statement received little coverage. It was a pattern that would recur during the campaign, appalling not only Republicans who watched the press ignore Democratic foibles in every presidential race, but also Democratic front-runner Hillary Clinton and her husband, Bill.

Still, the reference to the "wasting" of 3,000 lives forced the Obama campaign team into damage-control mode, not where it wanted to be on the first day of the race. During an interview with the *Des Moines Register*, Obama recanted. "Their sacrifices are never wasted; that was sort of a slip of the tongue as I was speaking," he said. "What I meant to say was those sacrifices have not been honored by the same attention to strategy, diplomacy and honesty on the part of civilian leadership."[9]

It would be but the first of a series of incidents in which candidate Obama's words or deeds offended the men and women in uniform. Sheer ignorance accounted at least partially for the gaffes. As someone who knew almost nothing about the military or war, Obama had a tendency to say things that did not appear especially awful to individuals of his social background and ideological persuasion, but that came across as grossly insulting to members of the armed forces.

At an August 2007 campaign appearance in New Hampshire, Obama sparked outrage within the military in the course of vowing to get tougher in Afghanistan. "We've got to get the job done there," he said, "and that requires us to have enough troops so that we're not just air-raiding villages and killing civilians, which is causing enormous pressure over there."[10] While many U.S. military personnel agreed on the need for more troops in Afghanistan, they took umbrage at the insinuation that the American forces in Afghanistan were simply firing into villages recklessly and killing civilians. With U.S. assets on the ground and in the air collecting information on what the military called the "human terrain," the U.S. military in Afghanistan went to considerable lengths to distinguish combatants from civilians. U.S. forces adhered to stringent regulations on the use of firepower, often putting the safety of Americans at risk for the benefit of the safety of Afghan civilians.

In July 2008, Obama's cancellation of a visit to injured troops at the U.S. military hospital in Landstuhl, Germany, fed suspicions that he viewed the military with disdain. In response to an outcry from veterans and Republican candidate John McCain, the Obama campaign offered competing explanations for the cancellation. Campaign strategist Robert Gibbs first asserted that Obama had "decided out of respect for these servicemen and women that it would be inappropriate to make a stop to visit troops at a U.S. military facility as part of a trip funded by the campaign." Gibbs subsequently said that the campaign had been swayed by military officials who had objected to the visit on the grounds that it would violate campaign rules.[11] Military officials, however, told the press that they had not recommended canceling the visit, and had been making preparations to receive the senator when they received notice that he would not be coming. According to their accounts, Obama's staff had canceled the visit after being informed that Obama "could only bring two or three of his Senate staff members, no campaign officials or workers" and "could not bring any media" with him except military photographers, because of rules prohibiting the use of military installations as campaign backdrops.[12]

Obama then sought to defuse the controversy by saying that when he was told he could not bring along retired Air Force Major General Scott Gration, a campaign volunteer, it "triggered then a concern that maybe our visit was going to be perceived as political, and the last thing that I want to do is have injured soldiers and the staff at these wonderful institutions having to sort through whether this is political or not or get caught in the crossfire between campaigns."[13] Skeptics wondered how a visitation of wounded American troops without campaign workers or media could have been construed as partisan politics, particularly given that military officers had explained what he could do to make sure the visit was not considered a campaign event. Jeff Zeleny of the *New York Times,* one of the few media figures to call Obama's explanation into question, chided the Obama campaign for failing to answer this simple question: "Why didn't Obama leave his aides behind, even the retired general, and make the visit by himself?"[14]

Further evidence of Obama's aversion to interaction with the military during the campaign would emerge later in a book by reporter Michael Hastings. As recounted in the book, Hastings had been favorably disposed toward Obama early in the race, but disillusionment began to set in during the summer of 2008, when he learned that Obama had consciously avoided spending time with the troops during a visit to Iraq. After giving a talk at the U.S. embassy, Obama bristled when asked to take pictures with soldiers and embassy staffers. "He didn't want to take pictures with any more soldiers; he was complaining about it," a State Department official told Hastings. "Look, I was excited to meet him.

I wanted to like him. Let's just say the scales fell from my eyes after I did. These are people over here who've been fighting the war, or working every day for the war effort, and he didn't want to take fucking pictures with them?"[15]

It may have been that Obama avoided spending time with the troops simply because he was an introvert with little appetite for small talk. In future years, his disinclination to socialize even with friends and supporters would irritate many within the White House and in Congress. Nevertheless, these episodes furthered a growing perception that Obama held the military in low esteem, if not contempt.

During the Democratic primary, Obama faced little criticism for his positions on national security or his slights of the military. Hillary Clinton agreed with most of his national security platform except for the rapid withdrawal from Iraq, and she was not going to talk much about that subject because Obama's position on Iraq was more popular with Democratic voters than hers. Nor was she in a position to bring up the question of contempt for the military, since she had been accused of turning a cold shoulder to military personnel during her time as First Lady. She concentrated her fire on Obama's inexperience in foreign policy and his complete lack of leadership experience.

The former First Lady would go so far as to liken Obama to the man whom their mutual party had vilified more than any other figure in recent memory, President George W. Bush. "We've seen the tragic result of having a president who had neither the experience nor the wisdom to manage our foreign policy and safeguard our national security," Clinton told students at George Washington University on February 25, 2008. "We cannot let that happen again. America has already taken that chance one time too many."[16]

Obama responded to these barbs with barbs of his own about how Clinton herself lacked the experience to be commander in chief. He derided Clinton's claim that eight years in the White House as First Lady had given her valuable national security experience, and he contrasted the supposed luxuriousness of that position with his hardscrabble travel abroad. Whereas he had profited from "understanding the lives of the people like my grandmother who lives in a tiny hut in Africa," Obama said, Clinton could boast only of "what world leaders I went and talked to in the ambassador's house I had tea with." Clinton backers assailed that remark with blog posts such as "Obama Turns to Sexism in Final Push," and "Never mind that this woman has been serving this country for years, has traveled around the world giving speeches and impact-ing the lives of women, including in China, you know, going to places Barack has only read about in books."[17]

Obama adviser Greg Craig, a high-powered defense lawyer who had represented the likes of John Hinckley, Ted Kennedy, and Kofi Annan, conducted a point-by-point demolition of Hillary Clinton's national security resume as if she were a key prosecution witness. "There is no reason to believe," Craig asserted, "that she was a key player in foreign policy at any time during the Clinton Administration. She did not sit in on National Security Council meetings. She did not have a security clearance. She did not attend meetings in the Situation Room. She did not manage any part of the national security bureaucracy, nor did she have her own national security staff. She did not do any heavy-lifting with foreign governments, whether they were friendly or not. She never managed a foreign policy crisis, and there is no evidence to suggest that she participated in the decision-making that occurred in connection with any such crisis."[18]

National security would play only a minor role in Obama's contest with Arizona senator John McCain in the general election of 2008. The financial crisis of the fall of 2008 drowned out national security, to such an extent that the one presidential debate that had been reserved for national security ended up covering both the economy and national se-curity. In that debate, held at the University of Mississippi, Obama went on the attack against McCain for supporting the Iraq War.

"Six years ago, I stood up and opposed this war at a time when it was politically risky to do so because I said that not only did we not know how much it was going to cost, what our exit strategy might be, how it would affect our relationships around the world, and whether our intelli-gence was sound, but also because we hadn't finished the job in Afghanistan," Obama said. "We've spent over $600 billion so far, soon to be $1 trillion. We have lost over 4,000 lives. We have seen 30,000 wounded, and most importantly, from a strategic national security perspective, al Qaeda is resurgent, stronger now than at any time since 2001." As president, Obama said, he would remove all U.S. troops from Iraq within sixteen months.

McCain parried, "The next president of the United States is not going to have to address the issue as to whether we went into Iraq or not. The next president of the United States is going to have to decide how we leave, when we leave, and what we leave behind. That's the decision of the next president of the United States." The senator from Arizona noted that Obama had opposed the Iraq troop surge of 2007 on the grounds that it would fail, but recently had been forced to concede that it had succeeded spectacularly in quelling the violence. McCain also pointed out that top U.S. military leaders believed that a rapid withdrawal from Iraq of the sort Obama envisioned could cause the recent gains to crumble, imperiling the United States once more.

On Afghanistan, there was considerably less disagreement between the two candidates. "We have seen Afghanistan worsen, deteriorate," Obama said. "We need more troops there. We need more resources there." He vowed to send two to three additional American brigades to Afghanistan. McCain concurred on the need for additional forces for Afghanistan, though he said that Obama did not understand how they needed to be used.

McCain waited until the end of the debate to hammer Obama on his lack of experience. "There are some advantages to experience, and knowledge, and judgment," said McCain, a Vietnam War hero with decades of national security experience. "I honestly don't believe that Senator Obama has the knowledge or experience and has made the wrong judgments in a number of areas." McCain cited Obama's opposition to the Iraq surge, as well as his reluctance to criticize Russia for its invasion of Georgia earlier in the year.

With the debate clock winding down, Obama had one more turn. Rather than avail himself of the opportunity to counter McCain's remarks about experience, Obama talked vaguely about improving America's global image through spending on education. "Part of what we need to do," he said, "what the next president has to do—and this is part of our judgment, this is part of how we're going to keep America safe—is to send a message to the world that we are going to invest in issues like education, we are going to invest in issues that relate to how ordinary people are able to live out their dreams. And that is something that I'm going to be committed to as president of the United States."

According to post-debate surveys, viewers thought that Obama came across better on the economy, while McCain outperformed Obama on Iraq.[19] With the economy tanking, those perceptions boded ill for McCain. Nor did it help that the incumbent Republican president, George W. Bush, had become very unpopular, or that the media made a concerted effort to tear down McCain's vice presidential candidate, Sarah Palin.

When the votes were tallied on the evening of November 4, Obama came out the clear victor, with 52.9 percent of the popular vote and 365 of 538 electoral votes.

2

THE STRATEGY OF TEAM OBAMA

Very few presidents have demonstrated equal interest in foreign affairs and domestic affairs. For presidents like John Adams, John F. Kennedy, Richard Nixon, and George H. W. Bush, foreign policy was an overriding passion that consumed most of their time and political capital. For Woodrow Wilson, Lyndon Johnson, Jimmy Carter, and Bill Clinton, domestic affairs took precedence. Domestically oriented presidents have most often viewed foreign policy as a nuisance that must be kept from interfering with the domestic agenda. They have not portrayed wars and other national security crises as momentous struggles that must be won in their own right, because of the risk of concentrating the nation's attention abroad at the expense of change at home.

Obama very much fit into the group for whom international affairs was a secondary priority. When he took office on January 20, 2009, all of his principal objectives lay in the domestic sphere. He wanted to expand health care coverage and enlarge welfare programs. He intended to pour money into public works programs and other job-creating activities, for the purpose of combating soaring unemployment. With large banks and auto companies on the verge of collapse, Obama believed that the federal government had to step in and bail them out. He sought to increase governmental protections for minorities, women, gays, and illegal immigrants. To pay for it all, he would boost taxes on the rich. The Democrats had majorities in both houses of Congress, and might well not have majorities after the midterm congressional elections, so Obama had a two-year window into which he intended to cram his domestic legislative agenda.

Robert Gates, who had served as secretary of defense for the last two years of the George W. Bush presidency and would stay in that job for the first two and a half years of Obama's, observed a marked contrast between the two men in their interest in national security. George W. Bush had been "passionate about the war in Iraq," Gates observed. At military ceremonies, Bush's eyes would sometimes well up. Not so with Obama. "I worked for Obama longer than Bush, and I never saw his eyes well up," Gates recounted. "The only military matter, apart from leaks, about which I ever sensed a deep passion on his part was 'Don't Ask, Don't Tell.' For him, changing that law seemed to be the inevitable next step in the civil rights movement."[1]

Obama's lack of passion was evident in his unwillingness to deliver pep talks on the war in Afghanistan, a war to which he had chosen to send tens of thousands of additional American soldiers. He was like a football coach whose team was tied at halftime but chose not to join his team in the locker room to look them in the eye and talk about what had to be done in the second half.

"When soldiers put their lives on the line, they need to know that the commander in chief who sent them in harm's way believes in their mission," Gates remarked. "They need him to talk often to them and to the country, not just to express gratitude for their service and sacrifice but also to explain and affirm why that sacrifice is necessary, why their fight is noble, why their cause is just, and why they must prevail. President Obama never did that."[2]

While Obama did not want to say much about national security as president, he had no choice but to devote some time and effort to the war in Afghanistan and a host of other global troubles. He no longer could succeed merely by telling the story of his opposition to Iraq and his support for Afghanistan, or by criticizing George W. Bush's decisions. Now the decisions were his, and if he refrained from making decisions, then other countries would make the decisions for him, and the Republicans would flay him.

Both fans and critics of Obama's national security policies as president have sought to identify a set of principles, a grand strategy, or an "Obama doctrine" that guided his decisions. One of the principles most often cited as foundational to the administration's policies was "smart power." As defined by Harvard professor Joseph S. Nye Jr., "smart power" was the combination of coercive "hard power," such as military force and law enforcement, with persuasive "soft power," such as diplomacy, development aid, and trade. The administration officials who relentlessly touted "smart power" contended that the Bush administration had relied too much on the "hard power" of the military, which in their view had alienated most of the world's countries. Obama, they asserted, would rely much more than Bush on "soft power" solutions, which would mend relations with other countries and elicit their cooperation in multilateral enterprises.

The idea of combining hard and soft power was far less novel than the use of the term "smart power" suggested. Every leader of every nation has employed both types of power. The term was aimed more at praising liberals and denigrating the alleged heavy-handedness of the Bush administration than anything else. As James Mann noted, the purveyors of "smart power" liked to bandy the term about because it "conveyed well their conviction that the Bush Republicans had been dumb."[3] But smart power advocates did have a real impact on Obama's thinking, by encouraging him to rely less on hard power and more on soft power than George W. Bush and most other American presidents.

Less straightforward in their impact on Obama were the two foundational philosophies of international relations: realism and idealism. Some observers have asserted that President Obama is a realist, focused on American interests with little concern for the internal affairs of other states. Others have depicted him as an idealist, committed to supporting democracy and human rights around the world. Still others have maintained that he is committed to both realism and idealism, or that he has shifted from one to the other over time.

Obama has proven reluctant to articulate and implement realism or idealism with any consistency. At times, he has intervened in countries to promote democracy, while at others he has refrained from intervening. He has used force to prevent human rights atrocities in some countries but not in others. He has been willing to violate the sovereignty of certain nations in order to eliminate terrorists, but has stayed out of other nations where terrorists lurk.

Some have sought to explain these inconsistencies by asserting that Obama has been guided by "pragmatism," addressing foreign policy challenges based solely on the practical considerations of a situation. Thus, he supports democratization of a specific country if it is feasible and will benefit the United States and other countries. Obama's defenders have contended that this pragmatism has prevented the adoption of a "one-size-fits-all" approach, which would be ill-suited to a diverse world. Detractors have contended that Obama's pragmatism has sent mixed messages to other countries and resulted in violation of core American values. It has, they say, discouraged adoption of a coherent strategy that serves as the basis for proactive measures, and has led instead to a reactive foreign policy that enables aggressive enemies to take the first punches and dodge the belated counterpunches.

The modern U.S. presidents with the best records in national security—the two Roosevelts, Eisenhower, Nixon, and Reagan—studied history and took a long-term view of national security strategy. They understood that the United States, as a world power, could not always pick its enemies, nor could it always anticipate them. They understood that American military strength usually bolstered America's international influence and encouraged other nations to help it, while military weakness invariably undermined America's influence and caused other nations to shy away from it. They knew how to flex military muscle and deliver stern speeches to keep wars from happening, and recognized that they would need to use force on some occasions to protect the nation's interests and maintain its credibility. They had the depth of understanding of other countries to know which ones would, for reasons of interests, culture, or leadership, make the best allies.

They invested in military capabilities to prepare for an uncertain future and to deter potential enemies, having seen that the nations that disarmed in pursuit of peace often encouraged enemies to violate that peace. Theodore Roosevelt, Eisenhower, and Reagan were able to maintain high levels of military spending at times of relative peace and with no imminent threats on the horizon. In each case, their investment paid dividends for future presidents. Theodore Roosevelt's shipbuilding produced not only ships but also shipbuilding expertise and seafaring experience that would make the U.S. Navy a formidable naval power by the time of its monumental test in World War II. Eisenhower's massive investments in the Air Force paid off during Vietnam, when B-52 bombers wreaked havoc on the North Vietnamese Army and precision-guided munitions single-handedly demolished bridges in Hanoi that untold numbers of unguided bombs had missed. The funding that Reagan gave the military for computers, fiber-optic cables, satellites, and stealth aircraft in the 1980s would make possible the stunning U.S. victory in the Gulf War of 1991, when U.S. forces defeated the world's fourth-largest army in one hundred hours of ground combat and at a cost of just 147 American fatalities.

Presidents with less impressive national security report cards thought that the United States could stay out of war if it so desired. Those who presided over the ends of wars shrank the military as soon as the war ceased in the belief that no future wars would come, as in the case of Woodrow Wilson after World War I, Harry Truman after World War II, Jimmy Carter after Vietnam, and Bill Clinton after the Cold War. They believed that America could maintain a position of global leadership with less military power, by convincing others to disarm and by making better use of diplomacy, trade, and other forms of nonmilitary power. They scoffed at those who doubted predictions of permanent peace, and waited until the wolves were already nipping at Uncle Sam's heels before readying the nation for war.

In Wilson's case, the projected peace evaporated in two decades and was followed by the nastiest war in world history. After that war, Truman's peace lasted a mere five years, with the United States caught off guard and ill-prepared for a war on the Korean Peninsula. Carter's attempt to perpetuate peace through American retrenchment spurred Soviet expansionism in the third world and a global loss of confidence in the United States, culminating in the humiliating seizure of the U.S. embassy in the hitherto-friendly Iran. Clinton's gutting of the military left the nation ill-prepared for the wars in Afghanistan and Iraq.

The tendency to forsake a proactive strategy in favor of a foreign policy of ad hoc reaction is exacerbated when the president views foreign policy mainly as something that needs to be kept off the front page of the newspapers, as has been the case with most of the domestically focused presidents, including Obama. From day one of Obama's presidency, the administration was divided between political operatives whose primary concern was Obama's political popularity and policy wonks who wanted the government to focus on sound policies. Rahm Emanuel, Obama's first White House chief of staff, referred to the two groups as "Tammany Hall" and "the Aspen Institute." Tammany Hall, named after the nineteenth-century political machine that controlled New York City through patronage and graft, wanted Obama to abandon campaign promises on national security that had been popular with the Democratic base but were unpopular with the general electorate, such as trying terrorists in civilian courts and releasing sensitive information about CIA counterterrorism programs.[4] The Aspen Institute, which took its name from a posh retreat in the Rocky Mountains where international elites exchanged ideas, wanted Obama to stick to those promises and, more generally, to take actions most beneficial to the American people and the world.

The first person Obama selected for his new administration, namely his vice presidential candidate, had been a member of Tammany Hall since Obama was in elementary school. Joe Biden won his first political race in 1969, and in 1973 was elected to the U.S. Senate, where he would spend the next thirty-six years. Now in his mid-sixties, with decades of service on the Senate Foreign Relations Committee under his belt, Biden had the gray hair and foreign policy experience to compensate for Obama's youth and inexperience.

Biden was hewn from the same ideological oak as Obama, but in terms of temperament they could not have been more different. Whereas Obama liked to be alone with his thoughts or his reading materials, Biden preferred to mingle with the crowds, glad-handing with constituents or fellow politicians. Obama chose his words carefully and used them sparingly, like an artist who is keenly aware that every brush-stroke counts, while Biden was prone to gaffes and had a penchant for interminable monologues that left the listeners in no doubt as to the high opinion in which he held his own intellect. In the Senate, Biden's self-righteous grandstanding during public hearings had caused even his own political allies to look forlornly at their watches and wish that he would spend more time receiving and processing information prior to entering transmission mode.

Joe Biden organized his first presidential campaign in 1987. Trouble began when the staff of rival Michael Dukakis debunked Biden's claims to be the descendant of coal miners and the first person from his family to attend college. Those details, the press was informed, had been stolen from the biography of British Labor Party leader Neil Kinnock. Biden's own family tree contained no coal miners, and it did contain college graduates. Then it came out that Biden had lifted speech material from Robert Kennedy and Hubert Humphrey, and that in law school he had received an F in a course for plagiarizing five pages in a fifteen-page term paper. With his poll numbers in free fall, Biden withdrew from the race.[5]

Biden chose to test the presidential waters again in 2007. Competing with Obama and Hillary Clinton for the Democratic nomination, he spoiled his own chances with a string of ill-considered remarks. "In Delaware, the largest growth in population is Indian-Americans moving from India," he said on one occasion. "You cannot go to a 7-Eleven or a Dunkin' Donuts unless you have a slight Indian accent. I'm not joking." Further on in the campaign, he said of Obama, "I mean, you got the first mainstream African-American who is articulate and bright and clean and a nice-looking guy. I mean, that's a storybook, man." Such statements would undoubtedly have spelled political death for a Republican, as had befallen Dan Quayle and Sarah Palin following lesser gaffes. It was a measure of the media's double standard that Biden came through with his political heart still beating.

Biden never posed a serious threat to Obama or Clinton, dropping out of the race on January 3, 2008, after receiving less than 1 percent of the vote in the Iowa caucus. He reemerged on the scene in August, when Obama picked him as the vice presidential nominee based on his experience and national security credentials. If Obama had counted on the seriousness of the nomination to serve as a restraining influence on Biden's mouth, he was to be sorely mistaken.

During a fund-raising event in Seattle, Biden committed his most egregious oratorical blunder, one that would become a hallmark of Republican attack ads. "Mark my words, it will not be six months before the world tests Barack Obama like they did John Kennedy," Biden said ominously. "Watch, we're gonna have an international crisis, a generated crisis, to test the mettle of this guy. . . . I've forgotten more about foreign policy than most of my colleagues know, so I'm not being falsely humble with you. I think I can be value added, but this guy has it. This guy has it. But he's gonna need your help. Because I promise you, you all are gonna be sitting here a year from now going, 'Oh my God, why are they there in the polls? Why is the polling so down? Why is this thing so tough?'"

Obama was not a man who angered easily—his calm demeanor often drew comparisons with *Star Trek*'s Mr. Spock—but Biden's assertions at the Seattle fund-raiser pushed him over the edge. According to people who were with Obama when he heard the recording, he turned as angry as anyone had ever seen him. "How many times is Biden gonna say something stupid!" he exclaimed in a conference call with Biden's chief of staff, Patty Solis Doyle. Obama told her that Biden "can't be doing this," and then called Biden to lecture him coldly on the necessity of avoiding self-defeating statements.[6]

Upon becoming vice president, Biden would see himself as the protector of the new president, especially on matters pertaining to national security. Biden perceived that Obama, as a young liberal Democrat with no military experience and little knowledge of national security affairs, was ill-equipped to assert control over the military or discern whether national security professionals were manipulating him. Obama's unfamiliarity with national security also convinced Biden that Obama needed his expert advice on a continual basis.

The individuals whom Obama selected for the plum jobs within the national security apparatus—secretary of state, secretary of defense, and national security advisor—fell mainly into the Aspen Institute category. For secretary of state, he chose Hillary Clinton, who still had her own political ambitions but because of her position would have to subordinate them to sound policy. For Obama, Clinton made an appealing choice as secretary of state because her selection would please her dispirited supporters in the Democratic Party, who constituted a large section of the party, and because it would take her out of the Senate, where she could act as an independent power player.

On the day Obama announced Clinton's nomination as secretary of state, Peter Baker of the *New York Times* questioned him on the wisdom of appointing someone whose qualifications he and his campaign team had mocked just a few months earlier. "Going back to the campaign," Baker said, "you belittled her travels around the word, equating it to having teas with foreign leaders. And your new White House counsel said that her resume was grossly exaggerated when it came to foreign policy. I'm wondering whether you can talk about the evolution of your views of her credentials since the spring."

Obama replied, "Well, I mean, I think—this is fun for the press to try to stir up whatever quotes were generated during the course of the campaign. No, I understand. And you're having fun. And there's nothing wrong with that. I'm not faulting it. But, look, I think if you look at the statements that Hillary Clinton and I have made outside of the heat of a campaign, we share a view that America has to be safe and secure. And in order to do that we have to combine military power with strength and diplomacy. And we have to build and forge stronger alliances around the world so that we're not carrying the burdens and these challenges by ourselves."[7]

Clinton, like Obama, had been well to the left of the American center on national security during her college years, in the sixties in her case, but then had shifted toward the middle as she strove for national office. She supported the invasion of Iraq in 2003, as Obama had relentlessly pointed out to liberal voters during the Democratic primary. By 2007, though, she had come out fiercely against the war, and was using it as a cudgel for beating the Bush administration as most other Democrats were then doing. When General David Petraeus and Ambassador Ryan Crocker briefed Congress in September 2007 on the U.S. troop "surge" in Iraq, Clinton lectured them, "You have been made the de facto spokesmen for what many of us believe to be a failed policy. Despite what I view as your rather extraordinary efforts in your testimony both yesterday and today, I think that the reports that you provide to us really require a willing suspension of disbelief." She added that "any fair reading of the advantages and disadvantages accruing post-surge, in my view, end up on the downside."[8]

For the position of secretary of defense, Obama chose Robert Gates, the only member of the Bush cabinet whom Obama retained. Gates had gained the respect of Obama and other Democrats with his low-key style, which they found a refreshing change from the overbearing, autocratic style of his predecessor, Donald Rumsfeld. Obama told aides that continuity would be helpful with Iraq and Afghanistan, especially as troops were being withdrawn from Iraq. Keeping Gates also demonstrated a commitment to bipartisanship, something that Obama had promised to deliver during the election.

For national security adviser, Obama selected James L. Jones, a retired four-star general who had served as commandant of the Marine Corps and Supreme Allied Commander Europe. The selection helped show the administration's respect for the military, which would score political points with the public and ease the concerns within the U.S. armed forces over Obama's attitudes toward the military. Obama barely knew Jones. In fact, Jones was surprised that Obama would give this critical job to someone whom he knew so little.[9]

Since the creation of the position in 1955, the national security adviser had been a central figure in national security policy, chairing meetings of the National Security Council and directing the NSC staff. Past holders of the office had included some of the biggest names in the history of U.S. national security—McGeorge Bundy, Henry Kissinger, Brent Scowcroft, Zbigniew Brzezinski, Colin Powell, and Condoleezza Rice. Jones expected to wield the same expansive powers as his forerunners. He quickly found, however, that the President had stripped away much of his authority and handed it to other individuals, who were all too eager to push Jones to the margins.

One of those individuals was Rahm Emanuel, a former congressman and a leading Tammany Hall figure. Profane, clever, and vindictive, Emanuel had littered his political path with the carcasses of those who had crossed him or let him down. In one of the most famous stories from his early career, he had mailed a dead fish to a pollster who had failed his team. At a fund-raising event, Obama had once roasted Emanuel by remarking, "Very few people know Rahm studied ballet for years. In fact, he was the first to adapt Machiavelli's *The Prince* for dance. It was an intriguing piece. As you can imagine, there were a lot of kicks below the waist."

Emanuel was prepared to pursue Obama's political interests with the same unsentimental ruthlessness with which he had pursued his own. He did not have foreign policy expertise, and he would often sit in uncharacteristic silence at meetings on national security matters. But he gave counsel when it counted, and arranged the President's schedule in ways that privileged the people whose views aligned with his own. One administration official told a reporter, "If you were to ask me who the real national security adviser is, I would say there were three or four, of whom Rahm is one and of which General Jones is probably the least important."[10]

During the assembly of Obama's national security team, Emanuel gave Jones strong encouragement to select Tom Donilon as deputy national security adviser. A veteran of the Carter administration and Walter Mondale's 1984 presidential campaign, Donilon had latched on to Joe Biden in the middle of the 1980s, working on his 1988 presidential campaign until the plagiarism revelations torpedoed it. Donilon then worked at the prestigious Washington law firm O'Melveny & Myers, before becoming the chief lobbyist for Fannie Mae in 1999. Over a six-year stint at the mortgage giant, he raked in huge sums, though the scandals that subsequently rocked Fannie Mae would tarnish Donilon to such an extent that Obama would avoid nominating him for administration positions that required Senate confirmation.[11] Jones met Donilon and liked him, so he agreed to take Donilon as his deputy. It was a decision he would soon come to regret.

Donilon behaved in a manner that would have earned him a pink slip in previous administrations. He routinely bypassed his immediate superior in the bureaucratic chain of command, Jones, in discussing national security policies directly with Obama and White House chief of staff Rahm Emanuel. When Jones was away visiting foreign capitals, as he often was, Donilon made decisions on national security matters without consulting him.[12] Donilon was able to get away with it all because he enjoyed the protection of Vice President Biden and Obama himself.

As an indication of Donilon's influence inside the White House, and of Obama's preference for the Tammany Hall crowd over the Aspen Institute, Donilon was the only person from the national security realm who attended the 7:30 A.M. meeting of administration VIPs that was held in Emanuel's office each morning. The other attendees were all top Tammany Hall operatives as well, including David Axelrod, Valerie Jarrett, Pete Rouse, and Robert Gibbs.[13]

Obama also put two of his most trusted foreign policy aides from the campaign, Denis McDonough and Mark Lippert, into the National Security Council. He included them and another of his favorites from the campaign, Ben Rhodes, in his inner circle on foreign policy, while keeping Jones, Clinton, and Gates outside the circle. Before and after meetings with his cabinet advisers, Obama met with McDonough, Lippert, and Rhodes, and he often made final decisions while conferring with them.

The oldest and most influential of this triumvirate was McDonough, a thirty-nine-year-old career congressional staffer. McDonough served as one of the unofficial national security advisers who wielded power at the expense of Jones. Top officials were soon saying, "If you get a request from Jim Jones, he might or might not be speaking for the president. If you get a request from Denis McDonough, he's asking on behalf of the president himself."[14]

Lippert, a thirty-five-year-old naval reservist, had also spent most of his career as a congressional staff member. In the first summer of the Obama administration, Jones concluded that Lippert was behind a series of press stories that cast Jones as ineffectual and lethargic. He went to Emanuel and demanded that Lippert leave.

"You'll have to talk to the president," Emanuel said. "This is his guy." Jones went to Obama. Two months later, Obama announced that Lippert would be leaving to return to the Navy.[15] Later, after the furor had subsided, Obama quietly appointed Lippert to a high post at the Pentagon, the sort of position normally held by someone of much greater seniority and expertise.

Rhodes, just thirty-one years of age, had joined the Obama campaign in 2007 and had vaulted to stardom as a speechwriter. During the Obama presidency, he continued to write speeches, but went far beyond the role of the typical speechwriter, and not just by serving as a member of Obama's inner circle on national security. Rhodes helped script meetings of national security officials to ensure that Obama appeared organized and in command of the issues. He also crafted written accounts of those meetings to make Obama appear especially insightful and decisive, accounts that showed up in news stories and books. According to Bob Woodward, who received more of these accounts than any other author, Rhodes took notes of the President's comments and then reorganized and embellished them to give them additional "clarity and purpose."[16]

For Jones, accustomed to a military culture that respected rank and protocol, Obama's direct dealings with Donilon, McDonough, Lippert, and others who reported to Jones were maddening. They demeaned people like him who had spent decades of hard service accumulating experience and knowledge. The circumvention of normal lines of authority also disrupted the processes by which policy decisions were made, creating an atmosphere of disorder that Obama, a novice at organizational management and decision making, was often unable to tame.

Daniel Klaidman, one of the journalists most sympathetic to Obama, noted that on tough issues, "Obama often took the path of least resistance, opting for passivity. He bobbed and weaved among his own advisers, endlessly adjusted tactics, and played for time in the ever-diminishing hope that the politics might eventually turn his way." Klaidman also noted that Obama's "elusiveness created confusion about who was in control of policy, what strategy should be pursued, and ultimately, what Obama really wanted or believed. In this vacuum his advisers fought brutally, each side invoking the president in support of its cause."[17]

Most troubling for the Aspen Institute figures within the administration was that Obama often paid less heed to policy advice from the ostensible captains of the national security team—Gates, Jones, and Clinton—than to the political advice frrom Emanuel, Donilon, McDonough, Lippert, Rhodes, and other Tammany Hall members. Some of the acrimony was personal. No one in a senior position likes to see their subordinates hold more power than they do. The pill was especially bitter for Hillary Clinton, as it reinforced suspicions among her loyalists that Obama was intent on marginalizing her. Tina Brown, founder of the *Daily Beast*, would pronounce in July 2009, "It's time for Barack Obama to let Hillary Clinton take off her burqa."

Much more of the ill will stemmed from the subordination of policy to politics. While the Obama administration was hardly the first to politicize national security policy, it committed more flagrant fouls than most, if not all, of its predecessors. From the beginning, the Tammany Hall operatives treated the presidency like a reelection campaign, assessing every national security decision based on its impact on Obama's poll numbers and domestic agenda. Jones referred to the Tammany Hall members of Obama's national security team as "the water bugs," the "Politburo," the "Mafia," and the "campaign set." He recounted that "the water bugs did not understand war or foreign relations" and "were too interested in measuring the short-term political impact of the president's decisions in these areas." When Jones invited them to expert briefings on strategic and policy questions, they usually failed to show up.[18]

Other administration veterans have described the White House in much the same terms. "The president's habit of funneling major foreign policy decisions through a small cabal of relatively inexperienced advisers whose turf was strictly politics was truly disturbing," remarked Vali Nasr, who served as a senior official in the State Department from 2009 to 2011. "The primary concern of these advisers was how any action in Afghanistan or the Middle East would play on the nightly news, or which talking point it would give the Republicans in the relentless war they were waging against the president."[19]

General David Petraeus, the commander of U.S. Central Command when Obama took office, recounted that the White House tried to get him to espouse the Tammany Hall view of the world when speaking to the press. He recoiled at the recommendations he received from David Axelrod prior to appearances on the Sunday morning talk shows, finding them "unsophisticated and political." Petraeus told one aide that Axelrod was "a complete spin doctor."[20]

Another prominent and troubling feature of Obama's politicized national security aides were their disdain for the military leadership. Few of the Tammany Hallers had ever served in the armed forces, and most hailed from elite liberal circles that had a reflexive distrust of the military. Obama, unlike Bill and Hillary Clinton, did not openly demonstrate disrespect for the military establishment while in the White House, and he publicly professed admiration for the armed forces. But he himself never warmed to the military leadership. Rosa Brooks, a Georgetown University law professor whom Obama appointed to a Defense Department position in 2009, found that Obama made little effort to work with the generals. She recounted one general telling her that "the White House preferred the military to be seen but not heard."[21] Obama did not even pay attention to the commanding general in Afghanistan, his one major war. General Stanley McChrystal, who held that position early in Obama's presidency, revealed in September 2009 that Obama had spoken with him only once in the last seventy days.[22]

Suspicions of the military within the White House received reinforcement in the administration's early months from one of the most potent weapons in Washington—a book. Titled *Lessons in Disaster: McGeorge Bundy and the Path to the War in Vietnam*, the book had just been published in November 2008. It had started off as a joint effort between Gordon M. Goldstein, a scholar and former United Nations adviser, and McGeorge Bundy, who had served as Lyndon Johnson's national security adviser during the fateful decisions of 1964 and 1965 that plunged U.S. forces into the Vietnam War. Bundy had died before the book could be completed, so Goldstein had finished it on his own, but it still reflected the biases of Bundy, who, like former secretary of defense Robert S. McNamara and other leading civilian officials of the day, had sought to shift blame for Vietnam from the civilian leadership to the military.

Tom Donilon was one of the first to read Goldstein's book. He was so excited that he told everyone else in the White House to get their hands on the book. Many did, including Obama. Donilon, Obama, and others were particularly struck by Goldstein's assertion that Lyndon Johnson was the victim of erroneous predictions and misguided resource requests from the military. According to Goldstein's account, General William Westmoreland, the top U.S. commander in Vietnam in 1965, believed that the enemy would quickly succumb if subjected to greater military pressure. This confidence allegedly encouraged Johnson to enter the war and consent to an attrition strategy that produced a prolonged, bloody stalemate in the face of unexpectedly persistent enemy resistance.

Unbeknownst to the White House officials who would apply this argument to present-day affairs, Goldstein's book was highly deficient as a history. Westmoreland had not actually given the president a rose-colored vision of the war, but instead had warned that a war would be long and costly, at least so long as it was confined to South Vietnam. Johnson's generals had recommended intensified bombing of North Vietnam and insertion of U.S. ground forces into Laos to cut the Ho Chi Minh Trail in order to avoid protracted bloodletting, but civilian leaders had rejected those options based on doubts about their strategic risks and returns. Postwar disclosures from North Vietnamese sources would prove those doubts to have been unwarranted; North Vietnamese leaders believed that the actions recommended by the U.S. military would indeed have crippled North Vietnam.

In other words, the problem in 1965 was that the civilian leadership had paid too little heed to the military, not too much. The lesson the White House should have drawn from this historical episode was that civilian leaders would do well to listen closely to military experts before making decisions. It was an especially important lesson for administrations short on expertise in national security affairs, such as those of Lyndon Johnson and Barack Obama.

The misreading of the lessons of Vietnam was to poison relations between civil and military leaders throughout Obama's presidency. It would also taint Obama's handling of the most pressing national security problem facing him at the start of his first term, the war in Afghanistan.

3

THE AFGHANISTAN DEBATE

In its first year, the Obama administration engaged in protracted debates on Afghanistan that would do much to shape the U.S. national security policies of the next eight years. It is much too early to produce a definitive history of these events, as critical information about wartime decisions invariably remains hidden from view for decades afterward. Nevertheless, enough information has come to light to illuminate fundamental issues and key decisions. Partisans have sought to shape perceptions of these events from the beginning and to exploit them to justify new actions, so rather than surrender the field by avoiding the subject until decades in the future, it is preferable to examine the available evidence now and draw conclusions from it.

As Obama's own admirers have acknowledged, the new president resolved to intensify the war in Afghanistan without understanding much about either the country or the conflict. "Obama had come into office knowing little about the situation on the ground in Afghanistan," recounted Jonathan Alter, one of Obama's most admiring biographers. In the spring of 2009, Alter observed, Obama "stumbled into a large commitment without fully realizing what he was getting into."[1]

Although Obama and his inner circle knew next to nothing about the counterinsurgency (COIN) warfare that the United States was waging in Afghanistan, there were others in the administration who understood it well. Gates had presided over the defeat of Iraq's insurgents in 2007 and 2008, and the general who had orchestrated that effort,

General David Petraeus, now held the position of commander of U.S. Central Command. Petraeus and Gates, however, were problematic for the new administration from the start. Petraeus, especially, had become a public celebrity as a result of his successes in Iraq and his careful cultivation of the media. White House aides suspected that Petraeus had political ambitions of his own. Gates was also suspect among many of Obama's appointees because he had originally been selected by their bête noire, George W. Bush.

The new administration also received an infusion of counterinsurgency expertise from the Center for a New American Security, a think tank replete with well-known counterinsurgency thinkers like John Nagl, David Kilcullen, and Nathaniel Fick. The new undersecretary of defense for policy, Michèle Flournoy, had founded the think tank in 2008 along with Kurt Campbell as a means of preparing national security leaders for a Democratic administration. Flournoy and Campbell, both veterans of the Clinton administration who had been too young to take sides on the Vietnam War as it unfolded, belonged to a wing of the Democratic Party that rejected the knee-jerk opposition to the military of the party's baby boom elites. They wanted to restore the centrist internationalism that had prevailed in the Democratic Party prior to the presidential nomination of George McGovern in 1972.

Nagl, Kilcullen, and other so-called COINdinistas provided intellectual respectability to COIN by emphasizing the nonmilitary aspects of counterinsurgency and the importance of obtaining popular support. The COINdinistas had helped write the 2006 Army Marine Corps Counterinsurgency Field Manual, and they had convinced the media and the public that the "population-centric" counterinsurgency doctrine in the manual had led to victory in Iraq. The same doctrine could save the day in Afghanistan, they said. Nagl and Kilcullen had mastered the art of the television and radio interview, and were able to make COIN sound appealing even to liberal NPR listeners. Flournoy and the COINdinistas from her think tank would help convince Obama and his national security team to engage in a full-fledged counterinsurgency in Afghanistan.

Three days into Obama's presidency, at the new administration's

first National Security Council meeting on Afghanistan, Petraeus informed Obama that the United States needed more troops to achieve
the U.S. objective of keeping Afghanistan from reverting to a terrorist
sanctuary. He endorsed a request from General David McKiernan, the
top U.S. commander in Afghanistan, to deploy 30,000 additional troops.
U.S. military raids and drone-fired missiles had proven insufficient at
thwarting Al Qaeda and its Afghan allies, Petraeus explained. What was
required was a counterinsurgency approach, similar in its fundamentals
to what Petraeus had executed in Iraq. It would involve securing the
population with American ground forces, bolstering the Afghan national
security forces, and inducing the Afghan government to provide services
to the citizenry.

Vice President Joe Biden interjected that they needed to agree on
a new strategy before sending more troops. They had to think through
their strategic goals.[2] Although he was not one to read weighty books
or policy studies on counterinsurgency, Biden believed that he knew
enough to question whether counterinsurgency was the right approach
in Afghanistan. And he was convinced that he personally was obliged
to prevent the military's counterinsurgency gurus from steamrolling the
novice president with their expert knowledge. A few days later, Biden
told reporters accompanying him to the Munich Security Conference
that he was not going to let the military "bully" the administration into
sending more troops to Afghanistan with "artificial timelines."[3]

Obama decided to authorize the deployment of additional troops
to Afghanistan as Petraeus had recommended. The number would be
adjusted downward to 17,000 troops, after the Pentagon's math was determined to have been in error. In line with his desire to keep the war
out of the public eye, Obama gave no speech or press conference to announce the decision. The White House limited its dissemination of the
news to a four-paragraph written statement, released by the office of the
press secretary.[4]

At the same time, Obama heeded Biden's recommendation to re-
think U.S. strategy. He ordered a strategic review of Afghanistan and
Pakistan, to be led by Bruce Riedel, a South Asia expert who had spent

thirty years in the CIA. Riedel had earned Obama's trust during the campaign, when he had led the Obama campaign's South Asia team. Obama gave Riedel until the middle of March to complete his review.

Riedel and his team met with U.S. officials, military commanders, legislators, and think tank analysts, and hosted delegations from Afghanistan and Pakistan. They reviewed the latest intelligence, which indicated that Al Qaeda was even more dangerous than Riedel had thought during the campaign, when he had told Obama that Al Qaeda was as dangerous now as on September 10, 2001. Al Qaeda was recruiting Pakistanis who had emigrated to Europe and held European passports that would enable them to slip through American screening.

The review team described Pakistan as an unstable bomb that could explode at any moment. If terrorists based in Pakistan attacked the United States, the President would be faced with the decision of bombing major terrorist training sites inside Pakistan, which could further destabilize the country. If the Pakistani government teetered, an extremist government could take power, or a war with India could break out, in which nuclear weapons might be used.

Riedel concluded that firing missiles from drone aircraft at terrorists in Pakistan, a practice that had begun in earnest in 2008, could cause real harm to Al Qaeda but would not solve the problem of Al Qaeda because the missiles could not take out the core leadership. While most of the core leadership was believed to be located in Pakistan, it was protected by Afghan and Pakistani extremist groups that the Pakistani government refused to eliminate. Riedel likened the drone program to the killing of bees one at a time—you could kill plenty of bees, but you would not eliminate the bee problem since the hive continues to produce new ones. In addition, Riedel pointed out, the drone strikes were not a reliable strategic weapon because they required the assistance of intelligence collectors on the ground in Pakistan, who would have to cease operations overnight if Pakistan's government had a change of heart about the drones.

The only viable strategy, Riedel contended, was to change Pakistan's strategy, so that the Pakistanis would voluntarily stop condoning and abetting terrorists. That outcome could not be fully achieved in two years,

Riedel cautioned. It might take two decades, or might not be possible at all. Nevertheless, it had to be attempted. Riedel recommended greater U.S. assistance to Pakistan and concerted efforts to ramp up counterinsurgency in both Afghanistan and Pakistan as the best means of changing Pakistan's strategic outlook.[5]

The top members of Obama's national security team held several meetings in March to discuss Riedel's findings. All concurred in Riedel's recommendations except for Vice President Biden. "Just let me take two minutes here," Biden said in a meeting on March 12. "I only have a couple of things to say, and this'll only take me a minute or two." Over the next twenty-one minutes, the Vice President delivered a rambling explanation of his objections to Riedel's plan. If the Afghan government was weak, he contended, then sending more troops would be ineffective and irresponsible. Given that the main objective was defeating Al Qaeda, whose personnel were concentrated in Pakistan and not in Afghanistan, why did they need to send large numbers of troops to do nation building in Afghanistan? Biden advocated what he called "counterterrorism plus," which would maintain a "light footprint" in Afghanistan in order to use drones and small teams of special operations forces to attack Al Qaeda along the border between Afghanistan and Pakistan.[6]

Gates believed that Biden's strategic alternative was "ridiculous."[7] He and the generals contended that without a large counterinsurgency spearheaded by U.S. troops, the United States could not collect the intelligence necessary to pinpoint the terrorists in Afghanistan or Pakistan. They noted that Biden's approach had already been tried in Afghanistan, between 2002 and 2008, and that its failure had led to the current predicament. While the United States had been conducting precision strikes against extremist leaders, the Taliban had multiplied sixfold in strength and captured large areas of the Afghan countryside.

Obama decided to reject Biden's advice and adopt the Riedel strategy. He also decided to authorize deployment of another 4,000 U.S. troops for training purposes based on a recommendation from the military, but deferred decision on a further 10,000 requested by McKiernan until after the August elections in Afghanistan.

Obama announced the new strategy in a speech on March 27. "Multiple intelligence estimates have warned that al Qaeda is actively planning attacks on the United States homeland from its safe haven in Pakistan," Obama intoned. "And if the Afghan government falls to the Taliban—or allows al Qaeda to go unchallenged—that country will again be a base for terrorists who want to kill as many of our people as they possibly can." Obama also provided an idealist rationale, remarking, "For the Afghan people, a return to Taliban rule would condemn their country to brutal governance, international isolation, a paralyzed economy, and the denial of basic human rights to the Afghan people—especially women and girls." He said he was sending more U.S. military forces and increasing the U.S. civilian effort in Afghanistan in order to "disrupt, dismantle and defeat al Qaeda in Pakistan and Afghanistan, and to prevent their return to either country in the future."[8]

On the advice of Gates and Chairman of the Joint Chiefs of Staff Admiral Mike Mullen, Obama selected a new general to take command in Afghanistan. Gates and Mullen had concluded that General McKiernan did not have the personality or the political acumen to command in such a complex environment. To take McKiernan's spot, they decided on General Stanley McChrystal, the director of the Pentagon's Joint Staff.

The son of a two-star general, Stanley McChrystal had graduated from West Point in 1976. In 2003, he assumed command of the Joint Special Operations Command, home to the most elite of America's special operations forces. Deploying forward to oversee special operations forces in Iraq, he created the most efficient and effective counterterrorism program ever conceived. Within the Department of Defense, his name came to symbolize a new way of shadow warfare.

Within days of arriving on the ground in Afghanistan, McChrystal came to the conclusion that the country was in graver peril than he had been led to believe from reading official reports and news accounts in Washington. He proposed to Gates that he conduct a detailed review of the situation, which would spell out the challenges along with the strategy and resources required to overcome them. Gates thought it a good idea, and conveyed the proposal to Obama and Biden at a meeting in the White House.

"Whoa. Whoa. Whoa," Biden declared, nearly jumping from his chair when Gates brought up McChrystal's proposal. The Vice President said he had to tell them an old Senate story from the 1970s. As a freshman senator in his thirties, Biden recounted, he had gone to Senator John McClellan of Arkansas in an effort to obtain a position on a Senate subcommittee.

"Mr. Chairman, should I send you a letter?" Biden had asked.

McClellan pulled out a cigar and told Biden, "A bit of adviiiiice. Nevuh send a chairman a lettuh he doesn't want to receive."

McChrystal's report, Biden continued, would be the letter they didn't want to receive. The timing would be poor because it would come before the Afghan elections. In Biden's view, the proposed report was part of a plot by the generals to pressure Obama into sending more troops to Afghanistan.[9]

Obama objected to Gates that Congress would not support sending more troops. Both he and Biden said that congressional Democrats, who at the time held both the House and the Senate, were averse to further troop commitments. Gates kept his cool but later expressed disgust at this overriding preoccupation with domestic politics.[10]

In the end, Obama agreed to McChrystal's recommendation to conduct a strategic review, but took steps to discourage McChrystal from making a case for more troops. National Security Advisor Jim Jones paid a visit to McChrystal in Afghanistan and made clear that the President would not be pleased to hear requests for additional troops. The military had been given its chance to weigh in during the Riedel review, Jones said, and the situation had changed little since that time. McChrystal replied that he was finding the situation to be much worse than Washington officials thought. Rates of violence were rising sharply and the number of Taliban was higher than previously believed, as high as 25,000.[11]

McChrystal pulled together an eclectic team, replete with think tank analysts as well as military personnel, to produce the report. The team found that security was deteriorating in the countryside, and as a consequence popular support for the government was sinking. Afghan forces were largely ineffectual, and coalition forces were too small to fill the security gaps. "Because we had a small footprint, we couldn't provide security," McChrystal said later.[12]

In its sixty-six-page report, completed in September, McChrystal's review team concluded that the international coalition needed to shift to a counterinsurgency strategy that put more emphasis on securing the population and improving governance. McChrystal recommended an increase in U.S. troop strength of 40,000 in order to execute this strategy. He laid out options for fewer troops, but said that with substantially fewer troops the United States would fail.

In a separate paper, McChrystal explained why he thought precision counterterrorist strikes alone would not work and why counterinsurgency with conventional forces was required. Counterinsurgency was indispensable, McChrystal argued, because it offered the only way to wipe out the enemy in a place like Afghanistan. The local government needed to provide that security in the long run, which required large numbers of foreign forces to train them and provide security in the interim.[13] Petraeus chimed in to support McChrystal's position, noting that the United States had killed top insurgent leaders in Iraq in 2006 on a colossal scale and yet the situation had continued to get worse.[14] McChrystal's strategy and troop recommendation also received endorsements from Secretary of Defense Gates and Chairman of the Joint Chiefs Mullen.

Vice President Biden, however, remained unimpressed. In September, Biden expanded upon his "counterterrorism plus" strategy and championed it as an alternative to McChrystal's strategy, with some like-minded officials in the White House providing echoes of support. Rather than sending additional U.S. troops to Afghanistan and dispersing them among the populous areas as McChrystal was advocating, the "counterterrorism plus" strategy concentrated U.S. forces at two large counterterrorism bases, at Bagram and Kandahar. U.S. special operations forces would fly from these bases, like eagles from their nests, to strike

Al Qaeda wherever it reared its head. The United States would obtain
the necessary targeting data by maintaining human intelligence networks in Afghanistan and supporting Afghan forces.[15] Gates was "both
astounded and amused" that Biden and his staff thought they were better
qualified than McChrystal, the nation's leading counterterrorism practitioner, to formulate counterterrorism strategy.[16]

Biden also challenged the view that defeating the Taliban was necessary because they were closely tied to Al Qaeda. "They're actually very
distinct," Biden said. "We're assuming that if al Qaeda comes back into
Afghanistan, where it wasn't, it would be welcomed by the Taliban. Is
that a correct assumption? We have no basis for concluding that."[17] In
fact, however, most of the CIA's counterterrorism experts were convinced that Al Qaeda was closely intertwined with the Afghan Taliban
and other insurgent groups, including the Haqqani Network and the
Pakistani Taliban.

On September 18, someone photocopied McChrystal's sixty-six-
page report and handed it to Bob Woodward. White House officials
accused the office of the Joint Chiefs of Staff of leaking the document,
and asserted that the leak was intended to "box the president into the
policy that McChrystal had recommended."[18]

Its professions of outrage notwithstanding, the White House secretly welcomed the prospect of a public row with the military. In the
view of Obama and his inner circle, the President could allay public
concerns about his suitability for national leadership by firmly asserting
control over the military, like a young cowboy wrestling his first steer to
the ground at the country fair. Since the beginning of the year, Biden
and Obama's political inner circle had vigorously pursued a campaign
to show that Obama would keep a tight rein on the generals and crack
the whip when they wanted to be more aggressive than he preferred.
Rejecting their advice for major escalation in Afghanistan in favor of
more modest escalation would be an excellent way to show that he had
the steer by the horns. Obama said plainly to Gates in October that
"my poll numbers will be stronger if I take issue with the military over
Afghanistan policy."[19]

What became problematic for the White House's strategy was the willingness of military leaders to diverge from the script. The White House had expected the struggle to play out in the major newspapers, where the administration's leading civilian figures had more friends and influence than the military. The military leadership trampled those expectations by speaking publicly in favor of intensive counterinsurgency in Afghanistan, which ratcheted up public and congressional pressure on the President to accept McChrystal's troop recommendations.

On September 16, Obama summoned Mullen and Gates to complain about recent public comments by senior military officials in support of McChrystal's counterinsurgency strategy. "Is it a lack of respect for me?" Obama asked. "Are they trying to box me in?" Obama mentioned the possibility that perhaps the generals did not like the decision process, but then he returned to questions about more sinister motives. "Are they suspicious of my politics? Do they resent that I never served in the military? Do they think because I'm young that I don't see what they're doing?"

Gates and Mullen assured the President that the military had not meant to disrespect him and was not plotting to box him in. Gates told Obama privately that McChrystal was inexperienced in dealing with the press and politics, and that Mullen and Petraeus felt "ethically compelled to say exactly what they thought" when speaking to Congress or the press. In his book, Gates recounted, "My assurances fell pretty much on deaf ears, which I found enormously frustrating and discouraging."[20]

As the White House was mulling over McChrystal's report, Biden found a general who was willing to help him flesh out "counterterrorism plus," General James E. "Hoss" Cartwright. A four-star general who held the position of vice chairman of the Joint Chiefs of Staff, Cartwright had risen through the Marine Corps by nontraditional means. In a service that glorified the infantry, he was an aviator, and one who had spent most of his Marine Corps time in support jobs, not the coveted warfighting commands. Perhaps his most distinctive characteristic was his eagerness to please his political bosses without regard for the views or prerogatives of his fellow military officers.

"I'm not a military guy," Biden said to Cartwright. "Here's how I would approach this strategically, but we need a military plan." He wanted a detailed analysis, with numbers. "We'll provide that," responded Cartwright.

Cartwright put together a plan that assigned the mission of hunting the enemy to two Special Forces brigades, with 10,000 troops. They would be hunters, Cartwright explained, rather than sitting ducks as regular infantry were in counterinsurgency. "We can sort of use their tactics against them," Cartwright said. Another 10,000 troops would go as trainers for Afghanistan's forces.[21]

Cartwright did not share his plan with other members of the senior military leadership prior to presenting it to the White House. His military colleagues were flabbergasted and appalled when they learned that he had been working behind their backs. To make matters worse, his plan was amateurish and unrealistic. As a career aviator, Cartwright had no experience in counterinsurgency or counterterrorism, yet he was offering alternatives to the plans of the nation's top counterinsurgency and counterterrorism commanders.

Petraeus shredded Cartwright's plan at a meeting of the national security principals. "You start going out tromping around, disrupting the enemy, and you're making a lot of enemies," he said of the counterterrorism operations. "Because all you're doing is moving through, trying to kill or capture bad guys who will fade into the woodwork, and then you leave. And so what have you accomplished?" Petraeus pointed out that they could not make two entire brigades into precision-strike forces, as precision strikes required enormous amounts of air, intelligence, and other support assets. Only a company of a few hundred soldiers could be used for counterterrorism operations at one time.[22]

Gates told Obama that "counterterrorism plus" was just a rehash of the failed strategy of years past. He said that McChrystal's troop strategy was not tantamount to nation building or "fully resourced counterinsurgency," presumably to allay Obama's concerns that he was getting in too deep. Rather than trying to develop a strong and capable central Afghan government, said Gates, McChrystal would use the additional

U.S. forces to stabilize Afghanistan and buy time to develop the Afghan security forces and a few key Afghan ministries. Gates added that while he supported McChrystal's request for 40,000 U.S. troops, he thought Obama could get by with only 30,000.[23] They could try to get the other NATO countries to cough up the remainder.

Cutting 10,000 American troops from McChrystal's request would save a lot of money, a factor that was very much on Obama's mind at this time. Obama had earlier criticized the Bush administration for failing to provide enough resources for Afghanistan and had promised to apply all necessary resources, but now that he saw the price tag, he was having second thoughts. On October 26, Obama held up a two-page memo written by budget director Peter Orszag, which said that McChrystal's recommended strategy would cost $889 billion over the next ten years. "This is not what I'm looking for," Obama said. "I'm not doing 10 years. I'm not doing a long-term nation-building effort. I'm not spending a trillion dollars." Spending so much on Afghanistan, he said, would unduly weaken domestic programs.[24]

In the end, Obama decided that he would send 30,000 U.S. troops and ask NATO countries to provide 10,000 more. To further reduce the costs of his troop surge, he shortened its duration, from the five years recommended by the military to eighteen months. He also halved the time at which the U.S. troop levels would go below the current level of 68,000, from six years to three years. He intended to stick to those timetables no matter what.

"This needs to be a plan about how we're going to hand it off and get out of Afghanistan," he told a group of his senior advisers. "Everything that we're doing has to be focused on how we're going to get to the point where we can reduce our footprint. It's in our national security interest. There cannot be any wiggle room."[25]

According to Jonathan Alter's sympathetic account, Obama had more than just budgetary reasons for wishing to shorten the surge. It was no coincidence, Alter wrote, that the eighteen-month time frame meant that surge troops would begin withdrawing in 2011. That time frame would ensure that by the middle of the 2012 reelection campaign

Obama could point out to voters that U.S. involvement in Afghanistan was winding down.[26] In addition, Alter recounted, Obama believed that a shorter surge would enable him to "turn the tables on the military, to box them in after they had spent most of the year boxing him in." If the situation in Afghanistan stabilized after an abbreviated surge, then he could start bringing the troops home while claiming success. If the situation were not stabilized, then it "would undermine the Pentagon's belief in the effectiveness of a hundred thousand troops."[27] Either way, he would come out looking smarter than the military.

Obama apparently did not consider the possibility that Afghanistan would stabilize but would still need a prolonged presence, which was what the military had predicted and what actually happened. Or perhaps he considered that possibility but was not worried about bringing troops home prematurely because the damage to U.S. interests would not come until after his reelection.

Another journalist-author who usually gave Obama the benefit of the doubt, David Sanger, asserted that Obama did not think that the surge was a good idea when he authorized the additional 30,000 troops, but decided to go along with it in order to "fulfill his campaign promise to focus on the Afghan War." An unnamed Obama adviser expressed it more forcefully. "I think he hated the idea [of the troop surge] from the beginning," the adviser said. "The military was 'all in,' as they say, and Obama wasn't."[28]

Obama informed Petraeus, Gates, and Mullen that he wanted them to get behind the 30,000 troop figure and the shortened deployment timelines, and if they did not, then he would send only 10,000 troops. That was not much of a choice, so the top brass agreed to Obama's conditions. Obama then went to the extraordinary measure of insisting on a six-page "term sheet" to which all of the top national security officials would have to agree. It was not unusual for a president to ask subordinates to support a controversial policy, but insisting that they swear fealty to six pages of text was unheard-of. The term sheet asserted that the U.S. government would pursue an approach in Afghanistan that was "not fully resourced counterinsurgency or nation building, but a narrower approach tied more tightly to the core goal of disrupting, dismantling and eventually defeating al Qaeda and preventing al Qaeda's return to safe haven in Afghanistan or Pakistan." Obama had decided that this language would help prevent his generals from dragging the United States into an endless quagmire.[29]

Donilon thought that the term sheet was "a historic document and model for presidential decision making." He believed that it corrected the mistakes of Vietnam and Iraq, when presidents had allegedly failed to provide useful instructions to the military.[30] Yet the term sheet was more confusing than it was precise. While it claimed that the strategy was not counterinsurgency or nation building, its description of U.S. civil and military operations in Afghanistan sounded precisely like counterinsurgency and nation building. The document called upon the military to wrest control of population centers and lines of communication from the Taliban, disrupt and degrade the enemy, enlarge the Afghan security forces, build the capacity of the Afghan government, and combat corruption. It did not prohibit anything that one would normally associate with counterinsurgency and nation building.

The one key respect in which Obama's new Afghanistan strategy differed from most nation-building and counterinsurgency efforts was its compressed timeline. Nation building usually requires decades, since it is dependent on the slow process of developing new pools of human capital. Counterinsurgency, like all forms of war, is a contest in which the enemy and chance play enormous roles, and for that reason there can be little certainty about how soon objectives can be achieved. Generals and statesmen routinely underestimate how long wars can take, which is one reason why governments have often embarked willingly on wars that turned out to be extremely long and costly.

Obama also viewed his decision as historic. He had, he believed, changed the manner in which the civilian and military leadership did business. "For the past eight years, whatever the military asked for, they got," Obama said in an interview. He was presumably unaware that George W. Bush had gone against the recommendations of the top military leadership on two of the most critical decisions of his presidency—

in 2003 he had authorized many fewer troops for the invasion of Iraq than the generals had wanted, and in 2007 he had sent a troop surge to Iraq that the generals opposed.

Obama continued, "I had the time to work through all these issues and ask a bunch of tough questions and force people to sharpen their pencils until we arrived at the best possible solution." He described the process of the review: "first the policymakers developed a strategy, then they assessed the resources necessary to implement the strategy, and finally they discussed how to get out."[31]

Gates had a far less positive view. At the end of the deliberations, he wrote in a note to himself, "I'm really disgusted with this process, I'm tired of politics overriding the national interest, the White House staff outweighing the national security team, and NSS ([Tom] Donilon and [Douglas] Lute) micromanagement." Gates later stated, "I felt this major national security debate had been driven more by the White House staff and by domestic politics than any other in my entire experience."[32] Gates, it should be remembered, had served in senior positions under eight presidents since 1974.

On December 1, Obama announced the decision in a speech at West Point. "I am convinced that our security is at stake in Afghanistan and Pakistan," Obama told a sea of clean-shaven cadets, who sat attentively in their gray dress coats. "This is the epicenter of violent extremism practiced by al Qaeda." He noted that the Taliban and Al Qaeda were working together, and that in recent months the United States had apprehended extremists who had come to the United States from the border region of Afghanistan and Pakistan to kill Americans. Consequently, Obama asserted, "I have determined that it is in our vital national interest to send an additional 30,000 U.S. troops to Afghanistan." The surge troops would begin to return home after eighteen months, in July 2011. Obama added that the troop withdrawals would take into account the "conditions on the ground," a phrase that Gates had persuaded him to include.[33]

Obama's speech pleased few Americans. Liberals were upset that he was sending more troops. Conservatives and some moderates attacked him for not defining victory or even mentioning it, and denounced the eighteen-month limit on the surge, noting that it might be too short and that it would encourage the enemy to wait the United States out. Harvard professor David Gergen, a veteran of both Republican and Democratic administrations who had previously praised Obama in the most glowing of terms, faulted Obama for sending the message that "the cavalry is coming, but not for long."[34]

On the day after the speech, the Senate Armed Services Committee grilled Gates and Clinton about the President's new Afghanistan strategy, with special emphasis on the July 2011 marker. When questioned about that date, Clinton said, "I do not believe we have locked ourselves into leaving."[35] Later in the day, Gates told the House Committee on Foreign Affairs, "I have adamantly opposed deadlines. I opposed them in Iraq, and I oppose deadlines in Afghanistan." In Afghanistan, he said, "This will be a gradual process."[36] In the wake of these imprecise responses, White House Press Secretary Robert Gibbs felt compelled to issue a statement saying that the President had determined that troops would definitely begin coming home in July 2011. That date was "etched in stone," Gibbs said, and he even had the chisel.[37]

The outcome of the Afghanistan debate of 2009 did indeed etch America's Afghanistan policy in stone for the next several years. The results in Afghanistan would be tragic. In terms of broader U.S. national security strategy, the Obama administration's deliberations were important not only because they yielded a strategy, but also because they delineated light-footprint counterterrorism as a strategic alternative. The military experts had convinced Obama to adopt a counterinsurgency strategy, although Obama did not want to call it counterinsurgency and he set timelines that the military opposed. They had exposed fundamental flaws in light-footprint counterterrorism. But it was only the first year of what would become an eight-year presidency. While the battle lines had been drawn, most of the battles were yet to come, and they would eventually move beyond Afghanistan to encompass the entire world.

4

SLASHING THE BUDGET

While the costs of the Afghanistan troop surge played a significant role in the policy debate of 2009, the overall size of the defense budget was not a high priority for the Obama administration during its first year. Fulfilling the campaign promise to expand the war in Afghanistan precluded the sweeping cuts that many of Obama's Democratic allies in Congress would have preferred. Nevertheless, the White House did undertake some early and sizable cuts to the defense budget, concentrated on new technologies that had little to do with Afghanistan but much to do with future preparedness.

Over the course of 2009, the Obama administration canceled, delayed, or reduced more than fifty major acquisition programs, with a total lifetime value of over $300 billion. Those programs included a combat search-and-rescue helicopter; the F-22 fifth-generation fighter; the Army's future combat vehicle program; the multiple-kill vehicle for missile defense; an airborne laser aircraft; and the Navy's next-generation cruiser.[1] Some of the canceled programs had fallen far behind schedule or run way over budget, and some were not especially valuable. Nevertheless, cuts of that magnitude hit a number of programs that would have undoubtedly enhanced U.S. capabilities in the future.

The continuation of wartime defense spending was accompanied by huge increases in domestic spending, the result of Obama's new domestic initiatives, as well as sagging tax revenues, the result of an economic recession. Hence U.S. budget deficits went through the roof in 2009 and

2010. Those deficits fueled the rise of the so-called Tea Party movement, a loose-knit political conglomeration that united around the issue of reducing governmental spending. Exploiting the Internet and talk radio, the Tea Party mobilized a large constituency in preparation for the 2010 congressional elections. They backed numerous candidates who embraced their platform of thrift, almost all of them Republicans.

The Tea Party's fervor paid significant dividends when voters went to the ballot box in November 2010. Republicans took the majority in the House of Representatives from the Democrats, and narrowed the Democratic majority in the Senate to 51–47. Obama and the Democratic Party would no longer be able to ram through large spending bills and other legislation without compromises that attracted Republican support.

While many of the Republican congressmen who benefited from the Tea Party vote were traditional Republicans with a preference for a strong national defense, the Tea Party also brought into office a different breed of Republicans, with pronounced libertarian and isolationist tendencies. Libertarianism caused them to view defense spending with as much suspicion as other forms of governmental spending. Isolationism led them to doubt the need for the levels of defense spending required of an active superpower. For these reasons, Tea Party favorites would soon prove willing to join with doves from the Democratic Party in supporting drastic cuts to defense spending.

In recognition that the 2010 elections reflected a shifting of the political winds, President Obama began searching for ways to cut the deficit. From his perspective, the defense budget was the obvious place to seek the most savings. Democrats had opposed high levels of defense spending since the Vietnam War, and Obama was less concerned than before about demonstrating seriousness on national security, now that he had made his point by sending more troops to Afghanistan. Entitlement programs and other domestic spending accounted for most of the federal budget, but Obama wanted to protect these areas because cutting them would undermine cherished domestic initiatives and hamper his reelection prospects.

The road of U.S. history was dotted with billboards cautioning against the sort of large defense cuts Obama was contemplating. Past slashing of America's defense budget had usually led to large and unforeseen problems, with American men and women in uniform suffering the worst of the consequences. The gutting of the U.S. military between the world wars left it so weak that not even a surge in spending and recruitment from mid-1940 to December 1941 gave it a chance of matching its impending adversaries in military power. Tens of thousands of young American men perished in the early 1940s because the nation had failed to build up its military human capital and develop superior military technologies in the 1920s and 1930s.

American military officers who lived through these debacles vowed to prevent their repetition. Yet the same mistakes were repeated immediately after World War II. Between 1945 and 1948, U.S. defense spending fell from 37 percent of gross domestic product (GDP) to 3.5 percent of GDP. The U.S. armed forces, which had achieved a peak strength of 12 million during the war, shrank to 1.5 million by 1947, and to just 600,000 in 1950. As a consequence of demobilization, most of the remaining military slots were filled with inexperienced young men, and supplies were cut to the bare bones. General George Marshall, who served as both secretary of state and secretary of defense in the Truman administration, protested vainly, "demobilization has become, in effect, disintegration, not only of the armed forces but apparently of all conception of world responsibility and what it demands of us."[2] Secretary of Defense James V. Forrestal lamented in 1948, "We scrapped our war machine, mightiest in the history of the world, in a manifestation of confidence that we should not need it any longer. Our quick and complete demobilization was a testimonial to our good will rather than to our common sense."[3]

War returned with a swiftness that caught even many of the pessimists by surprise. On June 25, 1950, the North Korean Army crossed the thirty-eighth parallel with the ambition of unifying Korea under a communist dictatorship of the proletariat. The first American unit to be thrown into the path of the advancing North Koreans was Task Force

Smith, formed from an infantry battalion commanded by Lieutenant Colonel Charles B. Smith. Like many of the other units that would come into Korea after them, Task Force Smith was short on equipment and supplies and long on inexperienced youth.

Flown in lumbering C-54 transport aircraft to the southeastern tip of the Korean Peninsula, Task Force Smith boarded rail cars at Pusan and rode them north to Taejon, near the deepest North Korean penetration. They hastily set up defenses on a line of hills overlooking the main north–south highway. When a column of North Korean T-34 tanks reached the task force's defensive positions, the Americans fired six armor-piercing rounds at the front of the column. The good news was that the rounds knocked out two tanks. The bad news was that the task force had just expended all of the armor-piercing rounds in its inventory. Smith's men had not been issued any of the other antitank weapons that the United States had developed for its infantry to stop Axis tanks in World War II, such as 3.5-inch bazookas and antitank mines.

With North Korean tanks and infantry flowing down the road and attacking up the hills, the Americans soon depleted their supply of small arms ammunition. Smith ordered a general retreat, which took place under heavy enemy fire and devolved into general disorder, with Smith's young and inexperienced American soldiers abandoning much of their equipment on the hillsides. When the survivors gathered the next day, Smith determined that 150 of the 400 men in his infantry battalion had been killed, wounded, or captured.

Although some of the defeats suffered during the opening battles of the Korean War would be considerably larger in scale than the one suffered by Task Force Smith, the campaign's first victim would be its most famous. "No More Task Force Smiths" would be a rallying cry for a generation of American military officers who were intent on seeing that the United States should never again enter a war unprepared. They would not be the last generation to take that vow.

The nation quadrupled defense spending during the Korean War, and maintained large defense expenditures through the Vietnam War. The Carter administration, dismissive of the threat of communism and

confident that disarmament would promote peace, reduced defense
spending to 4.5 percent of GDP, making huge cuts to operations, maintenance, and training. The result was the so-called Hollow Army, an
undermanned, poorly prepared, demoralized force. Of the Army's eighteen divisions, only four retained the capability of deploying overseas.
Low pay rates discouraged the best and brightest from volunteering for
what had become "all-volunteer" armed forces after the termination of
the draft in 1973. In 1980, only 50 percent of the Army's soldiers were
high school graduates, and 40 percent of all soldiers were removed from
duty for reasons of indiscipline or incompetence during their first en-
listment.[4]

The high military expenditures of the Reagan era fixed most of
these problems and paved the way for the spectacular victory over Iraq
in 1991. During the mid-1990s, however, the Clinton administration
and the Democratic Congress pushed through large defense cuts, bringing spending down to 2.9 percent of GDP. The Clinton administration
saved money by, among other things, deferring the replacement of aging
equipment and vehicles. Consequently, when the U.S. military went into
Iraq in 2003, it had weapons that broke down repeatedly and vehicles
that could not protect their passengers from insurgent bombs. Many
young Americans lost limbs or lives as a consequence of the low spending of the previous decade.

In 2010 and 2011, those bitter experiences were very much on the
mind of the historically minded secretary of defense, Robert Gates. They
were not on the minds of Obama or his national security inner circle,
most of whom probably knew the Korean War only as the setting for
the television series *M*A*S*H*. Gates saw, as his predecessors Marshall
and Forrestal had seen, the perils of disarming based on euphoria about
a peace that was likely to be fleeting. Like Horatius at the Tiber, Gates
would stand alone against the rest of the Obama administration in the
battle over the defense budget.

In November 2009, Obama had promised Gates that the Defense
Department could keep the savings achieved by cutting inefficient
spending. It was a sensible way of encouraging the Defense Department

to make better use of its money. Gates and his staff spent the next year identifying and cataloging expenditures that deserved to be trimmed. At the end of 2010, however, Obama told Gates that the money saved by eliminating these inefficiencies would not be reinvested in other parts of the Defense Department, but would instead be subtracted from the department's budget.

Gates had no choice but to grit his teeth and accept the cuts. As a career Aspen Institute man, though, he had new cause to wonder whether he had made the right decision in agreeing to stay on as secretary of defense. "I felt [President Obama] had breached faith with me," he said later. "I felt that agreements with the Obama White House were good for only as long as they were politically convenient."[5]

Four months later, the White House hit the Defense Department with another surprise. On April 12, Gates was summoned to a meeting at the office of White House Chief of Staff Bill Daley, where Office of Management and Budget director Jack Lew told him that the President was going to announce new cuts in the defense budget of $400 billion in a speech the next day. The $400 billion, spread over a two-year period, greatly exceeded the total that Obama had said he would subtract four months earlier.

Gates, normally known for his low-key demeanor, was unable to bite his tongue any longer. Pointing his finger at Daley, the secretary of defense exclaimed, "This White House's word means nothing!"

He proceeded to berate Daley and Lew for reneging on the promises made in December. He also lit into the White House for failing to come up with $1 billion to fund operations in Libya as it had pledged, which meant that the Defense Department had to take another $1 billion out of its budget. "You didn't get us a fucking dime," Gates barked.

The secretary of defense continued the flaying by asserting that the Obama administration's approach to national security "was math, not strategy." Four hundred billion dollars in cuts, he said, would undermine the morale of the U.S. armed forces and damage America's standing in the world. It would send the message that "the United States is going home, cut a deal with Iran and China while you still can."

Gates then went to Obama and made the same points to him. The United States needed a large military to deal with contingencies, he told the President. "What if Iran forces you into a real war?" Gates asked. "The way we will compensate for force cuts today in the next war is with blood—more American kids will die because of our decisions."

Obama replied that he could not spare the Defense Department from cuts while he was making cuts to Medicare, Medicaid, and other domestic programs. He assured Gates that he would not seek to cut defense by as much as domestic spending. Defense, Obama suggested, might be cut by one dollar for every ten dollars in domestic cuts. At the time, defense spending accounted for only 20 percent of the federal budget.

As Gates would point out in the book he wrote after leaving office, Obama broke this promise, too. He ended up avoiding any significant cuts to the entitlement programs. In the budget deal Obama helped orchestrate later in the summer of 2011, the Defense Department sustained more than half of the reductions in spending.[6]

Gates had only a couple of months left in office. Frustrated by his inability to sway the President, he spoke his mind publicly during two speeches in May. In a commencement address at the University of Notre Dame on May 22, Gates pronounced, "More than any other secretary of defense, I have been a strong advocate of soft power—of the critical importance of diplomacy and development as fundamental components of our foreign policy and national security. But make no mistake, the ultimate guarantee against the success of aggressors, dictators and terrorists in the 21st century, as in the 20th, is hard power—the size, strength and global reach of the United States military."[7]

Two days later, Gates declared that if the U.S. government wanted to slash defense spending, then "we need to be honest with the president, with the Congress, with the American people, indeed with ourselves, about what those consequences are—that a smaller military, no matter how superb, will be able to go to fewer places and be able to do fewer things." Gates observed that "America does have a special position and set of responsibilities on this planet," and he approvingly cited Winston

Churchill's assertion that "the price of greatness is responsibility." While a strong United States was good for America's allies, "the greatest beneficiaries are the American people, in terms of our security, our prosperity, our freedom."[8]

Gates, the career national security official, would be replaced by a career Democratic politician who was less resistant to large-scale defense cuts—Leon Panetta. Many of the other senior officials who were most likely to oppose sweeping defense cuts also departed the Obama administration by the fall of 2011, their seats filled by people who were close to Obama or otherwise nonthreatening. Donilon, a member of Obama's inner circle, took over as national security adviser for James Jones, who had never been able to break into that circle. General John Allen took over command of the Afghanistan War from Petraeus, who headed to Langley to direct the CIA, where he could be more easily distanced from policy discussions. When independent-minded Admiral Mike Mullen's term as chairman of the Joint Chiefs ended in September, he was replaced by General Martin Dempsey, whom military colleagues described as "a by-the-book company man."[9]

During the summer of 2011, the ballooning federal debt compelled Obama to ask congressional leaders to raise the federal debt ceiling. He wanted an eighteen-month extension so that he would not have to get into another tussle with Congress over the debt before the next presidential election. But the House Republican majority wanted the President to agree to spending cuts, particularly to entitlement programs like Medicaid and Medicare, before they would agree to such a raise. Obama countered that he wanted to include tax increases in the deal as well, and if there were to be spending cuts he wanted them to hit the Defense Department rather than entitlements and other domestic programs. House Speaker John Boehner, an establishment Republican, was open to some tax increases, but he could not compromise very much on taxes because of stiff opposition to further taxation among the sizable Tea Party element in the House.

As negotiations dragged on with little progress on the most contentious issues, White House Chief of Staff Jack Lew and Director of

Legislative Affairs Rob Nabors came up with a stopgap compromise. Under their plan, congressional Republicans would raise the debt ceiling and in return the government would be bound to a certain amount of spending cuts. The details of those cuts would be left to a bipartisan "supercommittee," which presumably would be more capable of reaching compromise than the full Congress. A failure of the committee to reach a compromise would trigger "sequestration," in which $1.2 trillion was cut automatically from large sections of the budget. That outcome was thought to be so abhorrent that the bipartisan committee would feel compelled to reach a compromise. Half of the automatic cuts would come from defense, which Republicans would find unpalatable, and the other half from discretionary domestic spending, which Democrats would be unwilling to stomach. The largest and most unwieldy parts of the budget, Social Security and health care entitlements, were exempted.[10]

Senate Majority Leader Harry Reid was ready to accept the deal. Boehner was less enthusiastic. Obama's proposed budget cut $487 billion in defense spending from fiscal years 2012 to 2021 even without sequestration, bringing defense spending down to 3 percent of GDP. Defense hawks in Congress wanted to keep defense spending at 4 or 5 percent of GDP in order to maintain large forces and reinvest for an uncertain future. Under the White House proposal, defense would account for more than half of the spending reductions even though it comprised only 20 percent of the budget, whereas the entitlement programs that Republicans wished to trim got off virtually scot-free.

Boehner informed the White House he thought the budget proposal cut too much from defense. But Obama refused to budge. "We can't give there," Vice President Biden told Boehner. If the Republicans did not accede to White House demands for defense cuts, Biden said, the President was willing to accept a U.S. default on its debts.

As the clock ticked down, the White House made a concession to Boehner that the defense cuts would apply to "security," which included items beyond the Department of Defense, such as foreign aid and the Department of Veterans Affairs. Meanwhile, some of the recently elected libertarian and isolationist Republicans in the House were expressing support for the budget deal, because they were prepared to accept any spending cuts if it meant avoiding more taxation. They were too few in number, however, to produce a majority in the House. To avoid a default on the nation's debt, Boehner set out to sell the budget deal to Republican defense hawks.

Some of those hawks were willing to accept the $487 billion reduction in national security outlays in return for domestic cuts and the absence of additional taxes, but sequestration made them very nervous. If the proposed supercommittee could not agree on a compromise, defense spending would plummet well below 3 percent, its lowest level relative to GDP since the isolationist years of the 1930s. Nor did they like the idea of severe defense cuts without any corresponding cuts to the entitlement programs that were dear to Democrats.

Boehner pulled, pushed, and prodded the hawks to go along. But the fear that sequestration would tear the guts out of the military kept getting in the way. In desperation, Boehner made an extraordinary and extremely bold promise to the hawks, based solely on his forecasting of the political winds, rather than any hard facts. The supercommittee, he vowed, would reach an agreement that forestalled the automatic defense cuts.

That pledge convinced enough of the hawks to go along to obtain passage of the deal. On August 1, the House passed the new budget in what was called the Budget Control Act, and President Obama signed it into law the next day. The Budget Control Act gave the supercommittee until November 23 to come up with a package of cuts that would prevent the onset of sequestration.

According to the forecast upon which Boehner had made his promise, the supercommittee would reach a compromise out of fear of sequestration. As it turned out, he and other Capitol Hill meteorologists who shared that view had miscalculated. Substantial constituents in both parties found the sequestration cuts less distasteful than the compromises that were put forth. Tea Party Republicans decided that cutting defense spending was better than cutting taxes, and hence made clear that they would let the sequestration cuts take effect rather than agree to new taxation. Some liberals saw sequestration as an opportunity to cut defense that was too good to pass up, and they were willing to live with the cuts to domestic spending because they did not touch entitlement programs and to a large extent were merely reversing large spending increases that Obama and the Democratic Congress had pushed through in 2009 and 2010.

As the supercommittee's November 23 deadline approached and sequestration seemed increasingly possible, leading defense hawks warned of dire consequences for the Defense Department in the absence of a compromise agreement. Senators John McCain and Lindsey Graham predicted that the sequestration cuts would "set off a swift decline of the United States as the world's leading military power."[11] While such assertions might have been written off as partisan posturing, the same could not be said of similar remarks from the leadership of the Defense Department, which included not only the Joint Chiefs of Staff but also the Obama-appointed secretary of defense, Leon Panetta.[12]

The sequestration cuts "will truly devastate our national security," Panetta told the House Foreign Affairs Committee on October 13.[13] If sequestration took effect, Panetta said a month later, "we would have the smallest ground force since 1940, the smallest number of ships since 1915, and the smallest Air Force in its history" by the end of the decade.[14]

On the eve of the deadline, congressional hawks offered legislation to avert the defense cuts, hoping to win over some moderate Democrats. President Obama, however, blocked their efforts by promising to veto any such legislation unless it included tax increases on the wealthy. "The concern about national defense is understandable," White House spokesman Jay Carney said as the sequestration deadline loomed. "If the concern is so great about the need to maintain a certain level of defense spending, there is an easy way out here, which is be willing to ask the wealthiest Americans to pay a little bit more in order to achieve this comprehensive and balanced deficit reduction plan, and then the sequester will never kick in. It's very simple."[15] Republicans responded that the supercommittee had been charged only with identifying spending cuts, not tax increases, so it was disingenuous to hold a compromise deal hostage to new taxation.

In the end, the supercommittee failed to reach a compromise agree-ment. Congressional Democrats and the White House pointed fingers at congressional Republicans, who returned the favor. The sequestration cuts were not, however, to take effect for more than a year, on March 1, 2013. Defense hawks therefore held out hope that they could negotiate a deal with congressional Democrats in the interim to forestall the cuts. The Obama administration, on the other hand, would spend its time coming up with new strategic concepts that promised to do more with less.

5

LIGHTENING THE FOOTPRINTS

During the budget negotiations of the summer of 2011, Obama's national security team was already working on a new national security strategy, one that could accommodate drastic cuts to the defense budget. Ostensibly, they were operating under the assumption that the budget reductions would be limited to the $487 billion already enacted by Congress, but the strategy they were developing would be suitable in the event that the sequestration ax struck the Defense Department's budget in 2013. That fact, along with others, would contribute to suspicions that Obama was secretly rooting for the triggering of sequestration.

Obama's team embraced the strategic principles that had guided Vice President Biden's "counterterrorism plus" strategy in the Afghanistan debates of 2009. By late 2011, the key critics of Biden's strategy—Gates, Mullen, Petraeus, Jones, and McChrystal—had been replaced. Considerations of presidential popularity had dominated strategic decisions in 2009 and 2010, and hence Biden's strategy had posed an excessive risk of alienating a public that wanted strong national defense. In 2011, however, budget constraints would take on the leading role, which made Biden's minimalist approach much more alluring. National interests, which were supposed to be the beacons that guided the ship, remained secondary in importance in 2011 as they had been in the preceding two years.

In reviving his strategic concept, Biden had a powerful ally in the new national security adviser, his longtime friend Tom Donilon. He also enjoyed the support of most of the other key national security officials in the White House, including Denis McDonough, Ben Rhodes, homeland security adviser John Brennan, and Biden's own national security adviser, Tony Blinken. The new secretary of defense, Leon Panetta, was not as closely involved in the strategizing, at least in part because the strategic redesign was already in progress when he showed up at the Pentagon for his first day of work, but he too was comfortable with the emphasis on precision counterterrorism. As CIA director, Panetta had just presided over a huge increase in the CIA's drone program, which constituted a central element in the new strategy.

Biden, Donilon, and the others asserted that the U.S. government could maintain its security at much lower cost by adopting a national security strategy of light-footprint counterterrorism not only in Afghanistan but wherever the United States faced threats from extremists and other enemies. With a light footprint, the United States could continue to eliminate the nation's most dangerous opponents through drone strikes and special operations raids. Their most formidable piece of supporting evidence was the special operations raid that killed Osama Bin Laden on May 2, 2011. Another piece of supporting evidence arrived with the fall of Libya's Muammar Gaddafi in October 2011 to a NATO campaign that consisted mainly of precision air strikes.

According to Biden and his strategic kinsmen, the size of the U.S. military's conventional ground forces could and should be drastically reduced. The wars in Iraq and Afghanistan, they asserted, had demonstrated that troop-intensive counterinsurgency was costly and ineffective, and that military power more generally was not as valuable in international affairs as it used to be. Iraq and Afghanistan had also, in their view, exhausted the patience of the American people with troop-intensive counterinsurgency. What was more, Al Qaeda was on its heels and hence the most dangerous threat to the U.S. homeland had subsided. "Make no mistake, al-Qa'ida is in its decline," Brennan said in a speech at the Paul H. Nitze School of Advanced International Studies, in Washington, D.C., on June 29.[1] With terrorism and the Middle East becoming less important to the United States, they argued, the United States ought to shift its resources to an area that was gaining importance, the Asia-Pacific region.[2]

Obama clearly liked the direction in which his new national security team was heading, and he encouraged them to continue down that track. "Give me fewer Iraqi Freedoms and more Desert Storms," he told them. "Don't end up there for ten years trying to do nation building. We're just not going to be allowed to do that. We can't afford it."[3]

In an interview near the end of his first term, Obama explained that his aversion to Iraq and Afghanistan stemmed not just from their costs but from his belief that sending large numbers of troops was strategically counterproductive. Drones and special operations forces, he said, were much more effective strategically. "Special Forces are well designed to deal with very specific targets in difficult terrain and oftentimes can prevent us from making the bigger strategic mistakes of sending forces in, with big footprints and so forth," Obama said. "And so when you're talking about dealing with terrorist networks in failed states, or states that don't have capacity, you can see that as actually being less intrusive, less dangerous, less problematic for the country involved."[4]

The national security strategy that was germinating in late 2011 actually bore some resemblance to the strategy adopted one decade earlier by the one man in the Bush administration who may have been more disliked by Democrats than Bush himself—Donald Rumsfeld. As Bush's first secretary of defense, Rumsfeld had entered office as an enthusiastic proponent of what military theorists of the 1990s had termed "network-centric warfare." According to those theorists, America could achieve its strategic objectives with lower expenditures by exploiting revolutionary advances in the acquisition, transmission, and exploitation of information, which they said heralded a "revolution in military affairs," or RMA for short. The United States could replace traditional "platform-centric" warfare, in which weapons platforms like tanks and aircraft carriers dominated the combat environment, with "network-centric warfare," in which networks of intelligence and operations nodes moved data among themselves so rapidly that they could locate and destroy all enemies from great distances. The 1991 Gulf War and the bombing campaigns in the former Yugoslavia lent credence to this view.

Rumsfeld had spent the first months of 2001 laying the groundwork for a plan to turn the U.S. military from a lumbering Cold War titan into a network of highly mobile forces. Titled "Transformation," Rumsfeld's plan reduced the number of personnel in the military, particularly in ground units, and reduced the number and size of overseas bases. It replaced slow, heavily armored vehicles with fast and light vehicles like the Stryker armored personnel carrier. Speed was more important than the ability to withstand a blow, because in the new era of network-centric warfare, U.S. forces would mainly serve as information collectors, feeding data to other nodes in the network that would blow up the enemy before they could strike U.S. forces.

The attacks of September 11, 2001, compelled Rumsfeld to move his transformation plan to the back burner and turn his attention to Afghanistan. A war with Islamist extremists who were protected by one of the world's most primitive governments did not at first glance seem a suitable venue for the high-tech U.S. military. Afghanistan's Taliban did not have a large military infrastructure or big stocks of vehicles or equipment that could be wiped out with precision-guided bombs and missiles. But circumstances would permit the use of the new way of war to such an extent as to confirm its brilliance.

Once the Taliban made clear that they would not hand over Osama Bin Laden, the Bush administration made ready to invade the country and overthrow the government. But not even the world's most formidable military could invade a landlocked country like Afghanistan without months of preparation. Fortunately, a small army of 22,000 Afghans, known as the Northern Alliance, had been waging war against the Taliban for the past five years, and they were more than eager to serve as the ground force for an American-backed offensive to oust the Taliban.

The Northern Alliance had heretofore posed little threat to the Taliban, owing to disparities in the sizes of their armed forces. The Taliban had more than four times as many men at arms, holding 50,000 regulars and 40,000 militiamen on their rolls. Until very recently, it would have been folly for an army to launch an offensive against an adversary with such numerical superiority. The advances of the Revolution in Military Affairs, however, had given such an offensive a real chance of success. The U.S. government decided to send three hundred U.S. special operations troops and 110 CIA officers to Afghanistan to advise the Northern Alliance and direct America's precision weapons.[5] In addition to showcasing the wonders of U.S. military technology, this minimalist approach would avoid what Rumsfeld viewed as a vital flaw in the Soviet involvement in Afghanistan in the 1980s—the presence of a large number of foreign troops who were certain to arouse the population's nationalist and religious furor.

The Americans traveled on ponies or in pickup trucks to set up observation posts, from which their advanced observation devices could pinpoint hostile installations, troop concentrations, and vehicles. The devastation that they were able to rain down on the Taliban and Al Qaeda would be seen afterward as proof that information technology and precision weaponry had rendered conventional ground forces obsolete. But defeating an enemy that traveled in civilian vehicles and communicated by courier would require battling them in the streets and ferreting them out one by one. It would take concerted ground assaults by Northern Alliance forces, oftentimes without the benefit of air support, to dislodge the Taliban from its centers of power in Afghanistan's cities.[6]

In early December, as the Taliban abandoned the last of Afghanistan's cities, American attention shifted to the fleeing elements of Al Qaeda. Osama Bin Laden had remained in the city of Jalalabad in eastern Afghanistan until its fall was imminent, at which point he retreated to Tora Bora. A region of jagged mountains and deep caves near the border with Pakistan, Tora Bora had long been an Al Qaeda stronghold. A small CIA team pursued Bin Laden to Tora Bora, seeking to convince Afghan warlords to help ensnare the fleeing Al Qaeda leader.

The head CIA officer on the scene, Gary Berntsen, requested that the U.S. military send 800 Army Rangers to Tora Bora to search for Al Qaeda and block its escape. Brigadier General James Mattis, who had arrived by air at Camp Rhino in southern Afghanistan with 1,200

U.S. Marines on November 22, asked permission to move his troops to Tora Bora in order to seal the escape routes. But the commander of U.S. Central Command, General Tommy Franks, rejected these recommendations. Franks and his boss Rumsfeld were of the opinion that sending large U.S. forces was unnecessary, as well as inconsistent with the broader strategy of minimizing the U.S. military footprint in the country. They would continue relying on small CIA teams, which, after all, had sufficed so far.

The small group of CIA operators who reached Tora Bora paid Afghan warlords for information on Al Qaeda and called in air strikes. The Americans came to suspect, however, that the warlords were averting their gaze in exchange for bribes from Al Qaeda. But with no American troops present to watch the passes or patrol the trails, the United States had to depend on the Afghans. In the end, those Afghans failed to deliver the goods. Sometime between December 14 and 16, Bin Laden slipped out of Tora Bora and into Pakistan.[7]

Yaniv Barzilai, author of a book on Al Qaeda's escape from Afghanistan, concluded that the failure of the United States to get Bin Laden at Tora Bora "stemmed largely from the light-footprint approach used to topple the Taliban across Afghanistan." That approach, Barzilai observed, "was neither designed nor suitable for cordoning off swaths of land and capturing or killing the enemies within that region."[8]

When the drums of war began to sound again in early 2003, America's military faced the prospect of fighting an Iraqi military that was much stronger than the Taliban's armed forces. Iraq, moreover, had no equivalent of the Northern Alliance, a friendly indigenous ground force with which the United States could ally. A large U.S. ground force, therefore, would be required to topple the Iraqi government. But just how large it would be became a matter of intensive debate in the Pentagon.

Whereas U.S. forces had sought only to eject Iraqi forces from Kuwait in the 1991 Gulf War, they now needed to penetrate five hundred miles into the heart of Iraq to seize Baghdad, a feat that would require positioning large numbers of troops along Iraqi roads to guard logistical lines. Some military planners, therefore, believed that the United

States would have to send a force at least as large as what it had sent in 1990, with half a million troops or more. Rumsfeld viewed that request as unimaginative and detached from the reality of the RMA. Even with the need to guard extended supply lines, he asserted, the U.S. military required much fewer ground forces than in the past. Rumsfeld at first suggested a U.S. invasion force of just 50,000, before settling on a somewhat more cautious figure of 145,000.

The Americans preceded the invasion of Iraq with a hailstorm of precision-guided bombs and missiles, pulverizing all of the obvious targets. Then American columns of tanks, armored personnel carriers, and trucks streamed into the country. Rather than pause at every town and city to clobber the Iraqi resistance, they kept rolling toward Baghdad. The miserly allocation of troops to the invasion left the lengthening supply lines highly vulnerable to Iraqi troops who had been bypassed, but the poorly led Iraqi army did not concentrate troops for attacks on the supply lines.

The American arrowhead pierced the heart of Iraq in a mere three weeks. Barging into the center of Baghdad behind a curtain of precision munitions, the U.S. ground forces took the city with unexpectedly low losses. In living rooms from Florida to Alaska, Americans cheered as U.S. Marines tethered a massive statue of Saddam Hussein to a tank retriever and yanked it to the ground. The swiftness of victory and the scarcity of American casualties seemed to vindicate Rumsfeld's decision to hold down the troop numbers. It also provided fresh confirmation that the RMA had put large ground armies into the same basket of obsolescence as the phalanx and the horse cavalry.

Disconcerting signs of trouble, however, soon began to appear. The jubilant Iraqi throngs, which to the Americans had initially resembled the French celebrating the liberation of Paris in 1944, took on a darker hue. Unaccustomed to freedom, the Iraqi people were unable to exercise it responsibly. Frenzied Iraqis looted every conceivable object from public buildings, down to the water pipes. They stripped power lines of their copper and aluminum, turning neighborhoods dark and bringing industrial production to a standstill. They killed former government of-

Afghanistan had shown that reserve units lagged far behind active units in capabilities. Regenerating active component forces requires at least a decade of cultivating officers, as the disastrous performances of armies with inexperienced officers had demonstrated time and again.

The *Defense Strategic Guidance* designated special operations forces and drones as the weapons of choice against the remaining extremists. Whether in Africa, the Middle East, or South Asia, they could take out any terrorist leaders, and without the burdens and risks of a large military footprint. The special operations forces and drones would be spared from the budgetary ax in order to facilitate "innovative, low-cost, and small-footprint approaches."[13]

In a speech on January 5 at the Pentagon, Obama explained that the attrition of Islamist extremists had removed the need for large ground forces. "We've decimated al Qaeda's leadership," Obama said. "We've delivered justice to Osama bin Laden, and we've put that terrorist network on the path to defeat." After claiming credit for winding down the wars in Iraq and Afghanistan, he said, "As we look beyond the wars in Iraq and Afghanistan—and the end of long-term nation-building with large military footprints—we'll be able to ensure our security with smaller conventional ground forces."[14]

The leadership of the Department of Defense spent much of 2012 attempting to convince Congress and the President to nullify the sequestration cuts before they took effect. In February, Dempsey told Congress that if the sequestration cuts were implemented, it would mean that "we would no longer be a global power."[15] When defense hawks seized on his words to advocate higher defense spending, he backtracked somewhat, saying, "The idea that I really wanted to get across was that we wouldn't be the global power that we know ourselves to be today."[16] In March, Deputy Secretary of Defense Ashton Carter called sequestration the equivalent of "assisted suicide for the DoD."[17]

House Republicans passed a bill in May 2012 to replace sequestration, which would spare defense from large cuts and instead impose reductions on entitlements and other domestic spending. Obama killed its chances by repeating his earlier threat to block any attempt to shift pain to other budgetary categories unless the Republicans agreed to tax increases, which remained anathema to Republicans. Although the President did not offer his own alternative budget to forestall sequestration, he nonetheless put the blame entirely on the Republicans with a monotonous consistency. "The only thing that's standing in the way of us solving this problem right now," Obama would say, "is the unwillingness of some members of Congress to ask people like me—people who've done very well, millionaires, billionaires—to pay a little bit more, in part, to preserve the freedoms that we hold dear."[18]

In his 2014 memoir, Panetta would fault Obama for "failing to lead the Congress out of" sequestration, noting that it "highlighted what I regard as his most conspicuous weakness, a frustrating reticence to engage his opponents and rally support for his cause." Panetta was shocked that no one else in the cabinet was willing to speak up on the dangers of sequestration. "The agency heads who best understood how cuts would affect them and the services they provided opted to strike a low profile," Panetta observed. "As a result, neither Congress nor the public got the benefit of their insights into what was about to transpire." Panetta added that his cabinet colleagues "waited for permission to object. It never came."[19] The silence of Obama and most of his cabinet on sequestration's perils provided additional evidence that Obama was content to let sequestration transpire.

As the presidential election approached, Republican nominee Mitt Romney accused Obama of jeopardizing U.S. national security by failing to avert sequestration. To reverse America's military decline, Romney advocated a return to spending 4 percent of GDP on defense. He vowed, further, to cancel Obama's plans to cut 100,000 ground troops.

In a televised presidential debate on October 22, moderated by Bob Schieffer of CBS News, Romney launched a frontal attack on Obama for reducing defense spending. "Our Navy is smaller now than at any time since 1917," Romney said. "The Navy said they needed 313 ships to carry out their mission. We're now at under 285. We're headed down to the low 200s if we go through a sequestration." Romney pegged Obama's defense cuts at $1 trillion, the sum of the cuts already enacted and the sequestration cuts. Obama's siphoning of defense dollars, Romney concluded, "is making our future less certain and less secure."

"Bob, I just need to comment on this," Obama replied. "The sequester is not something I proposed, it's something that Congress proposed. It will not happen." Then, even more astonishingly, Obama crowed: "I think Governor Romney maybe hasn't spent enough time looking at how our military works. You mentioned the Navy, for example, and that we have fewer ships than we did in 1916. Well, Governor, we also have fewer horses and bayonets, because the nature of our military's changed. We have these things called aircraft carriers, where planes land on them. We have these ships that go underwater, nuclear submarines. And so the question is not a game of Battleship, where we're counting ships. It's what are our capabilities."

The Internet was quickly ablaze with retorts from service members who noted that 600,000 soldiers and Marines had bayonets in 2012, more than in 1916. What provoked the most rebuttals, however, was Obama's remark that sequestration would not happen. Buck McKeon, the House Armed Services Committee chairman, said after the debate, "The president and his party in the Senate have failed to offer even a single real solution that could resolve sequestration. If the president is determined that these cuts won't happen, why has he drug it out this long?"

Senator Lindsey Graham, one of the Republican Party's most respected voices on foreign policy, piped in, "Saying it's not going to happen in a debate and not lifting a finger to prevent it for weeks and months is disingenuous. I think it's going to happen unless there is some leadership, and the president has done nothing to lead on this issue."[20]

The President's claim that sequestration was a congressional proposal and not a presidential one also came under fire. Two days after the debate, White House Chief of Staff Jack Lew reiterated the claim, and said specifically that congressional Republicans had proposed sequestration. Not until February 19, 2013, long after the election, did a White House spokesman acknowledge that sequestration "was an idea that the White House put forward."[21]

National security would not be a decisive factor in the 2012 presi dential race, just as it had not been in the 2008 campaign. Recognizing the difficulty of making a strong case for why voters should reelect the President, given the disappointing results of his first term, the Obama campaign focused instead on making a strong case for why voters should not vote for Romney. Relentless attacks portrayed Romney as an aloof rich guy who was out of touch with the American people.

The Obama campaign's barrage of negativity won the day. On November 6, Obama won 26 states and 51 percent of the popular vote, to 24 states and 47 percent for Romney. The Republicans retained control of the House, while Democrats kept their majority in the Senate.

Romney's defeat and the Republican Party's failure to win a Senate majority dashed the hopes of defense hawks that all of the sequestration cuts could be undone through legislation. In an effort to reach a compromise before March 1, the House Republicans decided to soften their negotiating position on the federal budget. Now that the presidential campaign was over, Obama might be willing to compromise as well. Republican negotiators informed the White House that they would be open to a tax increase, the President's foremost demand for a new deal to supplant sequestration.

During December, Obama proposed a $680 billion tax increase as part of what was ostensibly a compromise package. The following month, Republicans agreed to $620 billion in tax increases on high-income earners, expecting that in coming close to Obama's figure they could get Obama to come close to their demands on defense and other spending. But the $620 billion tax increase was pushed through as a separate measure, not as part of a package, and after its passage Obama said that Republicans would have to agree to another $680 billion in tax increases before he would agree to the defense cuts.[22]

The Republicans, having upset many of their own supporters by consenting to the $620 billion tax increase, were in no mood to raise taxes again to obtain what the White House already owed them. They informed the President that they had held up their end of the bargain by raising taxes on the wealthy, and now it was time for him to compromise on sequestration. Obama avoided negotiation and instead took to the airwaves to blame Republican aversion to new taxes for the lack of a solution to the impasse. "So now Republicans in Congress face a simple choice," Obama told the White House press corps on February 19. "Are they willing to compromise to protect vital investments in education and health care and national security and all the jobs that depend on them? Or would they rather put hundreds of thousands of jobs and our entire economy at risk just to protect a few special-interest tax loopholes that benefit only the wealthiest Americans and biggest corporations? That's the choice."[23]

On another occasion, the President declared, "Are Republicans in Congress really willing to let these cuts fall on our kids' schools and mental health care just to protect tax loopholes for corporate jet owners? Are they really willing to slash military health care and the Border Patrol just because they refuse to eliminate tax breaks for big oil companies?"[24]

The assertion that Republican opposition to further tax cuts was the main impediment to averting sequestration came under fire from Bob Woodward, whose book *The Price of Politics* had provided the public with the most detailed description of the sequestration negotiations of 2011. In a *Washington Post* op-ed, Woodward asserted that the sequestration deal had been based on an agreement that taxes would not increase. "When the president asks that a substitute for the sequester include not just spending cuts but also new revenue, he is moving the goal posts," Woodward wrote.[25]

Even some Democrats found fault with the White House's strategy of demanding further tax increases while laying blame on Republicans. Scott Wilson and Philip Rucker of the *Washington Post* reported in early March, "Two former Obama White House officials used the same word—'hubris'—to describe what they viewed as the administration's highly public and sometimes misleading turn against congressional Republicans."[26]

When the March 1 deadline arrived and nothing close to a compromise had been negotiated, Obama took the opportunity to lambaste congressional Republicans once more. "We shouldn't be making a series of dumb, arbitrary cuts to things that businesses depend on and workers depend on, like education, and research, and infrastructure and defense," he said at a press conference in the Brady Room. "It's unnecessary. And at a time when too many Americans are still looking for work, it's inexcusable." Citing estimates from economists that sequestration could decrease economic growth by more than half a percentage point and forfeit 750,000 jobs, he stated, "Every time that we get a piece of economic news, over the next month, next two months, next six months, as long as the sequester is in place, we'll know that that economic news could have been better if Congress had not failed to act."[27]

Following the onset of sequestration, Secretary of Defense Chuck Hagel ordered a new strategic review that would reconsider the military's needs in light of the sequestration cuts. Hagel announced the review's findings in July. The review, he said, had determined that the military could still perform its key missions under sequestration, even if it meant shrinking the Army to between 420,000 and 450,000.[28] This conclusion was difficult to reconcile with Secretary of Defense Panetta's prior warning that the sequestration would "truly devastate our national security," or with the assertion in the *Defense Strategic Guidance* of January 2012 that achieving the administration's strategic objectives required an Army of 490,000 soldiers.

When the Joint Chiefs were called to testify on Capitol Hill in September, they challenged the conclusions of Hagel's review with stunning candor and specificity. The most outspoken was Army Chief of Staff Ray Odierno, whose service stood to lose the most from the sequestration cuts. For audiences whose senses had been dulled by years of hearing senior officers dissemble or recycle euphemisms when pressed about questionable guidance, his testimony was as startling as foul language in a Disney movie.

The July review, Odierno told the Congress, had involved "rosy assumptions" that "were really put in there so we could say we need a smaller Army. And that's concerning to me." The burly general warned that the sequestration cuts would compel the active-duty Army to eliminate nearly half of its forty-five brigade combat teams and render 85 percent of the remaining brigade combat teams unprepared for combat deployment. The cuts would "put at substantial risk our ability to conduct even one sustained major combat operation."

Admiral William McRaven, commander of the Special Operations Command (SOCOM), noted that although sequestration would not impose drastic budgetary reductions on special operations forces, it nonetheless undermined special operations because of the interdependence between special operations forces and conventional forces. Most of what the special operators did relied on direct or indirect support from conventional air and ground forces, whether it be the use of transport aircraft or the staging of operations from bases held by conventional forces.[29]

Congress would pass some short-term reductions in the sequestration cuts at the end of 2013, but they did not alter the plans for radical downsizing. The Defense Department remained on track to cut the Army to 420,000 soldiers and the Marine Corps to 175,000 troops by 2016. Aircraft and ship production were scheduled to decline, and the number of U.S. aircraft carriers was set to fall from eleven to ten.[30]

The strategic turn that began in the middle of 2011 was completed with the onset of sequestration in March 2013. Although some White House officials publicly had warned of harmful national security consequences arising from sequestration, Obama made little effort to keep it from happening, while working hard to use it to bludgeon Republicans. Obama found a strategic justification for sequestration by taking Vice President Biden's half-baked ideas on Afghanistan and turning them into a global strategy. That strategy would soon be applied in a series of high-priority countries, ensuring that assessment of its merits would not be long in coming.

6

———

MILITARY FOOTPRINTS MATTER

Iraq

The war that had most attracted Barack Obama's attention prior to 2009 was the war in Iraq. From 2002 onward, he had spoken out against that "dumb war," and when insurgency flared up in late 2003, he derided the Bush administration for seeking to suppress it with American troops. Obama was especially outspoken in criticizing the Bush administration's decision to send a surge of 30,000 troops to Iraq at the beginning of 2007. "We cannot impose a military solution on what has effectively become a civil war," Senator Obama declared in January 2007. "And until we acknowledge that reality, we can send 15,000 more troops, 20,000 more troops, 30,000 more troops. I don't know any expert on the region or any military officer that I've spoken to privately that believes that that is going to make a substantial difference on the situation on the ground."[1]

On January 30, 2007, Obama introduced the Iraq War De-Escalation Act, which called for the removal of all U.S. combat troops from Iraq by the end of March 2008, regardless of whether the U.S. military had achieved its objectives. The bill never made it out of committee. Few senators were prepared to call it quits just yet, particularly in light of the fact that Bush had just sent a new commander to Iraq, General David Petraeus, who was considered the best general in the U.S. Army.

In August 2007, just before the surge's results began to come into focus, Obama said in a speech in Washington, "There is no military solution in Iraq. Only Iraq's leaders can settle the grievances at the heart of Iraq's civil war. We must apply pressure on them to act, and our best leverage is reducing our troop presence." Several years later, as president, he would get to test the proposition that reducing the American troop presence in Iraq resulted in greater American leverage.

In the same speech, Obama contended that Al Qaeda "has little support" in Iraq, and what support it had was largely due to the American presence. Therefore, "Ending the war will help isolate al Qaeda and give Iraqis the incentive and opportunity to take them out."[2] Obama was also to test this theory once in office.

In June 2008, Obama visited Iraq with Senators Chuck Hagel and Jack Reed, both of whom shared his skepticism about American involvement in the country. During a meeting with General Petraeus and Ambassador Ryan Crocker, the senators recommended setting a date for the withdrawal of all American forces, which in their estimation would please Iraqi leaders. Crocker disagreed, asserting that such a timeline was not necessary and that it would unduly constrain the United States. The large U.S. military footprint in Iraq was at that time bestowing all sorts of critical advantages on the United States, including influence over Iraqi politics, freedom of movement for intelligence personnel, and the bolstering of confidence among Iraqis that they could participate in the new political order without fear of death.

Like a university professor lecturing from the podium, Obama told Petraeus and Crocker that Al Qaeda in Iraq—the Iraqi franchise of Bin Laden's terrorist organization—did not pose a threat to the United States. Therefore, the young senator continued, Iraq was less important than Afghanistan. Formerly the central lair of Al Qaeda, Afghanistan was still the neighbor of Pakistan, where Al Qaeda's leadership was now headquartered. "Afghanistan is the central front in the war on terror," Obama asserted.

"Iraq is what Al-Qaeda says is the central front," Petraeus retorted. Iraqi terrorists had been linked to a terrorist attack in Scotland, Petraeus observed, and more such attacks against the West could occur if Al Qaeda in Iraq were not defeated.[3]

As the end of 2008 approached and the Iraqi insurgencies subsided, a continued U.S. presence in Iraq remained vital as a guarantor of the political reconciliation that Obama, and George W. Bush, deemed vital to Iraq's long-term stability. Iraqi prime minister Nouri al-Maliki and other leading Shiite politicians viewed Iraq's Sunnis with a distrust that bordered on paranoia, suspecting the whole Sunni population of seeking a return to the Baathist days of Saddam Hussein. Maliki showed blatant favoritism toward Shiites in dispensing governmental services and resources, and had in the recent past provided support to Shiite militias that had committed atrocities against Sunnis, which ensured that the Sunnis held him in equal contempt. Both Sunnis and Kurds feared that Maliki's heavy-handed methods portended a return to dictatorship.

Events in the waning months of Bush's presidency showed just how much the United States could do to prevent the Iraqis from beating each other to a pulp. In August 2008, Maliki's "Counter-Terrorism" Office attempted to use Iraqi special operations forces to arrest Sunni politicians whom Maliki wished to take off the political scene. The United States caught wind of it, and used the threat of suspending aid to stop the practice. That same month, American military advisers convinced Kurdish militia forces and the Iraqi Army to back down after both had amassed heavy weaponry for an anticipated battle at the disputed town of Khanaqin.[4]

During the second half of 2008, the Bush administration bargained with Maliki over the future U.S. troop presence in Iraq. Bush offered to remove U.S. forces from Iraqi cities by the middle of 2009 and to keep 40,000 U.S. troops in Iraq after 2011 to provide assistance in training and logistics. Bush subsequently removed the provision on maintaining U.S. forces after 2011, in order to lessen opposition to the deal among Shiite parliamentarians. In November, the Iraqi parliament approved a revised U.S. term sheet that kept no U.S. forces in Iraq beyond 2011. American policy makers and Iraqi leaders, however, had a mutual understanding that the U.S. presence would be extended beyond 2011 in a later agreement.[5]

Barack Obama, on the other hand, continued to see no need for a prolonged U.S. troop presence in Iraq. On the campaign trail, he said that if elected he would start removing U.S. combat brigades at a rate of one or two per month, with the final brigade departing after sixteen months. In an effort to demonstrate that such a withdrawal would bring the war to what Obama called a "responsible close," Obama's aides cited congressional testimony from 2007 in which General Peter Pace had said that a withdrawal at this speed was feasible. The aides conveyed the impression that Pace considered such a withdrawal compatible with the mission of maintaining stability in Iraq, when in reality Pace had said only that it was feasible logistically.[6]

Once Obama took office, he backed away from his campaign pledge to remove all U.S. combat brigades in sixteen months, owing to expert advice about the value of a prolonged U.S. presence and the dangers of so rapid a withdrawal. But, in order to appease the voters to whom he had promised a swift end in Iraq, he set an interim date to end the "combat mission," after which U.S. forces would become "advise-and-assist units." A large number of combat troops would remain after that date, at least until the end of 2011, in accordance with the agreement negotiated by the Bush administration.

Petraeus, Odierno, and Crocker wanted to set the date for the transition to "advise-and-assist" at the end of 2010, twenty-three months away. At Obama's insistence, Odierno and Crocker assessed the option of ending the combat mission in sixteen months. "The overall risk is extremely high," Odierno and Crocker wrote in their reply. This option would prevent U.S. forces from doing much beyond preparing for their own exit. The Americans would be unable to help the Iraqis solidify security gains, and would "largely be unable to fulfill their role as 'honest brokers' in the resolution of contentious issues."[7]

Gates recommended a period of nineteen months, after Obama had made clear that he would not accept the twenty-three-month option. In *The Endgame*, a superb and largely neglected book on the last phase of American military involvement in Iraq, Michael Gordon and Bernard Trainor wrote that a nineteen-month option was appealing to the President because "it was closer to Obama's sixteen-month schedule and would enable the White House—two months before the November midterm congressional elections—to say that the combat mission in Iraq had come to a close."[8] Obama ultimately settled on nineteen months as the time frame for ending the "combat mission." In August 2010, U.S. forces would discontinue combat operations, with the major exception of special operations, which would be coordinated with the Iraqis.

Based on recommendations from military commanders who saw continued fragility in Iraqi security and politics, Obama established a target of 50,000 U.S. troops in Iraq after the nineteen months. That number did not go over well with liberal Democrats, who had wanted Obama to stick to his campaign promise to get all the troops out in sixteen months. Gates remembered that when House Speaker Nancy Pelosi learned of the 50,000 troops, "she alternately looked like she had swallowed an entire lemon or was simply going to explode."[9]

In his first year in office, Obama entrusted Iraq policy to Vice President Biden. The President was so comfortable with Biden's handling of Iraq that he held no meetings on Iraq during the second half of 2009.[10] To replace Ryan Crocker as U.S. ambassador to Iraq, Obama appointed Christopher Hill, a former Peace Corps volunteer who had earlier faced withering criticism for going easy on North Korea in nuclear weapons negotiations. Whereas Crocker had worked very closely with the military, Hill was intent on distancing himself from the U.S. military and reducing its influence in Iraq. Hill complained that the embassy he took over "was not acting like an embassy but as kind of an adjunct to the military."

Hill, with backing from Biden and Secretary of State Clinton, intended to boost the embassy at the military's expense, based on the general principle that civil leadership should enjoy primacy, rather than on the practical merits of the situation. The military was, in fact, much better suited to managing affairs in a country that still had large security problems. Odierno had been in Iraq more than three years when Hill arrived, and much of his staff was on its second or third deployment to Iraq. Over the years, they had spun large webs of relationships with Iraqi leaders, political as well as military. Hill and the senior staff he brought with him, by contrast, had spent no time in Iraq, and none spoke Arabic.[11]

The withdrawal of U.S. forces from Iraqi cities in the middle of 2009, part of the deal the outgoing Bush administration had negotiated, did not weaken Al Qaeda as Obama had predicted during the campaign. Instead, it allowed Al Qaeda to regain some of its strength and its ability to carry out terrorist attacks. Maliki exacerbated the problem by imposing new restrictions on U.S. special operations forces and replacing competent Iraqi military and police commanders with individuals of more certain loyalty to him.[12] The reduced U.S. military role also emboldened Maliki to take divisive political actions of which the Americans disapproved, including the arrests of Sunni leaders on trumped-up charges.

The U.S. military presence remained significant enough, however, to enable the United States to rein in Maliki and other key figures on the most critical issues. Over the course of 2009, U.S. military personnel averted several potentially violent showdowns between the Iraqi Army and Kurdish militias. When Maliki sought to put Iraqi Army forces at the Mosul Dam, whose German-built hydroelectric plant made electricity from the waters of the Tigris River, American forces accompanied them to prevent an outbreak of hostilities with the Kurdish militiamen who had long guarded it. The Americans then set up a commission composed of Arabs, Kurds, and Americans to prevent future conflicts.[13] During the lead-up to the parliamentary elections of March 7, 2010, U.S. pressure ensured the reinstatement of candidates whom Maliki had tried to disqualify.[14]

The two leading competitors heading into those parliamentary elections were Maliki's Dawa Party, dominated by religiously minded Shiites who feared a Sunni resurgence, and the secular nationalist Iraqiya Party, which enjoyed support from secular Shiites and large numbers of Sunnis. On the day of the election, both sides turned out voters in droves. The vote tally gave Iraqiya 91 seats, while Dawa received 89. Maliki alleged that some of Iraqiya's candidates were terrorists, and he used a governmental body to disqualify some of the Iraqiya winners on charges of terrorism, but he was overruled by Iraq's highest court.

With neither Iraqiya nor Dawa holding enough seats for a parliamentary majority, the two parties sought to form parliamentary majorities by building coalitions. For weeks and then months, Iraqiya and Dawa bargained in vain with other parties. Fearing that a prolonged delay would destabilize Iraq and open the door to Shiite and Sunni extremists, the Obama administration encouraged Iraqiya and Dawa to come together as partners in a grand coalition, thereby marginalizing more extreme groups. But the American position on who would lead that coalition government was less clear. Iraqiya leader Ayad Allawi, a secular Shiite and Iraqi nationalist, struck some Americans as a man who could unite Shiites and Sunnis. Many of these same Americans, and most of America's Sunni Arab allies, perceived in Maliki an oppressor of Sunnis who was too close to Iran and too intent on expanding his own powers.[15]

Ambassador Hill and Vice President Biden, on the other hand, viewed Allawi as a pawn of Sunni politicians who retained fond remembrances of Saddam Hussein. In Hill's view, Allawi's bid to lead a Sunni party as a secular Shiite "was like arranging for the Afrikaner party to make a comeback in South Africa with a black front man."[16] Biden and Hill held, in addition, that Maliki was not as sectarian as his critics alleged. When General James Mattis, commander of the U.S. Central Command (CENTCOM), warned Biden that Maliki's continued presence could serve Iranian interests in the region and damage the United States, Biden downplayed the possibility. Biden also contended that if Maliki remained in power, his government would surely extend the existing Status of Forces Agreement (SOFA) to permit American troops to stay in Iraq beyond 2011. "I'll bet you my vice presidency Maliki will extend the SOFA," Biden said.[17]

With Biden serving as Obama's point man on Iraq, his views on Iraq's leadership prevailed. The Obama administration eventually threw its weight behind Maliki, and was reinforced by the weight of the Iranian government, which recognized in Maliki a potent ally. Maliki retained the position of prime minister, while Allawi was put in charge of a nebulous National Council for Higher Policies, a token position with no real authority. Maliki soon amassed additional power for himself, taking control of previously independent agencies responsible for the central bank, elections, and anticorruption.

The Obama administration spent much of 2011 debating with itself over the post-2011 U.S. troop presence in Iraq. Gates, Clinton, Panetta, Biden, and most of the other senior U.S. leaders supported a sizable presence in order to ensure the stability of the Iraqi government and limit Iranian influence. The debate, therefore, centered on how big that force would be, not whether it would exist.

In early 2011, the senior U.S. military commander in Iraq, General Lloyd Austin, recommended that the United States maintain between 20,000 and 24,000 troops in Iraq after 2011, which he said would entail moderate risk for the United States. Washington asked him to pare down his numbers and provide several options. He came back with an option of 19,000, two options that began at 16,000 at the start of 2012 and tapered down over three years, and a 10,000 option. Austin said he preferred 19,000, and that he had a low opinion of the 10,000 option.[18]

Even those numbers, however, were higher than Obama and his inner circle wanted. The White House scheduled a meeting for April 29 to consider a new set of options, with 16,000, 10,000, and 8,000 troops. Mullen, who was concerned by the White House's apparent lack of respect for Austin's recommendations, wrote Donilon a memo in advance of the meeting in which he recommended keeping at least 16,000 troops in Iraq. Mullen warned that the lower options entailed undue risks, including risks to the safety of Americans in Iraq.

Although Mullen had expressed his position through classified channels and without leaks to the press, Donilon was outraged that the military had submitted the document at all. Fearing that a written recommendation could later be used as ammunition by the President's opponents, Donilon complained that the military was "boxing in the White House," as it had done during the Afghanistan deliberations of 2009. Donilon phoned Michèle Flournoy, the undersecretary of defense for policy, and told her that she should have prevented Mullen from issuing the document. Flournoy replied that Mullen, as chairman of the Joint Chiefs of Staff, had a legal responsibility to provide independent military advice to the President, directly and without interference from anyone else in the administration. Donilon then went to Gates and informed him that he did not want 16,000 troops. He asked Gates if he would be willing to accept a residual force of 10,000. Gates said he could accept it.[19]

In the spring, Maliki and most other Iraqi leaders were saying that they wanted the U.S. military to retain a presence in Iraq after 2011.[20] But they were hearing little from the Americans on the subject. In May, Secretary Clinton asked Graham and McCain to visit Iraq in order to help convince the Iraqi government to agree to a residual force of U.S. troops. When the senators met with Maliki, the Iraqi prime minister asked them, "How many troops are you willing to leave here?"

"You don't know?" Graham asked.

"No," Maliki said. "Nobody ever talked to me about that."

Graham and McCain were stunned to learn that the secretary of state had asked them to urge the Iraqis to authorize troops without having presented the Iraqi government with any troop figures. Graham looked at Austin and U.S. ambassador James Jeffrey for an explanation. Austin and Jeffrey said that the White House was still reviewing the topic and had not yet decided on a number.[21]

Upon returning to the United States, McCain and Graham went to see Biden at his house. "Joe, you know they seem to be warming up to this, they seem to be all realizing they have got to have some American troop presence," the senators told Biden. They noted that the Iraqi General Staff was preparing a formal request for American troops, which would make it easier for Maliki to sell his constituents on the need to extend the American military presence.

"We're on it, we're on it, we're on it," said Biden. He intended to meet with Obama in a few days, he said, and they would finalize the troop package. Once that was done, Graham would receive a call. Graham waited days and weeks for Biden's call. It never came.[22]

Obama did take action, though not of the sort Biden had said the President would be taking. On June 2, Obama had a secure videoconference with Maliki, the first time he had spoken with him all year. They discussed the U.S. presence after 2011, but Obama chose not to say how many U.S. troops he was prepared to keep in Iraq beyond the end of the year. He told Maliki that the United States would keep troops in Iraq after 2011 only if the Iraqi parliament approved it.

It was the equivalent of asking a third-world police chief to find a missing American and then insisting that the search be conducted according to the standard operating procedures of the New York City Police Department. In Maliki's view, going to parliament was politically unfeasible, owing to opposition from Shiite parliamentarians who viewed an extension of the U.S. military presence as an obstacle to consolidation of Shiite control over Iraq. Maliki was prepared to get the Americans what they wanted, but did not want to be told how to do it, particularly when they were telling him how to do it in ways that would not work.

In the coming weeks, Maliki repeatedly suggested to Ambassador Jeffrey the creation of a document, perhaps in the form of an agreement between the U.S. and Iraqi departments of defense, that authorized a U.S. troop presence after 2011 without parliamentary approval. Brett McGurk, a member of Jeffrey's negotiating team who participated in these discussions, thought Maliki's argument made sense. He urged the White House to abandon its insistence on parliamentary approval, which he considered much less important in the grand scheme of things than the strategic benefits to be had from keeping U.S. troops.[23]

Contrary to much that would be said later, obtaining the approval of Iraq's parliament was not a legal necessity. State Department lawyers could have secured Iraqi agreement to American terms through a deal in which the Iraqi foreign ministry signed off on the U.S. troop presence. A former senior Hill staffer told Josh Rogin of *Foreign Policy*, "If State says that this requires a treaty or a specific agreement by the Iraqi parliament as opposed to a statement by the Iraqi foreign ministry, it has its head up its ass."[24]

The White House nonetheless clung tenaciously to its demand for parliamentary approval, so tenaciously as to arouse suspicions that Obama wanted to use the absence of parliamentary approval as an excuse for withdrawing all U.S. troops. Those suspicions were to be found within the senior ranks of the Obama administration. Panetta later re-counted that he and others who favored retaining a U.S. presence in Iraq "viewed the White House as so eager to rid itself of Iraq that it was will-ing to withdraw rather than lock in arrangements that would preserve our influence and interests."[25]

When Maliki accommodated numerous other American demands but kept encountering American insistence on parliamentary approval of an enduring U.S. military presence, he began adjusting to the possi-bility that Iraq might soon have no more U.S. troops. As the year moved along, Maliki's willingness to heed American advice and demands de-clined, while his willingness to heed the words of the Iranians spiraled upward. In the middle of 2011, Maliki arrested Brigadier General Numan Dakhil Jawad, the commander of the Interior Ministry's top counterterrorism unit, on charges as fraudulent as the Ray-Ban sun-glasses for sale in Baghdad's open-air bazaars. The Americans surmised that Jawad, a Shiite, had been ousted because he had been willing to conduct raids against Shiite extremists as well as those of Sunni persua-sion. The officer who took Jawad's place, a man reported to be in league with a Shiite extremist group, discontinued all raids against the Shiite militias. Maliki subsequently removed the commanders of the Iraqi Ar-my's two best brigades, and those units likewise discontinued operations against Shiite targets.[26] These moves received plaudits from the Irani-ans, who had complained to Maliki about raids that had targeted Shiite groups supported by Iran. American diplomats lodged protests, which went nowhere.[27]

Obama, meanwhile, was preoccupied with further reductions in the post-2011 U.S. troop strength. By the late summer, he was saying that he wanted a force of only 3,500 troops in Iraq. Biden, McDonough, Blinken, and Cartwright were telling him that the United States could achieve its objectives with such a light footprint after 2011.[28] American contractors and civilian government employees, they maintained, could take over much of the work that had been done by the military, and they could do it more skillfully and less conspicuously. Sixteen thousand civilians could be sent. A massive new U.S. embassy, completed in 2009 at a cost of $750 million and eclipsing all other U.S. embassies in size, would permanently supplant the U.S. military headquarters as the locus of American power.

Obama came up with a new precondition for extending the U.S. troop presence. The Iraqi parliament, he said, would have to provide U.S. troops with immunity from prosecution in Iraqi courts. With Maliki having already insisted that parliament would not agree to a deal even without the immunity proviso, it was a proposal that was predestined to fail, and Obama knew it. The proposal, moreover, was not necessary from a legal or political point of view, despite many administration claims to that effect. When Iraq encountered new catastrophes in the summer of 2014, Obama would deploy American troops to Iraq without requiring the Iraqi parliament to grant them immunity.[29] As the end of 2011 neared, Obama waited and avoided contact with Maliki, until finally the U.S. military could wait no longer to execute its withdrawal plan.

On October 21, the White House informed the Iraqi government that the United States would be withdrawing all of its troops by the end of the year. Obama appeared in the Brady Press Briefing Room of the White House for just six minutes to announce the withdrawal. Making no mention of the futile negotiations for a troop extension, he depicted the outcome as the result of mutual agreement with the Iraqis. Hours earlier, Obama told the cameras, he had spoken with Maliki, and "We are in full agreement about how to move forward." Obama welcomed the end of the U.S. military presence as an opportunity to redirect the nation toward domestic affairs. "After a decade of war," Obama intoned, "the nation that we need to build—and the nation that we will build—is our own."

After Obama's speech, McDonough, Blinken, and Carney fielded questions from the press. One reporter asked whether Obama would have wanted to keep U.S. troops had the Iraqis accommodated U.S. stipulations on legal immunities. McDonough replied, "What the President preferred was for the best relationship for the United States and Iraq going forward. That's exactly what we have now. . . . We feel like we got exactly what we needed to protect our interests, and the Iraqis feel the same way." During recent reviews of Iraq, McDonough said, "one assessment after another about the Iraqi security forces came back saying these guys are ready, these guys are capable, these guys are proven."

When a reporter asked about the danger of Iraq returning to civil war, Blinken said, "what we've seen is that politics has taken hold in Iraq. That's been the big story over the last two to three years. And increasingly, Iraqis are figuring out how to resolve their differences through a political process." The "sectarian fuse" was "unlikely or less likely, certainly, to be lit again."[30]

Whether the White House was really convinced that the Iraqi forces were good enough to handle matters by themselves is doubtful. Few military experts shared that opinion, which was one of the reasons why the U.S. military leadership had felt so strongly that the United States ought to maintain large numbers of troops after 2011. Yet Obama seems to have concluded that keeping U.S. troops was not critical to the stability of Iraq or to other U.S. strategic objectives. "We, in fact, were not eager to have 10,000 troops in Iraq," a senior administration official told Michael Gordon of the *New York Times* shortly after Obama's announcement. "We came to the conclusion that achieving the goal of a security partnership with Iraq was not dependent on the size of our footprint in country, and that stability in Iraq did not depend on the presence of U.S. forces."[31]

Left unspoken, at least in public, was the role of U.S. public opinion in Obama's calculus. As Obama well knew, recent public opinion polls had indicated that the majority of the American people would be satisfied with the withdrawal of all U.S. troops. Iraq had not been in the news, and Obama had carefully avoided communicating the perils of withdrawal to the American people, leaving the American public ill-equipped to assess the strategic consequences.

After the fact, the American public clearly sensed that domestic politics had loomed large in the President's decision. A CNN/ORC poll taken in December 2011 asked Americans, "Do you think that Barack Obama's decision to withdraw all U.S. combat troops from Iraq was based mostly on politics or mostly on the national security interests of the United States?" Sixty-two percent said it was based mostly on politics while only 34 percent said it was based mostly on U.S. national security interests.[32] Tim Arango and Michael S. Schmidt of the *New York Times* noted that for U.S. diplomats, the complete withdrawal of U.S. troops "represented the triumph of politics over the reality of Iraq's fragile security."[33]

The nosedive of American influence began the moment that the U.S. military footprint was lifted off Iraq. On December 19, one day after the last American soldiers drove across the Kuwaiti border, Maliki took a brazen political leap that he would never have dared taken in the past. The prime minister issued warrants for the arrest of hundreds of Sunni politicians, including his own vice president, Tariq al-Hashimi, who was the country's foremost Sunni political figure. According to Maliki, Hashimi and the others had been implicated in terrorism, but to Iraq's Sunnis and to most foreign observers, the move was merely another underhanded ploy to undermine the Sunnis.

In the coming months, the United States sat idly by as Maliki continued to amass his personal power and round up Sunnis. Liz Sly reported in the *Washington Post* in April 2012, "Sunnis and Kurds, angered by what they see as Maliki's efforts to exclude them from power, accuse the United States of doing little or nothing to restrain his excesses or to press him to implement agreements under which he pledged to share power."[34] Hannah Allam of McClatchy reported, "Many Iraqis—Sunnis, Shiites and Kurds alike—fear that the U.S. withdrawal has given Prime Minister Nouri al Maliki free rein to consolidate power and turn himself into an intractable strongman."[35]

Maliki and his party took a much more positive view toward U.S. policy. "All American interference in the internal situation of Iraq is over," said Khaled al-Asadi, a lawmaker from Maliki's Dawa Party. Iraq's relations with the United States were "better than ever," he said. "They don't put pressure on us; they only offer advice. . . . Sometimes we take their advice, but only when it benefits our interest and it is positive."[36]

While Maliki was giving less and less attention to the United States, he was paying more and more heed to Iran. On July 30, an Iraqi court acquitted Ali Mussa Daqduq, a member of Iranian-backed Hezbollah who had orchestrated an attack in 2007 that killed five U.S. troops. The Obama administration had previously transferred Daqduq to Iraqi custody in return for a promise that he would remain in jail, and the United States still believed that he posed a serious threat to the United States. Vice President Biden appealed directly to the Iraqi government to keep him locked up. Maliki, finding this advice to be less than beneficial to Iraq's interests, ignored Biden.[37]

As the Syrian civil war heated up, Maliki received conflicting entreaties from Iran and the United States concerning the use of Iraqi airspace. The withdrawal of U.S. forces had, among its many other negative aspects, ended U.S. control of Iraq's skies. Once the Americans had handed over control of Iraqi air traffic, Ilyushin Il-76 strategic airlifters began to fly hundreds of tons of military equipment and supplies from Iran to Syria to support the beleaguered Assad regime. The manifests of these flights listed "agricultural equipment" and "flowers," but the United States possessed intelligence indicating that the flights were carrying mortar rounds, rockets, light antiaircraft guns, small arms, and ammunition.

U.S. diplomats asked Maliki to block flights from Iran to Syria through Iraqi airspace or subject them to inspection, to which Maliki replied that he would do no such thing because the flights carried only humanitarian aid.[38] Biden got on the phone himself to inform Maliki that the flights were a "high priority." Maliki responded that he would take it up with the Iranians. Three days later, Maliki issued a statement that Iran was not sending weapons through Iraqi airspace. Ken Pollack, senior fellow at the Brookings Institution's Saban Center for Middle East Policy, observed, "This is another sign that the U.S. has lost a tremendous amount of influence inside of Iraq. We're leaning on Maliki heavily but he's just not cooperating. . . . at the end of the day Iran is wielding a lot more influence in Iraq than we are."[39]

In September 2012, after the White House lodged renewed complaints about the flights, the Iraqi government promised Secretary of

State Clinton that it would inspect aircraft flying between Iran and Syria for weapons. In the ensuing months, however, the Iraqis inspected only two planes, one of which was returning to Iran from Syria. They uncovered no weapons. According to U.S. intelligence sources, Iraqi officials had tipped off the Iranians as to which aircraft would be inspected.[40]

The U.S. military withdrawal also spelled doom for the American civilians who stayed on to conduct their nation's work in Iraq. Responsibility for the security of all American civilian government employees and contractors now belonged to the State Department, which had a very different approach to security than the Defense Department. With fewer security capabilities and much lower risk tolerance than Defense, the State Department issued stringent regulations that made it exceedingly difficult for Americans to go outside their bases to interact with Iraqis.[41] When American officials tried to alleviate the problem by inviting their Iraqi counterparts to come visit American facilities, the Iraqis routinely came up with excuses as to why they could not come.

Because of the inability of American personnel to conduct business with Iraqis, the State Department decided in February 2012 to slice its planned diplomatic staff in half. Later in the year, the U.S. civilian personnel ceiling was reduced from the 16,000 originally envisioned to 6,320. The large majority of that new number would be responsible for security and support for the small minority charged with assisting the Iraqis and otherwise promoting U.S. interests.[42]

By the end of the year, American officials and their vehicles had all but vanished from the city streets. Barry Malone and Peter Apps of Reuters reported from Baghdad that the embassy "was supposed to be a sign of an enduring presence," but "instead, it has become a sign of how greatly Washington overestimated its post-war clout." Homing in on the source of the problem, Malone and Apps observed, "In Washington and other Western capitals, there are mounting worries a failure to negotiate a permanent U.S. military presence may leave them sidelined for good."[43]

The theory that counterterrorism operations could proceed in so perilous a country without a substantial military footprint suffered a grievous blow. The loss of U.S. military protection and the inability of U.S.

civilians to move around freely as before compelled the CIA to shut down most of its facilities in Iraq. Intelligence officers were pulled into Baghdad, where they were cloistered in the embassy, isolated from the Iraqis who could give them information.[44] The Iraqi government demanded that the Agency make formal requests for meetings with individuals who had been readily accessible in the past, and rejected many of the requests. In June, Siobhan Gorman and Adam Entous reported in the *Wall Street Journal* that the CIA was contemplating cutting its presence in Iraq to 40 percent of what it had been at its wartime peak of more than 700 personnel, because of restrictions imposed on its activities by the Iraqi government. Paul Pillar, a former top analyst at the CIA, remarked, "If you don't have that cooperation, you are probably wasting the resources you are allocating there and not accomplishing much."[45]

As a consequence of the CIA's evisceration, U.S. awareness of Al Qaeda's activities in Iraq plummeted. Obama, it may be recalled, had previously contended that removing American troops from Iraq would "give the Iraqis the incentive and opportunity to take [Al Qaeda] out." This prediction proved to be badly mistaken. Maliki had never lacked incentives to destroy Al Qaeda—the organization was dominated by Sunnis, whom he dreaded, and it was inveterately hostile to his Shiite regime. Maliki's opportunities for taking Al Qaeda out did not increase after the American troop withdrawal, but instead deteriorated in parallel with those of the Americans. The Iraqi government lacked the surveillance and other technical capabilities required to track down extremists on its own, and the United States was not going to hand those capabilities over to Maliki or share information with Iraqi forces that no longer had American advisers. The departure of American advisers, moreover, had removed the principal bridges of sectarian and political divides among the Iraqis in the intelligence agencies and operational forces. Internal divisions now poisoned relations among Iraqis whose cooperation with one another was essential for combating Al Qaeda.[46]

During 2012, Al Qaeda in Iraq stepped up its terrorist attacks on government employees, Shiite civilians, and Christians. Iraqi Christians attributed their misery to the departure of American troops, who had been their one certain protector. In March, international organizations estimated that Iraq's Christian population had sunk from an estimated 800,000 to 1.4 million in 2003 to less than 500,000. "The consequence of this flight may be the end of Christianity in Iraq," asserted the United States Commission on International Religious Freedom.[47]

Iraqi Sunnis who had joined the "Sons of Iraq"—American-sponsored security forces that had helped turn the tide of the war—found themselves sandwiched between Al Qaeda fighters, who despised them for siding with the Americans, and the central government, which was dominated by Shiites intent on making Sunnis into third-class citizens. Maliki had promised the Americans he would give the Sunnis jobs in the police, but he had since reneged. Former Sons of Iraq leaders were killed in substantial numbers, often under mysterious circumstances that could not be traced clearly to either Al Qaeda or the government. "I want the Americans to be back," said Muhammad Mahmoud, a generator line electrician, who like many Sunnis said he had felt safer when the American troops were in Iraq.[48]

Senior U.S. counterterrorism officials warned that Al Qaeda in Iraq was increasingly posing a threat beyond Iraq's borders. In October, law enforcement officials in Jordan captured eleven Jordanians who were plotting a terrorist attack on the U.S. embassy in Amman with help from Al Qaeda in Iraq. The conspirators had planned diversionary strikes on shopping centers and luxury hotels popular with foreign diplomats and tourists, followed closely by an assault on the embassy with mortar and machine-gun fire and enormous bombs built with materials and expertise provided by Al Qaeda–in–Iraq bomb experts.[49]

Relations between the Sunni population and the Shiite government sank to new lows during 2013. The event that began the slide was Maliki's decision to arrest 150 bodyguards and staff members who worked for finance minister Rafie al-Issawi, a widely respected moderate Sunni. In response, 60,000 Sunnis gathered in Fallujah to protest the Maliki government, and 100,000 demonstrated in Ramadi. Blocking highways, demonstrators burned Iranian flags and chanted "Out, out Iran!" and "Maliki you coward, don't take your advice from Iran."[50]

On January 25, Iraqi soldiers opened fire on protesters in Fallujah, killing five people and injuring sixty. Sunni tribal leaders in Anbar province, including some who had sided with the Americans as Sons of Iraq during the Sunni Awakening, demanded that the government bring the perpetrators to trial. Sheikh Ahmed Abu Risha, chair of the Awakening Council, warned that if the government did not punish the offenders, the Sunni tribes would "launch jihad against army units and posts in Anbar."[51]

Sectarian violence surged in early 2013. In April, 712 Iraqis were killed, the highest monthly tally since June 2008, and 1,045 perished in May.[52] Al Qaeda exploited sectarian hatreds and the weakness of the Iraqi government to amass new strength. In a July attack on the Abu Ghraib prison, site of the prisoner mistreatment scandal ten years earlier, Al Qaeda blasted open the gates with explosive-laden cars and freed hundreds of Al Qaeda inmates.[53] In November, Matt Olsen, head of the National Counterterrorism Center, told a Senate committee that Al Qaeda in Iraq was the strongest it had been since 2006.[54]

While President Obama and many other Americans had hoped to forget about Iraq, the return of news stories on car bombings and beheadings occasioned a resurgence of commentary on the U.S. withdrawal. Especially striking was the surfacing of complaints about premature withdrawal from U.S. military personnel who had served in Iraq. General John Allen, who had played a critical role in Iraq before serving as the top allied commander in Afghanistan, addressed the subject in May just a few weeks after his retirement. During an interview on ABC's *This Week*, Martha Raddatz asked him, "Would you have liked to have seen the military stay" in Iraq?

Allen replied, "I think we all did."

Raddatz continued, "So you think things would have been better off today, right now in Iraq?"

"I don't think there's any question," Allen said ruefully.[55]

The start of 2014 marked another slide. In the first week of the year, Al Qaeda in Iraq, which was now calling itself the "Islamic State of Iraq and the Levant," or ISIL, to reflect its burgeoning operations in Syria, launched attacks in Fallujah and Ramadi. It obtained the cooperation of local Sunni tribesmen by capitalizing on public outrage at the Iraqi police for dismantling a protest camp in Ramadi. Militants seized control of all of Fallujah and large sections of Ramadi, commandeering government vehicles and flying the black flag of Al Qaeda over government buildings.[56] They set up courts under the "Committee for the Promotion of Virtue and Prevention of Vice," which enforced Islamic law and executed dozens of people for alleged collaboration with the United States.[57]

Maliki sent army units to Fallujah and Ramadi and sought help from Sunni militiamen hostile to Al Qaeda. When neither the army nor Anbar's tribesmen displayed a willingness to crush the militants, Maliki sent elite units forces that had been trained by the Americans. Those units, however, were too small and lightly equipped to take back entire cities.[58]

On January 5, 2014, Secretary of State John Kerry announced that the United States would "do everything that is possible" to help the Iraqi government suppress Al Qaeda. "Everything" did not, however, include sending American troops back to Iraq. "We are not, obviously, contemplating returning," Kerry told reporters. "We're not contemplating putting boots on the ground. This is their fight, but we're going to help them in their fight."[59]

. . .

For Obama, Biden, and the newly installed national security officials who replaced the administration's last Aspen Institute remnants in 2011, Iraq offered an early opportunity to test the light-footprint approach. Rejecting the advice of the U.S. military leadership for a large force after 2011, they concluded that a force of a few thousand would suffice. As it turned out, they would not be able to test the light military footprint in Iraq, because there ended up being no military footprint at all. The United States did, however, leave a sizable civilian footprint, making Iraq a test case for another theory that enjoyed support in the White House—that a civilian footprint was an adequate substitute for a military footprint. That theory flunked the test by a wide margin.

For the United States, the costs of this misjudgment were enormous.

Although the original U.S. war objective in Iraq of taking weapons of mass destruction from the hands of Saddam Hussein had been based on erroneous intelligence, the U.S. occupation of the country had presented critical strategic opportunities. The suppression of sectarian violence in 2007 and 2008, purchased at great cost in American blood and treasure, had paved the way for the development of liberal democratic political institutions and the culture to sustain them, which had the potential to effect fundamental change not only in Iraq but in the entire Islamic world. It also placed U.S. forces in a position to exert influence over events in other critical places, such as Iran and Syria.

When the Obama administration lifted the U.S. military footprint off the country, it removed the political and military clamps that had held Iraq in place while the glue of liberal democratic culture was drying. With the glue still wet, the country became open to manipulation by the unscrupulous. Maliki imposed a sectarian and authoritarian government, fracturing the country along sectarian and ethnic lines and creating dis-illusionment with democracy that may prove permanent. The absence of a military footprint prevented the United States from obstructing Iranian support for Syria or combating the budding Sunni extremist groups in Syria, and it allowed Al Qaeda in Iraq to come back to life. It made possible the rise of the most dangerous terrorist state yet known to the world, the Islamic State of Iraq and Syria.

7

COIN CAN WORK

Iraq, Afghanistan

By escalating the "smart war" in Afghanistan in 2009, Obama had committed himself to counterinsurgency, even if he preferred not to call it that. Although the U.S. military had just finished extinguishing Iraq's insurgent groups in a conflict that would serve henceforth as a prime case study in counterinsurgency, the Obama administration, with its relentless preference for present events over history, showed little interest in the Iraq experience. In its eyes, Afghanistan would serve as the proving ground for counterinsurgency.

The administration's lack of knowledge about counterinsurgency did, however, compel it to rely on counterinsurgency experts who had studied past conflicts, especially the Vietnam War and the Iraq War. Among the most influential of these experts was John Nagl of the Center for a New American Security, a former Army officer who had been propelled to fame by a *New York Times* profile on his implementation in Iraq of counterinsurgency principles from his doctoral dissertation. In 2006, with American forces bogged down in the dust and heat of Iraqi cities, Nagl had helped produce a new counterinsurgency field manual, which the press was to advertise as the new bible of counterinsurgency. Nagl infused the manual with what he called "population-centric" counterinsurgency doctrine, according to which the allegiance of the population was the decisive factor in the war's outcome. The key to effective counterinsurgency, Nagl asserted, lay in building the government's legitimacy through nonmilitary activities that alleviated the population's social, political, and economic grievances. Force was to be used sparingly, and only to protect the population and the government's activities, because the use of force tended to alienate the population.

General David Petraeus had led the development of the counterinsurgency manual, and he intended to apply many of its principles when he took command of U.S. forces in Iraq in January 2007. At the time, great numbers of skeptics predicted that Petraeus's plan to employ U.S. forces in intensive counterinsurgency operations was certain to fail. According to some of the naysayers, the mere presence of foreign troops would make Iraqis more likely to become insurgents, because troops of alien cultures and religions would further inflame Iraqi political and sectarian conflicts. Among those to make this claim was Senator Barack Obama. "I am not persuaded that 20,000 additional troops in Iraq is going to solve the sectarian violence there," Obama said in January 2007, as President Bush's surge forces arrived. "In fact, I think it will do the reverse."[1]

In actuality, that hypothesis had already been tested in Iraq under Petraeus's predecessor, General George W. Casey Jr. From the middle of 2004 to the end of 2006, Casey had repeatedly pulled American troops back into big bases in the belief that it would alleviate the xenophobia that supposedly motivated the insurgents, as well as compel the Iraqi government to get its act together. But instead of causing insurgency and terrorism to subside, the removal of American forces had merely caused the insurgents to attack the Iraqi government with equal ferocity, resulting in a deterioration in security.

Petraeus would put an end to the claim that foreign troops could not succeed in COIN, through the stunningly effective suppression of Iraq's insurgents during 2007 and early 2008. By the middle of 2008, the once-mighty insurgents had been laid low, and Iraq's cities had reverted from barricaded war zones back to commercial hubs teeming with street vendors and small trucks. That turn of events would, however, give rise to new controversies about counterinsurgency.

Nagl and several other public figures were quick to argue that Petraeus's successes were the result of prioritizing population-centric counterinsurgency above enemy-centric operations. A small group of military officers, led by Colonel Gian Gentile, challenged that interpretation, contending that it understated the role of force in Iraq's counterinsurgency, and in counterinsurgency more generally. Nagl and Gentile participated in a series of public debates on the question of whether counterinsurgency needed to be enemy-centric or population-centric.

The real answer was that it needed to be both. While Nagl invoked Petraeus as an exemplary practitioner of population-centric counterinsurgency, the truth was that the general was an exemplary practitioner of blended counterinsurgency, in which enemy-centric and population-centric operations were carefully combined based upon local conditions. Petraeus also appreciated better than these theorists did that knowing what to do in counterinsurgency was much easier than doing it, and that the key to doing it was good leadership.[2]

Counterinsurgency had not foundered under General Casey because he had failed to adhere to population-centric doctrine, as many of his critics alleged. Rather, the problem was that Casey had left much of the work of population-centric counterinsurgency to Iraqi leaders who were incompetent or unmotivated. Poorly led Iraqi forces routinely failed to keep the population secure or reinstate effective governance after American forces drove the insurgents from an area. It was common during Casey's time for Iraqi soldiers and policemen to show up late for work or not at all, or to run away in the face of insurgent attacks.

Casey did have one other tool at his disposal, a tool unprecedented in the annals of counterinsurgency. Task Force 714, as it was called, had been formed in 2003 for the purpose of eliminating former leaders of Saddam Hussein's regime and other hostile Iraqi leaders. The tall, lean Special Forces officer who ran the task force, Major General Stanley A. McChrystal, turned it into an extremely lethal surgical strike force by exploiting advances in information technology.

When McChrystal first took charge of the task force in October 2003, the special operators who had captured documents, cell phones, and computers in the possession of insurgents would put the items in burlap sacks, empty sandbags, or trash bags and send them to a base in Baghdad. Some of the bags were never opened because of a lack of intelligence personnel, and if anyone did find useful information in the bags, it was rarely sent back to the operators in the field.[3]

Most troublesome for McChrystal was the low impact of the task force's decapitation strikes, which, for all their shortcomings, were quite substantial in number by historical standards. Replete with former Iraqi government officials and foreign extremists, the insurgents had enough human capital to replace the senior leaders whom the Americans were capturing and killing. McChrystal eventually determined that defeating the insurgent groups required eliminating mid-level and low-level insurgent leaders, of whom there were a great many. It was therefore necessary for the task force to increase the number of its operations exponentially, and for other forces to lend a hand in tearing the insurgent organizations apart.[4]

An exponential increase in the number of successful operations required an exponential increase in intelligence. In insurgent environments, where the enemy blended in with the population and employed sophisticated countermeasures to evade detection and capture, it had hitherto been unthinkable to obtain enough intelligence to pinpoint enemy targets in the numbers that McChrystal wanted. But with the information revolution, and some deft organizational work, the impossible was now within reach.

McChrystal obtained fleets of manned aircraft and drones to watch the targets whom his men were preparing to apprehend or kill.[5] Surmounting bureaucratic brick walls, McChrystal tapped into the data of the National Security Agency (NSA), the world's premier interceptor and decryptor of communications, and convinced the NSA's leadership to provide raw intelligence in real time. He also persuaded the NSA, CIA, and National Geospatial-Intelligence Agency to send representatives to a massive tent near Baghdad from which he conducted the orchestra of special operators.[6]

The results were phenomenal by any measure. In early 2004, Task

Force 714 had organized ten operations per month in Iraq. Two years later, it was conducting three hundred per month.[7] Insurgent organizations were sustaining staggering losses from top to bottom. And yet, as McChrystal himself acknowledged, the insurgents continued to fight on. They retained control over the population, and hence continued to recruit new members from within it, because only they were providing lasting security to the population. When the special operations teams showed up at a house for a few hours and then disappeared for weeks, they offered little hope of protection from an enemy who was always nearby save for the few hours when the counterinsurgents showed up.

When Petraeus took command in early 2007, he resolved to improve population-centric operations by assigning more U.S. units to population security and boosting Iraqi leadership quality. Petraeus convinced Iraq's prime minister, Nouri al-Maliki, to purge nefarious militia leaders from the police. The Sunni Awakening, which had begun before Petraeus arrived and continued on with his encouragement, brought large numbers of talented Iraqi leaders onto the side of the counterinsurgency. At the same time, Petraeus allocated some U.S. conventional forces to military operations against the enemy, and Task Force 714 continued its offensive operations.[8]

In combination, enemy-centric and population-centric operations proved to be mutually reinforcing. Attrition of insurgents through enemy-centric operations made it easier for Iraqi policemen and administrators to control the population. Assertion of control over the population through population-centric operations made it easier for counterinsurgent forces to collect information and enter neighborhoods undetected. The harmonization of the types of operations was, indeed, essential to the defeat of Iraq's insurgents. McChrystal recounted that the casualties inflicted by Task Force 714 had a strategic effect "only when we were partnered with an effective counterinsurgency approach."[9]

Afghanistan, in contrast to Iraq, enjoyed a period of relative quietude after the Americans toppled its government. From 2002 until 2005, the Taliban and Al Qaeda lay low in Pakistan, nursing their injuries and ruing the loss of their Islamist state. The United States stationed a small number of special operators at a string of outposts near the Afghanistan–Pakistan border, from which they conducted counter-terrorism raids against terrorists who lingered in the border region or attempted to cross from Pakistan into Afghanistan. Securing the Afghan population, a central component of counterinsurgency, was not part of their mission, nor could it have been, since the United States had only a light footprint in the country. Counterinsurgency did not seem necessary in any case, considering the lack of enemy activity.

In 2005, a rehabilitated Taliban pushed across the border with the intention of launching an insurgency in the Pashtun areas of southern and eastern Afghanistan, the areas from which they had first sprung and where they still could count on support from fellow tribesmen. Their reentry happened to coincide with the arrival of NATO forces, mainly Europeans and Canadians, who had accepted American invitations into Afghanistan for what they had thought would be a humdrum peace-keeping mission. Hobbled by restrictions from their governments on the types of activities in which they could engage, most NATO forces pulled back to central bases. The Afghan National Security Forces, which were composed largely of poorly trained and ill-disciplined former militia-men, were not strong enough to hold off the insurgents. The Taliban quickly grabbed hold of the countryside and milked its manpower.

American special operators initiated raids and ambushes against the emerging insurgents, repeatedly inflicting heavy losses, but they could not keep most of the insurgents from reaching Afghanistan's interior. Insurgent strength within Afghanistan increased month after month, and year after year. Edward Reeder, the commander of the Combined Joint Special Operations Task Force–Afghanistan, watched in exasper-ation as special operators smashed hostile forces time and again only to see them get back up with undiminished vigor, as if they were cartoon superheroes. "How many times had special forces done this? To what end?" he asked himself after a successful operation in 2007. "It seems like every time I come back here, the security situation is worse."[10]

In 2008, as the triumphs of counterinsurgency in Iraq reduced the need for U.S. forces in that country, big units of the U.S. Army and

Marine Corps started to arrive in Afghanistan. Their commanders had no intentions of sitting on their big bases and letting the insurgents run rampant through the countryside, as many of the European forces were still doing. But they were just beginning to gear up for battle when Barack Obama entered the White House.

The man whom Obama selected to run the war in Afghanistan, General Stanley McChrystal, had made his reputation by capturing and killing the enemy, but as commander of the whole war he would need to focus much of the American war machine on the population. He directed the commanders of America's conventional forces to concentrate on protecting the Afghan people rather than destroying the enemy, asserting that "an insurgency cannot be defeated by attrition." According to what McChrystal termed "attrition math," the number of insurgents killed through enemy-centric operations would be smaller than the number of new insurgents generated by the population's desire for vengeance. Field commanders received orders to withdraw their forces from offensive operations in the mountains and sparsely populated valleys and use them instead to protect towns and villages.

McChrystal put exceptional emphasis on population-centric activities in order to rein in commanders who were inordinately preoccupied with attacking the enemy, and to mollify various Afghan and foreign audiences for whom enemy-centric methods were barbaric, or at least unenlightened. As the man most responsible for the massive precision-strike machine in Iraq, McChrystal did not share the view of some counterinsurgency enthusiasts that military operations against the enemy were unnecessary. Some of his subordinate commanders, on the other hand, took the rhetoric about "attrition math" literally and imposed restrictions on the use of force that went well beyond what McChrystal had intended. In some areas, coalition forces refrained from conducting any operations outside populous areas, which afforded the enemy sanctuaries for reorganizing and recuperating.

The scarcity of enemy-centric operations by regular units was offset to a considerable degree by the enemy-centric operations of special operations forces. While McChrystal was talking publicly about "attrition math," he was quietly stepping up those operations, by virtue of the transfer of assets from Iraq to Afghanistan. During McChrystal's first year, the rate of operations by special operations forces against the Afghan insurgents increased threefold.[11]

The fact that the special operators were conducting precision strikes against "high-value targets" and were sometimes called "counterterrorism" units fed a misperception, in the White House among other places, that they were engaged in a "counterterrorism" mission that was completely separate from the counterinsurgency mission. In actuality, they were conducting enemy-centric operations that supported the counterinsurgency. For every Taliban guerrilla removed from the battlefield, Afghan officials and Afghan and American forces were less likely to come under hostile fire or trigger improvised explosive devices. Oftentimes, the special units were sent to remove enemies from areas where other forces were attempting to secure the population.

Biden, Donilon, and other advocates of counterterrorism without counterinsurgency made much of the fact that special operations forces were capturing or killing large numbers of hostile personnel in places where the population had not been secured. To them, it demonstrated that eliminating enemy leaders did not require troop-intensive counterinsurgency.[12] What they did not comprehend was that the special operations raids in Afghanistan were not removing senior terrorists or insurgents whose skills the enemy would struggle to replace. Most of those individuals were in Pakistan. Long ago, the enemy had figured out that the Americans were adept at picking off high-level leaders, and hence had delegated authority in Afghanistan to junior commanders, who typically commanded only fifteen or twenty fighters. The enemy could readily replace these commanders and their foot soldiers by recruiting new people in the areas that counterinsurgents had not secured.

The enemy also replaced the loss of personnel by infiltrating men from Pakistan, where radical madrassas served as assembly lines for young zealots. The infiltrators, however, had a harder time when they arrived in Afghanistan and found the population organized against them as the result of effective counterinsurgency. And once the Afghan government gained the ability to take charge of counterinsurgency in an area with local security, it could make the villages so inhospitable to the enemy that foreign special operations forces would be unnecessary.

The importance of the lasting security that counterinsurgency could provide, and of building indigenous capabilities to provide that security, came to the fore during the most prominent military operation of McChrystal's tenure, Operation Moshtarak. Led by the U.S. Marines, Operation Moshtarak focused on the southern Afghan town of Marjah, a Taliban stronghold that served as the central hub of the Taliban's opium trafficking. In the lead-up to the operation, McChrystal met with a group of elders in Marjah. They said they would support the operation to oust the insurgents from their district under one condition: "If you come, you must stay," they told McChrystal. "If you don't, the Taliban return and we will all be killed." McChrystal assured them that the Americans would meet that condition.[13]

In the predawn hours of February 13, 2010, an armada of helicopters ferried U.S. Marines and a collection of Afghan, British, and French forces to landing zones on the flat fields of Marjah. Recognizing that a large force with heavy firepower and night-vision equipment was arriving, the Taliban avoided major battle, withdrawing most of its fighters. The clearing of Marjah took only five days.

The problem in Marjah, as in so many other locations in Iraq and Afghanistan, was installing a sustainable governmental structure that could maintain control after the Americans left. McChrystal had vowed to bring a "government in a box" to Marjah. The box, however, turned out to be empty. The central Afghan government had promised to send civilian officials from its various ministries to staff the local administration, but no one arrived. The Afghan security forces whom the central government had sent to Marjah with the Marines were not up to the task of keeping the Taliban out without a great deal of U.S. help.

The COINdinistas who had been so eager to bring counterinsurgency to Afghanistan, and the members of the Obama administration who heeded their advice with varying degrees of enthusiasm, had failed to account adequately for the frailties of Afghanistan's leadership class.

Afghanistan's elites, from President Hamid Karzai down to the commanders of two-man checkpoints on dust-filled roads, were beset by selfishness, tribalism, ethnic chauvinism, and incompetence. The ravages of war had depleted the country of human capital, and the cronyism of the Karzai government kept much of what remained on the sidelines. In Iraq, the United States had eventually convinced a critical mass of insurgent leaders to switch sides, and had convinced the Iraqi government to replace bad leaders with good ones, but Iraq had possessed a large body of experienced and educated government and military officers. Afghanistan, a poorer country that had been ruled for a decade by primitives, had no such reservoir.

Afghanistan's shortage of human capital stood as a giant, and at first unseen, obstacle to the White House's plans to turn over the war to the Afghans quickly. In order to build Afghan security forces to which the American forces could hand the baton after Obama's surge, the U.S. government dumped huge sums into the training of Afghan soldiers and policemen. The money was much needed. But the Afghans needed something else as well—time. While soldiers and policemen can be recruited, trained, and issued equipment in six months, the development of their leaders takes a decade or more. History has shown, in Afghanistan and many other places, that fielding security forces with underprepared leaders results in soldiers who abuse the population and are abused by the enemy. As one American put it, the belief that throwing resources at Afghanistan's security forces would shorten the development time was akin to the belief that a baby could be produced in one month by assigning nine women to the task.

The American general in charge of the NATO Training Mission–Afghanistan, Lieutenant General William Caldwell, understood the importance of leadership in building new security forces, and he invested much of his command's efforts into bolstering Afghan leader development. General McChrystal also understood the problem and exhorted his Afghan counterparts to institute merit-based personnel practices. On one occasion, he told the press, "The hardest thing about developing an army is developing leaders, non-commissioned officers and officers, and that takes many years."[14]

Caldwell and McChrystal, however, came under great pressure from White House officials and members of Congress to accelerate the training of Afghan security forces. Lacking understanding of how organizations are built, the appliers of the pressure did not appreciate how the rush for quantity would undermine quality. Because of the demands to get more units into the field quickly, Afghan officer development was abbreviated. The resultant military ineptitude cost Afghan soldiers and policemen their lives, and the resultant indiscipline caused offense and injury to citizens, increasing their receptivity to the insurgents.

Washington's rush to shrink the U.S. footprint also had adverse psychological effects on Afghan leaders, both inside and outside the government. The announcement of the surge's short duration in Obama's December 2009 speech at West Point and the near-total absence of any other presidential pronouncements about Afghanistan sparked Afghan fears that the United States would abandon the country just as it had in the early 1990s, when it had ended its support for the anticommunist mujahideen and left Afghanistan to its own devices. For most Afghans, the main point of Obama's West Point speech was not the initiation of the troop surge, but the intent to start withdrawing troops in June 2011.

U.S. military officials attempted to ease these fears by telling Afghan officials that "the 18-month timeline was more for the American public opinion than any unmovable deadline for the Afghans."[15] During a visit to Kabul a few days after the West Point speech, Gates announced at a news conference, "We will fight by your side until the Afghan security forces are large enough and strong enough to secure the nation on their own." He said that the United States might continue to fund the Afghan army and police for another twenty years.[16] Most Afghans, however, paid attention only to what the U.S. president said, not to the remarks of his deputies. In Afghanistan, as in most countries with authoritarian cultures, the man at the top was the only one who really counted.

In the second half of 2010, numerous American military officers in Afghanistan reported that fear of an American departure in 2011 was keeping Afghan tribal elders from siding with the government. As a result, Afghan villagers did not tell American or Afghan troops where improvised explosive devices (IEDs) were located. They joined the Taliban and fought against the counterinsurgents, rather than enrolling in the Afghan government's national security forces or its local police program. The Afghan elites who possessed the skills required to repair and improve the country avoided firm commitments to the government or to the country's future and concentrated instead on how they could exit the country with their families and their money when the Americans left.

During November 2010, in belated recognition that Afghan fears of 2011 were crippling the American enterprise in Afghanistan, the Obama administration began discussing December 2014 as the date for turning the war over to the Afghan government. The move allayed those fears for a short time. Soon, however, Afghans were predicting doom after an American departure in December 2014. Comments from non-presidential U.S. officials that some U.S. forces would remain after 2014, in order to advise and support the Afghans, made little difference.

McChrystal had been expected to preside over the surge of 30,000 troops approved at the end of 2009. Many of those troops had not even reached Afghanistan, however, when McChrystal's tenure was cut short by scandal. It began in April 2010, when a young *Rolling Stone* reporter named Michael Hastings tagged along with McChrystal and his inner circle of advisers during a tour of European nations that had troops in Afghanistan. Characterizing himself as a strong supporter of the Afghan war and the U.S. military, Hastings ingratiated himself with the group. As he would recount in his 2012 book *The Operators: The Wild and Terrifying Inside Story of America's War in Afghanistan,* Hastings actually despised both the war and the military. He had similar feelings toward his journalistic contemporaries, whom he accused of abandoning the spirit of the Vietnam era, when "war had been exposed as the Giant Lying Machine" by journalists like David Halberstam and Neil Sheehan.[17]

Hastings happened to be with McChrystal in Paris on the date of the general's wedding anniversary. McChrystal's staff told Hastings that he could accompany General McChrystal, his wife Annie, and the staff to an anniversary party at an Irish pub, on the condition that he would treat the event as off-the-record. According to members of McChrystal's staff, Hastings agreed to that condition for this event, and for a number of others.[18]

Hastings described the party in detail in the article he wrote for *Rolling Stone*, a decision that he later defended by denying any recollection of an agreement to keep the event off-the-record. Members of Mc-Chrystal's team, he alleged in the article, were "completely s——-faced." A subsequent inspector general's report took issue with that depiction, concluding that the event was "celebratory," but not "drunken, disorderly, disgraceful, or offensive."[19]

The most incendiary sections of the article, however, concerned comments made by members of McChrystal's staff. The first one-on-one meeting between McChrystal and President Obama was "a 10-minute photo op," said an adviser to McChrystal. "Obama clearly didn't know anything about him, who he was. Here's the guy who's going to run his fucking war, but he didn't seem very engaged. The Boss was pretty disappointed."

National Security Advisor Jim Jones was "a clown" who was "stuck in 1985," said one aide. McChrystal believed that Richard Holbrooke, Obama's special representative for Afghanistan and Pakistan, was "like a wounded animal," according to a member of the general's team. "Holbrooke keeps hearing rumors that he's going to get fired, so that makes him dangerous." A dinner with a French minister was "fucking gay," an aide of McChrystal's remarked.

None of these quotes were attributed to specific individuals, leaving the reader with the impression that the whole team had run amok. In his book, however, Hastings provided names, which revealed that most of the offensive material—including all four of the above quotes—came from a single individual. The "member of McChrystal's staff," the "aide," and the "member of the general's team" were all one person, a thirty-three-year-old lieutenant commander. The book also revealed that the lieutenant commander had made many of the most salacious remarks over a dinner with Hastings after imbibing large amounts of alcohol. Between tirades about Obama administration officials, Hastings recounted, the lieutenant commander told a series of fantastic stories, three of which "somehow involved strip clubs and waking up smelling like strippers."

Rolling Stone released the text of "The Runaway General" on the morning of June 22. A few hours later, *Rolling Stone* editor Eric Bates told MSNBC that the magazine's fact-checkers had run the article's contents by McChrystal's staff ahead of time, an assertion that journalists and bloggers were spreading across the airwaves and the Internet within a matter of minutes. This rendition of the fact-checking process led the public and the White House to conclude that McChrystal did not dispute the incendiary quotes or the general characterization of his team.

McChrystal, meanwhile, was summoned to the White House to discuss the blowup. He promptly boarded an aircraft for the long flight back to Washington, which prevented him and his staff from checking the accuracy of Hastings's allegations and rebutting them. It also kept them from refuting Bates's claim that the general's staff had reviewed the article's contents. As the email trail would later show, the *Rolling Stone* fact-checkers had sent emails to McChrystal's staff, but the facts they had checked did not include any of the contentious quotes.[20]

Gates advised Obama to berate McChrystal but tell him he had one more chance. Obama responded that he was concerned about McChrystal not just because of the *Rolling Stone* article, but because of how the war was going. "I don't have the sense it's going well in Afghanistan," Obama said. McChrystal "doesn't seem to be making progress. Maybe his strategy is not really working."

Gates later said he was "floored" to hear Obama express these doubts about his own strategy and commander.[21] He concluded that Obama had been hoodwinked by Biden, Donilon, and other opponents of counterinsurgency, who had incessantly denigrated McChrystal's counterterrorism strategy as a means of gaining favor for their own strategy of light-footprint counterterrorism. Furthermore, Gates suspected that Obama actually relished the opportunity to fire McChrystal, finding in it another opportunity to show the public that he could push the military around.[22]

When McChrystal arrived in Washington, he told Obama that he accepted responsibility for what had occurred and was willing to resign or stay on, depending on what the President wanted. McChrystal could not refute the substance of Hastings's article because he had not had time to look into the details. Even had he known the details, though, he would have been reluctant to engage in vigorous self-defense, because in the military profession an attempt to absolve oneself was viewed as unseemly, a fact that civilians unfamiliar with the military, such as Obama, most often did not know. McChrystal's lack of self-defense, together with Bates's statement on television, appear to have given the President the impression that McChrystal believed the article to have been accurate. Obama told McChrystal that he was fired.

To take McChrystal's place, Obama appointed David Petraeus. Summoning Petraeus for a short meeting in the Oval Office, Obama told him to avoid clearing areas of Afghanistan that his troops could not hold.[23] The remark was noteworthy for its questionable intellectual parentage, having been derived from simplistic variants of population-centric counterinsurgency theory, and for its acknowledgment that the United States was engaged in the sort of counterinsurgency that Obama had said he was avoiding. Obama could have been forgiven for thinking that Petraeus would concur in that guidance, since Petraeus was still popularly reputed to be a leading exponent of population-centric counterinsurgency. Petraeus, in reality, knew from Iraq that counterinsurgents had to be prepared to clear any and all areas of a country, in order to maintain the initiative and deprive the enemy of sanctuaries.

When Petraeus arrived in Afghanistan, he found that population-centric counterinsurgency doctrine had done more than just discourage clearing operations. It had discouraged military operations of any sort. He had championed the counterinsurgency field manual in 2006 as a means of increasing the military's use of nonmilitary instruments, but had not intended to halt the use of military tools. The manual "doesn't say that the best weapons don't shoot," Petraeus remarked. "It says *sometimes* the best weapons don't shoot. Sometimes the best weapons do shoot."[24]

Petraeus relaxed restrictions on the use of force, and eschewed warnings about creating enemies inadvertently by killing insurgents. He emphasized the need to "pursue the enemy relentlessly," in tandem with the need to secure the population and promote good governance. Having learned that many of the restrictions on the use of force had been imposed at intermediate headquarters, between the national command and the field commanders, Petraeus declared those restrictions null and void and decreed that intermediate headquarters could not enforce any restrictions beyond those issued from the top. Almost overnight, these changes raised the morale of the conventional forces in the field and stimulated more aggressive patrolling and raids. Insurgent casualties climbed, while insurgent control over populous areas fell.

Petraeus intended to push ahead in southern Afghanistan, where McChrystal had been concentrating his forces for full-fledged counterinsurgency. In early 2011, with all of the new surge forces in place, NATO and Afghan forces made major gains in the strategically crucial southern provinces of Kandahar and Helmand. U.S. forces drove the insurgents from populous districts and facilitated the resuscitation of Afghan security forces, including locally recruited police forces known as the Afghan Local Police, and civil governance. The Americans capitalized on their military power to insist that the Afghan government appoint better police chiefs and governors in the provinces.[25]

Petraeus planned to shift the preponderance of U.S. forces to eastern Afghanistan once the south had been wrested from the enemy. Only with a large increase in American forces would it be possible to detoxify the eastern provinces abutting Pakistan. Petraeus anticipated another two years of bitter fighting, with daily lists of young Americans killed or wounded in action. He did not know that just as he and the rest of the military were steeling themselves for battles still to come, the White House was seeking ways to get America out of the fight.

8

HALF A COIN DOESN'T WORK

Afghanistan

In the autumn of 2010, President Obama ordered half a dozen trusted aides from the National Security Council staff to begin a strategic review of Afghanistan. In an extraordinary breach of organizational protocol, he kept the project hidden from the highest-ranking members of his national security team—Gates and Clinton—as well as from General Petraeus. Obama and the members of his inner circle whom he had selected for the review team had come to the conclusion that progress in southern Afghanistan was too slow and costly. They were already convinced of the need to accelerate the transition from counterinsurgency, with its requirements for tens of thousands of U.S. troops, to light-footprint counterterrorism, involving only precision military strikes from drones and small special operations teams. Acceleration at the pace they envisioned would deprive Petraeus of the forces required to conduct intensive counterinsurgency operations in eastern Afghanistan following the stabilization of the south.

Gates and Clinton were furious when they learned that a strategic reconsideration had commenced behind their backs. Gates, joined by Petraeus, objected strongly to claims by Obama's review team that the war was going poorly in the south, noting that the team had disregarded more positive assessments at Defense, State, and the CIA. Gates, Clinton, and Panetta also believed that the group's initial findings mischaracterized what their agencies were doing in Afghanistan.[1]

White House officials attempted to stave off these arguments by citing a CIA assessment that spoke of Taliban gains in the north and east. This assessment, they said, showed that the Taliban had offset their defeats in the south with successes elsewhere, and hence proved that the surge had not worked. Senior military officers who were intimately familiar with Afghanistan, however, believed these conclusions to be highly misleading. The advances in the south had been much larger in scale and strategic value than the setbacks in the north and east. The CIA report in question, moreover, acknowledged that the surge had stopped the Taliban's momentum, which was one of its main objectives.[2]

The "light footprint" advocates on the National Security Council staff further maintained that the United States did not need to pacify all of eastern Afghanistan. It needed only to make sure that the Taliban did not take the major cities in the east, which could be accomplished without the troop-intensive operations that Petraeus was overseeing in the south.[3] They contended, in addition, that the successes of surgical special operations demonstrated that counterterrorism, not counterinsurgency, was responsible for most of the advances against the Taliban and Al Qaeda.

As had become common practice, White House officials presented their case to the press via unattributed leaks. On May 31, Rajiv Chandrasekaran reported in the *Washington Post* that unspecified administration officials had told him that "recent gains against the Taliban and al-Qaeda have largely been the result of a counterterrorism strategy implemented by Special Operations forces, not the costly, large-footprint counterinsurgency mission that aims to secure the country district by district." As evidence, they invoked the killing of Osama Bin Laden a few weeks earlier. One official told Chandrasekaran, "Our mission is to disrupt and dismantle al-Qaeda, and what the bin Laden killing shows us is that you can do that with a small number of highly skilled guys. You don't need Army and Marine battalions in dozens of districts."[4]

This analysis ignored the fact that the Bin Laden raid had depended upon a heavy conventional footprint in Afghanistan and the counterinsurgency operations it made possible. Large numbers of conventional forces had guarded the airfield in Jalalabad where the helicopters employed in the raid had taken off and landed. Many more troops had helped secure roads that kept Jalalabad supplied with food, water, fuel, and ammunition, and the villages through which those roads passed. Those supplies had come from central depots at Kabul and Bagram, which also depended on numerous U.S. and Afghan forces for their protection. The intelligence, aviation, logistics, and other combat functions that enabled special operations forces to carry out the Bin Laden raid and their other operations required numerous additional troops. The small American outposts in Afghanistan near the Pakistani border, where much of the intelligence for the precision raids was collected, depended upon conventional military forces for logistics and protection.

At this very time, moreover, the insurgents were maintaining or increasing their strength in areas of Afghanistan that were subjected to counterterrorist raids but not counterinsurgency. Districts and valleys that had experienced night raids every night for months were still riddled with insurgents. The Tangi Valley, a flat and fertile area surrounded by angular mountains fifty miles from Kabul, was a case in point. "The area is completely under the control of the Taliban," Roshanak Wardak, a doctor from the Tangi Valley, said in the summer of 2011. "These night raids have not brought security. This is the duty of the police, but unfortunately, the police are sleeping."

Afforded great freedom of action by the lack of sustained counterinsurgency operations, the insurgents of the Tangi Valley struck back at U.S. special operations forces during a night raid on August 6. As a U.S. CH-47 Chinook helicopter flew over the valley, an insurgent hit its aft rotor with a rocket-propelled grenade, destroying the rotor and sending the helicopter crashing into a dry creek bed. Thirty Americans perished, the majority of them Navy SEALs.[5]

The debate over the size of the U.S. footprint in Afghanistan came to a head in June 2011, the month Obama had designated as the start date for withdrawing surge forces. Petraeus recommended keeping at least 25,000 of the 30,000 surge troops in Afghanistan until December 2012 in order to carry out major counterinsurgency operations in eastern Afghanistan. Biden, Brennan, and others in the White House called for pulling out 10,000 by the end of 2011 and all the rest by the summer of 2012. When Petraeus learned of that proposal, he informed the President that removing the troops so rapidly would jeopardize the accomplishment of the campaign plan as well as heighten the risk of an ultimate Taliban takeover.[6]

Gates, Clinton, Panetta, and most of the experts in their organizations preferred Petraeus's December 2012 date. Obama, however, had made clear he would not agree to December, so they pushed instead for keeping the troops until September. Gates warned that pulling troops out by July would keep them out of the fighting season entirely since they would have to be pulled off the line in the spring, thereby precluding dramatic counterinsurgency advances in the east.[7] What was left unsaid, but was still no doubt on some minds, was that if Obama heeded Biden's advice, he would be conceding that he had sent Americans into harm's way in the past two and a half years for a counterinsurgency enterprise that he had since decided to be unworthy of American casualties.

On June 21, Obama informed Gates, Clinton, Mullen, and Petraeus that he was leaning toward Biden's plan to remove all of the surge troops by July 2012. "If I decide this," Obama asked them, "will you support it publicly?" Gates, Clinton, and Mullen replied that they would. Petraeus said that he had a confirmation hearing for CIA director in two days, and if asked for his professional military judgment he would say that the withdrawal was "more aggressive" than he would have preferred. Obama said that was okay, but then asked if Petraeus would say the new plan would succeed. According to Gates, "Dave got argumentative with Obama at that point, and I came within a whisker of telling him to shut up."[8]

On June 22, 2011, Obama announced in a speech that he would bring all the surge troops home by July 2012. He did not mention his doubts about the effectiveness of counterinsurgency or the need for counterinsurgency in eastern Afghanistan, which were the leading factors behind his choice of timeline. Instead, he chalked up the decision to the successes that had been achieved. Obama stated that he was pulling out the surge troops because "we are meeting our goals" and "the light of a secure peace can be seen in the distance." Afterward, a senior White House official confided that although many White House personnel believed that the surge had failed, "the President's announcement needed to be made on the basis of 'the surge worked, and therefore we can bring 33,000 troops home as I promised the American people.'"[9]

In the speech, Obama said that the transition to the Afghan security forces would be completed "by 2014." He did not, however, say whether he meant the beginning, middle, or end of that year. Obama wrapped up with the now-familiar refrain that "it is time to focus on nation building here at home."[10]

Obama's speech renewed Afghan fears of American abandonment and an ensuing civil war. His lack of clarity about 2014 gave rise to concerns that the United States would be out by the beginning of 2014, rather than the end. Within a week of the speech, leaders of the country's principal minority groups—the Hazaras, Tajiks, and Uzbeks—formed a political alliance that harked back to the Northern Alliance of 2001. Alliance leaders explained that Obama's speech had caused a spike in fears that Karzai and other Pashtun leaders in the government would seek an accommodation with their fellow Pashtuns in the Taliban, resulting in an ethnic civil war between Pashtuns and the minorities.[11]

Fears about the Pashtuns proved to be well founded. Obama's speech did indeed cause Pashtun leaders within the government to put out feelers to the Taliban about a post-American bargain. According to a classified NATO report that was leaked to the press, "Many of [the government's] personnel have secretly reached out to insurgents, seeking long-term options in the event of a possible Taliban victory."[12]

During the second half of 2011, wealthy Afghans attempted to sell off their assets and move abroad in anticipation of the American withdrawal. In Kabul, house prices dropped by a third. Miraj Din, a forty-eight-year-old salesman of imported cars, saw sales plunge from a dozen vehicles per month to only one per month, as people who could afford cars worried that they would have to leave their car behind along with their country. "Now people think the 1980s and 1990s crisis will start again and people will fight," he lamented.[13]

The clear American intent to withdraw also had the effect of stiff-ening the Taliban's resolve to keep fighting and the Pakistani govern-ment's resolve to keep supporting the Taliban. When Karzai sent former Afghan president Burhanuddin Rabbani to negotiations with the Tal-iban in September, the Taliban sent an emissary with a bomb hidden in his turban, who detonated the explosives when he went to hug the former president, killing both men. Interrogation of insurgent detain-ees revealed that the Pakistani intelligence service was meeting regularly with the senior Taliban leadership to provide advice on strategy, and was giving the insurgents remote detonators, mines, suicide vests, and electronics. "Pakistan knows everything," said an Al Qaeda commander from Kunar province. "They control everything. I can't piss on a tree in Kunar without them watching."[14]

The administration avoided clarifying its 2014 plans for more than seven months, until February 1, 2012, when Panetta announced that the United States would shift from a combat role to an advisory role by the end of 2013. The Obama administration had not notified the Afghan government or America's own NATO allies of the decision prior to the public announcement, preventing anyone from mounting a campaign to forestall the change. The choice of the transition date and the lack of forewarning infuriated the Afghans. One Afghan general remarked that ending the American combat role so soon would spell "disaster for Af-ghanistan." Sediq Sediqqi, a spokesman for Afghanistan's interior min-istry, called for the Americans to transfer the combat mission one year later, at the end of 2014. The White House ignored the Afghan pleas.[15]

In May, at a NATO summit in Chicago, Obama suggested that the United States was actually going to make matters better in Afghanistan by removing most of its troops. "Frankly, the large footprint that we have in Afghanistan over time can be counterproductive," Obama said. The ten-year American presence in Afghanistan had put "a strain" on the country.[16] Obama announced that it was time to "responsibly bring this war to an end." As *Time* reporter Aryn Baker noted, however, "the only thing that will really be ending over the next two years is the West's responsibility to Afghanistan."[17]

During the spring of 2012, the United States also convinced its NATO partners to agree to a cut in annual spending on the Afghan security forces from the current $6 billion down to $4.1 billion after 2014. It would require a reduction in Afghan National Security Force strength from the 352,000 projected for late 2012 to 230,000 after 2014.[18] One honest White House official conceded that "it was a number dictated by politics, not by realities on the ground."[19] No one with any knowledge of Afghanistan believed that the Afghan government could survive a huge shrinkage of its security forces at the same time that all foreign combat troops were leaving and the insurgents continued to send reinforcements from Pakistan and recruit heavily in the eastern provinces that Obama had refused to clear out.

Fears of America's departure accelerated the exodus of Afghans from their native land during 2012. Most left by illicit means, for few nations offered visas to Afghans. Fifty thousand Afghans fled to Australia and Europe, twice as many as in preceding years, and an even larger number fled to Iran and Pakistan. The United Nations estimated that one-third of all refugees in the world were Afghans.[20] *Los Angeles Times* reporter Laura King, who had spent the past three years living in Afghanistan, reported in October that "most of the educated Afghans I know, men and women alike, are intently focused these days on contingency planning. The luckiest among them have foreign passports and foreign bank accounts, and in the last year, more acquaintances than ever before have approached me to plead for help in getting a U.S. visa."[21]

The Afghans who planned to stick around busied themselves with alliance building and arms stockpiling in anticipation of ethnic civil war. A senior Afghan defense official admitted to Dexter Filkins that Tajik officers within the armed forces had carefully organized themselves for the looming clash with the Pashtuns. "The only thing stopping the civil war is the presence of the Americans," he said. Nizamuddin Nashir, a district governor in Kunduz province, predicted that "the moment the Americans leave, the civil war will begin."[22]

As 2013 approached, attention turned to the number of U.S. military personnel to remain in Afghanistan over the longer term. Carter Malkasian and J. Kael Weston, two American civilians who had served with distinction in Afghanistan, advocated keeping 25,000 troops in Afghanistan after 2014. Those numbers were required to maintain an advisory presence with the Afghan security forces, provide critical military support functions that the Afghans were not yet capable of performing, and conduct precision strikes against enemy leaders.[23] An external review led by Lieutenant General James M. Dubik, who previously had overseen U.S. assistance to Iraq's armed forces, concluded that a force of between 24,000 and 31,000 was needed after 2014 to ensure achievement of NATO's strategic aims of bettering governance and development and combating extremist groups.[24]

The "light footprint" proponents in Washington made clear from the beginning that they had much smaller numbers in mind. General John Allen, the top U.S. commander in Afghanistan, believed that a large U.S. force needed to stay behind, but he was also mindful of White House pressure, so he avoided putting forward numbers at the upper end of what the military thought necessary. At the beginning of 2013, he presented the White House with a proposal to keep 20,000 troops after 2014. But that number was still far too high in the view of Obama's inner circle. The White House directed Allen to prepare new options for the post-2014 period, with U.S. troop strengths of 3,000, 6,000, and 9,000.

The White House leaked its arguments in favor of a small number to the media, although those arguments were not entirely consistent. One senior administration official told the press that Afghan forces "have made more progress than virtually anyone expected. That's why we may not need as many troops as we might have thought we needed at one point." Things were so good, according to some officials, that no U.S. troops might be needed at all. Other U.S. officials, as reported by Adam Entous and Julian E. Barnes in the *Wall Street Journal*, said that "the lower numbers reflect the political reality in the U.S., amid wariness of costly long-term commitments overseas at a time of a budget crisis at home."[25] Some of the anonymous sources sniped at Allen's recommendation, asserting that it was based upon the continuation of counterinsurgency when all that was required was a small U.S. counterterrorism force.

There was a certain amount of truth to the statement that the Afghan security forces were performing better than expected. They were continuing to hold on in the critical provinces of Helmand and Kandahar in the south. At the beginning of January 2013, Alissa J. Rubin of the *New York Times* reported from Helmand: "Over several recent days, a reporter was able to drive securely to places that in the past had been perilous without a military escort, and many of the roads were better paved, too." But, she added, the people of Helmand were decidedly pessimistic about the future because of the impending American departure. In interviews with dozens of tribal elders, farmers, teachers, and government officials, Rubin found a prevailing belief that the departure of foreign forces would be followed by a return of the Taliban, as the Afghan government and security forces were not yet ready to handle the Taliban on their own.[26]

Carlotta Gall, another *Times* reporter, visited Panjwayi district in Kandahar one month later. Panjwayi was the birthplace of the Taliban, and after the Taliban exodus of 2001 it had remained a bastion of Taliban support, even as American soldiers had poured into the district. The Afghan government had only recently been able to gain control over Panjwayi, thanks to the appointment of a new police chief, a beefy former mujahideen commander by the name of Sultan Mohammad, who had enlisted the support of his Achakzai tribesmen in driving the Taliban out. The people of Panjwayi had rejoiced at their liberation from Taliban rule, in part because the Taliban had misbehaved at times or imposed rules deemed too harsh by the locals, in part because it made good sense in Afghanistan to rejoice in front of whoever held power. There remained, however, a widespread fear that the Americans would leave before the Afghan government was strong enough, on its lonesome, to prevent a Taliban return. One Afghan likened the government to the newly formed mud wall of an Afghan house before it has had time to harden. "If the foreigners take their hands from their shoulders," he said, "the government will collapse like a wet wall."[27]

Americans who favored a large U.S. presence after 2014 noted that the narrow focus on counterterrorism strategy aired in the press by White House officials would leave little of value for the Afghans, so little that the Afghan government might refuse to let any Americans stay. The idea that Americans would sit on a few big bases and target only the individuals deemed a direct threat to the United States was far from appealing to an Afghan government concerned about protecting the entire country from a range of predators. "A presence of 3,000 to 6,000 troops is a counterterrorist policy that gives up on serious support for the Afghan military and focuses on killing our enemies," observed Ronald E. Neumann, former U.S. ambassador to Afghanistan. "It offers nothing to Afghans except endless killing and, hence, will face increasing Afghan rejection."[28]

During March, top military commanders voiced their own concerns about the options put forward by the White House. General Joseph Dunford, the successor of General Allen as commander of coalition forces in Afghanistan, told visiting congressmen that he favored keeping 13,600, as did James Cunningham, the U.S. ambassador to Afghanistan.[29] CENTCOM commander General James Mattis, who enjoyed unusual freedom to speak his mind publicly because Obama had already decided to remove him over other policy disagreements, made the same recommendation in front of the Senate Armed Services Committee.[30]

Contrary to White House predictions that removing the "strain" of the large U.S. military footprint in Afghanistan would ease divisions among Afghans and hence reduce the levels of violence, the Taliban and Haqqani Network stepped up their brutal attacks as the American presence shrank in 2013. The Afghanistan NGO Safety Office, a respected organization funded by European nations for the benefit of NGOs operating in dangerous environments, reported that armed opposition groups initiated 2,331 attacks in the first quarter of 2013, versus 1,581 in the same period the previous year.[31] Because Afghan forces lacked the airpower and sophisticated intelligence and operational capabilities of NATO forces, the enemy often attacked them directly, spraying them with machine guns and assault rifles, rather than relying mainly on IEDs as in the past. During the summer months, Afghan forces sustained one hundred killed and three hundred wounded per week, close to three times the combined casualty rates of Afghan and U.S. forces at the height of U.S. combat participation.[32]

In July, White House spokesman Jay Carney said that the United States was considering the "zero option," whereby no U.S. troops would remain after 2014. A frustrated General Dunford took his displeasure public, telling reporters that open discussion of the zero option was undermining Afghan morale and impeding U.S. mission accomplishment.[33] Former U.S. ambassador to Afghanistan Ryan Crocker addressed speculation about whether the zero option was a U.S. negotiating tactic, intended to pressure Karzai into meeting American demands, or a strategic initiative, aimed at removing the U.S. military from Afghanistan entirely. "If it's a tactic, it is mindless; if it is a strategy, it is criminal," Crocker said in an interview with Trudy Rubin of the *Philadelphia Inquirer*. "Nothing could encourage the Taliban more. The Pakistanis will dig in harder. It will send Karzai in completely the wrong direction. It invokes memories of the early 1990s. It's as if we're telling the Afghans, 'We're tired, we're going home, screw you.'"[34]

During the fall, the Obama administration attempted to secure an agreement from Karzai that would leave a small number of U.S. forces in Afghanistan after 2014 and give those forces authority for unilateral counterterrorism operations. Karzai replied that the United States would have to involve Afghan forces in any counterterrorist operations. He also wanted the United States to provide an alliance commitment comparable to NATO, which would show that the United States had more than just its own interests at stake. The Obama administration gave no ground on either issue. Negotiations over the enduring U.S. presence would remain stalemated for months to come.

At the end of 2013, Dunford proposed to President Obama that the United States keep 8,000 troops in Afghanistan after 2014, along with 4,000 from other foreign countries. Between 1,800 and 2,000 of those troops would be special operations forces assigned to counterterrorism missions, and the remainder would be assigned to training, advising, and supporting the Afghan security forces and protecting bases. With fewer than these 12,000, Dunford said, it would be impossible to protect bases and carry out the other missions, so if he could not keep 12,000 then he would prefer a token force of a few hundred.[35] White House officials concluded that the military was once again trying to box Obama in.[36] Reinforcement of those suspicions came from the leaking at year's end of a dire U.S. National Intelligence Estimate on Afghanistan, which predicted a rapid descent into chaos if the United States removed all of its troops after 2014, with hostile forces threatening the capital in 2015.[37]

Surreptitious White House suggestions to the press that Dunford was trying to force the President's hand failed to silence the commander. On March 12, Dunford spoke to the Senate Armed Services Committee with a candor that no doubt spawned panicked text messaging among the White House staff. Withdrawal of all U.S. forces after 2014, Dunford told the committee, would provide a huge psychological boost for Al Qaeda. It would allow Al Qaeda "to once again establish preeminence in the region and become the vanguard for the al-Qaeda movement from the region."[38] When asked whether he thought a full U.S. withdrawal would pave the way for another attack like 9/11, Dunford responded, "I absolutely believe there'll be another attack."[39]

Media reports also began to surface that the U.S. intelligence community favored a sizable military footprint in Afghanistan after 2014 because a U.S. military presence was essential to the continuation of counterterrorism and counterproliferation programs in both Afghanistan and Pakistan. U.S. officials acknowledged that if all American troops were withdrawn, the CIA would not be able to protect its drone bases in Afghanistan and thus would have to shut them down, leaving the United States bereft of drone bases within range of Al Qaeda's hideouts in Pakistan.[40] According to Kimberly Dozier of the Associated Press, administration officials had hoped that by 2015, Al Qaeda would be weak enough and Afghan forces would be strong enough that drones would no longer be necessary. The administration, however, had been forced to conclude that "al-Qaida is not weakened enough yet."[41]

In early 2014, the shrinkage of the U.S. military footprint and concerns that the "zero option" might come to fruition led the CIA to shut down its outlying Afghan bases and its secret army of Afghan counter-terrorists, who had been instrumental in finding and eliminating Taliban and Al Qaeda personnel. Administration officials had previously expected that those elite Afghan forces would be expanded as the U.S. military footprint diminished, but the exigencies of security and logistics convinced CIA director John Brennan to shut down everything outside of Kabul and the nearby base at Bagram.[42] One CIA source told David S. Cloud of the *Los Angeles Times* that the Agency's leadership had concluded, "We are not putting our people out there without U.S. forces."[43]

The combined urgings of the U.S. military, the CIA, and Afghan leaders, along with the unraveling of Iraq, ultimately convinced Obama to keep 9,800 U.S. troops after 2014. But he would keep them there only two more years, against the recommendation of General Dunford, who favored maintaining a U.S. military presence beyond 2016.[44] At the end of May, Obama announced that U.S. troop strength would decline from 9,800 at the beginning of 2015 to zero by the end of 2016. The two Afghans scheduled for a presidential runoff, Ashraf Ghani and Abdullah Abdullah, both agreed privately to the arrangement.

Although this plan was considerably better than the zero option, many Americans and Afghans worried that the post-2014 drawdown would be too rapid, given the lack of clarity from the White House about the pace at which troop strength would diminish between January 2015 and December 2016. *New York Times* correspondent Matthew Rosenberg, who interviewed Afghan officials and business leaders after the announcement, found that "one common reaction to the decision was the belief that too few American troops were being left behind for too few years. Some worried that announcing such a short deadline would allow the Taliban to easily wait out the American presence, or that the quick drawdown would put Afghanistan's weak economy at greater risk of failure."[45]

• • •

The intensification of the war in Afghanistan under the Obama administration showed that counterinsurgency can work, so long as sufficient resources and leadership are assigned to the task. U.S. forces achieved immediate results at the local level, because they already had the necessary resources and leadership. Afghanistan, like many of America's other third-world allies, lacked those resources and leadership. The United States could provide the Afghans with resources in a very short time, but bolstering the Afghan leadership was a much different story. In a country with as little human capital as Afghanistan, developing enough leaders to conduct a successful counterinsurgency demanded at least a decade of effective training and education, more than the Obama administration was willing to commit.

Achieving enduring results also required securing the entire country, in order to deprive the enemy of sanctuaries where operations could be organized and new fighters recruited. Obama chose not to secure all of Afghanistan, thereby forfeiting huge tracts in the east that bled like gaping wounds, infected by vicious insurgents who were incubating new recruits to spread the disease. The decision to keep U.S. troops past 2014 may have compelled the insurgents to adjust their timeline for ending the life of the Afghan government, but U.S. half measures left them with good reason to believe that the delay would not alter the final outcome.

9

HARD POWER CROSSES BORDERS

Pakistan

The projection of military power across borders is as old as war itself. For millennia, archers fired arrows from their homelands into someone else's, be it for reasons of offense, defense, or offensive defense. Cavalrymen and guerrillas crossed into foreign lands to raid or plunder. In the twentieth century, nations launched manned aircraft from their own territory to unleash massive devastation on the armed forces, industries, and societies of their neighbors, killing thousands of people and destroying centuries of labor in the space of an afternoon. With the development of intercontinental nuclear missiles, mankind gained the power to obliterate entire civilizations from abroad.

Of course, humanity soon decided that launching nuclear missiles at one another was a bad idea. It also discovered that those nuclear weapons prevented the great powers from going to war with one another. For those interested in the use of force across borders, the world was getting very boring.

But then came new technologies that offered stunning new opportunities for projecting military power across borders. By happenstance, they were coming into existence just as Osama Bin Laden and his bedraggled henchmen were trudging into Pakistan from Tora Bora. These new technologies employed cross-border force without the need for ground troops or pilots, a key consideration in a country like Pakistan that did not want foreign troops stationed on or ejection-parachuting onto its soil, and they did so with an accuracy never before seen in an unmanned weapon.

Following the attacks of September 11, 2001, the United States at first saw in Pakistan a base for projecting force into Afghanistan. The Bush administration called upon Pakistan to facilitate U.S. operations against the Taliban regime, and to discontinue support for the Taliban, which it had helped bring to power in the mid-1990s and had kept supporting since that time. As dust and smoke were still swirling around the rubble of the twin towers, Secretary of Defense Colin Powell phoned President Pervez Musharraf to tell him, "You are either with us or against us." Richard Armitage, the deputy secretary of state, notified the director of Pakistan's intelligence service that if his country did not choose to be with the United States, then it should be "prepared to be bombed back to the Stone Age."[1]

The U.S. ambassador to Pakistan, Wendy Chamberlin, presented Pakistan with a long list of demands. The Pakistani government would have to provide the United States with blanket overflight rights and grant U.S. military forces access to Pakistani territory, air bases, and ports for the purpose of taking down the Taliban government. It would have to cease all support for Al Qaeda and the Taliban. The Americans even demanded that Musharraf's government find a way to muffle Pakistani expressions of support for anti-American terrorism.[2]

In his memoirs, Musharraf said that he considered the option of defying the United States. Pakistan wanted the Taliban regime to remain in power, since it was an ally of Pakistan and a replacement regime was likely to be more favorably disposed toward Pakistan's nemesis, India. In the end, however, he decided he had to abandon the Taliban, because Pakistan lacked the military power, economic strength, and national unity to withstand a U.S. military onslaught. In its current state of mind, the United States was liable to destroy Pakistan's military forces and its nuclear arsenal, permanently crippling Pakistan in its rivalry with India. "Why should we put our national interest on the line for a primitive regime that would be defeated?" Musharraf said in rationalizing the abandonment of the Taliban.[3]

Musharraf informed the Americans that he was with them and would accommodate their demands. But he did not accommodate all of the demands. He refused to let the Americans use Pakistan's naval ports and military air bases, directing them instead to civilian facilities. He gave overflight permission only for select areas, which were far from sensitive sites like Pakistan's nuclear weapons. The Directorate for Inter-Services Intelligence (ISI), Pakistan's intelligence agency, helped the CIA apprehend members of Al Qaeda and the Taliban, but kept the CIA in the dark on other members of these groups and other extremist organizations operating inside Pakistan's borders.

Despite these limitations, Pakistan's cooperation proved highly valuable to the United States in the aftermath of 9/11, especially in comparison with what Pakistan would do later on. Access to Pakistani territory and airspace permitted the rapid destruction of the Taliban regime. Information provided by Pakistani intelligence enabled the CIA to apprehend hundreds of Al Qaeda members, including 9/11 mastermind Khalid Sheikh Mohammed.

After a few years, Pakistan's fear of the United States ebbed, and its desire to influence events in Afghanistan to its own advantage returned. In 2005, the apparent success of Hamid Karzai in stabilizing Afghanistan along with the exigencies of the Iraq War convinced the United States to transfer military activities in Afghanistan to the European and Canadian member states of NATO. The Pakistanis interpreted the decision as another American abandonment of the region, and concluded that it would cause India to take on a larger role in Afghanistan and intensify its espionage activities there. The Pakistani government therefore decided to encourage the Taliban, the Haqqani Network, and other extremist groups friendly to Pakistan to undertake insurgent warfare in Afghanistan. The ISI covertly provided advice and support to these groups.[4]

Pakistan's newfound interest in supporting the Taliban and the Haqqani Network also redounded to the benefit of Al Qaeda. After the flight from Afghanistan, Al Qaeda had entrenched itself in Pakistan's Federally Administered Tribal Areas (FATA), a region the size of New

Jersey that bordered on Afghanistan. The Arabs, Chechens, Uzbeks, and other foreigners loyal to Bin Laden ingratiated themselves with Pashtun tribes through intermarriage and illicit businesses. They strengthened their ties to Taliban and the Haqqani Network as well as Lashkar-e-Taiba, an Islamist militant group that had originally been focused on India but had begun to support attacks on the West after rubbing elbows with Al Qaeda and other Pakistan-based extremists.[5] The Haqqani Network and the Taliban provided safe houses for Al Qaeda and helped keep the Pakistani government and the CIA off their back. Al Qaeda and Lashkar-e-Taiba provided suicide-bombing volunteers to the Haqqani Network, which planned and organized suicide attacks in Afghanistan.[6]

The Bush administration was aware that Pakistani assistance in combating extremist groups began to wane in 2005, and that those groups were gaining in strength as a result. But its ability to intensify counterterrorism in either Pakistan or Afghanistan was constrained by the need to send resources to Iraq, which was deteriorating during the same period. In July 2007, near the climax of the Iraq War, the intelligence community issued a National Intelligence Estimate warning of a resurgent Al Qaeda threat to the United States. "Al-Qa'ida is and will remain the most serious terrorist threat to the Homeland," the estimate stated. "We assess the group has protected or regenerated key elements of its Homeland attack capability."[7]

To confront this rising threat, the Bush administration would turn to a new weapon, the armed drone. Development of the armed drone had begun in the final years of the twentieth century as an alternative means of eliminating Osama Bin Laden and other terrorists. The Clinton administration had opposed the use of special operations forces and CIA commandos in Afghanistan, and Bin Laden had evaded the cruise missiles that Clinton had fired at his suspected hideout, so the CIA looked for new ways to strike from the air. The drone promised the capability of pinpointing targets from the air in real time, with the precision of manned aircraft, and without the possible political fallout from the death or capture of a pilot.

During the mid-1990s, the U.S. Air Force began experimenting with an unarmed drone called the Predator. When CIA weapon experts set out to create an armed drone a few years later, they determined that the Predator was sufficiently capable of extended flight and offensive operations. More difficult was finding the right ordnance. Most of the bombs, missiles, and rockets owned by the Air Force were too heavy to be carried by the lightweight Predator. The Air Force tested an array of ordnance, but found none suitable for the Predator. After further searching, the CIA came across an Army weapon, the Hellfire missile, which had been developed for attack helicopters to fire at armored ground vehicles. Weighing just over one hundred pounds, it was light enough for the Predator to sling under its wings. The first successful test-firing of a Hellfire from a Predator occurred on February 17, 2001.[8]

Shortly before 9/11, the United States had objected vociferously to Israel's targeted killings of Palestinian extremists. Martin Indyk, the U.S. ambassador to Israel, said in July 2001: "The United States government is very clearly on record as against targeted assassinations. . . . They are extrajudicial killings and we do not support that." The matter looked very different to Americans once their own security had been violated. A few days after the 9/11 attacks, President Bush signed a secret Memorandum of Notification authorizing the CIA to kill Al Qaeda members nearly anywhere in the world. Administration lawyers argued that the United States had the right to use force in this manner because it amounted to "anticipatory self-defense."[9]

Because of Pakistan's cooperation in hunting Al Qaeda during the first years after 9/11, the CIA did not see an urgent need for drone strikes in Pakistan. The first U.S. drone strike in Pakistan took place in 2004, and it was followed by only a handful during the next few years. Musharraf approved the strikes, though in public the Pakistani government maintained that it knew nothing about them.[10] As Al Qaeda regained its strength in Pakistan from 2005 onward and the Pakistani government became less interested in helping the Americans combat extremism within Pakistan, the CIA and Pentagon recommended larger numbers of drone strikes and the initiation of ground raids into Pakistan. They made little headway with the White House, however, because of objections from the State Department that these actions would exacerbate anti-Americanism.

In the summer of 2008, President Bush's frustration with Pakistani inaction against Al Qaeda and other extremist organizations boiled over. On a blistering July day, Bush assembled his top national security advisers at the Yellow Oval Room, on the second floor of the White House. Bush did not normally hold critical meetings in this room, preferring the Oval Office or the underground Situation Room. But it had special significance: it was the room where FDR had resolved to take the war to Japan after the Pearl Harbor attack.

The White House had just received new intelligence of dire threats to the American homeland emanating from Pakistan. Bush asked Chairman of the Joint Chiefs Mullen and CIA deputy director Stephen Kappes about a visit they had recently paid to Pakistan, during which Pakistani leaders had pretended that they were doing their best against the terrorists. Mullen and Kappes presented the President a plan for special operations forces raids into Pakistan and drone strikes over the tribal areas, all of it to be undertaken without the consent of the Pakistani government. The United States would notify Pakistan's leaders at the time of the strikes or shortly thereafter, which would keep the ISI from tipping off the targets, as had occurred frequently in recent operations. After some debate among the principals, Bush approved the plan.[11]

The CIA unleashed a wave of Hellfire strikes in the tribal areas, hitting large numbers of targets before the enemy could implement effective countermeasures. The missiles killed at least nine major Al Qaeda figures during the second half of 2008.[12] It would be viewed by posterity as the golden age of the drone.

The ground raids did not go nearly so well. On September 3, U.S. Navy SEALs flew into a Pakistani village where members of Al Qaeda had reportedly been spotted. The mission planners expected it to be a stealthy and quick raid, but the SEALs ended up encountering sharp resistance. The enemy had more armed men on the scene than the intelligence had indicated, and the sound of the initial gunshots attracted the attention of neighbors who grabbed their weapons and joined in the fight against the Americans. The SEALs fought for several hours, killing more than two dozen suspected Al Qaeda militants and a few civilians, before their helicopters took them back to Afghanistan.[13]

Pakistanis of all persuasions and walks of life erupted in protest at the intrusion of American ground troops. The Pakistani military ordered its forces to open fire on any U.S. troops found entering the country covertly, and a Pakistani army spokesman made those orders public.[14] The threats and President Bush's own discontent with the civilian casualties caused his administration to discontinue the ground raids.[15]

In Pakistan, as in so many other countries, the new Obama administration would try to win over the government with diplomatic engagement and development assistance. As a result of the Riedel review in the first months of 2009, Obama authorized a huge increase in nonmilitary aid to Pakistan. Later in that year, while crafting the Afghanistan surge, the Obama administration set out to forge a new strategic partnership with Pakistan. On November 11, Obama sent President Asif Ali Zardari a letter calling for Pakistan and the United States to become "long-term strategic partners." The letter spoke glowingly of a "vision for South Asia," which entailed "new patterns of cooperation between and among India, Afghanistan and Pakistan to counter those who seek to create permanent tension and conflict on the subcontinent." But the letter was also full of warnings and demands. "Some countries have turned to proxy groups to do their fighting instead of choosing a path of peace and security," it stated. "The tolerance or support of such proxies cannot continue." The United States wanted cooperation in "defeating Al Qaeda, Tehrik-e-Taliban Pakistan, Lashkar-e-Taiba, the Haqqani Network, the Afghan Taliban and the assorted other militant groups that threaten security."[16] The American emissaries who delivered the letter to President Zardari informed him that the United States would give Pakistan all the items on its wish list of weapons, trade deals, and funding if it agreed to the partnership on these terms.

The Obama administration did not expect that diplomacy and aid alone would win over Pakistan. Convincing Pakistan that it need not fear a pro-Indian Afghanistan was a major reason behind Obama's decisions in 2009 to send more troops to Afghanistan. The willingness of the United States to stay in Afghanistan was, indeed, the most important factor in Pakistan's calculus on whether it needed to support insurgents there.

The other main element of hard power in Obama's Pakistan policy would be drone warfare. In the first week of the Obama administration, outgoing CIA director Michael Hayden briefed the President and White House Chief of Staff Rahm Emanuel on the drone strikes in Pakistan. Obama said approvingly that he intended to continue the program, and Emanuel exuded enthusiasm about the unmanned aircraft. Sensing that the value of drones might have been exaggerated in the minds of his listeners, Hayden cautioned against thinking that drone strikes alone could solve the problems in Pakistan. "Unless you're prepared to do this forever, you have to change the facts on the ground," Hayden said. "That requires successful counterinsurgency" in both Afghanistan and Pakistan.[17]

It is not clear whether Obama and Emanuel paid any heed to Hayden's admonitions that drone strikes could not eliminate the terrorists based in Pakistan. Later on, the Obama administration would in fact help the Pakistanis undertake counterinsurgency operations in areas where terrorists were located. What was clear was that the new White House team saw the drone as an invaluable tool for reducing the terrorist threat from Pakistan, and for shoring up the President's image on national security.

At the beginning of Obama's presidency, Emanuel was the foremost proponent of drone warfare as a means of enhancing presidential popularity. "Emanuel recognized that the muscular attacks could have a huge political upside for Obama, insulating him against charges that he was weak on terror," observed Daniel Klaidman, a *Newsweek* reporter with numerous sources inside the White House. A senior Pentagon official told Klaidman that "Rahm was transactional about these operational issues. He always wanted to know 'how's this going to help my guy,' the president."[18]

The Bush administration had chosen to make the drone program covert, and had kept quiet about it in the knowledge that disclosure of its existence would foster anti-American sentiment in Pakistan. The Obama administration maintained it as a covert CIA program, but Emanuel directed CIA public affairs officers to leak information about successful operations to the press, including spicy details that would be sure to attract the public's attention. After a drone killed Baitullah Mehsud of the Pakistani Taliban in August 2009, for instance, the press was informed that at the time of Mehsud's death, he was on the roof of his father-in-law's compound receiving a leg massage from his wife.[19]

Early on, Obama explored ways to increase the number of drone strikes. One possibility was to expand the strikes into Pakistan's Baluchistan province, where most of the Afghan Taliban's leadership was hiding.[20] But the Taliban were concentrated in the Baluch capital of Quetta, a city of 900,000, which meant that the risks of killing civilian bystanders were much higher than in the remote tribal areas where the Hellfire missiles had been fired to date. The Pakistani government, moreover, had yet to be convinced that it would have no future need for the Taliban, and thus would not consent to strikes that would expose the Taliban's leadership to slaughter. Obama could undertake drone strikes without Pakistani approval, but that could invite an extraordinarily harsh response from Pakistan, which would likely include depriving the CIA of the ability to obtain the information used in targeting the strikes. Consequently, Obama ruled out expansion of the drone program into Baluchistan.

Obama's national security team found other ways to increase the rate of the drone strikes. One was to expand the target list beyond Al Qaeda to extremists whom the Pakistani government wanted eliminated, such as the Pakistani Taliban, which unlike most of the others was intent on bringing down the Pakistani government. Fortuitously, the Pakistani Taliban launched an offensive in the Swat Valley in the spring of 2009, which led the Pakistani government to extend an open invitation for drone strikes in that area.

Taking control of villages and towns, the Pakistani Taliban executed government officials and established sharia courts that imposed floggings, amputations, and the like on violators of sharia law. They then pushed southward toward Islamabad, coming within sixty miles of the capital. The Pakistani Taliban presented a wealth of easy targets for the drones, as the governing of villages and towns required that they set up offices and conduct regular supply movements, the locations of which were passed from ISI informants to ISI handlers to the CIA.[21] Buildings that were teeming with insurgent commanders and messengers at one moment were piles of flaming rubble and charred flesh the next.

The drone strikes, though, played only a minor role in the blunting of the Pakistani Taliban offensive. What proved decisive was the deployment of two Pakistani divisions to the Swat Valley for counterinsurgency operations. Perceiving a mortal threat to the regime, the Pakistani military charged into the valley with claws fully extended, slaughtering large numbers of Taliban fighters and reasserting control of the population. The surviving members of the Pakistani Taliban fled the valley to reorganize and stir up trouble elsewhere in the country.[22]

A similar scenario unfolded in October, when the Pakistani government launched a counteroffensive against the Pakistani Taliban in South Waziristan. As had occurred in the Swat Valley campaign, Pakistani officials provided the Americans with intelligence on enemy positions, which was then used to guide drone strikes. Those strikes added to the body count of the drone campaign, but again were far from decisive. It was the participation of 45,000 Pakistani troops that dislodged the Pakistani Taliban from South Waziristan.[23]

Obama also increased the drone tallies by changing the targeting criteria. He granted the CIA permission to conduct "signature strikes," whereby individuals could be designated as targets without positively identifying them, based on suspicious behavior such as moving in armed convoys, visiting terrorist facilities, or employing certain types of communications equipment.[24] Over time, the signature strikes would account for the majority of drone killings. According to a 2011 report, they killed twice as many people as strikes on individuals who had been positively identified.[25]

The Obama administration could, and did, boast of killing more terrorists with drones than the Bush administration had. It would cite that fact during the strategic deliberations of 2011, when claiming that drone warfare could take the place of land warfare, and during the campaign of 2012, when arguing that Obama was strong on national security. The administration's mouthpieces did not mention that most of those killed by Obama were not members of America's number-one enemy, Al Qaeda, but rather of Pakistan's number-one enemy, the Pakistani Taliban. In terms of Al Qaeda, the drone strikes of 2009 did decidedly less harm than the strikes of 2008. Only 6 of the first 41 strikes in 2009 targeted Al Qaeda personnel. Of the 53 U.S. drone strikes during Obama's first year, 17 were aimed at a single Pakistani Taliban leader, Baitullah Mehsud, and most of the others were employed against the Pakistani Taliban in the Swat Valley and South Waziristan.[26] The broadening of the targeting criteria also meant that many of the victims held low ranks in the extremist organizations and hence their elimination could have but little impact on the enemy.[27]

In the wake of the Pakistani government's counterinsurgency operations in the Swat Valley and South Waziristan, the Obama administration urged the Pakistanis to send their troops and American drones into North Waziristan, where the Haqqani Network and Al Qaeda were at their strongest. The Pakistanis balked, saying they were overstretched and did not have enough troops for the operation. Skeptical Americans pointed out that Pakistan had no trouble assembling 50,000 troops for a military exercise near the border with India at this same time.[28]

Obama had an opportunity to convince Pakistan to forsake the Taliban and the Haqqani Network at the end of 2009, when he announced the troop surge in Afghanistan. Had he stated that U.S. forces would stay for the long haul, he could have dissipated Pakistani fears that Afghanistan would be handed over to India. "Rather than hedging their bets, the Pakistanis might have jumped on the powerful American bandwagon," observed Daniel Markey of the Council on Foreign Relations, who had previously covered South Asia on the State Department's Policy Planning Staff.[29]

Obama's eighteen-month timeline for withdrawing troops from Afghanistan and his more general lack of resolve would prevent Pakistan

from gaining confidence in American staying power. Pakistanis concluded that the United States was going to bail out as it had in the early
1990s, leaving Afghanistan up for grabs between Pakistan and India.
"Announcing the timeline for military departure from the outset was a
crucial blunder," Markey concluded. "The mixed message about American resolve relaxed what pressure Pakistan might otherwise have felt to
reconsider its own stance toward the Taliban insurgents and get onboard
with Washington's program."[30]

The Americans would intensify drone strikes in North Waziristan
during 2010, but the drones could not and did not have the same effect
as sending in troops on the ground. Only a small number of leaders from
Al Qaeda and allied groups were killed in the 118 strikes conducted in
Pakistan during the year. In the middle of 2010, a U.S. counterterrorism
official disclosed that of the 500 people who had been killed in drone
strikes since 2008, more than 90 percent were low-level fighters.[31] In the
first half of 2011, as the drone kill lists were further expanded to include
large numbers of Afghan Taliban fighters operating inside Pakistan, the
number of drone victims considered to be leaders of extremist groups fell
to less than 2 percent.[32]

The loosening of targeting rules was not the only reason for the pau-
city of leaders among the deceased extremists. Following the first big
wave of drone strikes in 2008, the enemy had devised countermeasures
that proved effective in limiting the damage, and in particular the damage to the leadership. Among the most obvious countermeasures were
eliminating cell phone usage and delegating greater authority to local
commanders. Other techniques were developed by studying the drone
program as it progressed. Discerning that the missiles often hit sizable
gatherings of men and that they rarely struck when women and children were present, the extremists avoided large assemblies and kept their
leaders in close proximity to women and children.[33]

Upon learning that individuals from Afghanistan were bringing
homing devices into Pakistan to guide the drone strikes, militant commanders began monitoring the movement of people from Afghanistan
into Pakistan, and they beheaded, hanged, or shot those caught carrying

the gadgets.[34] After one wily militant discovered that some American tracking devices contained infrared transmitters, they started scanning vehicles with infrared cameras.[35] Al Qaeda disseminated an illustrated guide to GPS devices that were used by the CIA for targeting drone strikes,[36] and some Pakistani militants even bought commercially available GPS jamming devices in an effort to disorient the drones.[37]

The most simple, most common, and most effective countermeasure was the relocation of leaders outside the zones where the Pakistani government was permitting the Americans to fly the drones. Once Hellfire missiles began killing members of the Haqqani Network in North Waziristan, the organization's leaders went to live in cities that were off-limits to the drone program. Rawalpindi, a city on the Potwar Plateau where some of the Pakistani government's leading figures resided, was their preferred destination.[38] Other senior Haqqani Network figures took up residence in upscale neighborhoods of the Pakistani capital, Islamabad, in plain view of the national leadership.[39]

Another attractive destination for extremist groups fleeing the Hellfires was Karachi. A diverse city of 20 million people, Karachi had 5 million Pashtun residents, whose ethnic commonality with many of the extremists made their neighborhoods excellent places for a few men to hide and obtain support.[40] The Pakistani Taliban moved much of their leadership to Karachi during the fighting in the Swat Valley, and they used their new urban footholds to assassinate secular politicians who were hostile to their movement, reducing the number of moderate representatives in the legislature.[41] By 2012, Al Qaeda had shifted many of its organizational activities from the tribal areas to Karachi. Capitalizing on its growing strength in the city, Al Qaeda indoctrinated and recruited followers at universities and madrassas.[42]

Al Qaeda also grew in strength in Lahore, a city of 7 million that served as the capital of Punjab and the unofficial cultural capital of Pakistan. Lahore was already home to the leadership of Lashkar-e-Taiba, the organization that had killed 166 people, including six Americans, in the Mumbai attacks of November 2008.[43] Hafiz Muhammad Saeed, the head of Lashkar-e-Taiba, claimed to have moved away from violence after

2008 in favor of nonviolent democratic political activity, but his organization continued to engage in attacks against U.S. and Indian targets
in Afghanistan. The United States had put a bounty of $10 million on
his head, and the United Nations had levied sanctions on his group. Still,
he enjoyed the obvious support of the Pakistani government, for whom he
served as a valuable weapon against India.

Saeed was so confident that the Pakistani government would not
touch him that he maintained a regular residence in Lahore, living in a
large compound with a fortified house, office, and mosque. He spoke at
large public gatherings and appeared on prime-time television. During
public appearances, he mocked the United States and called for an end
to its drone war. On the Friday after Bin Laden was killed, he led prayers
in mourning of the Al Qaeda leader.[44]

Because of the high probability that Hellfire missiles would kill
civilian bystanders when fired into crowded urban centers, the Obama
administration did not pressure the Pakistani government to authorize
strikes in the cities. It did, however, ask the Pakistanis for cooperation
in operations on the ground to capture or kill extremist leaders. The
Pakistani government had obstructed such operations in some cities
by preventing CIA personnel from leaving their bases, on the pretext
that they needed to be protected from terrorists. At the end of 2009,
Panetta proposed "joint ISI-CIA operations on the ground" to the Pakistanis for the purpose of targeting Al Qaeda, the Taliban, and the like
within Pakistani cities, but the Pakistanis rejected the proposal out of
hand.[45]

Further evidence of the drone program's limitations could be found
in its inability to foil terrorist plots even in the areas where the drones
were permitted to operate. Najibullah Zazi, who had been preparing
to blow up New York subway trains with backpack bombs in September 2009 when the FBI caught him, and Faisal Shahzad, who drove
a massive bomb to Times Square in May 2010 but failed to detonate
it, received their terrorist training in Pakistan's Federally Administered
Tribal Areas at the height of the drone campaign. So did militants of
the Islamic Movement of Uzbekistan whose plotting caused a terror-

ism scare in Europe in the fall of 2010. The drones had minimal effects on the mass production of Islamist fanatics in the Pashtun tribal areas, which continued to supply 80 percent of the suicide bombers in Afghanistan.[46]

For the White House, Faisal Shahzad's success in driving a bomb-laden Nissan Pathfinder into Times Square made clear that the drone campaign was not an adequate guarantor of safety from terrorism. Only a faulty detonator had prevented the killing of hundreds, if not thousands, of civilians. Following that event, Jones flew to Islamabad to meet with President Zardari and General Ashfaq Parvez Kayani, who as chief of Pakistan's army was the real boss. Jones told Zardari and Kayani that if the SUV had blown up in Times Square, Obama would have been compelled to take actions that Pakistan would have found highly disagreeable. "The president wants everyone in Pakistan to understand if such an attack connected to a Pakistani group is successful, there are some things even he would not be able to stop," Jones warned. "Just as there are political realities in Pakistan, there are political realities in the United States. No one will be able to stop the response and consequences. This is not a threat, just a statement of political fact."

Zardari replied that if the United States and Pakistan were strategic partners, shouldn't they come together at a time of crisis?

Jones said that Obama would have no choice. The United States could no longer tolerate Pakistan's support for terrorist groups of any kind. The Pakistanis were playing Russian roulette, Jones said, and so far they had managed to avoid pulling the trigger with a bullet in the chamber. One day, however, there would be a round in the chamber.[47]

The United States wanted four things from Pakistan, Jones told the Pakistanis. First, the ISI needed to share "all intelligence with us and we will share intelligence with you." Second, the Pakistani government needed to share all passenger data on flights departing from Pakistan. Third, counterterrorism cooperation had to be increased. Fourth, Pakistan needed to stop holding up visa requests for American intelligence and law enforcement personnel.

The Pakistanis replied that the ISI was already sharing all relevant

intelligence with the Americans and cooperating fully on counterterrorism. They refused to share passenger data, and did little to expedite the
visas.[48]

Separately, Panetta asked Kayani to expand the "boxes" where the
CIA carried out Predator drone strikes. Kayani said he would look into
it. Nothing was done.[49] A few months later, the CIA asked the Pakistani
government to let more of its officers into the country to collect information for drone strikes. The Pakistanis refused that request, too.[50]

In the midst of this desert of setbacks, the Obama administration
was to find one oasis, the existence of which would be touted to such
a degree as to divert most of the attention from the surrounding sands.
It was, admittedly, a big oasis. In August 2010, CIA director Panetta
notified Obama that the CIA had a promising lead on the whereabouts
of Osama Bin Laden. After losing Bin Laden's scent at the end of 2001,
the CIA had concentrated its searches on remote villages and cave complexes in Pakistan's tribal areas, where most of the world suspected him
to be. But the location that the CIA had just identified was in Abbottabad, a city in northwestern Pakistan.[51]

Founded by the British officer James Abbott in 1853, Abbottabad
was an unlikely hiding place for the world's most wanted terrorist—
which was what made it such an excellent choice. The section of the
city where Bin Laden had taken up residence was populated mainly by
retired army officers and businessmen, and his compound stood just one
kilometer from Pakistan's military academy. The proximity to the military academy would later fuel much speculation that Pakistan's government had known all along who was living in the compound. Countries
like Pakistan, with its constant fear of Indian subversion, did not normally permit construction of large and foreboding buildings within a
kilometer of their military facilities without knowing the owners and
occupants. "Nobody can believe he was there without people knowing,"
commented Ejaz Shah, former head of the Pakistani equivalent of the
FBI. "In a Pakistani village, they notice even a stray dog."[52] Materials
recovered from Bin Laden's compound would lead the United States
to conclude that Pakistani intelligence knew of Bin Laden's presence,

though the Obama administration chose to avoid disclosing this information publicly.[53]

Neighbors rarely saw any of the residents of the concrete compound. A twelve-foot-high wall surrounded the buildings, shielding the grounds from gazes out of nearby windows, and a seven-foot-high wall encircled the third terrace, providing Bin Laden a place to stroll unobserved. Bulletproof vehicles occasionally arrived, for which security gates quickly opened and closed. Bin Laden and the women in the compound never went outside the walls, and the children played only with each other.[54]

The Americans had found Bin Laden's compound by tracking down the courier whom he used in lieu of electronic communications. In one of history's more notable ironies, the raid that Obama would advertise as his signature achievement in national security was made possible through the CIA's use of interrogation techniques that Obama had denounced in the 2008 campaign and banned in 2009. During Bush's presidency, several senior Al Qaeda detainees had disclosed the identity of Bin Laden's courier only after those techniques had been used.[55]

Admiral William McRaven, the commander of the Joint Special Operations Command, first learned of the Abbottabad compound in January 2011. Summoned to CIA headquarters for a briefing, he listened attentively to the details. By the time the briefers had finished, McRaven concluded that a raid by special operations forces was much preferable to the other likely option—an air strike on the compound. Destroying the compound and any tunnels and bunkers that might be below it would require 50,000 tons or more of bombs, which would kill numerous civilians nearby and create an enormous political backlash in Pakistan. The United States would be unable to conduct a detailed search for Bin Laden's DNA after the strike, and thus would be unable to justify the bombing to the Pakistanis with conclusive evidence.[56]

McRaven expressed confidence that his forces could handle the mission. "This is a relatively straightforward raid from JSOC's perspective," he told the CIA briefers. "We do these ten, twelve, fourteen times a night. The thing that makes this complicated is it's one hundred and fifty miles inside Pakistan, and logistically getting there, and then the politics of explaining the raid, is the complicating factor."[57]

Obama's communications team would later tell the press that the President had decided on a ground raid over the objections of nearly all his advisers. In actuality, the ground raid was the preferred option of most of them, including Donilon, McDonough, Rhodes, Blinken, Brennan, Panetta, Clinton, Mullen, Director of National Intelligence James Clapper, Under Secretary of Defense for Intelligence Mike Vickers, and Under Secretary of Defense for Policy Michèle Flournoy, in addition to McRaven. These individuals noted that a ground raid would be easier for the United States to deny than an air strike in the event that Bin Laden was not present at the compound, and it would leave no uncertainty as to whether he was really there. If Bin Laden was there, then ground forces would be able to seize documents and computer drives containing invaluable information on his global terrorist network.[58]

The main skeptics of the ground raid were Gates and Biden. Gates was concerned that U.S. ground forces would trigger booby traps or get into a fight with Pakistani forces.[59] Both Gates and Biden warned Obama that a raid would permanently damage U.S. relations with Pakistan. The Pakistani government could retaliate by denying the United States access to the land and air corridors critical to the supply of American forces in Afghanistan, and it could shut down the U.S. drone program.[60] Gates and Biden preferred an air strike.

The other option was to do nothing. Unlike the ground raid and the air strike, it entailed no risk for either U.S. forces or U.S. relations with Pakistan. But it did pose huge risks for Obama's own political fortunes. The Democrats had derided George W. Bush mercilessly for the failure to catch Bin Laden at Tora Bora in 2001. If the American people learned that Obama had received credible information on Bin Laden's location and refused to act upon it—as they would inevitably learn when a disillusioned national security official told a press contact—then they might well vote him out of office in 2012. During the deliberations, Panetta told Obama that he needed to ask himself, "What would the average American say if he knew we had the best chance of getting bin Laden since Tora Bora and we didn't take a shot?"[61] Neither Obama nor any of his advisers came down in favor of the do-nothing option.

Obama was swayed by McRaven's argument that the possibility of killing civilians in neighboring compounds made a bombing strike prohibitively risky.[62] Outrage over such casualties, in Pakistan and elsewhere, would have devastating diplomatic blowback, which would be multiplied if it turned out that the mysterious tall man in the compound were someone other than Bin Laden. Obama decided to launch a ground force raid at the beginning of May.

On the first of May, at 11 P.M. local time, two Black Hawk helicopters lifted off the airfield at the Afghan city of Jalalabad. The pilots flew "nap-of-the-earth," keeping the helicopter skids just a few feet above the tree-tops, riverbeds, and foothills of the Hindu Kush mountain range as they raced toward Abbottabad, 150 miles to the east. After ninety minutes of uneventful flight, the first of the two Black Hawks attempted to set down in the largest courtyard of Bin Laden's compound. Its tail clipped a wall, instantly wrecking the tail rotor and rendering the helicopter unfly-able. The pilot, however, was able to land the helicopter without serious injury to any of the passengers, and the mission proceeded as planned.

Twenty-three Navy SEALs disembarked from the helicopter. They fanned out through the compound and, after taking fire from several men, shot all of the adult males dead, including Osama Bin Laden. Scouring the compound's buildings, they stuffed satchels with computers, flash drives, CDs, documents, and anything else that might be of value in the ongoing war against Al Qaeda. Forty minutes after their arrival, the SEALs hopped back onto helicopters and departed into the night.[63]

Obama delivered a speech on the night of the raid. "Shortly after taking office," the President said, "I directed Leon Panetta, the director of the CIA, to make the killing or capture of Bin Laden the top priority of our war against Al Qaeda." Obama went into detail on his own in-volvement in the operation, which would spawn allegations of narcissism and self-promotion, even from his own political allies. "Last August, after years of painstaking work by our intelligence community, I was briefed on a possible lead to Bin Laden," Obama said. "I met repeatedly with my national security team as we developed more information about the possibility that we had located Bin Laden hiding within a compound deep inside of Pakistan. And finally, last week, I determined that we had enough intelligence to take action, and authorized an operation to get Osama bin Laden and bring him to justice. Today, at my direction, the United States launched a targeted operation against that compound in Abbottabad, Pakistan."[64]

On the day before the raid, the top members of Obama's national security team had agreed to keep quiet about the specifics of the raid, in order to protect operational methods that were used routinely in Afghanistan and elsewhere. But within a matter of hours, senior administration officials broke the promise. John Brennan, in a meeting with reporters in his office, rattled off a string of operational details. Some of his assertions turned out to be inaccurate, such as a claim that Bin Laden had used one of his own wives as a human shield.[65]

Obama's staff also propagated a bogus claim that Obama deserved special credit for the intelligence that had led to Bin Laden. The main piece of evidence invoked in support of the claim was a June 2009 memo in which Obama had directed Panetta to "provide me within thirty days a detailed operation plan for locating and bringing to justice Osama bin Laden."[66] Peter Bergen, who had defended Obama from criticism on many other occasions, characterized this line of reasoning as absurd. "Five senior U.S. intelligence officials who worked for both Bush and Obama say that the idea that the CIA needed to be pushed to do more on Bin Laden is laughable," Bergen wrote in his book on the Bin Laden raid. "The Agency was doing as much as it could already."[67]

Administration sources informed the press that the Bin Laden raid showed the value of light-footprint counterterrorism. On June 19, the *New York Times* reported that "high-ranking officials" said that "the intense campaign of drone strikes and other covert operations in Pakistan—most dramatically the raid that killed Osama bin Laden—had left Al Qaeda paralyzed, with its leaders either dead or pinned down in the frontier area near Afghanistan."[68] Although the death of Bin Laden certainly was a psychological and organizational blow, Al Qaeda was hardly lying in paralysis near the Afghan border. By this time, Al Qaeda had relocated many of its operations from the Afghan border to Karachi, Lahore, and other Pakistani cities, where they were largely beyond the reach of the United States. The fact that Bin Laden himself had lived comfortably in a Pakistani city for six years also should have led Americans to be more concerned about active or tacit support for Al Qaeda within the Pakistani government, the entity whose cooperation was most vital to U.S. efforts against Al Qaeda. Much of Al Qaeda's core leadership, moreover, was located in other countries, having been dispersed by Bin Laden in order to expand and guide the movement.

The Obama administration would have far less to say to the press about the negative consequences of the raid. The biggest of these was the antagonizing of Pakistan, which proved to be as harmful as Gates and Biden had predicted. One of the few administration officials to discuss the subject conceded, "We certainly anticipated that the Pakistani leadership would find what we did unwelcome, and would feel bruised and resentful. I think the depth and breadth of that has probably gone further than we had anticipated."[69]

In surveys taken a week after the Bin Laden raid, 64 percent of Pakistanis said that they disapproved of the operation, whereas only 10 percent approved.[70] The Pakistani military suffered a severe and humiliating loss of prestige among the Pakistani people because of its inability to detect or disrupt the American operation. Pakistanis were appalled that the American helicopters had been able to fly into the middle of a Pakistani city under the noses of Pakistan's armed forces without anyone so much as catching a whiff. If the Americans could penetrate the home of the Pakistani military academy unnoticed, then they might also be able to sneak in and steal or destroy Pakistan's nuclear weapons.[71]

The resentments resulting from the raid would have enduring effects on relations between the United States and Pakistan, the full extent of which will not be known for decades. There were also immediate results. The Pakistani government ejected U.S. special operations personnel who had been in Pakistan, and put new restrictions on the movements of foreign diplomats and aid workers.[72] A report published by the U.S.

Government Accountability Office (GAO) in May 2012 stated that "the reduced number of U.S. military personnel and trainers, along with continued delays in obtaining visas, hindered the United States' provision of security-related assistance to Pakistan," including U.S. efforts to bolster Pakistani counterinsurgency capabilities in areas of high importance to the United States. The report concluded, "The progress achieved since 2010 in training, advising, and equipping Pakistan security forces has eroded, particularly in the area of counterinsurgency effectiveness for tactical- and operational-level combat forces."[73]

The adverse consequences for the drone program were particularly severe. When Senator John Kerry visited Pakistan two weeks after the raid, Pakistan's leaders demanded that the United States shut down the drone program.[74] When the Obama administration refused, the Pakistanis forced the Americans to leave the Shamsi Air Base in the Baluchistan desert, from which the CIA had flown the drone strikes over Pakistan's tribal areas. The United States had to move all of its drones to bases in Afghanistan, whose government for the moment had no choice but to accept the arrangement, but which was expressing desires to remove drone bases in the future.[75] The relocation of all drone aircraft to Afghanistan created new logistical and operational hurdles that forced reductions in the number of drone strikes over Pakistan.[76]

As another consequence of the Bin Laden raid, the ISI launched a concerted effort to undermine the CIA inside Pakistan. ISI agents harassed CIA employees and blocked visa applications for new CIA personnel, both of which impeded acquisition of targeting information for the drones.[77] The ISI also initiated a covert media campaign to stimulate domestic and international criticism of the drone strikes, leveling exaggerated claims of civilian casualties.[78]

The ISI's charges contributed to an acceleration in opposition to the drones, opposition that had already been gaining momentum in numerous countries, including the United States. Put on the defensive, the Obama administration maintained that the drone targeters took great care to avoid civilian casualties, while acknowledging that somewhere between 20 and 50 civilian bystanders had been killed.[79] Independent experts jumped on the administration in the spring of 2012 after a senior administration official told the *New York Times* that the number of civilians killed by Obama's drone war in Pakistan was in the "single digits." That tally was based on the presumption that all military-aged males killed in the strikes were combatants, an assumption adopted at the personal behest of Obama, despite complaints from intelligence officials and others within the administration about its validity. The New America Foundation, which tracked the drone war closely, estimated in 2012 that between 293 and 471 civilians had been killed by drone-fired missiles.[80]

Indignation about the drone program, in Pakistan and around the world, would lead to its curtailment in early November 2011. The State Department, which was less enamored of drone strikes than the White House, received greater influence over the targeting. Obama also agreed to give the Pakistanis advance notification of future strikes.[81]

Frustrated by the diminishing returns from the drone program, the Obama administration publicly floated the idea of U.S. ground operations into North Waziristan against the Haqqani Network. In public testimony, Admiral Mullen called out the Haqqani Network for a truck bombing on September 10, 2011, that had wounded seventy-seven Americans, and a subsequent attack on the U.S. embassy and other targets in Kabul that had killed two dozen Afghans. According to Mullen, cell phone evidence showed conclusively that the ISI had supported the attacks. The Pakistani government vehemently denied providing any support to the Haqqani Network, and sternly warned the Americans against any ground operations in North Waziristan. If the Americans set foot in North Waziristan, General Kayani snarled, "they will find it 10 times more costly and difficult" than their wars in Afghanistan and Iraq.[82]

Obama decided not to send ground forces into North Waziristan, but the U.S. military did intensify operations in Afghanistan near the Pakistani border in order to debilitate the Haqqani Network.[83] American forces repeatedly took fire from Haqqani forces on the Pakistani side of the border, some of whom were in plain sight of Pakistani police or military forces who did nothing to stop them. U.S. suspicions that Pakistan's government was tipping off the insurgents caused the Americans to stop providing the Pakistanis with NATO troop locations, which led to a calamitous fight between NATO and Pakistani forces. On November 26, 2011, Pakistani soldiers opened fire across the border on NATO forces, whom they apparently believed to belong to a hostile extremist group, and the NATO forces returned fire in a more accurate fashion, killing twenty-four Pakistani soldiers.[84]

The Pakistani government blamed the United States for the tragedy and shut down the movement of U.S. supplies to Afghanistan through Pakistani territory, compelling the United States to rely on more costly routes to the north of Afghanistan. The U.S. monthly supply transportation bill increased from $17 million per month to $104 million per month.[85] Pakistan demanded an apology for the deaths of the twenty-four soldiers, and an increase in the fee paid by the United States for each truck that moved through the country, from $250 to $5,000.[86] The White House refused to accept those terms. U.S. taxpayers had to foot the extra $87 million per month until July 2012, when Secretary of State Clinton issued an official apology and agreed to unfreeze $1.2 billion in military aid for Pakistan.[87]

In the meantime, Pakistan continued to support the operations of the Haqqani Network and the Taliban in Afghanistan, and to shelter their leaders inside Pakistan. In early 2012, U.S. Ambassador to Afghanistan Ryan Crocker wrote in a cable to Washington that the presence of hostile forces in Pakistan, especially the Haqqani Network, threatened the viability of U.S. strategy in Afghanistan.[88] The Obama administration could do little to address the problem, with the drone program on the decline and ground operations into Pakistan off the table. The total number of drone strikes for 2012 would reach only 46, down from 64 in the previous year.[89]

The number of drone strikes in Pakistan slid further in 2013, to twenty-seven, thanks in no small part to reductions in the U.S. footprint in Afghanistan during the year.[90] The withdrawal of U.S. forces from Afghan districts along the Pakistani border compelled the CIA to close bases that had collected intelligence on hostile organizations as well as other strategic matters like Pakistan's nuclear arsenal and Islamist subversion of the Pakistani government.[91] The closure of these bases also resulted in the disbanding of the CIA's elite Afghan counterterrorism teams, which in the past had gone across the border to obtain targeting data for the CIA's drones.[92]

The decline of the drone program and the Pakistani government's obstruction of other counterterrorist measures allowed all of the big extremist groups to gain in strength during 2013. Al Qaeda was regenerating in Pakistani cities beneath the shields of the Afghan Taliban, Lashkar-e-Taiba, and other extremist outfits.[93] In August, Al Qaeda leader Ayman al-Zawahiri, who was believed to be located somewhere in Pakistan, fomented a plot to attack U.S. diplomatic facilities in the Middle East and North Africa. Fortunately, the United States received word of the plot before it could be hatched, and it preempted the terrorists by closing nineteen U.S. embassies and evacuating American civilians and governmental personnel from Yemen.[94]

American drones did not fire a single missile into Pakistan during the first five months of 2014. The Obama administration cited the killing of Al Qaeda leaders and reduced enemy activity in Pakistan's tribal areas as reasons for the lack of strikes. Those explanations, however, were merely smoke screens for the harsh truth that Pakistani opposition to the drones, American retrenchment in Afghanistan, and the urbanization of Pakistan's extremists had neutered the drone program.[95]

In the summer of 2014, U.S. drones fired a few missiles into North Waziristan, in concert with a new Pakistani ground offensive. The Pakistani government advertised the offensive as the granting of long-standing American requests to crush the Haqqani Network in its main base area. The offensive would not achieve that objective, however, and undoubtedly it had not been meant to do so. The Haqqani Network and other extremists had been forewarned of the operation weeks in advance. Cutting away their distinctive long hair and beards, they had blended in with hundreds of thousands of civilians who fled the area prior to the arrival of Pakistan's ground forces. One barber in the town of Bannu told a foreign journalist, "I have trimmed the hair and beards of more than 700 local and Uzbek militants ahead of the security forces' operation."[96]

During the offensive, the Pakistani army brought foreign correspondents to Miram Shah, a town in North Waziristan that served as the de facto capital of the Haqqani Network. One hundred thousand people had lived in Miram Shah prior to the offensive, but journalists from the *New York Times* reported that the only inhabitant now visible on Miram Shah's streets was a stray donkey. "Yes, they did escape," Major General Zafarullah Khan, commander of the offensive, admitted as he escorted the reporters through the town. "They had smelled that the operation was about to be launched," so "the leadership abandoned this place."[97]

The disappearance of U.S. bases in Afghanistan also brought down the curtain on the one other counterterrorist tactic that the United States had used against terrorists in Pakistan, the ground raid. The air facilities, supply depots, and intelligence centers that had made the Bin Laden raid possible had been shut down, their personnel and equipment trucked or flown out of the country. "Raids like the one on Abbottabad," Bruce Riedel wrote in early 2014, "will be much more difficult to conduct without bases in Afghanistan. Instead of a short flight from a base in Afghanistan, they will need to be flown from carrier battle groups hundreds of miles away in the Arabian Sea. In all likelihood, the Abbottabad raid would have failed had it been flown from the Arabian Sea just like the Iranian hostage rescue mission failed in 1980."[98]

With the drone program all but moribund and ground raids nearly impossible both diplomatically and militarily, the outlook for U.S. counterterrorism was bleak indeed. Riedel, who had been chief of South Asia strategy for Obama in 2008 and 2009, was now among the most pessimistic. As the American counterterrorism programs in Pakistan came to an end, Riedel asserted, Al Qaeda's "regeneration will be fast given the huge jihadi infrastructure in Pakistan and the ISI's incompetence and/or collusion with the jihadists."[99]

. . .

When President Obama decided in 2009 to raise the U.S. troop strength in Afghanistan to 100,000, he cited the interdependence of Afghanistan and Pakistan as a critical strategic rationale. That same interdependence has remained, even as recognition of its importance has faded. Had Obama displayed a resolve to bring the Afghanistan war to a successful conclusion, he could have used the cross-border power of America's perceived military strength to gain Pakistani cooperation in combating Al Qaeda and other extremist groups. Instead, he focused his words and deeds on getting the U.S. military out of Afghanistan, while citing misleading statistics about drones as proof that surgical strikes from afar were a viable substitute for ground forces. He left the United States bereft of influence in a country with nuclear weapons, a fragile government, a perilous rivalry with nuclear-armed India, widespread hatred of the United States, and thriving terrorist organizations with aspirations to bloody the American homeland.

10

DRONES ARE NOT ENOUGH

Yemen

While Pakistan was the destination of choice for Al Qaeda members seeking to get away from Afghanistan at the end of 2001, Osama Bin Laden did not want to put all of his kebabs on one skewer. He sent some of his adherents, including some of the most talented, to other countries where they would be hard for the Americans to find, and where sympathetic Muslim populations could be enlisted in the cause. The two largest recipients of Bin Laden's lieutenants were the countries fronting the Gulf of Aden—Yemen and Somalia. As U.S. counterterrorism operations heated up in Pakistan in the succeeding years, additional Al Qaeda faithful would migrate to these locations.

Al Qaeda's franchise in Yemen, known as Al Qaeda in the Arabian Peninsula (AQAP), remained obscure during the Bush years. It sprang onto the global scene in 2009, thanks to a charismatic cleric of American birth named Anwar al-Awlaki. Born in Las Cruces, New Mexico, in 1971, Awlaki was the son of a prominent Yemeni scion who had gone to study agricultural economics at New Mexico State University. At the age of seven, Awlaki had returned to Yemen, where his father eventually became the country's economics minister. When it was the son's turn to attend college, he went back to the United States to study at Colorado State University. For his major, Awlaki chose what so many other Islamic terrorists have taken as their primary field of study—engineering.

Anwar al-Awlaki went on to earn a master's degree in education at San Diego State University. While in San Diego, he turned toward a career as an imam, preaching at a local mosque where the attendees included several future 9/11 hijackers. Although he espoused a radical variant of Islam that emphasized moral purity, the San Diego police arrested him in 1996 and again in 1997 for soliciting prostitutes. Awlaki returned to Yemen in 2004, taking a job at al-Iman University, a religious school in Sana'a run by an Al Qaeda sympathizer.

Had he been born a generation earlier, Awlaki most likely would have lived out his days teaching religious doctrine to Yemeni youths, or causing mischief within the confines of Yemen's capital. But the World Wide Web turned him into a figure of global influence and reputation. Web videos and Internet chat rooms enabled him to reach across the oceans into all nations, to touch disillusioned Muslims who were sitting at computers in search of ideas and kindred spirits. As one of the few Arab extremists who could speak English fluently and relate culturally to Americans, he stood out among the Internet's other purveyors of Islamic radicalism.

Awlaki was to inspire many of the terrorists who attempted to kill Americans during Obama's presidency. One of those individuals was Abdulhakim Mujahid Muhammad, a U.S. citizen who had been born in Memphis, Tennessee, under the name Carlos Leon Bledsoe. The son of middle-class Baptists, Bledsoe converted to Islam at the age of nineteen after visiting a mosque in Nashville. On the sixth anniversary of the 9/11 attacks, he traveled to Yemen, where he was mesmerized by Awlaki's teachings. His dealings with radical Islamists aroused the suspicions of the Yemeni police, who arrested him and held him until his deportation to the United States in January 2009. The FBI, which knew of Muhammad's interest in extremism, interviewed him on his return, but then let him go.

On June 1, 2009, Muhammad drove a black Ford Explorer Sport Trac to a military recruiting office in Little Rock, Arkansas. Two U.S. Army privates, William A. Long, twenty-three, of Conway, Arkansas, and Quinton Ezeagwula, eighteen, of Jacksonville, Arkansas, were standing outside in military fatigues, enjoying a smoke. Muhammad pointed an SKS assault rifle out the window of the Explorer and opened fire on the two men. The bullets killed Long and left Ezeagwula lying injured in a pool of blood. He sped away, heading toward Memphis, 150 miles away.

Muhammad planned to switch cars in his city of birth in case anyone had seen the Explorer, and then would continue his killing spree. On his way to Memphis, however, he made a wrong turn in a construction zone and ran into the police, to whom he surrendered. After his arrest, he wrote to the judge presiding over his case that he was affiliated with AQAP and he wanted to plead guilty to the murder charges.[1]

Another terrorist whom Awlaki influenced was Nidal Malik Hasan, a Palestinian-American who joined the U.S. Army after high school and served as an Army psychiatrist for six years prior to his rendezvous with destiny on November 5, 2009. At 1:34 P.M. that afternoon, Hasan walked into Fort Hood's Soldier Readiness Center, where three hundred service members were lined up to receive shots and eye exams. Shouting "Allahu Akbar!" he pulled out a pistol and opened fire. He killed 13 American military personnel and wounded 33 before he himself was shot and paralyzed. It was the largest act of terrorism on U.S. soil since the 9/11 attacks.

Umar Farouk Abdulmutallab, a young Nigerian, was so enthralled by watching Awlaki's sermons online that he traveled from Dubai to Yemen in the summer of 2009 to seek Awlaki's assistance in carrying out a suicide attack. Awlaki probed Abdulmutallab to see if he had sufficient conviction, and then linked him up with AQAP bomb maker Ibrahim al-Asiri, one of the most innovative and dangerous terrorists in the world. Al-Asiri provided Abdulmutallab with a pouch of PETN explosive that he could sew into his underwear, along with a syringe filled with flammable chemicals. Abdulmutallab managed to smuggle these ingredients aboard Northwest Airlines Flight 253, from Amsterdam to Detroit, on Christmas Day of 2009. As the aircraft approached Detroit Metropolitan Airport, Abdulmutallab covered himself with a blanket and mixed the chemicals. The concoction caught fire, but failed to detonate the explosives, leaving a severely burned Abdulmutallab as the sole casualty.[2] With 289 passengers on board, Flight 283 had come very close to sustaining more deaths than the Fort Hood shootings and the suicide airplane crashes at the Pentagon and Shanksville, Pennsylvania, on 9/11.

Awlaki also influenced the Boston Marathon bombers, Tamerlan and Dzhokhar Tsarnaev. On April 15, 2013, the Chechen brothers detonated two pressure cookers packed with carpenter nails and ball bearings, killing three Americans who were standing near the marathon's finish line and injuring 260 others. Identified via surveillance videos, the Tsarnaev brothers led police on a manhunt that paralyzed the city of Boston for several days.[3] After Dzhokhar was apprehended and hospitalized for gunshot wounds, he told FBI investigators that he and his brother had been swayed by Awlaki's Internet sermons.[4] The investigators found some of Awlaki's writings among Dzhokhar's belongings.

During 2009, the Obama administration was highly reluctant to link any terrorist attacks to Awlaki or AQAP more broadly. After the Fort Hood shooting, it eschewed the use of the word *terrorism* at all, calling the killing spree instead an act of "workplace violence." Administration spokespersons focused their rhetoric on the need for Americans to avoid blaming the Islamic faith and its adherents for the massacre. "Obviously, we object to—and do not believe—that anti-Muslim sentiment should emanate from this," said Secretary of Homeland Security Janet Napolitano. "This was an individual who does not, obviously, represent the Muslim faith." She emphasized that her agency was working with state and local organizations to discourage Americans from becoming angry at Muslims over the shooting.[5]

When Abdulmutallab's underwear bomb plot fizzled, Obama at first suggested that it was not linked to a broader terrorist movement. "This incident, like several that have preceded it, demonstrates that an alert and courageous citizenry are far more resilient than an isolated extremist," he said in a speech in Honolulu on December 28. But when intelligence agencies and the media accumulated evidence that AQAP had been directly involved in the plot, including the supply of the bomb, Obama admitted publicly that it was an AQAP attack.

The underwear bomb plot was something of a wake-up call for

Obama. Once AQAP had undertaken a clear attack on the U.S. home-land, Yemen entered a different category as far as the White House was concerned. General David Petraeus, as commander of U.S. Central Command, flew to the Yemeni capital of Sana'a shortly after the failed underwear bomb plot to discuss expanded American counterterrorist operations in the country. Yemeni president Ali Abdullah Saleh told Pe-traeus that missiles had shown themselves poorly suited to fighting the terrorists, as they had killed civilians. The only way the United States could help eliminate the terrorists and their bases while simultaneously preventing civilian casualties, Saleh said, would be to give Yemen twelve helicopter gunships for use by Yemeni forces.

Petraeus countered that U.S. special operations forces and spies should be inserted into Yemen to find and neutralize the terrorist sites. But Saleh rejected that option, asserting that he would not allow U.S. forces and intelligence agencies to venture outside an operations center that had been established for them near the capital. Saleh did, however, offer something of a compromise: the U.S. could use drones to hit terror-ist leaders when there was specific intelligence on their location. He even said he would help conceal the American role by claiming publicly that the strikes had been conducted by the Yemeni government.[6]

The U.S. implemented a limited regimen of drone strikes in Yemen over the course of 2010. Owing to Saleh's refusal to let U.S. agencies out of their pen in Sana'a, the Americans were dependent on the Ye-meni government for targeting data. Lacking familiarity with AQAP and the rest of Yemen, the U.S. drone targeters had little way of know-ing whether the Yemenis were vectoring them onto AQAP leaders, or onto other enemies of the Yemeni regime.[7] On May 25, 2010, an Amer-ican drone fired a missile at someone whom Yemeni intelligence had described as an important AQAP commander, but who turned out to be a Yemeni deputy governor whom Saleh had viewed as a rival.[8] The Americans suspected that Saleh had deliberately misled them on this and several other occasions.[9]

AQAP proved adroit at finding effective drone countermeasures, be-yond the usual ones like staying away from cell phones. They discerned that the drones did not fire on moving targets, which was the result of seconds-long delays in the transmission of data via satellite. When drones approached, therefore, the militants hopped in trucks and drove off. They exploited the reluctance of drone operators to strike areas replete with civilian bystanders by keeping their facilities and their leaders in densely populated areas.[10]

The capture of an AQAP document revealed that the Yemeni militants had learned from their Pakistani brethren how to frustrate the spies who located targets for the drones. "The drones used in the attacks in Swat Valley depend on electronic chips or radioactive dyes placed at the target by the spy or the agent, then the guided missiles come directly toward these targets," the author explained. "The spy, therefore, is the main pillar of this operation." The best way to counteract this espionage was to track down the spy and hang him "in a public place with a sign hanging from his neck identifying him as an 'American Spy.'"[11]

The drone campaign in Yemen was to highlight another shortcoming of drones, their inability to yield prisoners. In the past, much of the information that had enabled the United States to understand and counter terrorist organizations had come from the mouths of individuals apprehended by military forces or law enforcement agencies. The Obama administration made extensive use of information extracted from prisoners who had been apprehended under the Bush administration, and it was more than happy to exploit information from new detainees, yet it displayed a pronounced aversion to the taking of prisoners.

At the start of his administration, Obama had issued an executive order mandating closure of the U.S. military's detention facility at Guantanamo Bay within one year. Candidate Obama had made much of Guantanamo Bay, asserting in 2008 that "[t]he first step to reclaiming America's standing in the world has to be closing this facility." But Gitmo, as the facility was often called, would end up staying open well into Obama's second term because closing it was more difficult than anticipated. Early in his presidency, Obama also directed the CIA to close all of its existing detention facilities, the so-called black sites, and prohibited the CIA from operating any detention facilities in the future.

The shuttering of the black sites removed the best facilities for detaining and interrogating terrorists and the only good alternative to Guantanamo Bay, to which Obama refused to send any more prisoners.[12]

In another executive order, Obama restricted interrogators to the use of the interrogation methods in the U.S. Army Field Manual, thereby forbidding the "enhanced interrogation techniques" of the Bush era, such as waterboarding and exposure to cold temperatures. Top intelligence officials warned the new administration against describing those interrogation techniques as torture, as it would impugn the integrity of CIA officers who had been conducting procedures approved by the White House. Obama ignored their advice. "We ended torture" became a common refrain in Obama's media songbook. In disregard of warnings from the current CIA leadership and seven former CIA directors about adverse effects on organizational morale and the image of the United States, Obama released the so-called torture memos written by Bush administration officials in support of the enhanced interrogation techniques, and he authorized Attorney General Eric Holder to conduct criminal investigations into some of the Bush-era interrogations.

CIA counterterrorism officials saw hypocrisy in criticisms of "torture" from a man who was simultaneously boasting about killing people with drones without attempting to capture them or try them in court. "An administration that thinks it was 'torture' to interfere with the sleep cycle of a handful of the worst terrorists on the planet has no problem with authorizing the firing of Hellfire missiles into a group of thirty or forty suspects gathered around a campfire," objected Jose Rodriguez, former director of the CIA's National Clandestine Service.[13] Rodriguez noted that the administration's unwillingness to send prisoners to Guantanamo or alternative locations was encouraging the killing of individuals with drones. "Unable or unwilling to capture, hold, and interrogate terrorists," the Obama administration had "over-relied on technical means to kill suspected terrorists from afar."[14]

Several government officials who were close to Obama made the same point to the President in private. "We do not have a plausible capture strategy," General Cartwright warned the President in the middle of 2009.[15] Some of Obama's advisers urged him to develop a viable detention option, whether abroad or in the United States, but Obama temporized, unwilling to alienate his liberal base by authorizing a preventive detention system that could be likened to Gitmo.[16]

The United States did not capture a significant terrorist suspect outside the United States or the active combat zone of Afghanistan until April 19, 2011, when it apprehended Ahmed Warsame en route from Somalia to Yemen. State Department lawyers recommended bringing Warsame to the United States for trial in a civil court, but the White House rejected that option because many in Congress opposed trying terrorists in U.S. civil courts. Secretary of Defense Gates and some in the White House urged Obama to try Warsame in a military court, but that too did not sit well with Obama because it was unpopular with his political allies on the left.

In the meantime, interrogators from the military, CIA, and FBI were flown to the USS *Boxer*, a 40,000-ton amphibious assault ship where Warsame was in custody. After a few weeks of questioning, Warsame began to give them information. But the interrogators had not read Warsame his legal rights prior to interrogation, so his words could not be used against him in a civilian court. The administration therefore sent a new FBI team to interrogate Warsame and this time they read him his legal rights before proceeding, enabling them to obtain information for use in a civil trial. On June 30, after holding Warsame at sea for seventy days, the national security principals decided to fly Warsame secretly to New York for a civil trial using his own statements as evidence.[17]

Conservatives denounced Obama for bringing Warsame into the United States and giving him all the rights of a U.S. citizen, while liberals accused Obama of imitating Bush with a "floating Guantanamo." Administration officials hailed the outcome as a success, but the negative reactions from both sides of the political spectrum, along with the possibility that the next captive might not choose to incriminate himself, appear to have convinced Obama that it was an outcome not worth

repeating. For a long time afterward the administration would not follow up with further attempts to capture terrorism suspects. In the middle of 2012, by which time no further suspects had been apprehended,
Jo Becker and Scott Shane wrote in the *New York Times*: "the administration's very success at killing terrorism suspects has been shadowed by
a suspicion: that Mr. Obama has avoided the complications of detention
by deciding, in effect, to take no prisoners alive."[18]

Warsame's case would also show once more the value of taking prisoners alive. Having served as an intermediary between Al Qaeda's affiliates in Yemen and Somalia, Warsame gave his interrogators a wealth of
information about AQAP and its leading light, Awlaki. That information would help the CIA find the elusive Yemeni preacher.[19]

The case of Anwar al-Awlaki presented the Obama administration
with yet more legal and moral problems. Although Awlaki had been
living in Yemen since 2004 and had been implicated in terrorist activities, he still held U.S. citizenship, which made it considerably harder for
the U.S. government to justify killing him without a trial. Such a killing
could be construed by lawyers as a violation of the Fifth Amendment's
guarantee of due process to all U.S. citizens, and by the general public as
a presidential usurpation of judicial powers.

Obama wanted to kill Awlaki with a drone strike, so lawyers in
the State and Justice Departments were asked to produce arguments
demonstrating that killing him did not violate the Fifth Amendment.
At the State Department, the task fell to Harold Koh, who had taken
a leave of absence from his position as dean of Yale Law School to join
the Obama administration. During the presidency of George W. Bush,
Koh had lambasted the White House for violating the Constitution by,
among other things, holding prisoners without charges and keeping the
American people in the dark about counterterrorism programs. The next
administration, he told a House panel in 2008, must "restore the rule of
law in the national security arena," end "excessive government secrecy,"
and abandon the "claims of unfettered executive power." Once he joined
Obama's team, however, Koh had taken to justifying counterterrorism
policies, secrecy practices, and claims of executive power that Obama

had chosen to carry over from Bush, often by employing the same arguments that the Bush administration's lawyers had employed.[20]

When it came to lethal drone strikes, Koh devised a number of clever explanations as to why the Obama administration's policy complied with all applicable domestic and international laws. He decided that he could create his own standard for determining which individuals could be lawfully targeted: the person had to be "evil, with ironclad intelligence to prove it." In a speech to an association of international lawyers in March 2010, though, Koh did not enumerate that standard, choosing instead to provide abstruse legalistic justifications for U.S. targeting practices.[21]

Eric Holder's Justice Department lawyers, who did their own review of the matter, concluded that Awlaki could be killed because he was engaged in Al Qaeda's war against the United States and posed a dire threat to Americans. They added, however, that he could be killed only if capturing him was infeasible. The United States had sent special operations forces on the ground to get Bin Laden in Pakistan and a host of enemies in Afghanistan, and it could easily have sent forces into Yemen. But, as the Bin Laden raid had shown, such an operation could have highly negative political consequences.[22] For reasons that were not made clear, Obama chose not to attempt the capture of Awlaki when U.S. intelligence caught up with him in September 2011. Instead, he ordered that Awlaki be killed by drone. The President also directed that the administration's legal justification for the action be kept secret.

With the help of the information gleaned from the interrogations of Warsame, the United States pinpointed Awlaki's location on September 30, 2011. A flock of Predator and Reaper drones headed toward the cluster of parked trucks where Awlaki was having breakfast. Hearing the humming of a drone engine, Awlaki and his colleagues dashed for the vehicles and attempted to speed off in different directions. Awlaki had narrowly escaped an earlier strike by hightailing it in a truck. This time, however, a missile hit Awlaki's truck before it could get away, killing him.[23]

In the United States, some liberals denounced Awlaki's killing as a violation of constitutional protections. "The United States is abandoning its role as the global champion of human rights," Jimmy Carter chomped. "Revelations that top officials are targeting people to be assassinated abroad, including American citizens, are only the most recent, disturbing proof of how far our nation's violation of human rights has extended."[24]

Media figures who were generally sympathetic to Obama denounced the administration for failing to provide any public justification. *New York Times* veteran reporter David Rohde asserted, "After criticizing the Bush administration for keeping the details of its surveillance, interrogation, and detention practices secret, Obama is doing the same thing."[25] Doyle McManus wrote in the *Los Angeles Times*, "It's odd that the Obama administration, which came into office promising to be more open and more attentive to civil liberties than the previous one, has been so reluctant to explain its policies in this area. Obama and his aides have refused to answer questions about drone strikes because they are part of a covert program, yet they have repeatedly taken credit for their victories in public."[26]

Even some of the most hawkish Americans found fault with the Awlaki strike. "We needed a court order to eavesdrop on him, but we didn't need a court order to kill him," remarked Michael Hayden, the former CIA director. "Isn't that something?"[27]

Two weeks after the killing of Anwar al-Awlaki, the drone targeters believed that they had located another Al Qaeda leader on Yemeni territory, an Egyptian named Ibrahim al-Banna. An American missile hit a small outdoor restaurant in Shabwa where he was reported to be dining, killing a dozen people. But it turned out that the Egyptian was not among the dead. Whether by strange coincidence or a sinister extremist plot that has yet to be unmasked, one of the twelve civilians killed was Abdulrahman al-Awlaki, the sixteen-year-old son of the recently deceased radical. A U.S. citizen like his father, the boy had not been implicated in terrorist activity and was not on U.S. target lists.

The boy's death was a public relations disaster in Yemen, the United States, and the rest of the world. The Obama administration multiplied the damage by informing the press that Abdulrahman al-Awlaki had

been twenty-one. The dead youth's relatives discredited the claim in the most embarrassing manner possible, by publicly releasing his U.S. birth certificate.[28]

While the death of the elder Awlaki robbed AQAP of one of its most talented and inspirational leaders, neither his death nor any of the others resulting from the drone program succeeded in halting AQAP in its quest for control of Yemen's territory and people.[29] During 2010, AQAP covertly infiltrated villages and towns to build up their support base, in the classic manner of guerrillas. In February 2011, it began conquering territory and governing it overtly.

The first place to come under overt AQAP rule was the town of Jaar. From studying the history of Al Qaeda and other insurgent groups, AQAP's leadership had learned that winning the people's support required positive acts of governance, not merely beheading spies or violators of Islamic law. So they initiated public works projects. To get the projects going, two hundred men showed up in Jaar wearing black robes that came down to the knees.

"They started extending water mains," recounted Nabil al-Amoudi a lawyer from Jaar. "They installed their own pipes. They succeeded in bringing electricity to areas that had not had power before." AQAP members took photographs of gleaming lightbulbs and spinning fans which they displayed in propaganda videos and an online newsletter. In one of their video clips, AQAP fighters placed ladders against electrical poles and shouted "Allah Akbar" each time that they connected downed electrical wires.[30]

On May 27, AQAP advanced on a much bigger prize, the coastal Yemeni city of Zanjubar. Militants quickly overran several military posts and the governor's office, sending soldiers and officials scattering. The heavy weapons and ammunition left behind by the Yemen army made welcome additions to Al Qaeda's arsenal. AQAP set up checkpoints on the three roads leading out of the city and searched thousands of fleeing residents for soldiers. At the provincial bank, they laid their hands on billions of Yemeni rials, which would enable them to finance operations across Yemen. Establishing sharia courts, the

executed suspected government collaborators and crucified a man for homosexuality.[31]

The enforcement of Islamic law was so severe that it would come under criticism from AQAP's own chief executive, Nasser al-Wahishi. Controlling a population, he admonished his fellow jihadists, required moderation in governance, especially in places where the people had not received a rigorous Islamic education. "You have to be kind," Wahishi remonstrated. "You can't beat people for drinking alcohol when they don't even know the basics of how to pray."[32]

The Yemeni army's Twenty-Fifth Mechanized Brigade was located near Zanjubar along the coastal highway, presenting a formidable obstacle to an Al Qaeda advance toward the vital port of Aden, which was only thirty-two miles away. The brigade's soldiers fended off some initial Al Qaeda probes but did not undertake a major counterattack to dislodge Al Qaeda from the city. When Yemen's southern command attempted to send reinforcements from Aden to shore up the Twenty-Fifth Brigade and organize a counterattack on Zanjubar, Al Qaeda fighters ambushed them from the narrow sand berms adjoining the highway, which compelled them to turn back. In the meantime, the militants prepared for a concerted assault on the brigade's base and blocked the approaches to prevent it from receiving supplies.[33]

Senior U.S. military leaders were riveted to the unfolding situation in Yemen. Mullen and Mattis warned that "if AQAP wasn't stopped in its tracks, it would establish a dangerous toehold on the coast," which would "allow the group to vastly strengthen its operational ties to Al-Shabaab in Somalia."[34] The enemy advance also offered the United States an opportunity to cause great harm to AQAP. By massing forces and holding territory, AQAP had exposed its fighters to the concentrated application of military force.

On June 10, General Mattis recommended a set of air strikes in Zanjubar, including a large number concentrated on the city's soccer stadium, which AQAP was using to lob mortar rounds into the base of the Twenty-Fifth Mechanized Brigade. Brennan and other senior civilians, however, expressed doubt that the hostile forces at Zanjubar posed a

serious threat to the United States. AQAP had tribal elements that were focused on local events, not on international terrorism, they said. Brennan concluded that Mattis's proposal would commit the United States too heavily, putting it on a "slippery slope to counterinsurgency." He was able to sway Obama, who ended up approving a much smaller set of targets in Zanjubar than Mattis had advised, consisting exclusively of four individual extremists.[35]

A few days later, when a military officer mentioned the "campaign" in Yemen at one of the White House's "Terror Tuesday" meetings, Obama interrupted heatedly to say that there was no "campaign" in Yemen. "We're not in Yemen to get involved in some domestic conflict," Obama growled. "We're going to continue to stay focused on threats to the homeland—that's where the real priority is."[36]

In July, the isolated Twenty-Fifth Mechanized Brigade ran critically short of water and food.[37] The United States agreed to airdrop parcels of food to the brigade. Saudi Arabia, which was keen on stopping the spread of AQAP, used its aircraft to bomb AQAP targets near Zanjubar. The Americans and Saudis advised the Yemeni military to send a large relief force to Zanjubar to break the siege, but the Yemeni government was in disarray as the result of a rocket attack on President Saleh's palace, during which Saleh had sustained burns to 40 percent of his body as well as internal bleeding in his brain, requiring his evacuation to Saudi Arabia for emergency surgery. Finally, on September 10, pressure from the United States and Saudi Arabia induced the Yemeni army to send a large relief force toward Zanjubar. The army met little resistance from AQAP, which had decided that the force was too large to engage in open battle. The Al Qaeda fighters and organizers melted back into the population.[38]

Although the relief force had lifted the siege and occupied central points in the city, AQAP retained control of most of Zanjubar. They fired rockets and mortars at government forces on a daily basis and bombarded them with propaganda over loudspeakers. "They say they are the followers of Osama bin Laden," attested Wadhan Ali Said, a skinny twenty-year-old Yemeni soldier. "They give us lectures on Islam. Then, they tell us they will enter the base tonight."

The Yemeni government sent elite counterterrorism forces to Zanjubar to help fight AQAP, but they were too small in number to make much of a difference. "We are like an island in a sea of al-Qaeda," said Lieutenant Abdul Mohamed Saleh at the end of 2011. "We are surrounded from every direction."[39]

During the fall, the State Department suspended military aid to Yemen because Saleh had used force against political protesters. The aid would remain shut off until the installation of a democratically elected president, Abd Rabbuh Mansur Hadi, in the spring of 2012.[40] The withdrawal of American support for the Yemeni military led to further deterioration of the security situation during the first months of 2012. Faring poorly in a sequence of battles with AQAP, Yemeni forces lost large quantities of military equipment. AQAP increased its control of territory and recruited droves of new fighters in those areas.[41]

In April, a double agent revealed that AQAP was plotting to down an airline with an underwear bomb. Although similar in concept to the one Abdulmutallab had used, the bomb had been given a better detonator than the one that had fizzled over Detroit. The CIA intercepted and seized the device in early May before it could be taken aboard an aircraft.[42]

The discovery of the plot renewed concerns about AQAP threats to the U.S. homeland and led Obama to loosen the restrictions on drone strikes in Yemen. New guidance permitted the targeting of "fighters whose names aren't known but who are deemed to be high-value terrorism targets or threats to the U.S."[43] The newly elected Yemeni government eased its restrictions on the drone program, giving the Americans unprecedented latitude. The Obama administration sent at least twenty U.S. special operations troops to Yemen to obtain targeting data for drones and advise Yemeni commanders on the disposition of their forces.[44]

"We're pursuing a focused counter-terrorism campaign in Yemen designed to prevent and deter terrorist plots that directly threaten U.S. interests at home and abroad," announced Tommy Vietor, the NSC spokesman. "We have not, and will not, get involved in a broader counterinsurgency effort."[45] But the distinction between "counterterrorism" and "counterinsurgency" turned out to be less clear-cut than such pronouncements suggested. U.S. officials attributed the expansion of the drone program to "rising concern over AQAP's territorial expansion."[46] Yet depriving the enemy of territory required counterinsurgency, not just counterterrorism. U.S. precision strikes and U.S. training of Yemeni forces were aimed at helping the Yemenis secure territory, not merely at knocking off a few terrorist leaders, even if U.S. assistance to Yemen's counterinsurgency efforts were very small relative to the demands of the situation. And the expansion of targeting parameters to include individuals considered to be "threats to the U.S." resulted in the targeting of rank-and-file AQAP fighters, based on the argument that all AQAP fighters were threats to U.S. personnel in Yemen. In early June, U.S. officials divulged that the twenty-two drone strikes undertaken in recent months had killed only three "high-value" terrorists.[47]

A shift in emphasis from counterterrorism to counterinsurgency was, indeed, badly needed at this time. Drone strikes against enemy leaders had not only failed to prevent AQAP from gaining territory, but had also driven citizens into the arms of AQAP. When Sudarsan Raghavan of the *Washington Post* interviewed Yemeni tribal leaders and government officials in the spring of 2012, he found widespread anger over the drone strikes, based mainly on the belief that the drones had killed large numbers of women and children.[48] Noted Yemen experts such as former U.S. ambassador to Yemen Edmund J. Hull and Princeton scholar Gregory D. Johnsen reported similar findings.[49]

Raghavan's interviews also suggested that the population would have accepted the killing of AQAP members had it led to the annihilation of the enemy, for in that case it would have brought peace. Without governmental security forces on the ground to secure the population, however, it had only led to more Al Qaeda recruitment and the continuation of violence. "There is more hostility against America because the attacks have not stopped al-Qaeda, but rather they have expanded," observed Anssaf Ali Mayo, head of one of the main parties in the Yemeni government.[50]

Obama's increased use of drones against low-level fighters caused a spike in the incidence of civilian casualties. In August 2012, a drone strike mistakenly killed Sheikh Salem Ahmed bin Ali Jaber, a Yemeni cleric who had preached against Al Qaeda in local villages. His vocal opposition to Al Qaeda had, in fact, led to his tragic demise. Shortly before, his preaching had come to the attention of Al Qaeda, prompting three militants to demand a meeting with him. He had agreed to the meeting, taking a cousin with him for protection. At least one of the three militants, it turned out, had been targeted by the U.S. drone program. As soon as the five men converged, four missiles struck in quick succession, killing everyone. Afterward, the dead cleric's brother-in-law said, "everyone who saw that there is no differentiating between us and al-Qaida are asking, 'Why don't we just join al-Qaida since it makes no difference?'"[51]

On September 2, a missile hit a Toyota truck carrying fourteen people on a desert road from the town of Radda. The strike flipped the truck over and set it on fire. Moments later, a second missile slammed into the truck and exploded. Twelve of the passengers perished, including a twelve-year-old boy, a seven-year-old girl, and the girl's mother. The Yemeni government initially announced that the truck had been carrying Al Qaeda militants, and that Soviet-era jets from the Yemeni air force had fired the missiles. But tribal leaders soon were saying that the truck had been carrying only innocent civilians, and Yemeni officials eventually came to that conclusion as well. They also conceded publicly that it had been an American strike, aimed at the car of an Al Qaeda leader who was reported to be traveling on the same road. The government sent 101 guns to the nearby community, a traditional gesture of apology.

AQAP capitalized on the Radda debacle with the speed and skill of Hollywood publicists. Militants snapped digital photographs of the mangled corpses and posted them on extremist websites and Facebook. On the day after the attack, they blocked the roads around Radda and set up a tent where they gave speeches condemning the government and the United States. They handed out fliers that read, "See what the government has done? That's why we are fighting. . . . They are the agents of America and the enemy of Islam. . . . They fight whoever says 'Allah is my God,' according to America's instructions."

AQAP's publicity campaign helped the organization recruit large numbers of men in communities near Radda. "Our entire village is angry at the government and the Americans," said Sultan Ahmed Mohammed, one of the two survivors of the strike. "If the Americans are responsible, I would have no choice but to sympathize with al-Qaeda because al-Qaeda is fighting America."[52]

The next drone strike to attract international attention, in November, killed only the intended AQAP suspect, Adnan al-Qadhi, near Beit al-Ahmar. It was the manner of his elimination that generated controversy. Beit al-Ahmar, less than an hour's drive from the capital of Sana'a, was home to much of the top leadership of the Yemeni armed forces. Why, Yemenis asked, did Americans use a drone to kill him, when the government could have sent a police car to arrest him? "It is nearly inconceivable to imagine that he could not have been taken into custody alive," Abdulghani al-Iryani, a Yemeni political analyst, remarked to McClatchy correspondent Adam Baron.[53]

By the end of 2012, the killing of AQAP leaders through drone strikes had made only a small dent in the organization's leadership. AQAP and its affiliates retained a powerful presence in most of the country, and proved capable of assassinating top government leaders in the capital.[54] Between the end of 2009 and the end 2012, during which time the number of drone strikes skyrocketed, the estimated AQAP strength in Yemen increased from 300 to more than 1,000.[55] Some intelligence analysts believed that AQAP had several thousand fighters in early 2013.[56]

In light of numerous analyses indicating the unpopularity of the drone program among Yemenis, the United States tapered off the rate of strikes in the first months of 2013, and grounded the drones altogether for several months in the summer. While the change may have made it more difficult for AQAP to attract recruits, it also removed pressure on AQAP at a time when the Yemeni armed forces remained unable to apply much pressure of their own. AQAP took advantage of the pause to cook up new trouble.

The drone strikes resumed after U.S. intelligence detected AQAP's August 2013 plot to attack U.S. diplomatic facilities in the Middle East and North Africa.[57] This resurgence of the drone program went over with the Yemenis like a steak dinner at a banquet for vegetarians. The evacuation of U.S. personnel from Yemen also upset the Yemeni government and populace, who took it as an affront to the government's capabilities. In an official statement, the Yemeni government declared that the decision to remove the Americans "serves the interests of the extremists and undermines the exceptional cooperation between Yemen and the international alliance against terrorism."[58]

The drone war came to a halt once more in December, as the result of another controversy. On December 12, Hellfire missiles struck a convoy of vehicles that was reported to be carrying militants, but which according to Yemenis who surveyed the wreckage was carrying only the members of a wedding party. Although the United States did not admit wrongdoing, it agreed to stop the strikes, and the Yemeni government paid out more than $1 million to the fifteen Yemenis who were wounded and the families of the twelve Yemenis who were killed.[59]

. . .

The war against AQAP in Yemen has provided the clearest evidence of the limitations of drone warfare. Although more drone strikes have taken place in Pakistan, the Pakistani case has been complicated by the Pakistani government's imposition of onerous restrictions on the drone program and by its efforts to shield some of the targeted groups. In Yemen, American and Yemeni restrictions on the drone program diminished over time, such that by 2012 virtually anyone in AQAP could be targeted. Yet even under those conditions, the strikes failed to halt the growth of the AQAP insurgency, and they eventually provoked so much outrage that severe restrictions had to be reintroduced.

So far the American homeland has been able to dodge AQAP's bullets without going beyond the light footprint, in part because of luck, like the luck that foiled the underwear bomber. But by refusing to enter the enemy's lair with overwhelming and permanent force, be it supplied by Yemenis or even Saudis, it will likely face more bullets. The next time, the United States may not be so lucky.

11

ALLIES ARE UNRELIABLE

Afghanistan, Libya, Somalia

"Ultimately, the challenges of the 21st century can't be met without collective action," Barack Obama told a gathering of world leaders in London on April 2, 2009. "In a world that is as complex as it is, it is very important for us to be able to forge partnerships as opposed to simply dictating solutions." The part about "dictating solutions" was a tacit jab at George W. Bush, whom Obama had repeatedly accused of forcing his ideas on foreign countries instead of collaborating with them. Then Obama proceeded to slug his predecessor directly. The Bush administration, Obama said, had "lowered our standing in the world."

The President went on to express confidence in his own ability to undo the damage. "I would like to think that with my election and the early decisions that we've made, that you're starting to see some restoration of America's standing in the world," Obama said. "International polls seem to indicate that you're seeing people more hopeful about America's leadership." In an assurance to the foreign audience and an admonition to the American people, Obama emphasized that Americans needed to recognize that "we are going to have to act in partnership with other countries."

American relations with the rest of the world were not as dire when Bush left office as Obama's rhetoric suggested. Bush had spent much of his second term repairing relations with foreign governments that had been alienated by the Iraq War and other foreign policy initiatives of Bush's first term. Still, it was true that numerous world leaders and large segments of their publics viewed Obama as a welcome change from Bush. Obama's Ivy League polish and multicultural life story appealed to foreign elites who had been put off by Bush's cowboy persona, and Obama's professed renunciation of unilateralism encouraged the belief that the United States would incorporate the concerns of other nations into its decisions.

Obama and his foreign policy team were convinced that heavy reliance on allies was preferable to the self-reliance of the Bush years because it required smaller American military and economic commitments, and because it jibed with their ideological sensibilities. Multilateralism had been a staple of liberal American foreign policy thinking since the 1960s, a derivative of the notions that unilateralism was morally arrogant and that U.S. power was declining relative to that of other states. While predictions of American decline had been grossly overstated in the late twentieth century, there was a stronger case to be made that American power was declining in relative terms in 2009 because of the rapid economic growth in China, India, Brazil, and other emerging nations. Those nations, plus the more established powers of Russia, Japan, and the European Union, could overrule the United States by virtue of their collective size if they worked together. Multilateral institutions like the United Nations and World Bank that made big decisions were no longer sure bets to heed America's signal calling as they once had been.

Of course, collaboration with other nations to achieve strategic objectives had by no means been the exclusive purview of liberals. President Dwight D. Eisenhower erected a series of regional alliances in the 1950s as bulwarks against communist expansionism. Central to Richard Nixon's foreign policy was the making of common cause with China in containing the Soviet Union. Ronald Reagan collaborated with Pakistan in supporting the anticommunist rebels in Afghanistan, and with Honduras in supporting anticommunist rebels in Nicaragua. Both Bush administrations mobilized international coalitions against rogue nations. But Obama would differ from those predecessors in his expectation that other nations would take on very large commitments and leadership responsibilities.

Obama's multilateralism did help the United States accomplish some foreign policy objectives. His popularity in Europe, for instance, contributed to the willingness of European countries to negotiate trade agreements with the United States. But in terms of obtaining assistance from foreign nations in the deployment and use of military forces—a fundamentally different proposition from changing rules or transferring money—the administration has found success hard to come by.

At the start of his administration, Obama expected that diplomacy and his personal popularity would yield large foreign contributions to multinational military ventures, thereby reducing the need for U.S. military contributions. Expanding the military commitments of other nations would, in addition, facilitate the transfer of leadership duties from the United States to those nations or to multilateral bodies. This line of reasoning relied on three assumptions that would prove fatally flawed. First, that foreign goodwill toward the United States would increase the willingness of foreign nations to employ military power in places of importance to the United States. Second, that foreign nations were capable of employing military power at adequate levels. Third, that leadership by others was a viable substitute for American leadership.

Had one looked back just one administration before that of George W. Bush, one would have found considerable evidence to suggest that not even a liberal Democratic president with high approval ratings among the world's cosmopolitan elites could induce the rest of the world to shoulder much of America's international burdens. During the Clinton presidency, America's European allies were unwilling to chip in much for international initiatives for which the United States desperately wanted European contributions. Bloated welfare states had squeezed European military budgets, and Europeans had lost the enthusiasm in overseas military ventures that had led them to dominate the world prior to 1945. Decades of reliance on American military power for protection had contributed to the view that Europe no longer needed its own military power.

The military frailty of Europe became strikingly clear when Europe's once-great nations could not handle security challenges that arrived in their own backyard. Following the breakup of the former Yugoslavia, European nations contributed most of the troops for a UN peacekeeping force that was incapable of keeping peace among Serbs, Croats, and Muslims. Dispersed in small detachments across Bosnia and Croatia, the European troops were easy to intimidate. Peacekeepers who objected to the killing of civilians or tried to intervene were told that they themselves would be next if they did not back off. The Europeans had to turn to the United States for help with Bosnia, leading to an intensive U.S.-led bombing campaign in the summer of 1995 that convinced the war criminals to desist.

In September 1996, during a United Nations meeting at Ireland's Dublin Castle, the UN leadership appealed for contributions for the retraining and reforming of Bosnia's police. The United States offered to provide 225 police advisers and $19 million for equipment and training. The various European representatives made far more modest offers. Some said they needed more time to view the UN request. The Germans offered fifty Volkswagen vans. The French complained about the fact that the United States had been allowed to speak before the other nations, asking in what language the United States came first alphabetically. Several other European nations offered to host Bosnians at their police academies. All told, the offers of money from European countries totaled only a few hundred thousand dollars.[1]

For Obama, Afghanistan presented an early test of the policy of relying on foreign allies for military contributions. When Obama tried to obtain 10,000 additional NATO troops to fill out General McChrystal's request for 40,000 more troops, European nations that had gushed with enthusiasm for Obama during his run for the presidency now said sheepishly that they could not provide the help he requested. As had been the case when Clinton was president, the Europeans had no appetite for increasing their military commitments, preferring to keep their tax revenues flowing into their welfare states.

Europeans were similarly unwilling to heed Obama's requests to make better use of troops already present in Afghanistan. During George W. Bush's presidency, only a handful of NATO countries had been willing to insert their troops into the thick of Afghanistan's fighting. Having originally committed to send troops to Afghanistan at a time of relative peace, many NATO governments had attached a remarkable number of strings to their forces to keep them out of harm's way. European military commanders often imposed additional constraints on the use of force, owing to the popularity in Europe of the theory that conflicts could and should be resolved by nonviolent means. Because the Europeans had been put in charge of large sections of Afghanistan, entire regions were left wide open to insurgent penetration.

Appeals by Obama, Secretary of State Clinton, and other top officials failed to persuade European leaders to increase their participation in combat operations. The American troops who poured into Afghanistan in 2009 and 2010 quipped that ISAF, the acronym of the multinational International Security Assistance Force, really stood for "I Saw Americans Fighting," or "I Suck at Fighting." In 2010, recognition that some European forces had failed to secure their assigned regions caused the United States to deploy large numbers of troops to those regions.

In areas where Europeans held the command of multinational forces, the overly restrained European approach to counterinsurgency impinged on the activities of the U.S. forces sent under Obama's surge. In Helmand province, site of the most intensive fighting during 2010, the U.S. Marines chafed under the leadership of the British commander of Regional Command South, Major General Nick Carter. Whereas the Marines viewed the use of force as an essential component of counterinsurgency, Carter thought that they could prevail primarily through more enlightened instruments such as political compromise and economic development.

"We're not in the business of conducting an attritional campaign," Carter said on one occasion. "The business we're doing here is about bringing people into the tent and using the full range of political levers to achieve that effect. So we will not be going head-to-head with insurgents in vineyards and orchards. What we will be doing will be a rather more sophisticated approach that plays to the enemy's weaknesses."[2] On another day, when a reporter asked Carter a question about insurgent casualties, he replied, "I'm not going to go into the number of insurgents that have been killed or detained, because at the end of the day what we're trying to do here is we're trying to measure our success by the extent to which we protect a population, rather than kill or defeat insurgents. Because ultimately what I'd like to see happen, and the Afghan government in particular would like to see happen, is that people simply put their weapons down and come over to the side of the government."[3]

During the planning for the seizure of Marjah in early 2010, the U.S. Marines wanted to move in quietly and swiftly and crush the insurgents before they could prepare for battle. Carter, however, decided to announce the operation in advance, in order to encourage the insurgents to leave. If the enemy fled, Carter said, that was fine with him, because it was the population, not the enemy, that mattered. With the enemy gone, it would be much easier to bring in Afghan civil servants and officials.

This approach did succeed in getting the enemy to leave some towns and villages without a fight. But when Afghan civil servants and policemen eventually arrived, the insurgents quietly returned in force to terrorize them and any civilians who assisted them. The newly arrived government officials could not do their jobs, and others who had planned to go to these areas refused to go.

After the Europeans had made clear that they were not going to increase their participation in combat operations, the Obama administration concentrated on convincing them to contribute troops for training Afghan security forces. During 2010, American diplomats repeatedly asked their NATO counterparts to pony up 1,500 specialized trainers ahead of a summit of Afghanistan's international supporters in November. When the diplomats arrived in Lisbon for the summit, however, 900 of the specialized training slots remained unfilled, and NATO countries pledged only 100 more during the summit. French diplomats tried to fill some of the remaining 800 positions by "repledging" troops who were already training Afghan troops in the United Arab Emirates, but the U.S. military did not bite. "We don't count those," a U.S. military official snapped.[4]

At a gathering of NATO leaders in Brussels on March 11, 2011, Secretary of Defense Gates berated the NATO allies for their continued failure to provide troops for Afghanistan. He noted that the United States had almost 100,000 troops in Afghanistan, more than twice the combined total of all the other NATO member states. Gates also faulted America's NATO allies for concentrating on planning their departure instead of demonstrating the unity and commitment that would give the psychological upper hand to the Afghan government. "Frankly, there is too much talk about leaving and not enough talk about getting the job done right," Gates said. "Too much concern about when and how many troops might redeploy, and not enough about what needs to be done before they leave."[5]

At this same point in time, European leaders were seeking American help in a military intervention in Libya to topple Muammar Gaddafi. On February 17, 2011, protesters inspired by the Arab Spring had taken to the streets of Tripoli and the largest city of eastern Libya, Benghazi, to demand political change. Gaddafi's security forces responded by firing on crowds, arresting gunshot victims at city hospitals, and detaining protesters for the purposes of torture and execution. In Tripoli, the government's forces were able to hold the rebels at bay. In Benghazi, however, Gaddafi's power crumbled when the central security complex, known as the "fist of Gaddafi," was breached by a car bomb and overrun by a vicious mob.[6] By the end of February, all of eastern Libya lay in the hands of anti-Gaddafi rebels.

In the first days of March, Gaddafi laid plans for a large offensive to retake Benghazi and the rest of eastern Libya. His armored forces began assembling on the outskirts of Benghazi on March 15 in preparation for an onslaught in which Gaddafi vowed to show "no mercy" to the rebels.[7] U.S. officials feared that a massive bloodletting was imminent, having received numerous reports of atrocities by Gaddafi's forces, including one in which Gaddafi had painted his helicopters to look like Red Cross aircraft and then sent them to strafe aid convoys.

Samantha Power, Obama's "Senior Director for Multilateral Engagement," supported military intervention in Libya as a matter of humanitarian principle. Before entering the Obama administration, Power had risen to fame by writing a Pulitzer Prize–winning book titled *A*

Problem from Hell: America and the Age of Genocide, in which she had excoriated U.S. presidents for failing to stop genocidal violence. Power now asserted that the United States was bound by a moral "responsibility to protect" civilians from atrocities. Among those in the know, Power's doctrine was called R2P.

Power's other claim to fame had been her description of Hillary Clinton as a "monster" during the 2008 Democratic primary. She had since apologized to the secretary of state, who, if she bore any lingering grudge, did not let personal animus get in the way of policy on Libya. Clinton backed Power's recommendation for a humanitarian military intervention, as did UN ambassador Susan Rice. According to Jonathan Allen and Amie Parnes, authors of a highly positive book on Hillary Clinton's time at the State Department, Hillary told her aides that Libya "presented a unique opportunity for America to exercise a new kind of international leadership that relied on building a partnership in which the bulk of the might and money would come from other countries." Libya was a "particularly inviting crucible in which to test the theories of smart power, multilateralism, and democracy promotion that informed Hillary's philosophy of American leadership."[8]

Some leading administration figures, however, opposed military intervention in Libya. Their number included National Security Advisor Tom Donilon, Deputy National Security Advisor Denis McDonough, and Secretary of Defense Robert Gates. The United States did not have vital interests at stake in Libya, they contended, and intervention would put the United States on the side of rebels whose motives and capabilities were largely unknown. Given the influence of these individuals with the President and the President's prior reluctance to employ the military, the smart money had Obama staying his hand.

Obama convened the decisive meeting on the evening of March 15, just as Libyan tanks were gathering along the roads into Benghazi. The humanitarians and realists engaged in protracted verbal jousting while the President listened. At the end, to general surprise, Obama came out in favor of military intervention.[9] He directed that the United States cooperate with France and Britain in establishing a "no-fly zone" over

Libya and launching air attacks on the Libyan forces that were preparing to attack Benghazi.

Obama struck a deal with French president Nicolas Sarkozy and British prime minister David Cameron whereby the United States would take the lead in the air campaign for the first few days and then turn it over to France and Britain. According to U.S. officials, Obama let France and Britain take over because he thought the U.S. image in the world would suffer if the United States were perceived as leading a third war in an Islamic country, and because he viewed it as a way of encouraging other nations to participate in multinational operations of this sort.[10] One of Obama's senior advisers told Ryan Lizza of the *New Yorker* that Obama's Libya strategy was one of "leading from behind." Lizza commented, "That's not a slogan designed for signs at the 2012 Democratic Convention, but it does accurately describe the balance that Obama now seems to be finding."[11]

Clinton and Rice worked with diplomats from UN Security Council members to obtain a resolution authorizing a no-fly zone over Libya, which they said was intended to prevent the slaughter of innocent civilians. On March 17, the UN Security Council took a vote, with ten countries voting in favor, and China, Russia, Brazil, India, and Germany abstaining. Obama did not seek authorization from his own Congress before using force in Libya, something that Democrats had routinely demanded of Republicans for actions of this type since the passage of the War Powers Act in 1973. Administration officials justified the omission by asserting that the bombing of targets in Libya did not amount to war or "hostilities," but rather was merely "kinetic military action."[12]

The air campaign commenced on March 19 with French aircraft and U.S. Tomahawk missiles making mincemeat of Gaddafi's forces on the outskirts of Benghazi.[13] The strikes ensured the safety of Benghazi for the time being. But NATO airpower and the no-fly zone failed to tip the military scales against Gaddafi with the rapidity that some proponents had hoped. Forces loyal to Gaddafi retained control over much of the country, and civilian casualties mounted. As the civil war intensified, NATO leaders decided to shift the emphasis of the air strikes from atrocity prevention to regime change.

When the change in the objectives of the air campaign became evident, the leading NATO countries faced accusations of exceeding the original UN mandate to protect civilians. The Obama administration performed new rhetorical gymnastics to refute that charge. Some administration officials said that because Gaddafi was such a menace, the only way to protect civilians was to remove him from power. Others characterized the use of force to oust Gaddafi, to include the bombing of his home, as merely giving Gaddafi incentives to desist from atrocities.[14]

As the months wore on and Gaddafi remained in power, the frailty of Europe's military organizations was laid bare. European air forces could not marshal nearly as many aircraft for Libya as the United States had ponied up for the former Yugoslavia in the 1990s, resulting in a daily average of air sorties less than one-quarter of what it had been in Kosovo. Although all of the NATO member nations had voted in favor of the air campaign, fewer than one-third of them contributed any strike aircraft. The Obama administration, insistent that the Europeans remain in the lead, refused to send large numbers of additional U.S. aircraft to compensate for the scarcity of European planes. When all was said and done, the United States provided one-quarter of the air sorties.[15]

Had the bombing campaign been more intensive, Gaddafi and his loyalists might have been subdued much earlier and the war would have been much shorter. As it turned out, 25,000 Libyans would perish during the eight-month civil war.[16]

In June 2011, at his last meeting with NATO leaders before stepping down, Gates remarked that "the mightiest military alliance in history is only 11 weeks into an operation against a poorly armed regime in a sparsely populated country—yet many allies are beginning to run short of munitions, requiring the U.S., once more, to make up the difference." He lamented that NATO had become "a two-tiered alliance," divided "between those willing and able to pay the price and bear the burdens of alliance commitments, and those who enjoy the benefits of NATO membership—be they security guarantees or headquarters billets—but don't want to share the risks and the costs." He warned that if Europeans did not start spending more on their military capabilities, then the American public and Congress would lose their appetite for expending money "on behalf of nations that are apparently unwilling to devote the necessary resources or make the necessary changes to be serious and capable partners in their own defense."[17]

These unusually blunt admonitions made no more impact than had his gentler urgings of the past. European military spending continued to sag in the coming years, falling below Asian military spending in 2012 for the first time in history.[18] To counter perceptions that anemic defense spending had shriveled the capabilities of NATO's European members, NATO leaders announced a policy of "Smart Defense," whereby they would pool military resources to make up for reductions in the resources of individual nations. "In this age of austerity, the choice is stark: Smart Defense or less defense," asserted Anders Fogh Rasmussen, the secretary-general of NATO. He explained that "by creating an even stronger culture of co-operation, allies will be able to provide a level of military capability that would be too expensive for any of them to deliver alone."[19]

In reality, Smart Defense proved to be the same as less defense. NATO countries cooperated much less than advertised, unwilling to surrender national assets to the collective. "The actual agreed-upon initiatives are very modest and the money saved won't come close to matching the size of European defense cuts," observed Clara Marina O'Donnell of the Brookings Institution. "The bottom line is still an overall deterioration in European defense capabilities."[20]

. . .

In sub-Saharan Africa, the Obama administration looked to European and African allies for help in promoting stability and security. Like George W. Bush before him, Obama sought to prevent poorly governed and insecure African nations from becoming sanctuaries and incubators for international terrorist organizations. Like Bush, too, he did not want to send American ground forces into Africa because of concerns that it would antagonize the U.S. public, which remained haunted by the dragging of dead American soldiers through the streets of Mogadishu in 1993. In the so-called Battle of Mogadishu of October 3–4, 1993, Somalis had inflicted nearly one hundred casualties on American special operations forces, who, it might be added, had been sent to Somalia in the mistaken belief that surgical strikes could bring peace to a conflict-ridden country.

Only a few African countries had the capability to deploy large numbers of troops beyond their borders, and none of them wished to maintain foreign troop commitments indefinitely. The European countries that sent troops or trainers to assist in the securing of African countries often lacked the resources or political will to complete the assigned tasks. If the Europeans could not organize a serious war effort to deal with ethnic wars on their own continent, they could not be expected to do very much on another continent that was much more difficult to reach and much less important to their own well-being.

Since 9/11, Somalia had been the African nation of highest interest to the United States, owing to Bin Laden's decision to make it a leading destination for the Al Qaeda diaspora. Somalia's large Muslim population provided Al Qaeda with ready sources of recruitment and plentiful hiding places. Somalia had not had a viable central government since 1991 and Somalian society was deeply fractured along tribal lines, leaving the country devoid of governmental or security personnel who could assist the United States or other countries in pursuing terrorists.

In 2006, Islamic extremists had seized control of Mogadishu under the banner of the Council of Islamic Courts (CIC), and then had extended their tentacles into southern and central Somalia, driving Somalia's internationally backed provisional government into a few scattered pockets. But the CIC overreached at the end of 2006, with an attempt to overrun the headquarters of the provisional government. Ethiopia, the principal guardian of that government, responded to the CIC's offensive with a much larger offensive of its own. Sweeping across the border in massive numbers, the Ethiopian army routed the CIC forces in open battle and stood triumphant in Mogadishu within just a few days.[21]

The presence of a large Ethiopian footprint in Somalia was a boon for the U.S. military. U.S. special operations forces arrived in Mogadishu together with the Ethiopian forces like sucker fish on the side of a whale. The Ethiopians held bases and roads that the U.S. forces needed, and they fought thousands of Islamists who would otherwise have homed in on the Americans. By capitalizing on these advantages, the U.S. forces eliminated a substantial number of Al Qaeda leadership figures.[22]

The Ethiopians were to discover, however, that occupation was far harder than regime change. The provisional government that followed the Ethiopians into Mogadishu was incapable of governing effectively or organizing large security forces that could take the place of Ethiopian forces. By contrast, Al Shabaab and other Islamist insurgent groups were vigorous and effective in waging guerrilla war on the Ethiopian occupation forces, upon whom they inflicted heavy casualties. Widespread allegations of human rights violations by Ethiopia's predominantly Christian troops sparked outrage among Muslims in Somalia and drew foreign jihadists to the country.

The Ethiopians sought to get other nations involved so that they could hand over at least some of the hard work. In 2007, the UN Security Council authorized the deployment of 8,000 African Union troops to Somalia for what was dubbed the African Union Mission to Somalia (AMISOM). Sixteen hundred Ugandan troops deployed during that year, and thousands more, from a variety of other nations, would follow in future years. The United States provided most of the funding for AMISOM, and it funded contractors who provided training and logistical assistance.[23]

Later in 2007, the Somali government requested UN peacekeepers as a supplement to AMISOM. But the UN did not have the stomach for the mission.[24] During 2008, at the request of the Security Council, UN secretary-general Ban Ki-moon sent out a request to fifty of the world's wealthiest nations for financial resources, personnel, equipment, and services for a long-term multinational peacekeeping force in Somalia, but only fourteen countries bothered to respond, and only two of them offered anything of substance—the United States, which offered funding, equipment, and logistical support, and the Netherlands, which offered funding alone.[25]

Tired of the guerrilla war, Ethiopia negotiated a peace agreement with the Islamists and withdrew its forces in early 2009. The Ethiopian troops had scarcely finished stepping across the border into their homeland when the Somali Islamists began their flouting of the peace agreement. UN-trained Somali security forces were supposed to protect the transitional government, but they quickly crumbled once the Ethiopian buttresses had been removed. The UN Monitoring Group reported that "government security forces remain ineffective, disorganized and corrupt—a composite of independent militias loyal to senior government officials and military officers who profit from the business of war and resist their integration under a single command."[26] The African Union peacekeepers who remained in Somalia, somewhat more competent, did not pose much more of a threat to Al Shabaab. When they ventured into combat, they made lavish use of artillery with little regard for civilian bystanders, alienating the civilian population.[27]

Once the Ethiopians had pulled out, the Islamists wasted little time in seizing control of Mogadishu and most of Somalia's other territory. The transitional government and the peacekeeping forces retreated into isolated enclaves. Al Shabaab, an ascendant offshoot of the Islamic Courts Union, assumed leadership in Mogadishu and set its sights on targets beyond Africa. Al Shabaab leader Sheikh Moktar Ali Zubeyr openly pledged his fealty to Osama Bin Laden and other Al Qaeda chieftains.[28]

Al Shabaab's rise to power induced large numbers of foreign radicals to make their way to Somalia. Western intelligence services grew concerned about ethnic Somalis with Western passports who were training with Al Shabaab in Somalia in preparation for terrorist attacks in the West. According to the FBI, at least thirty Americans had joined Al Shabaab by 2011, three of whom had carried out suicide attacks against African Union forces. Abdisalan Hussein Ali, a twenty-two-year-old American of Somali extraction, who had briefly studied chemistry at the University of Minnesota before disappearing in 2008, recorded a message to inspire future jihadists prior to blowing himself up. "Don't just sit around, you know, and be, you know, a couch potato and just like, just chill all day," he said. "Today jihad is what is most important. It's not important that you become a doctor, or some sort of engineer."[29]

More than one hundred Britons were reported to be undergoing terrorist training in Somalia. In September 2011, the head of the British intelligence agency MI5, Jonathan Evans, warned that Somalia now was suspected of harboring as many terrorist plots against the United Kingdom as Pakistan. Evans remarked, "I am concerned that it's only a matter of time before we see terrorism on our streets inspired by those who are today fighting alongside al-Shabaab."[30]

Following Anwar al-Awlaki's death, an American member of Al Shabaab named Omar Hammami took over as the top English-language Islamist on the Internet preaching scene. He told Muslims living in the West that they had to "get out of the belly of the beast and start living in the crisis zones with the Muslims." Adherents of Islam could not fulfill their divine purpose "by walking down orderly sidewalks and buying Subway sandwiches on your way back from the gym." Muslims should not be troubled by terrorist violence that killed "Joe and Sally," his preferred terms for non-Muslim civilian bystanders, because those nonbelievers were "part of a civilization that is at war with Islam."[31]

The withdrawal of Ethiopian forces from Somalia and the coming to power of Al Shabaab greatly reduced U.S. opportunities to hunt down extremists on Somali territory.[32] Obama was unwilling to establish a military footprint in the country, so intelligence collection had to take place at a distance, and operational forces had to fly in from elsewhere, reducing their stealth. U.S. special operations forces conducted only occasional strikes against terrorist suspects in Somalia.[33]

Like the Islamic Courts Union before them, Al Shabaab poked Somalia's neighbors too hard and in so doing spoiled their own chances of consolidating control. This time it was Uganda that was pushed over the edge. At some point in the first half of 2010, Al Shabaab decided that loosing terrorist arrows at the heart of Uganda would demoralize the Ugandans and convince them to withdraw their AMISOM troop contingent, the largest in Somalia. On July 11, 2010, Al Shabaab suicide bombers walked into a rugby club and an Ethiopian restaurant in

Kampala where Ugandans and expatriates were watching the World Cup final between the Netherlands and Spain. With the eyes of the spectators fixed on the big-screen televisions, the bombers positioned themselves in the middle of the crowds to achieve maximum effect, then detonated their explosive vests.

The blasts killed 76 people and injured 85. Among the dead was Nate Henn, a twenty-five-year-old from Pennsylvania. Henn had attended the University of Delaware, where he played rugby, and after college had raised money to undertake Christian missionary trips. Just one week earlier, Henn had arrived in Uganda to work as a volunteer for Invisible Children, a charitable organization that sought to stop Ugandan rebels from abducting children and forcing them to become soldiers. "He was passionate for doing the work that the Lord did and helping people," said Brenda Kibler, who had gone on Christian missions with Henn. "I know for a fact he would be proud to know he died, living the life that he did. And that people are proud of him and know for a fact that he lived a selfless life."[34]

Al Shabaab had badly underestimated the Ugandans. Instead of cowering, the Ugandans showed a newfound resolve to fight Al Shabaab. They sent more troops to Somalia, increasing the size of AMISOM to 20,000, and prepared the plans for a major AMISOM offensive in which Uganda would assume the leading role. Somalia's Transitional Federal Government would ostensibly be in the lead, but as a disorganized and impotent hodgepodge of clan militias, it was only a façade, as everyone knew. When the offensive kicked off in the summer of 2011, locals joked that the war was really one between AMISOM and Islamisom.[35] AMISOM made quick work of Al Shabaab in central Mogadishu, driving it out in August.

Ugandan forces took on the task of training Somali youths for a Somalian national army. The U.S. military advocated insertion of U.S. military personnel in Somalia to train and advise both Somali and African Union forces, but the request was rejected by a White House that was averse to any military footprint in Somalia. "The international community showed no serious interest in prioritising training of Somali troops as a way of solving the Somalia problem, so Uganda took it on," said Lieutenant Colonel Paddy Ankunda, a spokesman for the Ugandan military.[36]

The Ugandan military did not, however, have the resources to give proper training to Somali recruits, and no other foreign donor was providing resources for the mission. The Ugandans did not even have rifles to train the Somalis. When Ugandans positioned Somali trainees to conduct assaults on sand dunes, the "attackers" had to use sticks or their own fingers as make-believe rifles. "They're training them in drama not military skills," remarked Ugandan intelligence officer Michael Baguma. "If you engage them with the enemy, they will lose because they'll shoot each other." Baguma lamented, "It's inhuman. This is sacrifice of these young boys."[37]

AMISOM lacked enough troops to extend central authority outside the main urban centers, so Al Shabaab was able to hang on to much of the countryside. In addition, the will of the troop-contributing nations to maintain troops in Somalia began to erode again in 2013. Ethiopia withdrew some of its forces from Somalia, stretching out the other African Union forces too thinly to permit continuation of offensive operations.[38] Al Shabaab was regaining strength in the second half of 2013, pushing African Union and Somali government forces back.[39]

These gains did not receive much international attention until September 21, when Al Shabaab stormed the Westgate Mall in Kenya. An upscale three-story shopping center in downtown Nairobi, the Westgate Mall was popular with affluent Kenyans and foreign tourists.[40] The Al Shabaab assault force, numbering between ten and fifteen individuals, intended to kill as many people as possible, though they were also determined to avoid harming Muslims, because Al Qaeda had provoked widespread condemnation in the Muslim world for killing Muslim civilians in recent years. The gunmen rounded up shoppers and asked them questions about Islam, such as the names of Mohammad's relatives or the text of Quranic verses. They set free those who knew the answers, and shot the rest.[41]

During the three-day mall siege, the attackers killed 67 people, including 18 foreigners, and wounded another 200. When investigators entered the mall afterward, they found that some of the deceased showed signs of torture, including severed hands and noses. The Kenyan government reported that some of the attackers had been killed and that additional suspects had been detained, but it provided fluctuating figures on both of those groups, and did not make clear whether any of the perpetrators had escaped.[42]

The White House took the unusual step of portraying the three-day terrorist attack as evidence of successful counterterrorism. "We've actually had a very aggressive effort to go after al Shabaab in Somalia," said Ben Rhodes. "And, frankly, I think it was that pressure on al-Shabaab that, in terms of their own professed motivation, led them to pursue an attack against Kenya."[43]

Few observers in Africa viewed the attack as evidence of either successful counterterrorism or Al Shabaab's weakness. Nick Kay, the UN special representative for Somalia, concluded that as a result of the Westgate attack, the international community needed to send more troops to Somalia to fight Al Shabaab, especially outside Mogadishu where the extremists were registering their biggest gains. "I don't think we will remove that threat until we actually deal with al-Shabab outside Mogadishu," he said.[44] In November, the African Union asked the UN to increase the number of AMISOM personnel from 17,731 to 26,000. Erastus Mwencha, deputy chairman of the African Union, explained that the increase was needed to cope with an Al Shabaab organization that was regaining its strength. The UN Security Council agreed to authorize an increase, though only to a strength of 22,126.[45]

While the Obama administration had downplayed the Westgate attack in public, some U.S. officials privately voiced great concerns about Al Shabaab's rising power. Some recommended decapitation strikes. The ability of Al Shabaab leaders to mingle with the population, however, discouraged the use of drone strikes, as did the growing international revulsion at drone warfare.

Problems arising from enemy intermingling with civilians also stood in the way of precision-strike missions by U.S. special operations forces. The most valuable targets, moreover, were located in enemy-held territory, which would afford the enemy greater opportunities to detect and resist raiding forces. In spite of those obstacles, Obama authorized a raid on October 5, 2013, to nab the Al Shabaab commander Abdulkadir Mohamed Abdulkadir, whom U.S. intelligence had located in Baraawe, a Somali city of 200,000 residents. Once a major hub of the international slave trade, Baraawe now counted fishing as its principal commercial enterprise. The city had been an Al Shabaab redoubt since 2008, and African Union forces and the Somali government were absent for seventy miles in every direction.[46]

At two in the morning, a speedboat deposited twenty U.S. Navy SEALs at one of Baraawe's beaches. According to the carefully rehearsed plan, the SEALs would head to a house two hundred meters from the beach, where Abdulkadir was believed to be located. They would suppress any sentries or bodyguards, grab their target, and take him back to the beach for exfiltration. Success depended on speed; anything that slowed them down increased the likelihood that local Al Shabaab supporters would come to Abdulkadir's rescue.

Maintaining strict noise discipline in the black of night, the SEALs reached the compound where the house was located without coming to anyone's attention. As they approached the house, they caught sight of an Al Shabaab sentry, and everyone froze. Puffing on a cigarette, the sentry appeared not to have seen the SEALs. When he went inside, the SEALs prayed that he was checking his Facebook page, or going to bed, or doing something else that would get him out of their way. But moments later the sentry reemerged with his AK-47 blazing.

The eruption of gunfire awoke other militants in the compound and neighboring compounds. Men in robes began running toward the sound of the guns, their own assault rifles in hand. Knowing that the number of hostile gunmen would now be increasing by the second, the SEALs cast caution aside and stormed the house where their prize was located. Six of the SEALs exchanged fire with militants inside the house.

The enemy fighters kept the SEALs sufficiently busy to allow Abdulkadir to slip away. With the hostile forces multiplying and the exit point two hundred meters away, the SEALs could not afford to stay long. Within minutes, the SEAL commander decided to withdraw his men to the beach. He considered calling in an air strike on the compound for the purpose of killing Abdulkadir, who might still have been holed up in one of the buildings, but decided against it because of the probability that it would kill large numbers of women and children. The SEALs bolted for the beach, where they reassembled and prepared to board the boat. A head count revealed that all of the SEALs were present and unharmed. It also indicated that no prisoners had been taken.

Al Shabaab responded to the raid with new countermeasures and a wave of propaganda. In Baraawe, Al Shabaab fighters stepped up their patrolling and positioned sentries and antiaircraft weapons on the beach. They instituted curfews and hunted for informants who might have tipped off the Americans, arresting one man who had frequently been seen at an Internet café. Al Shabaab propagandists touted the escape of their leader and the American withdrawal as evidence of Al Shabaab's mighty power.[47]

In December 2013, the White House finally agreed to send a small number of U.S. troops to Somalia. It was a belated acknowledgment that the African Union forces could not secure the whole country or build viable Somalian security forces on their own. It was also an acknowledgment that defeating Al Shabaab required counterinsurgency, not just counterterrorism. But the Obama administration's desire to avoid entanglement limited the deployment to three U.S. advisers, not the sort of number that could restore a viable government and security forces in a place like Somalia.[48]

Somalia is not a typical state, and American involvement in the country should not be treated as a model to be applied in other states. Some African forces have been able to put down insurrections and defeat insurgents in their own countries without foreign troops, or with help from European or other African forces. But even in these countries, U.S. support has often been critical.

· · ·

The history of the Obama administration has shown repeatedly that a multilateral enterprise is likely to end in failure if it lacks strong American leadership. Time after time, Obama handed the mantle of leadership to nations or international organizations that fell well short of expectations. The allies upon whom the United States has been most inclined to rely, the NATO member nations, have proven incapable of leading in most major crises, owing to insufficient fortitude, resources, and public support. The United Nations has been even worse, its Security Council routinely stifled by the vetoes of member nations with conflicting interests.

When the United States has refused to lead, as it often has under the Obama administration, it has diminished the very international cooperation that multilateralism ostensibly promotes. No one wants to join the basketball team whose captain refuses to run his hardest and expects others to provide the inspiration and the points. People want to join the team with the captain who dives for every loose ball, shouts encouragement to teammates, and volunteers to take the last-second shot when the game is on the line.

On May 11, 2014, Martha Raddatz of ABC News asked Secretary of Defense Hagel to comment on "all the heat President Obama has been taking over his foreign policy choices, even from the usually friendly *New York Times* editorial page." She read from a *Times* editorial that stated, "The perception of weakness, dithering, inaction, there are many names for it, has indisputably had a negative effect on Mr. Obama's global standing."

Hagel responded, "I don't subscribe to the *New York Times'* analysis because it isn't an easy matter of just what your perception is in the world. And I don't think you can run foreign policy or lead a nation or be president of the United States based on what other people think of you." It was a far cry from Obama's statements in 2009 about the need to "forge partnerships as opposed to simply dictating solutions."

"When I travel overseas, people say different things about America," Raddatz continued. "They say it's not as forceful."

"I have seen some of it, yes," Hagel said. "I do think there is a sense out there, that you have correctly identified, by some, that somehow America's power is eroding or we're not going to use our power or we're too timid about our power."[49]

12

BIGGER IS BETTER

Libya

Following NATO's decimation of Muammar Gaddafi's forces outside Benghazi on March 19, 2011, the city of Benghazi became the hub of planning for a rebel counteroffensive. The largest city in eastern Libya, Benghazi had served as the seat of the Senussi monarchy until 1954. Benghazi had garnered American attention in 1967, when a mob angered by U.S. support for Israel overran the U.S. consulate, poured gasoline on it, and set it on fire.

Benghazi's more recent history had been noteworthy for its mixture of sports with politics. The Al Ahly Benghazi soccer club had often accused Muammar Gaddafi and his son Saadi of bribing or bullying referees to ensure the victory of clubs owned by Saadi, resulting in denunciations of Gaddafi that aroused the dictator's ire from time to time. In 1996, Saadi's bodyguards opened fire on Al Ahly Benghazi fans inside a crowded stadium after they jeered his father, killing several of them. In 2000, Al Ahly Benghazi's fans incurred Gaddafi's wrath for painting the colors of one of Saadi's clubs on a donkey and parading it through the stadium. Gaddafi's goons ransacked the club's headquarters, smashing the trophies and memorabilia, and then bulldozers flattened it.

More serious in their consequences had been Gaddafi's armed clashes with Islamists in Benghazi and other towns in eastern Libya. In 1997, Gaddafi used helicopter gunships and napalm against Islamist forces in eastern Libya. In the early 2000s, a new group calling itself Al Qaeda in

Eastern Libya emerged to join other Islamist groups like the Muslim Brotherhood and the Libyan Islamic Fighting Group.[1] Gaddafi's tough measures against the Islamic extremists in the early post-9/11 era were applauded in Washington, which had its hands full helping less committed countries deal with their extremist problems.

At the end of February 2011, leaders of the anti-Gaddafi forces met in Benghazi to form a National Transitional Council, which laid claim to the role of interim government until Gaddafi could be ousted from Tripoli. The council's leadership included intellectuals, professionals, tribal leaders, and disgruntled government officials. Like many interim governing bodies, it was better at talking about a bright future than at building one. Nevertheless, it was able to convince foreign countries to recognize it as the sole legitimate government of Libya.

On April 5, a Greek cargo ship pulled in to Benghazi to deliver the U.S. special envoy to the Libyan National Transitional Council, J. Christopher Stevens. The American embassy in Tripoli had closed two months earlier, so Stevens was now the principal U.S. representative in the country. Sensing that his arrival signified American support for the rebel cause, the resistance leaders rushed to embrace him.[2] They complained to Stevens that the European-led air campaign was too weak to bring Gaddafi down, and called for the United States to provide more military muscle.

Obama, however, remained disinclined to veer from the strategy of "leading from behind." He had no desire to send U.S. ground forces into Libya to assist the rebels, because he feared that such a deployment would lead to a quagmire along the lines of Iraq. In public, Obama said time and again that the United States would not send ground forces to Libya, which scored political points in the United States, but which in Libya encouraged Gaddafi in his belief that he could survive if he stayed the course.

The U.S. government and European governments did pursue other avenues of aiding the rebels as Libya's civil war dragged on. They enlisted the assistance of Qatar and the United Arab Emirates in providing weapons to various groups. But without a U.S. military presence on the ground, the United States had a very limited understanding of who was receiving the weapons, and it could do little to control the distribution. American officials eventually became concerned that Qatar was sending weapons to Islamist entities that, according to one U.S. official source, were "more antidemocratic, more hard-line, closer to an extreme version of Islam" than the rebels whom the United States had intended to support. Some of these weapons would eventually reach anti-American militants in Mali and Syria.[3]

Intensified NATO bombing of government forces finally broke the stalemate at the end of July, permitting rebel forces to break out of the port city of Misrata and pierce Gaddafi's defensive perimeter in the mountains south of Tripoli. Ensuing air strikes on government communications and logistical facilities discombobulated loyalist troops retreating toward the capital. On August 20, rebel forces entered Tripoli, and three days later they took Gaddafi's headquarters at Bab al-Azizia, in the city's southern suburbs.

Gaddafi himself, however, continued to slip through the rebel nets, protected by military units and militias with ties to his favored tribes. The tribes most loyal to Gaddafi had come to his rescue in the past, and he was counting on them to do so again. In an audio message released on a still-friendly television channel on August 25, Gaddafi called on the tribes to "organize a million man march that will fight this time, that will fill the streets and fill the squares." Indicative of both his desperation and his belief in the gullibility of his people, he added, "Do not fear the shelling" from the rebel artillery. "These are blank shells that scare you."[4]

Gaddafi's rallying cries failed to arouse enough tribesmen to save Tripoli. The dictator soon fled the capital and headed to his hometown of Sirte, a city on the coast midway between Tripoli and Benghazi that Gaddafi had built into the Libyan government's cultural and administrative center. The rebels cast a noose around the city, and began to pull it tight in the middle of October. Their weapons transformed Sirte's ministry buildings, conference centers, monuments, and housing complexes from pristine edifices into bullet-ridden hulks.

On October 20, Gaddafi concluded that the remaining loyalist forces could not hold Sirte much longer, so he ordered a breakout. He evidently intended to continue waging war from another site, as he did not sneak out with a few bodyguards as would a man who had given up, but instead departed in a convoy of 175 vehicles. Soon after departing from Sirte, the convoy caught the attention of a U.S. drone, which then transmitted its location to the staff at a NATO headquarters, who in turn dispatched a French Mirage jet to bomb the convoy. The bombs wiped out a few vehicles at the front of the column, causing Gaddafi and everyone else in the convoy to scurry out vehicle doors and seek cover.

A rebel militia that had been pursuing Gaddafi caught up with the group and hunted them down like bobcats in a field full of wild turkeys. Gaddafi attempted to hide in a drainage pipe with his bodyguards, but the rebels soon found him. "You are my sons," the once-mighty leader pleaded to his captors. "Show me mercy." The rebels, who had seen little mercy from Gaddafi over the decades, beat him and pulled his hair. "This is for Misrata," one yelled.

The rebels threw Gaddafi on the hood of a four-by-four vehicle and pressed down on him with shoes as a symbol of disrespect. Some of the rebels wanted to keep him alive, but they were overruled by a man who shot Gaddafi in the forehead. The rebels then took Gaddafi's corpse and that of his son Mu'tassim to Misrata, where they were put on display in the frozen-foods locker of a butcher's shop. The bodies sat in the freezer for a week while Libyans came to have a last look at the nation's long-time ruler.[5]

The downfall of Gaddafi and his regime seemed, at first, to have vindicated the NATO military intervention and its reliance on airpower rather than land power. "The dark shadow of tyranny has been lifted," Obama said during an address from the Rose Garden on the day of Gaddafi's death. "Without putting a single U.S. service member on the ground, we achieved our objectives, and our NATO mission will soon come to an end."[6]

"The light U.S. footprint had benefits beyond less U.S. lives and resources," Ben Rhodes informed the media. "We believe the Libyan revolution is viewed as more legitimate. The U.S. is more welcome. And there is less potential for an insurgency because there aren't foreign forces present."[7]

Secretary of State Hillary Clinton told the *Washington Post* that "we set into motion a policy that was on the right side of history, on the right side of our values, on the right side of our strategic interests in the region."[8] In a television interview, she gloated over Gaddafi's death. "We came, we saw, he died," she chuckled, clapping her hands together.[9] Jonathan Allen and Amie Parnes, semiofficial chroniclers of Clinton's tenure as secretary of state, observed that Clinton thought Libya was "on track to be the success that defined her legacy," and "the jewel in her crown." It would put an end to "the big knock on her," which had been that "she didn't have a major foreign policy breakthrough under her belt."[10]

Neither the United States nor its European partners elected to put peacekeepers or other significant ground forces in Libya. They either had high expectations for Libyan self-governance, or believed that sending ground forces was too politically unpopular in their own countries, or both. The lack of a NATO ground presence following Gaddafi's demise ensured that NATO forces did not find themselves in the cross fire of competing factions, as had occurred in Iraq. But it also deprived NATO of key advantages that the U.S. forces in Iraq had conferred. The U.S. Army and Marine Corps battalions in Iraq had safeguarded the American civilian personnel responsible for restoring Iraqi civil governance and collecting information. They had provided a protective bubble within which a new central government could be formed and developed, and served as a large training force that could help develop national security forces. Their presence gave the United States political clout, which it used to marginalize some of the most nefarious actors.

The Obama administration did deploy a small CIA contingent to Libya to track down terrorists and dangerous weapons that could fall into the hands of terrorists. A small number of State Department diplomats went as well. The CIA and State Department sent security personnel to guard these individuals, but not enough to guard all the installations occupied by Americans or to secure all the roads they traveled. Providing that sort of security would have required a much larger footprint than the White House was willing to accept. Protection of CIA and State personnel therefore required extensive reliance on Libyan security forces, which in the short term meant militias because Libya did not yet have a viable national army or professional police forces.

The most immediate problem arising from the lack of NATO ground forces was the inability to secure critical facilities. The rebels did not assert control over prisons in which Gaddafi had incarcerated numerous members of Al Qaeda and other violent extremist organizations, but instead unlocked the prison gates and let the inmates go free. Also of great concern were Gaddafi's armories, which contained heavy weapons and surface-to-air missiles that could shoot down commercial as well as military aircraft. Rebel militias looted the armories and sold some of the weapons for cash to extremist groups. Investigators would later conclude that heavy weapons and surface-to-air missiles formerly belonging to Gaddafi were smuggled out to Mali, Lebanon, and other dangerous locations in Africa and the Middle East.[11]

While Gaddafi's death had removed a vicious tyrant from Libya, it also had removed the cause behind which the rebels had united. After the initial jubilation of Gaddafi's death had passed, rebel factions stopped holding hands and started shaking their fists. Their behavior would do serious injury to the Obama administration's argument that keeping foreign troops away was the key to preventing insurgency from sprouting.

The National Transitional Council demanded that the tribal militias hand over their weapons, but the tribes paid no heed. When it attempted to form national security forces that could impose the government's will on the tribes, the militias assassinated government officials until the attempts ceased. Tribal hatreds that had flared during the civil war continued to burn afterward, igniting further acts of violence and mutilation among pro-Gaddafi and anti-Gaddafi tribes. Meanwhile, the hopes of Westerners and Libyan intellectuals that the Libyan people would rally around a democratic government, as if they were Americans or Frenchmen, were soon dashed. A poll conducted by British researchers a few months after the war found that only 15 percent of Libyans wanted democracy within the next year, and only one-third wanted it within five years, while the majority preferred authoritarian rule.[12]

Some of the militias that lorded over Libya's cities were dominated by Islamist extremists. Islamist militias were strongest in Darna, an old Barbary port in eastern Libya where Gaddafi had suppressed an Islamist insurrection in the 1990s. Darna's militiamen assassinated officials, policemen, and journalists who dared to defy them.[13]

A somewhat more diverse group of Islamist militias held sway in Benghazi. With NATO unwilling to put its troops on the ground, the security of the small Western diplomatic corps in Benghazi depended heavily on tribal militias of purported pro-Western sympathies. The policy of counting upon friendly militiamen for security did not get off to a promising start. Attacks on Western installations and personnel in Benghazi surged in late 2011 and the first half of 2012. During June 2012, Islamist militiamen in Benghazi attempted to assassinate the British ambassador, causing the British to shut their Benghazi consulate, and they blew a hole in the U.S. diplomatic compound.

Chris Stevens returned to Libya in May 2012 as U.S. ambassador. As he quickly learned, the risks to U.S. personnel and installations in Benghazi and Tripoli now ranked among the embassy's most pressing concerns. On July 9, Stevens submitted a request for thirteen additional U.S. security personnel for the two cities. Marine Lieutenant General Robert Neller, the Joint Staff's director of operations, responded with a proposal to beef up the military presence in Libya with either a military Site Security Team, a Marine Security Detachment, or a Marine Fleet Antiterrorism Security Team.[14] The State Department's leaders in Washington, however, rejected Neller's offer and told Stevens not to ask for military forces again.[15] The following month, the State Department turned down another offer of U.S. military security personnel, this time from General Carter Ham, the commander of the U.S. military's Africa Command. Ham had proffered the troops after learning that U.S. embassy officials deemed security inadequate at the Benghazi mission, a diplomatic facility that was at times erroneously called a consulate.[16]

Eric Nordstrom, the chief security officer at the U.S. embassy in

Tripoli, later told congressional investigators that Deputy Assistant Secretary for International Programs Charlene Lamb "wanted to keep the
number of U.S. security personnel in Benghazi artificially low."[17] The
State Department's leaders were worried that sending military forces
would call into question claims by Secretary Clinton and others that
Libya was a splendid trophy. As Mark Hosenball of Reuters reported
after interviewing U.S. officials, the State Department preferred a light
security footprint in Benghazi in order to "project an appearance of nor-
mality in U.S. dealings with Libya."[18]

The extent and nature of guidance that Lamb received from Secretary
of State Clinton and other top State Department officials have remained
a mystery. Clinton did, however, defend the level of security at Benghazi
at a news conference in the middle of September 2012. "We had no ac-
tionable intelligence that an attack on our post in Benghazi was planned
or imminent," she said as justification for the State Department's refusal
to send more security personnel.[19] Senator Dianne Feinstein, a Democrat and the chairwoman of the Senate Intelligence Committee, took
issue with that interpretation after seeing the intelligence that had been
available. "The problem was the right people apparently either didn't
make the decision or didn't analyze the intelligence, because I think if
you looked at the intelligence, you would have substantially beefed up
the security in that particular mission, in Benghazi," Feinstein said.[20]

Ambassador Stevens headed to Benghazi on September 10 for several days of meetings with local and foreign leaders. On the evening of
September 11, he dined with the Benghazi City Council at a local hotel,
then returned to the mission for a meeting with a Turkish diplomat. At
7:40 P.M., Stevens escorted the Turkish guest to the front gate of the
mission compound to say good-bye. The street was quiet.[21] Stevens then
retired to his room.

At 8 P.M., 150 bearded men began setting up roadblocks on the streets
leading to the mission. They crisscrossed the streets with pickup trucks,
which bore the logo of the Islamist group Ansar al-Shariah on their
doors and carried heavy machine guns in their beds. Commanders prepared the men for battle. No one participated in activities that could

have been construed as political protest, a matter that was soon to acquire global significance. Khaled al-Haddar, a lawyer who saw the armed men as he was walking home, said, "I am certain they had planned to do something like this, I don't know if it was hours or days, but it was definitely planned. From the way they set up the checkpoints and gathered people, it was very professional."[22]

The U.S. mission compound contained four buildings, separated from one another by large courtyards with carefully manicured grass and emerald-green shrubs. Nine-foot walls surrounded the compound, several of which contained gates wide enough to accommodate vehicles. Libyan militiamen were supposed to be watching all the walls and gates. The Americans inside the compound, however, never received reports of the enemy's arrival.

At 9:40, a man appeared at one of the compound's gates. He banged his rifle on the glass of a guard booth, drawing the attention of the Libyan guard. "Open the gate, you fucker!" he screamed, pointing his AK-47 at the guard's forehead. The man did as he was told. Several men burst into the compound and made their way to a second gate, which they opened. Four vehicles sped up to that gate and dropped off more than a dozen fighters.[23]

At 9:42, gunshots and an explosion pierced the evening quiet. Alec Henderson, a Diplomatic Security officer inside the compound's tactical operations center, looked up at the security monitors to see armed men moving through the compound and making ready to assault its four buildings. According to a subsequent review of footage from U.S. surveillance cameras, approximately sixty individuals entered the compound.[24] As Henderson also saw on the screens, Libyan militiamen who were supposed to be guarding the compound were running away at maximum speed.

Henderson sounded an alarm, which flooded the compound with a shrill siren similar to that of a police vehicle as well as a repetitive voice recording that announced "Duck and cover! Get away from the windows!" Henderson also contacted the U.S. embassy in Tripoli and another U.S. facility nearby. "Benghazi under fire, terrorist attack," read his message.[25]

According to a prearranged plan, Diplomatic Security special agent Scott Wickland was supposed to locate Ambassador Stevens and information officer Sean Smith and get them to a safe area. Wickland found both men quickly. He told them to put on their body armor, then guided them to a safe room that had been fortified and stocked with food and water to get them through a protracted siege.

With the supposedly pro-American Libyan militiamen nowhere to be found, the militants had free rein over the compound. A militant search party soon located the safe room where the ambassador was hiding. Peering into the locked grates, they saw only darkness. They pulled and banged on the grates, but to no effect. Then they came up with a clever solution, one perhaps inspired by the sacking of the American consulate in 1967.

Next to the mission's generators sat cans of diesel fuel, free for the taking. Leaving flammable liquids unsecured at a high-risk facility was one more adverse consequence of outsourcing the security of Americans. Militants had already used some of the fuel to burn vehicles and one of the mission's other buildings. Now they hauled cans to the villa with the mysterious barricaded room, where they splashed it across the floors and the overstuffed furniture before setting it alight.

Diesel smoke seeped into the safe room, becoming so thick that Wickland, Stevens, and Smith could barely see or breathe. Fearing asphyxiation, Wickland led Stevens and Smith to a bathroom, locked the three of them inside, and put towels under the door. They opened the window to get some clean air, but as soon as they opened it, smoke poured in from outside. Convinced that they needed to get out of the building as soon as possible, Wickland told Stevens and Smith that they would head into a nearby bedroom and escape through a window.

Crawling on their hands and knees, the three men could not see one another. Wickland reached the window first, and shouted its location to Stevens and Smith. He climbed out the window, in expectation that Stevens and Smith would follow. But no one else climbed out after him.

Wickland pulled himself back in the window to look for the ambassador and the information officer. Hemmed in by smoke and heat, he was unable to find either man. Wickland then contacted the few other security personnel inside the compound. Although barely intelligible because of smoke inhalation, Wickland managed to communicate his position accurately. The other Americans found him and joined him in searching through the smoke for Stevens and Smith. Eventually they found Smith, but by then he was dead from smoke inhalation. They could not locate the ambassador.[26]

One mile from the mission stood a secret site called "the annex." A two-acre compound that a wealthy Libyan hotel owner had rented to the United States, the annex housed U.S. intelligence personnel looking for weapons that had gone missing from Gaddafi's arsenals. It was also the home base of a seven-man quick-reaction force from the CIA's Global Response Staff, which had responsibility for protecting both the annex and the mission.[27] Receiving word of the attack within moments of the first gunshots, the members of the security team had immediately grabbed their weapons, body armor, night-vision goggles, and medical kits and boarded two armored vehicles.

Intimately aware that the mission's defenses were too weak to hold off a concerted attack for long, the security team's members wanted to drive to the mission compound at once. But the senior CIA officer at the base, known as "Bob," decided to wait until he could gather additional information and obtain support from friendly Libyan militias.

After several minutes of awaiting permission to drive to the mission compound, the security team began to voice its displeasure. "Hey, we gotta go now!" said John Tiegen, a former Marine. "It's too fucking late to come up with a plan. We need to get in the fucking area and then come up with a plan."

"No," replied Bob, "hold up. We're going to have the local militia handle it." Bob was trying to get the 17 February Martyrs Brigade, a friendly Libyan militia, to send overwhelming force to the mission to secure it.

Kris Paronto, a former U.S. Army Ranger who was on the security team, protested that this militia had let them down before and could not be entrusted with so critical a task. "We need to go," he said. "We're not letting 17 Feb handle it."[28]

The Global Response Staffers had compelling and admirable reasons
to act immediately, but Bob had compelling reasons to wait for Libyan
help. The decision of the State Department to minimize the footprint
of the U.S. military in Libya had ensured that the use of small security
teams against armed militias would be a highly risky proposition. Without any American troops in Benghazi to put fear into America's enemies
or come to the rescue of Americans in extremis, a half dozen security
contractors would be an inviting target for militias that might already
have hundreds of fighters on the scene. The Global Response Staffers
may have been veterans of America's elite special operations forces, but
past debacles in cities like Mogadishu and Fallujah had shown that even
the world's most elite soldiers could not survive indefinitely against far
more numerous opponents who enjoyed home-field advantage.

The agitation mounted as more bad news came in over the radio.
The attack on the mission's buildings was intensifying and no friendlies,
from the 17 February Martyrs Brigade or any other organization, were
coming to the rescue. Roughly twenty minutes into the attack, someone
at the compound notified the annex, "If you guys do not get here, we're
going to die!"[29]

Bob still refused to unleash the Global Response Staff. The Staff,
however, had seen enough. They were going to bite through the leash.
"We need to go," Paronto told their team leader, who had been awaiting
orders from Bob. "Get in the fucking car." The team leader evidently was
fed up with Bob's dithering as well. He got in, and the two vehicles drove
toward the mission compound.[30]

The black Mercedes G-Class sport-utility and dark blue BMW
sedan would have blended in had they been cruising through Malibu or
Manhattan. On the streets of Benghazi, though, they were sure to attract
unwanted attention. Taking a circuitous route to minimize encounters
with hostile forces, the vehicles bowled through militia checkpoints and
barricades as necessary. They arrived at the compound at 10:25, by which
time the villa was in full blaze and Stevens had been declared missing.

Members of the Global Response Staff team would later say that
they could have saved the ambassador had they been allowed to drive

to the mission right away.[31] They reached the compound approximately twenty-five minutes after smoke began to enter the villa's safe room, the same number of minutes that had elapsed while Bob had kept them penned at the annex.[32] So they certainly would have had a chance.

At the time of the team's arrival on the scene, no one was sure whether the ambassador was beyond saving. Bolting out of the armored vehicles, six heavily armed men pushed toward the burning villa in which the ambassador had last been seen. Militants who dared oppose them were greeted immediately with highly accurate fire that either put them down or chased them away. Within fifteen minutes, the annex security team had secured the villa.

Still engulfed in flames and choking smoke, the building could be entered only in brief forays. The Americans took turns darting in and out to find the ambassador, each time emerging with stinging eyes and lungs. After fifty minutes of fruitless searching, with reports coming in that enemy forces were planning a new assault on the mission, the Americans loaded up in vehicles and headed back to the annex.[33]

Shortly after midnight, as fiery beams gave way to smoldering embers, looters descended on the mission compound. The entire Benghazi metropolitan area had been alerted to the overrunning of an American "consulate" and "spy den" through text messages and video messages showing militants waving AK-47s in celebration.[34] Combing through the villa where Stevens had last been seen, they ripped televisions from walls. They pulled suits from wardrobes on their hangers and stripped the cupboards of food. One man was seen pouring Hershey's chocolate syrup in his mouth.[35]

At least some of the looters proved well disposed toward the Americans, possibly because the throng included individuals who were supposed to have been guarding the compound. One person paused when he saw a blond-haired man in a white shirt and gray pants lying unconscious on the ground. The man's mouth, like the rest of his body, was covered with thick black soot, but he was still breathing. "The man is alive!" someone yelled. "Move out of the way!" Several others shouted: "Alive! Alive! God is great!"

A group of Libyans rushed Ambassador Stevens to a nearby hospital. By the time of his arrival at the emergency room in the early morning hours, his breathing had stopped. The emergency room doctors spent nearly ninety minutes attempting to resuscitate him. They injected him with epinephrine to jump-start his heart, and inserted a tube down his throat to get his lungs going, while continuously administering CPR. But it was to no avail. A friend of the U.S. embassy who had made his way to the hospital reported that he had positively identified the blond man as Ambassador Stevens, and that he was dead.[36]

News of the ambassador's death soon reached the only reinforcements that the world's greatest superpower had sent to Benghazi that night, a team of seven special operators and CIA security contractors who had flown from Tripoli at 12:30 A.M. The men had landed in Benghazi forty-five minutes later, but were stranded at the airport for several hours because Libyan officials slow-rolled their requests for permission to enter the city. After learning that Stevens was dead, they considered going to the hospital to retrieve his body, but by the time they were able to leave the airport, they had received another report that the hospital was surrounded by Ansar al-Shariah fighters, so they drove instead toward the annex, arriving at 5:04 A.M.

They were just beginning to take up firing positions on the roof when the enemy attacked the annex with what witnesses described as impressive military professionalism. Fifteen rocket-propelled grenades hit the annex between 5:15 and 5:17. Highly accurate mortar fire came down on top of the annex's rooftop defensive positions. The fourth mortar round landed on the roof where Tyrone Woods, a former Navy SEAL from the annex's security team, was firing an Mk 46 light machine gun at suspected enemy positions. Shell fragments ripped through Woods, and he slumped over on the barrel of his gun. Glen Doherty, one of the seven men who had just flown in from Tripoli and also a former SEAL, rushed over to Woods. It was no use, as Woods had been killed instantly. Moments later, the fifth mortar round landed on the same roof, spraying sharp metal shards in all directions. The shrapnel killed Doherty and severely wounded two other Americans.[37]

The precision of the mortar fire alarmed the dwindling number of American security personnel. Another few dozen mortar rounds could wipe the remaining Americans off the rooftop firing positions, and then the enemy would be able to launch a coordinated ground assault with machine guns and rocket-propelled grenades. Jack Silva, a thirty-eight-year-old former Navy SEAL, thought to himself that the annex's defenses were too thin to hold off that type of assault for long. The annex, he feared, would soon be overrun, all of its occupants put to the sword.[38]

After eleven minutes, however, the enemy fire abated. The attackers had caught sight of a convoy of fifty heavily armed trucks from the Libyan intelligence service, which the Libyan government had belatedly sent to rescue the Americans. Lacking comparable firepower, the militants scattered and disappeared into the city like water sinking into sand.

The convoy arrived at the annex at 6 A.M. Thirty-two Americans, including the intelligence specialists who had resided at the annex, boarded the trucks. They carried with them the most sensitive computer drives and spy equipment, having already destroyed everything else of value. The bodies of Smith, Woods, and Doherty were loaded into the back of a sport-utility vehicle. The convoy headed to the Benghazi airport, where it linked up with a group of pro-American Libyans who had retrieved the body of Ambassador Stevens. By day's end, the entirety of the American presence in Benghazi had departed the city by air.

Most of the congressional and media attention to Benghazi would focus on the White House's description of the event in the following days. Most of the remainder concerned what the administration did and did not do on the night of September 11. The controversy drew in conspiracy theorists and vitriolic blowhards whose tirades often yielded more confusion than clarity. What was almost entirely ignored was the low availability of U.S. relief forces that night, which was ultimately the most important and most troubling issue.

In Washington, Secretary of Defense Panetta had been visiting the White House when word of the attack came. Consulting General Martin Dempsey and other senior military officers about the options

for sending military reinforcements, he learned that the nearest ground
forces were in Europe and would need nearly a day to get to Libya. At
3 A.M. Libya time, more than five hours after the battle began, Panetta
ordered a small special operations strike force to fly from Central Europe to the Sigonella Naval Air Station in Sicily. It would not arrive
until nearly twenty-four hours after the start of the Benghazi attacks, by
which time the guns had fallen silent. A Marine rapid-reaction force in
Rota, Spain, was sent to Tripoli, arriving at about that same time.[39]

The Pentagon sent no combat aircraft to Benghazi because none
were anywhere close. The nearest AC-130 gunships were more than one
thousand miles away and the United States did not have sufficient weapons or fuel facilities in the region to support them. Sending F-16 aircraft
from Aviano, Italy, would have taken at least twenty hours.

When Republican senators asked Panetta and Dempsey at a February 2013 hearing why more military assets were not in the area in
light of the reports of threats in Benghazi, Dempsey replied that it was
not practical for the military be in "every place" in the world.[40] Panetta
remarked, "The United States military is not and should not be a global
911 service capable of arriving on the scene within minutes to every
possible contingency around the world."[41] But Benghazi was not just
another place or another contingency. It was the second most important
city in a country of considerable strategic importance, and on the date
of the attack was visited by a U.S. ambassador at a time of severe threat
warnings. The Marine Fleet Antiterrorism Security Team that General
Neller had offered to send to Libya two months before the attack, and
that the State Department had refused to accept, was intended for use in
these very circumstances.

The United States had, as a matter of fact, maintained precisely such
a 911 service in the Mediterranean just one year earlier, during the air
campaign against Libya. On March 21, 2011, an American F-15 had
gone down twenty-five miles from Benghazi. Within thirty minutes, two
Harrier jets, two Ospreys, and two Super Stallion helicopters took off
from the amphibious assault ship USS *Kearsarge* with a quick-reaction
force of over one hundred Marines. The rescue force retrieved the two

downed pilots without incident and was back aboard the *Kearsarge* just ninety minutes after it had left.[42]

The first person to ask publicly why the United States had not maintained this type of capability in the Mediterranean in September 2012 was not a national security analyst or journalist or congressman, as one might have expected, but rather novelist Mark Helprin, author of such literary classics as *A Winter's Tale* and *Freddy and Fredericka*. Helprin pointed out that the U.S. Sixth Fleet had continuously maintained a carrier battle group and a Marine Expeditionary Unit (MEU) in the Mediterranean until 2009, when the Obama administration downsized the fleet and curtailed its operations. On September 11, 2012, Helprin noted, "No MEU could respond to Benghazi because none was assigned to, or by chance in, the Mediterranean."[43]

Because the Benghazi attacks lasted less than ten hours and took place at night in a city with few foreign journalists, the international media did not have a chance to cover the unfolding drama. Press attention, therefore, focused initially on the question of who had carried out the attack. The answer had special significance because the U.S. presidential election was only two months away and President Obama was touting his successes against Al Qaeda as evidence of his national security prowess. Five days before the overrunning of the Benghazi mission, Obama had told the Democratic National Convention, "A new tower rises above the New York skyline; al Qaeda is on the path to defeat; and Osama bin Laden is dead."[44] That line of argument, and the credibility of Obama's campaign rhetoric, would suffer grievously were it revealed that Al Qaeda had just been party to the killing of an American ambassador.

Within hours of the death of Ambassador Stevens, the White House received a dozen intelligence reports indicating that the ranks of the attackers had included militants linked to Al Qaeda. Some intelligence analysts quickly decided that these reports were conclusive. A number of analysts in the Directorate of National Intelligence, however, were less sure that the attackers were linked to Al Qaeda, and they believed that the attack had grown out of a spontaneous protest over an anti-Islamic video produced by Florida pastor Terry Jones. Such a protest had been reported in some local Libyan media outlets.

The White House gravitated toward the position that the attack had been the result of a protest over the video, rather than a terrorist attack by Al Qaeda–linked militants. This explanation not only averted damage to the campaign narrative about Al Qaeda in decline, it also shifted the purported target of Islamic hostility from the U.S. government to a man in Florida who had widely been derided in the media as a crackpot. In a September 14 press briefing on recent events in Libya and Egypt, Jay Carney explained, "This is not a case of protests directed at the United States writ large or at U.S. policy. This is in response to a video that is offensive."

The White House stuck to this interpretation in the face of mounting evidence that no protest had occurred in Benghazi on September 11. On Friday, September 14, CIA officers in Libya reported their certainty that no protest had taken place outside the mission compound before the attack. On September 15, the CIA chief of station embraced their conclusion in a written report to Washington.[45]

The White House asked Secretary of State Hillary Clinton to go on the Sunday television shows to give the administration's version of what happened at Benghazi. Clinton refused, saying that she was exhausted from managing the crisis.[46] The fact that the Sunday shows took place five days after the night of crisis called the sincerity of that claim into question. *Politico* later reported that three people close to the situation said that it was "less a matter of fatigue, and more a matter of Clinton not wanting to go on the shows."[47]

Those sources did not explain why Secretary Clinton wished to avoid the appearances, leaving the issue open to speculation. One probable reason was that she did not want to face questions about the level of State Department security at Benghazi. Another was concern over the accumulating evidence that the actual events in Benghazi did not conform to the narrative that the White House still wanted to convey. The person who went on the Sunday shows instead of Clinton, Susan Rice, would come under such enormous criticism for misrepresenting the truth as to prevent her from becoming Clinton's successor as secretary of state.

In the days leading up to Rice's television appearances, CIA deputy director Mike Morell shepherded the drafting of talking points for the interviews. White House spokesman Jay Carney would later assert that the White House and State Department had not been involved in producing the talking points, in an effort to quash emergent Republican allegations that the talking points had been doctored for partisan political gain. Carney's story began to fall apart in May 2013, however, with the publication by ABC News of an email showing that the State Department had, in fact, influenced the content of the talking points for political reasons. In the email, State Department spokeswoman Victoria Nuland objected to an initial draft of the talking points that mentioned prior CIA warnings about Benghazi and implicated the Al Qaeda affiliate Ansar al-Shariah. This material needed to be excised, Nuland explained, because it "could be abused by members [of Congress] to beat up the State Department for not paying attention to warnings."[48]

In response to Nuland's complaints, it was learned, Morell had deleted the references to the CIA's warnings and Ansar al-Shariah. Morell then sent the updated version to the CIA director, Petraeus. After reading the revised text, Petraeus wrote back to Morell that he did not like the changes. "Frankly, I'd just as soon not use this," Petraeus stated, though he added that it was ultimately up to the National Security Council to decide what to do with the revised talking points.[49] Despite Petraeus's dissatisfaction with the document, the White House chose to proceed with the modified points and to characterize them as a CIA product.

In 2014, evidence surfaced of deep White House involvement in crafting and managing the talking points. In their book *HRC*, which was based on interviews with numerous Obama administration insiders, Jonathan Allen and Amie Parnes revealed that Nuland's email had been only one small part of a parsing of the talking points by officials from the State Department, the White House, and the CIA. On the evening of September 14, Ben Rhodes had informed those involved in reviewing the talking points that the matter would be resolved at a deputies meeting the next morning, rather than via email. As Allen and Parnes noted, the calling of the meeting "ensured that any decision making would be done face-to-face, without the risk of e-mail chains being leaked or later made public in archives or through press requests under the Freedom of Information Act."[50]

In response to congressional inquiries, the White House turned over a data dump on May 15, 2013, which according to administration officials contained all the emails pertaining to Benghazi. But one of the most important emails was withheld until its release in April 2014 in response to a Freedom of Information Act request from the conservative organization Judicial Watch. The email had been sent on September 14, 2012, at 8:09 P.M. by Ben Rhodes to senior White House public relations staff, with the subject line "RE: PREP CALL with Susan: Saturday at 4:00 pm ET." In the message, Rhodes had enumerated several goals for Rice's press appearances, which included: "underscore that these protests are rooted in an Internet video, and not a broader failure of policy," and "reinforce the president and the administration's strength and steadiness in dealing with difficult challenges."[51] That this message influenced Rice's talk show appearances could be discerned from the fact that some of Rice's statements on the Sunday shows were contained in this message, but not in the talking points. Foremost among these would be her reference to the anti-Islamic video.

It also came to light later that while Morell was working on the talking points, he received a report from the CIA station chief in Benghazi stating that no protests had preceded the Benghazi attacks. Morell did not accept this interpretation and chose to stick with the prior interpretation of CIA analysts in the United States that the attacks had evolved from nonviolent protests.[52] His dismissal of what turned out to be an accurate report from the man on the scene, in favor of what an analyst in Virginia was saying, raised a lot of eyebrows in Congress.

When called to testify about the matter on Capitol Hill on April 2, 2014, Morell maintained that political considerations had played no role in the disregarding of the station chief's report. Morell was a career CIA employee, which meant that he had fewer incentives than a political appointee to twist the facts for his bosses. But a number of developments would raise questions about his motives. For one, Morell initially claimed that the White House had not been involved in preparing the talking points, but later, after more evidence of White House involvement had emerged, he acknowledged that the points had been shared with White House officials and edited based on their comments.[53] When Morell left the CIA, he went to work for Beacon Global Strategies, a ten-person strategic advisory firm populated mostly by Democrats who had held political appointments in the Obama administration and were closely tied to Hillary Clinton. The firm's cofounder and managing director was Philippe I. Reines, who had served as Hillary Clinton's press secretary from 2002 to 2009 and as her head of strategic communications during her tenure as secretary of state. A senior Republican House staffer told the press that Morell "would be a lot more believable if his paychecks weren't signed by Hillary Clinton's right-hand man."[54]

The final version of the talking points contained two key sentences, which read as follows: "The currently available information suggests that the demonstrations in Benghazi were spontaneously inspired by the protests at the U.S. Embassy in Cairo and evolved into a direct assault against the U.S. Consulate and subsequently its annex. There are indications that extremists participated in the violent demonstrations."[55] They did not make reference to a video, though one could infer from them that the Benghazi events were at least indirectly tied to the video since the Cairo protests had been driven by its content.

On September 16, Rice appeared on all five of the Sunday morning political talk shows. She delivered the same points in each appearance. "What sparked the recent violence was the airing on the Internet of a very hateful very offensive video that has offended many people around the world," Rice said on *Fox News Sunday*. The violence at Benghazi "was a spontaneous reaction to what had just transpired in Cairo as a consequence of the video. People gathered outside the embassy and then it grew very violent and those with extremist ties joined the fray."[56]

By the end of September, the U.S. intelligence community would come to a unanimous consensus that no protest had preceded the attacks. The anti-Islamic video and the protests it aroused earlier on September 11 in Cairo may have played a role in the timing of the attack, the intelligence analysts concluded, but they were not the cause of the attack.[57] The U.S. intelligence postmortems also determined that the perpetrators included individuals from two Al Qaeda organizations—AQAP and Al Qaeda in the Islamic Maghreb (AQIM)—and two organizations closely linked to Al Qaeda—the Mohammed Jamal Network and Ansar al-Shariah.[58]

Obama vowed repeatedly that he would bring the perpetrators of the Benghazi attacks to justice. At one of his debates with Republican presidential candidate Mitt Romney, he declared, "we are going to find out who did this, and we are going to hunt them down, because one of the things that I've said throughout my presidency is when folks mess with Americans, we go after them."

His ability to hunt down the perpetrators was, however, severely constrained by the lightness of the American footprint. Having been light from the start, the U.S. footprint in Libya was further lightened on September 12 with the removal of the entire intelligence and security footprint from Benghazi, where most of the attackers were still believed to be located. That removal was a "catastrophic intelligence loss," observed an American official who had served previously in Libya. "We got our eyes poked out."[59] In the months ahead, the loss of U.S. intelligence capabilities would repeatedly be cited as a leading reason why the U.S. government had not apprehended any of the men who had killed the four Americans.[60]

The lack of a military footprint also hindered efforts to interview witnesses and conduct forensic investigations at the mission compound. An FBI team that was sent to investigate the catastrophe was stuck in Tripoli for weeks because of inadequate security in Benghazi. The U.S. national leadership refused to send ground troops to provide security for the FBI or to secure the mission, where looting and the elements were taking a daily toll on the physical evidence. The Libyan national leadership promised to help investigate the crime, but without viable national security forces or real authority over Benghazi's militias, it could not conduct an investigation or provide protection for U.S. investigators.[61]

When the FBI officers finally made their first visit to Benghazi, on

October 4, they stayed in the city only for the day, returning to Tripoli in the evening because of security concerns. Their investigation of the scene of the attack revealed that the evidence had been badly "degraded," according to one official. The brief duration of their visit precluded the extended interviewing of witnesses.[62]

American impotence in Benghazi in the last months of 2012 was so complete that one of the prime suspects in the attack was casually walking around the city and mocking the Americans. On October 18, *New York Times* correspondent David D. Kirkpatrick chatted on the patio of a bustling luxury hotel with Ahmed Abu Khattala, a known Ansar al-Shariah leader whom numerous witnesses had seen directing fighters at the mission compound. Sipping a strawberry frappe, Khattala scoffed at the idea that the American and Libyan governments would bring him to justice. Libya's national army, he said, was a "national chicken." Kirkpatrick's mention of an ostensible investigation by the Libyan government brought a smirk to Khattala's face. No one from the Libyan government had questioned him, he said. Khattala also took a turn as a disinterested political analyst, commenting that U.S. political leaders were "using the consulate attack just to gather votes for their elections." Khattala claimed that he himself was not a member of Al Qaeda, but added that he would be proud to be associated with Al Qaeda's religious zealotry.[63]

The weapon of choice for light-footprint counterterrorism, the drone, proved ill-suited to the hunt for the perpetrators of the Benghazi attacks. Surmising that American drones would fire missiles at the suspects, the Libyan government explicitly warned the U.S. government against resorting to drone warfare. Drone strikes "would be a disaster," declared Saad el-Shlmani, a spokesman for the Libyan foreign ministry. "Any unilateral action by any country, but especially by the United States, would really be damaging."[64] Even Libyans who were hostile to the extremists worried that drone-fired missiles would cause a massive increase in recruiting by Islamist groups. "If there are drone strikes, people will see it as Libyan sovereignty that's being threatened," said Ebtisam Stieta, a member of the General National Congress. "It might compel people to join these groups rather than go against them."[65]

Libyan protestations convinced the U.S. government to keep its weaponized drones out of Libya. Concerns about Libyan opinion also dissuaded the Obama administration from sending U.S. special operations forces into the country to capture or kill the suspects on the ground. By the spring of 2013, U.S. officials said they had enough incriminating evidence to justify detaining five suspects for the Benghazi attacks, but they were not sending U.S. troops to make the apprehensions because putting U.S. boots on the ground could "harm fledgling relations with Libya and other post-Arab-Spring governments."[66] The inaction frayed nerves among the FBI and military personnel who were working to track down the guilty. In September 2013, Michael S. Schmidt and Eric Schmitt wrote in the *New York Times* that "some military and law enforcement officials have grown frustrated with what they believe is the White House's unwillingness to pressure the Libyan government to make the arrests or allow American forces to do so."[67]

The Obama administration's own frustration with the inaction of the Libyan government led finally to a unilateral U.S. counterterrorism mission in Libya, though the target was not one of the Benghazi ringleaders. On October 5, 2013, American special operations forces moved into the center of Tripoli and kidnapped Abu Anas al-Libi, who had been indicted for two Al Qaeda attacks on U.S. embassies in Africa in 1998. The special operators reportedly were planning an operation against Benghazi perpetrator Ahmed Abu Khattala within days of getting al-Libi, but the abduction of al-Libi on Libyan soil produced a groundswell of anti-Americanism so great as to convince the Obama administration that another operation would bring down the Libyan government. Consequently, the operation against Khattala was canceled.[68]

Over the course of 2013, the U.S. government stepped up funding for Libya's national security forces, which in the absence of a viable American military presence offered the only possible means of apprehending the Benghazi suspects and preventing further attacks on U.S. interests. Those forces were also essential to the protection of the Libyan national leadership from kidnapping and murder.[69] Regrettably, little progress was made. The most auspicious place for assisting Libyan forces was in

Libya, but the Obama administration's aversion to sending American troops or contractors into Libya made it impossible to conduct training there. When Libya's prime minister asked the United States in March 2013 to help train Libyan security forces, Obama offered to train between 6,000 and 8,000 Libyans somewhere outside Libya. Organizing the training outside the country proved to be more difficult than anticipated; in the summer of 2014, U.S. officials acknowledged that the training had not yet begun, and asserted that the start date for training had been pushed into 2015.[70]

Al Qaeda profited from the disorder in Libya by moving personnel and training facilities into the country. In mid-2014, AQAP, AQIM, and an AQIM splinter group called the Masked Brigade were all reported to be making extensive use of Libyan territory. In the words of one American counterterrorism specialist in Africa, Libya had become a "Scumbag Woodstock."[71] At this time, it was also revealed that a base the United States had originally intended for use in training Libyan special operations forces had fallen into the hands of Ibrahim Ali Abu Bakr Tantoush, a longtime Al Qaeda leader who had been indicted for the 1998 U.S. embassy bombings in Africa.[72]

Following contentious elections in June 2014, civil warfare intensified within Libya. Tribal militias and Islamists exchanged fire, with little concern for the lives of civilians or foreigners. The United States evacuated its embassy in July "temporarily," further disrupting efforts to assist the Libyan government. One month after the evacuation, with the embassy still vacant, State Department spokeswoman Jen Psaki told the media that "the relocation of our staff is temporary," and "we continue to work with a range of officials on the ground." She conceded, though, that "obviously, being in country provides a different opportunity to do that, but we remain engaged even though our officials are not in country."[73]

. . .

In October 2012, one year after the fall of Muammar Gaddafi, the RAND Corporation published a report on Libya which stated aptly that the "lighter-footprint approach has made Libya a test case for a new post-Iraq and Afghanistan model of nation-building."⁷⁴ By 2014, the test had been completed, and its results evaluated. The light-footprint approach had failed.

The problems began while the civil war was still raging. Obama's public forswearing of American ground force deployments stiffened the resolve of Gaddafi and hence may have prolonged the war. The absence of U.S. boots on the ground gave the United States little control over which anti-Gaddafi rebels received weapons from the Americans and other foreign suppliers, with the result that many weapons fell into the hands of anti-American fanatics. It also deprived the United States of opportunities to secure Libya's jails, from which Al Qaeda prisoners would escape, and Libya's arsenals, from which extremists would arm themselves.

The decision to rely on a light footprint after the civil war prevented the United States from providing the security and training required to form a viable national government and security forces. The light U.S. footprint in Libya left Ambassador Stevens with an inordinately small security detail and put his safety in the hands of Libyan militiamen who proved undependable in time of crisis. The light U.S. footprint in the region left the Pentagon without the emergency response capabilities that such a dangerous region demands. When the light footprint came under attack in Benghazi, it suffered such devastating losses that the entire footprint had to be withdrawn from the city, leaving the United States without eyes or ears in a critical location. The preferred tools of the light-footprint approach, drones and special operations forces, could not be used to bring the perpetrators of the Benghazi attacks, or anyone else, to justice, on account of overwhelming popular opposition to those tools.

Putting American ground forces into a country during or after a civil war is not a matter to be taken lightly. Certainly there are cases in which the strategic stakes are too low or the risks too high to justify the insertion of American forces. But in the case of Libya, the large concentrations of extremists from Al Qaeda and its affiliates, together with the opportunities for extremists to acquire powerful weapons, gave the country significant strategic stakes, and the risks to American troops would not have been especially high—certainly not as high as the risks to the American civilians whom the Obama administration sent to Benghazi in 2011 and the first nine months of 2012. In light of public wariness of another war, though, it would have taken a bold president with little concern for short-term public opinion to send U.S. ground troops to Libya.

While reasonable people may disagree over the proper role for U.S. government personnel in influencing another nation's internal conflicts, there is little disagreement that the United States needs to protect whatever personnel and assets it sends abroad. Only the U.S. military has a good track record of providing that protection in dangerous countries. As Benghazi made painfully clear, not even the CIA's elite security force of former special operators has sufficient manpower, firepower, and risk tolerance to keep Americans safe from the world's miscreants. Only the military can hold off sustained attacks on American facilities and personnel. Only the military can fly one hundred heavily armed young men to rescue isolated Americans in a matter of minutes or hours, as it did in March 2011 when it rescued the two F-15 pilots who went down near Benghazi. If the United States is to maintain a presence throughout the world, as a superpower must, it needs a military that can come to the rescue wherever and whenever an American official dials 911.

13

NOT SO SMART POWER

Afghanistan, Pakistan, Yemen, Mali, Latin America

For Barack Obama, Hillary Clinton, and other adherents of "smart power," terrorism and a variety of other international security problems were the result of nonsecurity ills such as poverty and human rights violations. Thus they had to be solved primarily by agencies that alleviated poverty and supported good governance, not by brute force. As Micah Zenko of the Council on Foreign Relations and Michael A. Cohen of the Century Foundation put it, "American foreign policy needs fewer people who can jump out of airplanes and more who can convene round-table discussions and lead negotiations."[1] In the name of smart power, administration officials routinely called for "whole of government" approaches, with participation by all U.S. federal agencies engaged overseas. The underlying message was that civil agencies needed to reclaim seats at the head table of national security from the Department of Defense.

The idea that farm tools and coed schoolhouses undercut terrorism better than firearms and police stations had long been popular with career aid officials, who like many highly educated Americans were inveterately suspicious of the military. It had gained in popularity in recent years thanks to the book *Three Cups of Tea*, in which author Greg Mortenson claimed to have thwarted the Taliban by building schools for girls, although much of his story was later exposed as fraudulent, including the part about forestalling Taliban violence through school construction. Application of this idea in the real world, however, had been limited by the lack of strong support at the top levels of government. Now it enjoyed the backing of the secretary of state, and of a president who remained true to his conviction, as expressed after the September 11 attacks, that terrorism "grows from a climate of poverty and ignorance" and thus the United States needed to "devote far more attention to the monumental task of raising the hopes and prospects of embittered children across the globe."

Clinton and Obama might have gotten off to a better start had they taken a serious look at George W. Bush's attempt to promote "whole of government" solutions, instead of writing Bush off as a Neanderthal concerned only with hard power. Bush had, in fact, asked the State Department and other civil agencies to contribute large amounts of personnel to Afghanistan and Iraq for nation building. He had found that sending civilians was much harder than sending military personnel, for unlike the military, the civil agencies had employee unions that resisted personnel assignments to dangerous places.

When the Foreign Service's director general announced in 2007 that compulsory personnel assignments to Iraq would begin if additional volunteers were not forthcoming, a deluge of opposition from Foreign Service Officers compelled the State Department's leadership to convene a town hall meeting on the subject. An Associated Press correspondent who happened to be present reported that many attendees "expressed serious concern about the ethics of sending diplomats against their will to work in a war zone." Jack Croddy, a senior Foreign Service Officer, went before the microphone to say, "It's one thing if someone believes in what's going on over there and volunteers, but it's another thing to send someone over there on a forced assignment. I'm sorry, but basically that's a potential death sentence and you know it. Who will raise our children if we are dead or seriously wounded?" According to the Associated Press report, "Croddy's remarks were met with loud and sustained applause from the estimated 300 people at the meeting."[2] As a consequence of the opposition from the Foreign Service Officers and their union, the State Department canceled its plan for compulsory deployments to Iraq.[3]

Bush directed the State Department to form the Office of the Coordinator for Reconstruction and Stabilization (S/CRS) to provide a civilian expeditionary capability for unstable environments. It too fell victim to opposition within the Foreign Service. Following that failed experiment, State and other civil agencies sought to compensate for personnel scarcities by relying heavily on contractors. Oftentimes, those contractors were ill-qualified for their jobs, especially when they had to be hired quickly and in large numbers. In Iraq and Afghanistan, for example, the inferiority of contractors assigned to police training resulted in failures so spectacular that the U.S. military eventually took over police training in both countries.

Shortly after Obama took office, Clinton sought to increase the size and influence of U.S. civil agencies in Afghanistan through a "civilian surge," which would increase the number of U.S. civilians in Afghanistan from 531 to 1300. They sent diplomats to run "regional platforms" alongside two-star military generals, with the mission of spending money on development projects as quickly as possible. Most members of the civilian surge were expected to serve in the rural districts.

Clinton obtained a huge increase in U.S. governmental spending on Afghan development, from $1.25 billion in 2008 to $4.1 billion in 2010, in the belief that underdevelopment was a root cause of the Afghan insurgency. She and Special Representative for Afghanistan and Pakistan Richard Holbrooke prodded U.S. Ambassador to Afghanistan Karl Eikenberry to prod aid officers in Afghanistan to spend money much more rapidly than before. "We have an opportunity to think unconstrained," Eikenberry told officials from the U.S. Agency for International Development (USAID) and the State Department at a May 2009 strategy meeting. "If you used to ask for $22 million and now you're asking for $24 million, that's not thinking boldly."[4]

The civilian surge was to fall far short of expectations. The civilians sent to run the regional platforms—who were generally much younger and less experienced than their military counterparts—alienated military officers by claiming to be "the equivalent of two-star generals." USAID and the State Department could not convince many of their experienced hands to fill the "civilian surge" positions, and they were too small on the whole to allocate so large a number of individuals to one country, so they had to hire contractors and temporary government employees in bulk.

Out in the field, at the district and provincial levels, hundreds of slots that had been reserved for members of the civilian surge sat vacant because the assigned personnel were sent to safer areas, on account of State Department regulations that enabled civilians to stay far from danger if that was their preference. A total of 920 of the 1,300 civilian surge personnel ended up in Kabul. A sizable fraction of the other 380 worked at regional headquarters that were nearly as removed from the countryside as was Kabul.[5]

In early 2011, Brigadier General Kenneth Dahl received word that fifty-seven American civilians from the civilian surge would be coming to help his unit, the Tenth Mountain Division. But as days and weeks went by, nobody showed up. Dahl contacted the senior U.S. State Department official in Kandahar, who covered the area where the Tenth Mountain Division was operating. The official told him to "expect nothing" from the U.S. embassy. A few weeks later, when Ambassador Eikenberry paid a visit to Kandahar, Dahl took the opportunity to express displeasure about the civilian no-shows.

Eikenberry, attempting to defend the civilian surge, replied, "General Dahl, the civilians are at the high-water mark right now."

"That's great," Dahl said. "I can feel it lapping at my ankles."[6]

Some very idealistic and dedicated civilians did make it to the districts and provinces. Oftentimes they had to beg permission from superiors and ignore advice from senior officials who said that working in the field was too dangerous or career-inhibiting. Carter Malkasian, a military historian with a Ph.D. from Oxford, volunteered to work alongside the Marines in Helmand province, one of the most dangerous provinces in the country. Learning the local language, Malkasian spent most of his time working with local elders and Afghan officials to solve problems that had undermined support for the government. He became so effective that the elders referred to him as a *sahib*, a term of respect and honor rarely bestowed on foreigners, and urged the Americans to keep him in their district indefinitely. With a wife and young daughter in the United States, Malkasian could not stay forever, and when his two-year tour came to an end in the fall of 2011, the State Department said there was no one to take his place.

Anne Smedinghoff, who grew up in a well-to-do family in suburban Chicago, joined the Foreign Service after graduating from Johns Hopkins University in 2009. Following an initial tour in Caracas, Venezuela, she was posted to Afghanistan. At twenty-five years of age, Smedinghoff embodied the best of the United States, radiating a buoyant optimism and a desire to tell the world about the goodness that America had to offer. That passion led her to go outside protected areas on foot to meet with Afghans, a practice that won her respect and praise from military colleagues.

On April 6, 2013, Smedinghoff was en route to a book donation ceremony in Qalat, the capital of Zabul province, when a man approached her group and blew himself up. The blast killed Smedinghoff and several U.S. military personnel. She was the first U.S. diplomat to be killed in Afghanistan during more than a decade of war.

By the time of Smedinghoff's death, the State Department had already begun withdrawing its personnel from outlying areas. With the overall U.S. military presence shrinking, all foreign civilians were being pulled from district and provincial capitals into regional and national headquarters. The killing of Anne Smedinghoff led to acceleration of the State Department's withdrawal, such that within a few months nearly all U.S. civilians had been removed from the districts and provinces.

Throughout the "civilian surge," the shortage of U.S. civilians in the districts and the inexperience of many who made it to the districts ensured that the massive infusion of American cash would not be spent well. Owing to poor oversight, large amounts of funds fell into the pockets of insurgents, predatory warlords, or corrupt government officials. The Afghan government, moreover, failed to provide staff for the health clinics and schools that had been built with American money.

Misbehavior by Afghan administrators or policemen often trumped any positive achievements that might have come with the development projects. And security trumped everything. Where the Taliban had the power to kill at will, Afghan officials could not govern, aid workers could not build schools, and the people would not support the government. The counterinsurgency gains of 2010 and 2011 hinged almost entirely on improvements in security spearheaded by the U.S. military. The improvements in Afghan governance and development that the security made possible were also dependent on support from the American military, since the military had a much larger presence than America's civil agencies.

. . .

The theory that U.S. development aid could solve security problems, and could solve them better than military aid, was applied in many other countries in the early years of the Obama administration. During 2009, Secretary of State Clinton convinced Congress to triple nonmilitary assistance to Pakistan to $1.5 billion per year for a period of five years, on the grounds that development programs would undercut radicalism as well as promote positive views of the United States. The cochairs of the Senate Foreign Relations Committee, John Kerry and Richard Lugar, and the chair of the House Foreign Affairs Committee, Howard Berman, sponsored the legislation for the aid, which became known as "Kerry-Lugar-Berman" aid.

USAID, the contractors and NGOs that it hired, and the Pakistani government were not prepared to administer aid on the scale of the Kerry-Lugar-Berman package. Delays and confusion proliferated, tarnishing the image of the aid program. By virtually all accounts, the Kerry-Lugar-Berman aid failed to make significant improvements to Pakistani opinion of the United States. Pakistani politicians and ordinary citizens evidenced little gratitude, and they complained that it was not enough. When the U.S. government supplemented Kerry-Lugar-Berman by providing the lion's share of a $1.7 billion emergency flood relief effort in the middle of 2010, the Pakistanis seemed no more favorably disposed to the United States than before.[7]

The aid also did little to undermine the appeal of Islamic extremism.

The Pakistani army refused to provide protection for U.S.-funded development agencies in the villages where madrassas churned out aspiring terrorists for duty in Pakistan, Afghanistan, and every other place where extremist groups had a demand for manpower. Knowing that aid workers who went into those villages without security forces were likely to be threatened or killed, the development agencies stayed away.[8]

· · ·

The Obama administration's initial strategic review of Yemen concluded that "a new, whole-of-government approach to Yemen" was required. Under the Bush administration, the review's authors asserted, the United States had paid too little attention to the poverty, illiteracy, and human rights abuses that fostered terrorism. According to Jeffrey Feltman, assistant secretary of state for Near Eastern affairs, the administration resolved to "address security and counterterrorism concerns, but also the profound political, economic, and social challenges that help al-Qaeda and related affiliates to operate and flourish."[9]

To help implement the new approach, the United States boosted spending on development and other forms of civil assistance to Yemen. Later, when the Obama administration came under criticism for its heavy reliance on drones in Yemen, administration officials would defend U.S. policy by touting the large American expenditures on non-military programs. "This year alone, U.S. assistance to Yemen is more than $337 million," John Brennan said in August 2012. "Over half this money, $178 million, is for political transition, humanitarian assistance and development."[10]

The nonmilitary assistance to Yemen would achieve little because of a lack of security in the areas where extremism had the largest fan base. By maintaining only a light U.S. footprint and deliberately avoiding involvement in counterinsurgency, the Obama administration left most of the country under enemy control. A 2012 GAO report found that "the deteriorating security situation denied program implementers access to certain areas, and they could not travel or establish a long-term presence in more remote locales." Because of insecurity in the rural areas, where

Al Qaeda was concentrated, "USAID began to focus assistance activities on large urban areas, which were more secure and accessible."[11]

. . .

In the early years of the Obama administration, U.S. policy toward Mali was based on the theory that social and economic development, not security, held the key to stability. On November 17, 2009, Assistant Secretary of State for African Affairs Johnnie Carson told the Senate Committee on Foreign Relations that the ability of Al Qaeda's North African franchise, AQIM, to recruit followers in Mali "can largely be traced to its ability to capitalize on the frustration among the young over insufficient educational or vocational opportunities."[12] The administration believed it could best help the Malian government quell rising opposition from Al Qaeda and other groups by stepping up aid for social and economic programs.

By 2011, the U.S. government was spending $221 million per year on development in Mali, while spending less than $4 million annually for security.[13] Most of the security total, moreover, covered the Trans-Sahara Counterterrorism Partnership, which in the words of the Obama administration "aims to provide Malians with the means to overcome the acute poverty and weak institutional capacity exploited by extremist groups," with primary emphasis on "enhancing civic engagement and economic opportunities among Malian youth."[14] Trans-Sahara Counterterrorism Partnership funds paid for basic education, ten FM radio stations, "interactive radio instruction" for two hundred thousand students at madrassas, vocational training, microenterprise development, and "conflict prevention."[15]

The Malian government itself did not spend much on defense, which accorded with recommendations from Western experts that most state resources should be allocated to development. In 2011, Mali spent just 1.9 percent of its small GDP on defense. Corruption, moreover, siphoned off some of that amount. An internal audit conducted in 2009 found that Mali's government had suffered a loss of $224 million in the past year because of mismanagement or theft of government funds.[16]

Because of Mali's low defense spending, the low amount of military aid it received, and corruption, the Malian armed forces were hobbled by chronic resource shortages. "In Mali, they barely have AKs that have butt stocks," an American officer remarked in 2011. "They have old Chinese ammo where one of every three rounds work." The Malian army did not use the forty-two vehicles that the Americans had provided, because of a lack of fuel.[17]

The dearth of foreign military assistance also left the Malian armed forces short on military professionalism. Before and during the Obama era, the U.S. military administered very limited training and education to the Malian armed forces. "We provided training and equip support for many years, but in relatively modest quantities," Deputy Assistant Secretary of Defense for Africa Amanda Dory testified in December 2012. She added, "I don't think that level of resourcing was commensurate with the threat."[18]

Admiral William McRaven, commander of SOCOM, observed that U.S. special operations forces came too infrequently to Mali to effect major improvements. "It has been difficult for us in some countries to have a persistent presence, and Mali is a case in point," McRaven said. "We had an episodic presence in Mali."[19] Major Simon J. Powelson, a Special Forces officer who oversaw much of the American training of Malian forces, later wrote a master's thesis on the lessons of Mali under the title "Enduring Engagement Yes, Episodic Engagement No." Powelson noted that the few Malian units to receive continuous training acquitted themselves well in the field, whereas the other units could not perform even basic tasks.[20]

The low attention given to Mali's armed forces in Washington and the Malian capital of Bamako might have been excusable had Mali been an island paradise, existing in splendid isolation from those who might wish it ill. But Mali in actuality contained hostile and internationally menacing elements within its own borders, and several of its next-door neighbors hosted nefarious characters who coveted Malian territory. Tuareg separatists, who had been in various states of conflict for most of Mali's existence as an independent nation, skirmished intermittently with

Mali's armed forces in the north. Islamic extremist groups that operated in Mali included the Algerian-based AQIM, an Al Qaeda splinter group called the Movement for Unity and Jihad in West Africa (MUJAO), and Ansar al-Dine, which was based in Mali but, like the others, contained a mixture of foreigners and Malians. Largely self-funded, the Islamic militants reaped large profits from kidnapping and collusion with drug traffickers. Most of the kidnapping targets were Western Europeans, but on occasion the kidnappers targeted Americans.

On the morning of June 23, 2009, a thirty-nine-year-old native of Cleveland, Tennessee, by the name of Chris Leggett was walking through the Mauritanian capital of Nouakchott, where he had lived with his wife and children for the past six years. Like so many other Americans living in Africa, Leggett was motivated by Christian compassion for the poor and disadvantaged. He directed a nongovernmental humanitarian organization that sought to assist young women and boys in Mauritania's prisons, and he also taught at a school specializing in computer science in the lower-class neighborhood of El Kasr.

That morning, Leggett was approached by two AQIM gunmen. Pointing their weapons in his face, they intended to kidnap him and exact a ransom. Leggett, however, refused to go along. The gunmen shot him in the head and fled the scene, leaving the father of four dead in the middle of the street, next to piles of trash.

Someone draped Leggett's body with a white-and-red checkered tablecloth, the sort one would find at a Sunday picnic in Kansas. The cloth concealed his face in the photo that appeared next to the lone U.S. press report on the event. American officials eventually showed up to retrieve the body, but the U.S. government refrained from discussing the murder.

AQIM, on the other hand, released a statement saying that it had killed Leggett because he had tried to convert Muslims to Christianity. "Two knights of the Islamic Maghreb succeeded Tuesday morning at 8 a.m. to kill the infidel American Christopher Leggett for his Christianizing activities," the statement read.[21]

The ineptitude of Mali's military came home to roost in early 2012.

Between January and the middle of March, Tuareg and Islamist rebels overran several key military bases in northern Mali, the task made easier by the failure of Mali's military logistical system to keep army garrisons stocked with supplies. On March 21, soldiers at the Kati barracks prepared to march in protest against the government for the corruption and inefficiency that had deprived soldiers in the north of ammunition. In an effort to head off the march, the defense minister drove to the barracks, twelve miles from his Bamako office. Speaking before a large group, he unwisely chose to lecture them with the condescension of an overbearing middle school teacher. The soldiers replied with catcalls, stones, and the firing of guns in the air, forcing the minister to run to his car and order the chauffeur to drive off posthaste.

In an indication of the sorry state of Mali's military, the senior officers on the scene did not attempt to restore discipline after the minister fled, but instead they too ran away. The man who emerged to grab the reins of the frenzied crowd was Captain Amadou Haya Sanogo, a man whose very presence was another testament to the weakness of Mali's armed forces. Early in his career, Sanogo had failed several of the exams that are intended to prevent the inept from attaining officer status in military organizations, but he had nonetheless been allowed to become an officer. In 2011, five soldiers under his authority had died during a hazing ritual, which had resulted not in stiff punishment for Sanogo but instead in reassignment to a sinecure at the Kati barracks. With nothing else to do, Sanogo had spent recent months spreading contempt for the government and acquiring supporters.

That afternoon, Sanogo led a mob of soldiers to the presidential palace. The presidential guard exchanged taunts and warning shots with the mob while President Amadou Toumani Touré sneaked out the back. Once the president was safe, the guards took off, too, allowing the mob to take full possession of the palace. Soldiers, some of them reeking of booze, looted flat-screen televisions, computers, and photocopying machines.

Touré, his term nearly at an end, chose to go into exile rather than organize military forces against Sanogo. Although Mali's populace was considered one of the most prodemocratic in Africa, few Malians mourned the overthrow of the democratically elected Touré. The gross ineffectiveness and corruption of his government had discredited the idea that democracy and good governance went hand in hand.

The Obama administration did not appreciate the depth of Mali's disillusionment with democracy, nor did it accept the view that a military coup might be preferable to democratic elections. Obama chose to terminate assistance to Mali's government on April 10. He cited congressional legislation that prohibited aid following military coups, but presidents had disregarded that legislation when it suited their purpose and Obama could have done the same had he doubted the advisability of terminating aid. Administration officials announced that American assistance would be suspended until the inauguration of an elected civil government.

The termination of U.S. assistance amounted to another kick to the head of a Malian military that was already on its hands and knees. The suspension of U.S. security assistance further reduced the government's chances of reversing the military momentum in northern Mali, a fact eventually acknowledged even by Hillary Clinton's State Department, whose championing of terminating Mali's military aid had driven the policy.[22] In the weeks after the coup, the Islamist and separatist rebels took control of all of northern Mali, whereupon they recruited and kidnapped large numbers of northern youth for service in their armed forces. To train new members, Islamists set up a "jihad academy" in what had been one of Timbuktu's police stations.[23]

In the summer of 2012, the interim Malian government granted permission to the Economic Community of West African States (ECOWAS) to send 3,000 troops to retake northern Mali. The African Union and the French government backed the plan, and they urged the Americans to provide operational support. The Obama administration, however, refused to go along, arguing that the problem should be solved politically rather than militarily. Once democratic elections restored political stability in Mali, administration spokesmen said, the parties could negotiate a political solution in the north.

"We support regional and international efforts to negotiate a resolution with those groups who have expressed a willingness to enter
into dialogue with the Malian government," asserted Assistant Secretary of State Carson on June 29, 2012. In lieu of military action to
mop up the extremists in northern Mali, the United States was pursuing
an "outside-in strategy," in which it supported border patrolling in the
countries surrounding Mali to contain the spill. Within Mali, Carson
said, the United States needed to "increase economic development and
provide economic opportunities to disaffected youth populations" and
"help build resilience in Mali's democratic institutions."[24]

The negotiating track went nowhere. None of the major rebel
groups was prepared to yield control of territory so recently won.[25] The
"outside-in" security strategy suffered from the assumption that African
countries with modest security forces could seal long borders that smug-
glers had been able to penetrate undetected since the dawn of history.
During the fall, it would become clear that extremists were freely moving back and forth between Mali and Libya. On September 26, Clinton acknowledged that AQIM was using Mali as a base for operations
into Libya and, most ominously, that it may have used Mali as a staging
ground for the Benghazi attacks on September 11.[26]

Plans to bolster economic development and provide economic opportunities also ran aground. Without the protection of friendly security
forces, aid projects were doomed. In Toya, a model village of the Millennium Villages Project, rebels showed what they would do to foreign-
financed development projects that did not have armed men guarding
them. The militants made off with one hundred tons of fertilizer that
had been donated by the Minnesota firm Mosaic Company, and confis-
cated the Ericsson cell phones that had been given to community health
workers. The diesel fuel that had powered the village's water pumps disappeared, halting the irrigation of fields and turning crops brown. "All of
our gains are lost," lamented Amadou Niang, the director of the Millennium Villages Project in West Africa. "Five years and four or five million
dollars of interventions and everything is lost."[27]

In December, the French persuaded the United States to go along with a UN Security Council resolution authorizing an African-led security mission to Mali, by inserting a provision that allowed the Americans to veto the operational plan. The mission, dubbed the African-led International Support Mission in Mali (AFISMA), was to be composed of troops from ECOWAS member states and several other African nations. Despite the fact that the United States had dragged its feet for nine months already, the AFISMA forces were not scheduled to deploy to southern Mali for another nine months, with operations to retake the north commencing another six months after that.

The rebels had a much more aggressive timetable. By the end of 2012, the rebel ranks had swollen to the levels required for a drive on Bamako, thanks to the recruitment of local Malians and an influx of foreign jihadists from France, Pakistan, Afghanistan, and a multitude of African countries.[28] Estimates of their strength at year's end ranged from 4,000 to 15,000.[29] AQIM took charge of organizing a January offensive to conquer the whole country, with Ansar al-Dine and MUJAO providing the bulk of the fighters.

On January 7, rebel fighters entered Bourei, a village near the unofficial dividing line between northern and southern Mali. "There are numerous Islamists in Bourei aboard all-terrain vehicles and even armored vehicles that they have stolen from the Malian military," reported Mamadou Guindo, an employee of Binke Transport, a bus company.[30] The next day, the rebels pushed toward Konna, twenty-five miles to the south, and overwhelmed a contingent of Malian armed forces that had tried to get in their way. Konna fell the next day.

The armada of rebel sport-utility vehicles and pickup trucks pressed on toward Mopti, a small city at the confluence of the Niger and Bani rivers. Mopti and the adjacent military base at Séveré offered the only major line of defense against a rebel advance on Bamako, and the line was thinly defended. Within a day of fighting, the Malian armed forces made clear that they were not strong enough to hold the line.

On January 10, Mali's interim president, Dioncounda Traoré, called French president François Hollande to ask for emergency assistance. He did not place a call to President Obama. Hollande received word from his own ambassador in Mali that the enemy was on the verge of taking Mopti and would then be able to cruise down the highway into Bamako without so much as a speed bump. Hollande phoned Obama to inform him that the French were about to undertake military action in Mali.[31]

The only problem for Hollande was that the French military had been so stripped down by budgetary cuts that it could not conduct even such a limited overseas operation on its own. The French, therefore, had to ask the Americans for help. They requested airlift to move troops into Mali, aerial refueling for their aircraft, and intelligence on the disposition of enemy forces.[32]

The Obama administration told the French they would have to pay for the transportation of troops, and that the United States would need more information about whom the French bombers and fighters were planning to destroy before it would meet their requests for refueling and intelligence. The French were stunned, having expected to receive robust American support from the outset.[33] French officials disclosed to American journalists that during the fall of 2012, Panetta and Michael Sheehan, the assistant secretary of defense for special operations and low-intensity conflict, had urged French officials to help fight AQIM in Mali. Panetta reportedly had said the United States would provide "whatever it takes" to help the French in Mali.[34] Panetta, in fact, reiterated that pledge in slightly different terms on January 14, 2013, when he said that the United States had promised to give the French "whatever assistance we can."[35]

When confronted with the recounting of the fall 2012 statements of Panetta and Sheehan, Obama administration officials protested that American messages to France may have been "lost in translation." During the meetings, according to these U.S. officials, "neither Mr. Panetta nor Mr. Sheehan directly urged France to use force and didn't promise specific support." Panetta's aides said that "his comments were meant to convey general U.S. support for the aims of the French in Mali."[36] They did not, however, deny Panetta's offer of "whatever it takes," nor did they retract Panetta's statement of January 14.

In another series of unattributed press interviews, the White House made known its rationale for avoiding the prompt and full support of the

French effort. Among the administration's concerns was that the French offensive might harm elements of the rebel coalition that were not as radical as AQIM, and who thus might be crucial negotiating partners. Another White House concern, which ran contrary to statements by Panetta and others about the dangers of AQIM, was that the militants did not pose a serious threat.[37]

While the Obama administration awaited more information from the French about their intended bombing targets, the war continued. A small number of French special operations troops landed in Mali within a matter of hours of Hollande's green light.[38] Hollande's initial plan was to limit the participation of French troops to the spotting of targets for French aircraft in the hope that airpower alone would stop the rebels in their tracks. But the rebels continued to advance in the face of French air strikes. On January 14, rebel forces took the town of Diabaly, 120 miles west of Mopti and 220 miles north of Bamako. The Malian army's sizable garrison chose to remove their uniforms and skedaddle rather than fight.

Upon hearing that airpower was proving insufficient, President Hollande decided to use French troops on the ground. In contrast to Obama, Hollande considered imminent military defeat a greater threat than the deaths of enemy combatants who might eventually choose to negotiate. Hollande also ordered an increase in French troop strength in Mali from 800 to 2,500.[39] The Obama administration continued to withhold support to France.

Two days after the fall of Diabaly, one of the Malian extremist groups committed some of its fighting strength to a surprise attack next door in Algeria. On January 16, thirty-two Islamists from the Masked Brigade attacked a gas plant in the Algerian desert where substantial numbers of American, British, and Norwegian experts were working.[40] Hailing from North Africa, the Middle East, and Canada, the attackers served under the leadership of Mokhtar Belmokhtar, who had split from AQIM just a month earlier to form the Masked Brigade.[41] The terrorists quickly overwhelmed the guards and took several hundred hostages, including ten Americans.

Belmokhtar had ordered his men to blow up the gas facility. He envisioned a massive fireball, so profuse in its splendor and horror that its image would fill every television screen and Web browser in the world. The name Belmokhtar would enter the global lexicon, occupying the same rarefied page as the name Bin Laden. His shock troops, however, had made the mistake of blowing up the plant's generators during the initial attack, which shut down the processes required to ignite a large quantity of gas. The militants tried to blow up the facility with a car bomb, which they parked beneath two gas towers together with three Norwegian and two American plant executives. The blast sent tremors through the desert floor and killed all five of the hostages, but it failed to create the intended fireball. Shortly thereafter, the Algerian army stormed the plant and shot the militants dead. Three of the ten Americans working at the gas facility perished during the siege, as did another thirty-five workers.[42]

Although Mali-based insurgents now had American blood on their hands, the White House remained unwilling to support French operations in Mali. Another week passed before the United States finally granted the French request for refueling aircraft. After the American tankers had begun refueling French jets, the House Foreign Affairs Committee questioned Deputy Assistant Secretary of Defense Amanda Dory about the delay. She replied that each French request "was met as quickly as feasible." She averred that "the French have expressed their gratitude and their support in multiple different conversations with DoD officials, with State Department officials, and with the White House."[43] Impartial press accounts, however, painted a different picture of the French reaction. Mark Hosenball and Tabassum Zakaria of Reuters reported: "According to interviews with officials from both sides, the French have privately complained about what they see as paltry and belated American military support for their troop deployment."[44]

By the time that the United States began meeting the French request for refueling, French ground forces had already driven rebel forces out of southern Mali and pushed up the Niger river past Mopti and into the northern city of Timbuktu. The remaining population centers of northern Mali fell to the French at the end of January. The Islamist fighters had decided to disappear rather than stand toe-to-toe against French forces, who had demonstrated that their combination of air and land power would annihilate anyone who tried to fight them in pitched battle. The fighters fled into the Ifoghas and Tigharghar mountains, or hid their weapons and melted into the population.

African nations, which in the past had often opposed Western intervention in African conflicts for fear of "neocolonialism," applauded Hollande's intervention in Mali. Many of Mali's neighbors lined up to send troops for the follow-on mission. "All of the African continent, all its heads of state, are happy about the speed with which France acted and with France's political courage," said Thomas Boni Yayi, who was the African Union chairman as well as the president of Benin.[45]

The French planned to transfer responsibility for Mali's security to 12,600 AFISMA troops, whose arrival was greatly accelerated so that 6,000 arrived in Mali by the end of March.[46] The AFISMA troops, however, proved a poor substitute for the French. Michael Sheehan described the West African forces assigned to AFISMA as "completely incapable."[47] In the face of AFISMA's ineptitude, President Hollande decided to maintain a large French military presence longer than previously forecast. France still had 1,600 troops in Mali in 2014.[48]

A few thousand troops were much too few to assert control over Mali, a country twice the size of Texas. Over the course of 2013, rebels who had gone underground early in the year began to organize terrorist attacks, including rocket attacks and suicide bombings. They prevented international organizations from providing relief and undertaking the development projects that, in some opinions, were still the main solution to Mali's security problems. "Insecurity is still critical in some areas," said a humanitarian worker, who did not wish to be named. "Even local organisations cannot get access there."[49]

• • •

In Latin America, counternarcotics has long been the main U.S. national security concern. In addition to the more than $200 billion that illicit drugs cost the United States each year in health care, productivity losses, and law enforcement expenses, the drug trade provides funding to extremist groups around the world. Ingenious money-laundering schemes have made it exceedingly difficult to determine how much money has gone to whom. Nevertheless, some rough numbers give an idea of the magnitude of the illicit funds that are up for grabs. Americans consume approximately $65 billion of illegal drugs per year, most of them of Latin American origin, but law enforcement is able to seize only $1 billion of that amount. The remaining $64 billion disappears into mazes of shell companies and fly-by-night banks, traversing the money-laundering epicenter of Panama and a plethora of other countries, including the United States.[50] Import-export businesses, car dealerships, construction companies, casinos, and all manner of other enterprises have been implicated in money-laundering schemes that fund, among other things, Islamic terrorist organizations.

The Obama administration sought to shift the weight of U.S. assistance in Latin America from hard-power programs like military aid and drug interdiction to soft-power programs such as alternative crop development and infrastructure improvement. It made a concerted effort to minimize the participation of Latin American military organizations in counternarcotics, based on the notion that military organizations should stay out of internal affairs lest they become instruments of oppression. "I'm not interested in militarizing the struggle against drug trafficking," President Obama declared. "This is a law enforcement problem."[51]

The Obama administration's approach to Central America, where the drug traffickers were enjoying the most freedom of action, was heavily tilted toward social and economic development. In 2012, for instance, the administration's $68 million aid request for Honduras included $56 million for development. The administration provided Honduras an additional $40 million for agricultural skills and transportation through the Millennium Challenge Corporation.

This "smart power" approach flew in the face of the history of counternarcotics in Latin America. During the 1980s, when surging U.S. cocaine use brought Colombia to America's attention, the United States had at first limited its support to Colombian law enforcement, only to watch the large Colombian drug cartels murder Colombia's most dedicated police officers and buy off the rest. In 1986, President Reagan ordered the U.S. military to assist Colombia's military in taking down the big drug traffickers, a decision that would prove instrumental in the ultimate dismantling of the cartels. American special operations forces trained and supported Search Bloc, the elite military unit that hunted down Pablo Escobar and shot him dead during his final scamper across the rooftops of Medellín on December 5, 1993.

After Escobar's demise, the Clinton administration concluded that the worst had passed, so it withdrew most of the U.S. military support to the Colombian government. In the mid-1990s, the Revolutionary Armed Forces of Colombia, known better by the Spanish acronym FARC, took charge of Colombia's drug-trafficking industry. At first the U.S. government downplayed the threat and chastised the Colombian government for employing the military against what the American leadership believed to be a law enforcement problem. In 1998, the Clinton administration allocated 90 percent of all its aid to Colombia to the Colombian National Police.[52]

A string of insurgent victories over Colombian military and police forces during 1998 ended the American complacency. In March, FARC forces won a pitched battle with an elite government battalion for the first time, killing 62 and capturing 43 at El Billar. In August, they assembled a force of 500 fighters and decimated an army company and a police counternarcotics unit. In November, a FARC force of 1,500 annihilated the police force in Mitú and occupied the city.

These alarming events led the United States and Colombia to form a new strategic partnership, which included the largest aid package ever provided to a Latin American country. U.S. aid and Colombian tax revenues would breathe life into a new strategic plan called Plan Colombia, which bolstered Colombia's military as well as its civil agencies. Plan Colombia outfitted new Colombian air assault battalions with helicopters that provided rapid access to distant coca plantations and smuggling routes that the police had been unable or unwilling to contest. The number of U.S. military advisers would rise from 160 to 800 under Plan Colombia.

Rather than waiting for Colombia's military forces to secure the areas controlled by the FARC, the Clinton administration pushed ahead with a $500 million alternative crop program that employed financial incentives and laws to convince coca farmers to switch to other crops. But when the Colombians attempted to implement the program in FARC-held areas, it flopped. Farmers would not change their crops when the only people with guns in their vicinity belonged to the FARC. USAID eventually gave up trying in these areas and instead concentrated on economic development in secure areas, in the vain hope that aid programs would lure coca farmers there.

When Alvaro Uribe won election to the presidency in 2002, he gave much higher priority to military than nonmilitary measures, to the dismay of Colombian intellectuals and American experts who objected to the "militarization" of counternarcotics and counterinsurgency. The George W. Bush administration, on the other hand, enthusiastically supported Uribe's push for a larger military, increasing the cap on U.S. military advisers to 1,400. Under Uribe, the Colombian security forces drove the FARC from urban slums, destroyed its bases, killed many of its leaders, and forced it into remote jungles. The FARC, which just a few years earlier had posed a dire threat to national survival, became a mangy band of outmoded revolutionaries, chewing on jungle roots in their isolation. Once the FARC had been pushed out, it became possible to restore civil governance and convince farmers to change their crops.

Colombia's counternarcotics successes in the 1990s and early 2000s led to a shifting of power from Colombian cartel bosses to Mexican drug lords. When Colombia's cartels disintegrated, savvy and ruthless criminal organizations like the Sinaloa Cartel and the Gulf Cartel took charge of the Latin American drug industry. They organized the transportation of cocaine from Colombia into Mexico, and ensured its safe passage through Mexico by buying off Mexican policemen and politicians.

In 1995, the Mexican government and most of Mexican society decided that the Mexican police were not up to the task of combating the big narco-traffickers. The only institution that possessed the physical and moral capabilities to do the job was the military. Beginning in the spring of 1995, Mexican military officers took charge of planning counternarcotics operations, and Mexican military units went into action against the criminals by land, sea, and air. The Mexican government sought to clean up the police by inserting thousands of military officers into the federal and state police forces, and by using the military to hire and train new police personnel.[53]

Felipe Calderón, elected president in 2006, expanded the Mexican military's participation in the drug war. The Bush administration rewarded Calderón's determination with $1.5 billion in counternarcotics aid under the Merida Initiative. Calderón assigned military officers to supervise the police, while employing polygraph and drug tests to purge corrupt elements from the military, police, and judiciary.[54] He sent thousands of additional military personnel to patrol the streets and man checkpoints in highly insecure areas.

Although Calderón's militarized drug war did not put an end to large-scale drug trafficking, it caused serious harm to the drug industry, and it gained the confidence of the Mexican people. Near the end of Calderón's presidency, 83 percent of Mexicans expressed approval of the use of the Mexican military against the drug-trafficking organizations.[55] Seventy-one percent said they trusted the armed forces, close to the 75 percent of U.S. residents who expressed trust in their nation's armed forces.[56]

Calderón's battering of Mexico's illicit narcotics industry led drug traffickers to shift many of their operations into Central America, a shift that was in progress when Obama took office. Instead of shipping drugs straight from Colombia to Mexico, the Mexican traffickers used speedboats to carry bundles of cocaine along the Pacific or Caribbean littorals to Honduras, Guatemala, and Belize, where they were off-loaded, moved to warehouses, and divided into smaller parcels for shipment northward via truck or automobile. Money laundering, drug processing, and other activities in the drug industry "value chain" moved into the nations of Central America.

Honduras and Guatemala were the two Central American countries hit hardest by the new waves of drug trafficking. As in Colombia and Mexico before them, the ineffectiveness and corruption of the Honduran and Guatemalan police forces generated interest in the militarization of counternarcotics. In 2011, Honduran legislators voted to increase the military's role in domestic counternarcotics, and the Guatemalan people elected Otto Pérez Molina, a former general who had vowed during the presidential campaign to use the military more vigorously against the drug traffickers.

Honduras, Guatemala, and other Central American countries asked the Obama administration for training and military equipment to build their security capabilities beyond the few elite units that already received extensive foreign support. The Department of Defense supported many of the requests, but the White House turned most of them down on the principle that it did not want to militarize counternarcotics. As far as "hard power" was concerned, the Obama administration relied primarily on civil assistance to a handful of small law enforcement and security agencies. Those organizations nabbed a few high-profile traffickers, but the drug-trafficking organizations easily replaced those losses. The bulk of the Central American security forces, the potential instruments for broad national campaigns to tear down the drug-trafficking businesses, remained weak and corrupt.

As had occurred when the United States had pushed soft power without hard power in Colombia and Mexico, development programs in Honduras, Guatemala, and other Central American countries made little headway in areas dominated by drug traffickers because the criminals could bring superior force against them. In January 2012, the U.S. Peace Corps withdrew all of its personnel from Honduras as a result of acts of rape and murder against Peace Corps volunteers. Peace Corps director Aaron S. Williams stated that the agency was pulling out because "the safety and security of all Peace Corps volunteers is the agency's highest priority."[57]

The Obama administration's discomfort with military participation in the Latin American drug wars, combined with budgetary pressures, undercut the most successful counternarcotics outfit in the world, the Joint Interagency Task Force South. Located improbably in Key West, Florida, the task force is just a short walk from the bikini shops, Jimmy Buffett bars, and key lime pie vendors that line the crowded island streets. JIATF-South, as it is known in military parlance, oversees the ships and aircraft that interdict drug shipments across Latin America, which in the past inflicted a massive toll on the drug-trafficking industry. In 2009, JIATF-South seized 220 tons of cocaine, accounting for more than 40 percent of all cocaine seized in the entire world, and more than five times what all the other U.S. law enforcement agencies hauled in combined.[58]

Since 2011, cuts to the defense budget and the shift of assets to the Pacific have shorn away most of the U.S. Navy and Coast Guard vessels that had been dedicated to drug interdiction in the Western Hemisphere. At the beginning of 2013, only six Navy and Coast Guard ships remained committed to the drug interdiction mission,[59] and over the course of 2013, JIATF-South seized only 132 tons of cocaine.[60] In March 2014, by which time only three U.S. ships were still interdicting drugs, General John F. Kelly of the U.S. Southern Command (SOUTH-COM) said that he needed thirteen more ships and a twentyfold increase in intelligence resources to prosecute the maritime interdiction campaign to the fullest. "Because of asset shortfalls, we're unable to get after 74 percent of suspected maritime drug smuggling," Kelly told the Senate Armed Services Committee. "I simply sit and watch it go by."[61]

. . .

The Obama presidency provided "smart power" advocates with a host of proving grounds for the theory that the United States could achieve better results by relying more on soft power and less on hard power. The results of the administration's experiments did not turn out as they had hoped or expected. Since Obama took office, most of those proving grounds have witnessed as much or more warfare, terrorism, and drug trafficking than before. The United States has been forced to relearn the lesson that soft power consistently fails when hard power is not present to protect it. Civilians cannot run schools or introduce new farming techniques in the face of intimidation and violence. Law enforcement organizations cannot bring justice if guerrillas are free to assassinate judges and police officers.

It has become fashionable, even in the U.S. military, to assert that "today's enemies cannot be defeated with purely military means." That statement is generally accurate. But, given the influence of "smart power" thinking, a more important assertion to remember is that today's enemies cannot be defeated with purely nonmilitary means.

14

DANGEROUS NATIONS

Iran, China, North Korea, Pakistan, Syria, Russia

It has been said, by advocates of reduced U.S. defense spending, that a smaller U.S. military is acceptable because no foreign nations pose serious threats to the safety of the United States. Long gone, they say, are the days when Nazi Germany or the Soviet Union demanded a large U.S. military, and those days are never going to return. During the debates over the draconian budget cuts stipulated by sequestration, liberal defense analysts contended that even those cuts would not cause serious harm to the military because U.S. military spending would remain higher than that of all its nearest competitors combined. "We would still have the world's only global force at a time when we are facing no real existential threats," asserted Gordon Adams, a professor at American University and distinguished fellow at the Stimson Center.[1]

Nuclear weapons have indeed made major war much less likely. This fact is frequently lost on proponents of nuclear disarmament, even as recent history has shown that countries that disarm are at far greater peril of war. Libya's abandonment of its nuclear arsenal allowed NATO to bomb the country and seek regime change without fear of a nuclear conflagration. Ukraine's relinquishment of nuclear weapons left it vulnerable to invasion by Russia. Those who seek to rid additional countries of nuclear weapons should be prepared for more war, not less.

Obama's dream of a world without nuclear weapons is unlikely to come to pass in the near future, so another world war appears highly improbable for the moment. It would be folly, however, to assume that the United States will not have to fight another war requiring large forces in the coming years. The United States could well face a war or other crisis requiring large forces in one of the recognized trouble spots, or in a country to which no one is currently paying much attention.

Predicting the next war is about as difficult as predicting the next great technology stock. In 1945, no one expected that the United States would be fighting a major war in Korea within five years. Until September 11, 2001, no one foresaw a war in Afghanistan or Iraq. General James Mattis, commander of U.S. Central Command, told the Senate Armed Services Committee in 2011: "I think, as we look toward the future, I have been a horrible prophet. I have never fought anywhere I expected to in all my years."[2]

Despite the impossibility of knowing where the next war will take place, it is worth examining the most likely locales. Such an exercise facilitates contingency planning, and helps demonstrate the need for continued military spending to Americans who are inclined to believe that the United States will not have to fight another big war.

. . .

Iran is among the most likely of candidates to engage the United States in a ground war. The Iranians have been working hard to develop nuclear weapons, despite American economic pressure and repeated American warnings that a nuclear-armed Iran will not be tolerated. In Iranian eyes, nuclear weapons are an invaluable deterrent against attacks by the United States and Israel. No strategic genius is required to discern that the United States readily attacked countries that did not have nuclear weapons, like Afghanistan, Iraq, and Libya, while it has been reluctant to undertake even mild provocations against nuclear-armed countries like North Korea and Pakistan.

Israel is mortally opposed to Iranian possession of nuclear weapons for several reasons. A nuclear Iran would be more confident of its security and therefore more likely to support attacks on Israel by Hezbollah and other militant groups. It could use the threat of nuclear retaliation to discourage provocations by Israel and other enemies. Of greatest concern to Israel is the possibility that Iran would be willing to use nuclear weapons to obliterate the Israeli nation. Some in the West have dismissed that fear as absurd, contending that rational calculations of self-interest will prevent Iranians from such a course of action since it would result in a devastating Israeli nuclear counterattack on Iran. The Iranians no doubt are far from enthused about the prospect of Iran's cities and towns vanishing in mushroom clouds. Yet there are legitimate reasons to question whether Iran would automatically rule out an offensive nuclear strike on Israel.

Among Iranians, hatred of Israel has acquired an intensity that may be comparable to the anti-Semitism of Nazi Germany. In the latter stages of World War II, it should be recalled, Hitler pushed ahead with the extermination of Jews in the knowledge that it was undercutting military efforts and could lead to Germany's destruction, based on his conviction that Jewish extermination would be permanent while a German military defeat, even at the hands of vengeful Russians, would be temporary. Iran could well arrive at such a conclusion regarding Israel. Former Iranian president Akbar Hashemi Rafsanjani provided evidence to support this view with his remark, "If one day, the Islamic world is also equipped with weapons like those that Israel possesses now, then the imperialists' strategy will reach a standstill because the use of even one nuclear bomb inside Israel will destroy everything. However, it will only harm the Islamic world. It is not irrational to contemplate such an eventuality."[3]

During the 2008 election, Obama had criticized the Bush administration's hard-line approach to Iran and vowed to "extend a hand" to Iran. He said that he would offer the Iranians unconditional talks, aimed at a reconciliation that would alleviate the fears that drove Iran's pursuit of nuclear weapons. Soon after taking office, Obama made several gestures aimed at improving relations with the Iranian leadership, including a letter to Supreme Leader Ali Khamenei and an appearance in a YouTube video on the Persian New Year. When democracy activists took to Iranian streets in June 2009 to demand political liberalization, Obama avoided getting behind their cause for fear of antagonizing the Iranian government.

The Iranians chose to smack the extended American hand rather than shake it. Over time, Iran's intransigence on its nuclear program caused Obama to veer toward the hard line of the Bush years, such that by 2011 he was denouncing Iran's nuclear program with the adamance he had found objectionable in 2008. During an interview in March 2012, Obama made his boldest statement yet, calling Iranian acquisition of nuclear weapons "unacceptable."[4]

Obama, like Bush before him, refused to tell Israel the United States would condone an Israeli strike on Iran's program. Administration officials said publicly that the development of an Iranian nuclear weapon was too far off to justify so provocative and perilous an action as an Israeli or U.S. military strike. But with the Iranians intent on producing such a weapon and the outside world incapable of thwarting Iran's program by covert means, procrastination will not be an option indefinitely. At some point, Israel will most likely take military action against Iran whether or not the United States consents.

The ability of the United States to protect its interests and its people after an Israeli attack on Iran will depend on the size and capabilities of the U.S. military. Maintaining the forces necessary to invade and occupy Iran could spell the difference between whether Iran retaliates with terrorist attacks on the U.S. homeland or sits on its hands. Since 1979, the threat of invasion has been a central, if not always explicit, component of U.S. deterrence policy toward Iran, and that threat diminishes each time the number of U.S. troops stationed in the Middle East decreases.[5]

If the Iranians were to carry out terrorist attacks in the United States, the U.S. president would face widespread public pressure to undertake action on the ground against Iran, as was the case with Afghanistan after 9/11. Given the size of Iran's territory, population, and armed forces, the United States would need more than special operations forces even for a punitive raid. If the United States sought regime change, it would need to send an invasion force much larger than it sent to Iraq in 2003, in order to secure population centers and nip insurgency in the bud.

The Obama administration touted economic sanctions against Iran as a safer alternative to military force, while failing to mention that a robust sanctions regime had begun under Bush. The economic sanctions of Obama's first term failed to halt or even slow Iran's nuclear program; Iranian uranium enrichment tripled from 2009 to 2012.[6] In November 2013, Iran agreed to some restrictions on its nuclear program and greater international oversight in return for limited curbing of sanctions, which the Obama administration cited as evidence that its sanctions had compelled Iran to yield on the nuclear question. But the deal was too modest to justify that conclusion. The concessions on both sides were exceedingly small; the Iranian right to enrich uranium was still recognized, and the United States kept 95 percent of its sanctions in place.

The Obama administration characterized this agreement as the first step toward a bigger, comprehensive deal, which the United States hoped to reach within the next six months. That bigger deal, however, did not materialize after six months, nor did it materialize during the seven-month extension that the Obama administration granted when the first six months of negotiations failed to bear fruit. While American officials formulated one package after another to obtain satisfactory terms from the Iranians, the Iranian negotiators gave them enough encouragement to string the negotiations along while avoiding any commitments that would impede Iranian's nuclear program.

. . .

America's military presence in the Middle East, and hence its deterrent power, has been shrinking as the result of budget cuts and the "pivot to Asia." The Obama administration chose to concentrate U.S. air and naval assets around Asia based on the perception that those assets were critical to the protection of U.S. interests in Asia and the Pacific. That perception was accurate enough. U.S. naval and air forces serve as a critical counterweight to the rise of Chinese power on a continent long known for hardheaded calculation of force. They discourage China's intimidation of its neighbors, with whom it has a host of disputes, and give Asian leaders the confidence to rebuff Chinese demands.

The burgeoning Chinese economy has developed an enormous thirst for imported energy and raw materials, giving China a newfound interest in foreign lands and seas. By the time Obama took office, China was jostling with the nations of Southeast Asia over hydrocarbon and fishing rights in the South China Sea, and with Japan over the same prizes in the East China Sea. Chinese leaders were continuing their decades-long preparations for the seizure of Taiwan, implanting so many missiles on the Chinese mainland that American ships and aircraft would be certain to sustain crippling losses if war broke out over the coveted island. The United States had dominated the global air and the seas for decades without a serious competitor, but China was building air and naval forces on a scale that would make them a serious rival within two decades.

Chinese leaders perceived Obama's announcement of a "pivot to Asia" as an upping of the ante in the Pacific. They decided that they needed to increase military spending further in order to prevent the American pivot from undermining China's prestige and to render America's position in Asia untenable over the long term. In a manifestation of China's rising military strength, Beijing's leaders broke with their long-standing policy of *taoguang yanghui*, meaning "hiding capabilities and biding one's time," and instead pounded the nation's chest in public.

In March 2013, the Communist Party anointed a new leader, Xi Jinping, who made no bones about his desire to surpass the United States. He publicly praised "the China Dream," a nationalist creed that, according to the military officer who first articulated it, aimed at pushing China ahead of the United States as the world's foremost military power. "This dream can be said to be the dream of a strong nation," Xi Jinping said in a speech to Chinese sailors. "And for the military, it is a dream of a strong military."[7] Xi emphasized the importance of increasing China's naval power. "The oceans and seas," he told the Politburo in July 2013, "have an increasingly important strategic status concerning global competition in the spheres of politics, economic development, military, and technology."[8]

Other leading Chinese officials expressed similar sentiments. In early 2013, General Liu Yazhou, the political commissar of China's National Defense University and a close adviser of the nation's new leader, wrote, "the competition between China and the U.S. in the 21st century should be a race, that is, a contest to see whose development results are better, whose comprehensive national power can rise faster, and to finally decide who can become the champion country to lead world progress." In February 2013, the Chinese army published an article in *Qiushi*, the party Central Committee's official journal, that stated, "History and reality show us that what determines the political and economic pattern of the world is, in the final analysis, a comparison of great powers' strength, and ultimately depends on force."[9]

The international research firm IHS Global Insight estimated that Obama's announcement of the "pivot to Asia" caused China to increase the annual growth rate of its military spending to 18.75 percent for the next three years. At that pace, it would reach $238.2 billion in 2015, exceeding the combined total of the next twelve largest defense budgets in the region, and equaling four times the amount of the region's second-largest defense spender, Japan.[10]

While Obama's pivot to Asia resulted in a large budgetary increase for China's military, it did little for the U.S. military or for U.S. allies in the region. When reporters and Asian officials pressed the Obama administration for specifics on the additional U.S. resources that would flow to the region as a result of the pivot, administration officials had very little to offer. No new bases were to be established. U.S. forces were to undertake new rotations through a few friendly nations, but they were small and temporary, and hence insignificant. Obama authorized the rotation of 2,500 U.S. ground troops through Australia, a pittance in the shadow of a continent with 4 billion people. The U.S. Navy was told to rotate four of its new "littoral combat ships" (LCS) through Singapore. Lightly armed coastal vessels, the LCS were mocked by detractors within the Navy as "little crappy ships." Secretary of Defense Panetta vowed to increase the percentage of U.S. ships in the Pacific from 52 percent to 60 percent but would not say how much of that increase would come from building new ships, how much would come from transferring ships to the Pacific from other regions, and how much would come from decommissioning ships outside the Pacific.

With the Middle East and North Africa on fire and the U.S. defense budget stricken by sequestration, the Obama administration struggled to find any military resources to reposition. The cuts to the defense budget ultimately compelled the administration to roll back even its modest plans for adding military strength in Asia. The 2,500-troop deployment to Australia, the hallmark of the pivot to Asia, was radically downsized. Only 200 U.S. troops rotated into Australia in 2013, and after they completed their tour in October they were not replaced.[11]

Prior to sequestration, the U.S. Navy had planned to increase its total number of ships from 285 to 313 by 2020. A widely hailed bipartisan study, led by former national security advisor Stephen Hadley and former secretary of defense William Perry, had concluded in 2010 that the Navy needed 346 ships to achieve the nation's strategic objectives.[12] But in February 2012, Secretary of Defense Panetta announced that the Navy's expansion plans had been scrapped because of budget cuts. Shipbuilding would be slowed and additional ships would be retired, keeping the Navy at its existing strength of 285 ships over the long term.[13] During 2013, Chief of Naval Operations Admiral Jonathan Greenert estimated that the advent of sequestration would compel the shrinkage of the Navy to somewhere between 255 and 260 ships.[14] With that type of downsizing, any thoughts of major increases in a Pacific naval presence would be vaporized.

"We are going to have to think about how to remain a global power with fewer resources," General Dempsey said during a visit to Japan in May 2013. A Pentagon spokeswoman was given the hapless task of announcing, "The budget constraints of sequestration may require a change in the pace and scope of some of the Department of Defense's activities in Asia-Pacific, but it will not change the priority of the region to the United States."[15]

On March 4, 2014, Assistant Secretary of Defense for Acquisition Katrina McFarland described the status of the Asia pivot at a conference in Washington, D.C. "Right now," she told the attendees, "the pivot is being looked at again, because candidly it can't happen."[16]

That reality was widely understood within the U.S. Defense Department and in Asian capitals, but it had not been acknowledged previously by the White House. Hence it prompted Republicans to engage in denunciation, and the administration to engage in damage control. As an uproar spread across cable TV and the Internet, McFarland announced that she was rescinding the statement. To justify the rescindment, she redefined the pivot to Asia as a pivot in terms of approach, rather than in terms of resources. The new approach, according to McFarland, consisted of adherence to Secretary of Defense Chuck Hagel's guidance to "adapt, innovate, and make difficult decisions."[17]

The Obama administration's failure to muster additional military resources in Asia prevented the pivot from exerting the positive influence on friendly Asian nations that had been intended. Asian newspapers and television newscasts ran story after story on American defense cuts and canceled American military initiatives, which encouraged Asia's lesser powers to conclude that American strength was declining and hence they would be well-advised to adopt a more accommodating stance toward China. Compounding the damage was Obama's cancellation of a planned trip to four Asian nations and two Asian summits in October 2013, a decision the President attributed to the shutdown of the U.S. government. Prime Minister Lee Hsien Loong of Singapore remarked, "Obviously we prefer a U.S. government which is working to one which is not. And we prefer a U.S. President who is able to travel to fulfill his international duties to one who is preoccupied with his domestic preoccupations."[18]

The sputtering of the pivot led the Obama administration to focus increasingly on strengthening relations with Asian countries whose military forces could help offset China's growing military. At the top of the list stood India. In June 2012, Panetta traveled to New Delhi to seek a closer military partnership for the purpose of containing China. Meeting with India's top leaders over a period of two days, the U.S. secretary of defense characterized security cooperation with India as "a linchpin" of a new U.S. strategy to contain the Chinese behemoth.

The Indians, however, did not put as much value on containment of China as the Americans did, and they showed little interest in becoming a pillar in the American containment edifice. "Senior Indian officials made it clear," reported David S. Cloud and Mark Magnier in the *Los Angeles Times*, "that they will continue to set their own course on U.S. national security priorities, sometimes in tandem with Washington and sometimes not." When Panetta brought up the idea of military cooperation aimed at containing China, India's "response was decidedly cool."[19]

Armed conflict between the United States and China does not appear to be on the immediate horizon. For the moment, China's strategy appears to involve small provocations that will expand its power at the expense of its neighbors, provocations that are too small and infrequent for the United States to contemplate going to war against a nuclear power. That approach has already yielded a few successes. Among the most notable took place in April 2012 at the Scarborough Shoal.

A collection of tiny outcrops 120 miles west of Subic Bay, the Scarborough Shoal had been considered Philippine territory since the days of U.S. imperialism. On April 8, 2012, the Philippine navy sent BRP *Gregorio del Pilar*, a decommissioned U.S. Coast Guard cutter, to arrest the crewmen of eight Chinese fishing vessels after a naval surveillance plane spotted them near the shoal hauling in endangered giant clams, corals, and live sharks. The Chinese coast guard, however, had positioned some of its own naval vessels nearby, and when the Philippine cutter approached, Chinese ships entered the area to prevent the boarding of the fishing boats. Additional Philippine ships arrived, but they were soon outnumbered by a much larger Chinese flotilla.

The Chinese government made spurious allegations that the Philippine government had unfairly "militarized" a territorial dispute by sending a naval ship to the shoal. The United States attempted to mediate the dispute, eventually convincing the Chinese and Philippine governments to agree to a June withdrawal date. The Philippine government, which could ill afford lengthy naval deployments or the trade sanctions imposed by China during the standoff, withdrew as agreed. The Chinese, on the other hand, kept their ships at the Scarborough Shoal, where they have remained ever since.[20]

Despite China's reliance on a strategy of nibbling, the possibility of major conflict between China and the United States in the next decade is still real. The most obvious flashpoint is Taiwan. Conceivably, China could invade Taiwan, with the hope that the United States would sit on its hands as it did in the cases of Georgia and Ukraine, or would at least refrain from using nuclear weapons, in which case China might be able to hold off American air and naval forces with volleys of missiles. China now is believed to have antiship ballistic missiles that can disable an aircraft carrier at a distance of more than one thousand miles.[21] As China's missile stocks increase and America's military power stagnates, the chances of a Chinese invasion of Taiwan creep upward.

A more likely scenario, at least for now, would involve a Chinese attempt to strangle Taiwan economically by shutting down maritime traffic. Michael O'Hanlon of the Brookings Institution has calculated that preventing Taiwan's strangulation could require the deployment of all ten of America's aircraft carriers, along with much of its other naval and air strength.[22] Such a deployment would expose America's aircraft carriers to China's antiship missiles and expose American interests to enemy opportunism in the rest of the world.

Another possibility is that China will spark a showdown through repeated seizures of disputed islands in the East China Sea or the South China Sea. America and its allies may at some point decide that China has taken too much and must be stopped. Obama, given his aversion to conflict and the troubles arising from his past issuance of threats, is unlikely to draw a line in the sand. His successor, however, may be more inclined to deliver an ultimatum.

· · ·

Another possible locale for a major war is North Korea. The North Korean regime could start a war with South Korea that would suck in the American forces currently located in that country, and many more U.S. units. Possessing nuclear weapons and one of the world's largest armies, North Korea has repeatedly menaced its neighbors to the south through nuclear tests, missile firings, and occasional acts of violence like the torpedoing of the South Korean ship *Cheonan* in 2010. Kim Jong Un, who inherited the position of supreme leader from his father Kim Jong Il in 2011, has killed people on grounds of state security with such barbarity and caprice as to arouse grave concerns about his mental stability and character.

The first of the murders came within weeks of his assumption of office. Upon his father's death, Kim Jong Un had decreed that the entire country enter into a three-month period of mourning, during which no one was permitted to engage in "singing or dancing, merrymaking or recreation." A short time later, he received reports that Kim Chol, a deputy defense minister, had consumed alcohol during the mourning period, whereupon the supreme leader ordered the execution of the deputy minister and several others. Rather than use the standard firing squad, Kim Jong Un directed that the victims be shot at close range with mortars.

In December 2013, Kim Jong Un executed his uncle Jang Song Thaek on suspicion of plotting a coup. Jang also was accused of womanizing, misappropriating resources, abusing his power, and "dreaming different dreams" from those of the supreme leader. Kim Jong Un sent security forces to the homes of Jang's closest blood relatives to arrest them, with orders to shoot those who resisted. According to South Korean media reports, Kim Jong Un then ordered the execution of all the detainees, including the grandchildren. In what he may have considered an act of magnanimity, he spared the lives of some individuals who had only married into Jang's family, sending them to live in remote villages.[23]

As in the case of the Chinese, the North Koreans may be tempted to launch a military conquest by U.S. acquiescence to Russian land seizures and by diminishing U.S. military strength. In the event of a North Korean invasion of South Korea, the United States would need to rush all available units from the shrunken Army and Marine Corps to the Korean Peninsula, which would invite aggression in other regions. The aftermath of a major war with North Korea, moreover, would demand the long-term commitment of American ground forces for counterinsurgency, humanitarian, or peacekeeping purposes.

Another possible scenario in which U.S. troops would be required in North Korea, and one that most experts consider more likely than an invasion, is the collapse of the North Korean state. One assassination plot against Kim Jong Un nearly came to fruition in March 2013. Should another plot succeed, the state might enter into a civil war, in which rival factions within the state apparatus turn against one another. The resultant chaos could very well compel the United States to intervene in North Korea, according to Bruce E. Bechtol Jr., one of the foremost experts on Korean security.[24] Bruce Barnett of the RAND Corporation has calculated that political disintegration in North Korea would require the United States to send at least eight brigade combat teams, and possibly as many as twenty, in order to disarm North Korean forces, secure North Korea's nuclear sites, provide humanitarian relief, control refugee flows, and participate in stability operations.[25]

. . .

A breakdown of the central government is one of several eventualities in Pakistan that could demand American military intervention. Another would be the inability or unwillingness of the Pakistani government to keep control over its nuclear arsenal. Pakistan's tactical nuclear weapons are considered especially vulnerable to theft by Islamist sympathizers within the Pakistani government, who might be willing to hand over such weapons to terrorist organizations. Pakistan's nuclear arsenal has been a great worry to the U.S. government since a 2009 scare in which nuclear materials reportedly went missing from a Pakistani facility.[26] A third reason why the United States might intervene militarily in Pakistan would be a mass-casualty strike on the U.S. homeland by one of the formidable Pakistan-based extremist organizations.

Other countries with internationally minded terrorists would also be strong candidates for U.S. intervention on the ground should extremists in their midst strike the United States. The secondary Al Qaeda theaters of Somalia and Yemen make this list. So do Libya, Mali, and Iraq.

And then there is Syria. During the Arab Spring, Syrians took to the streets to demand better and more democratic governance, much as Arabs were doing in other countries. Syrian president Bashar al-Assad chose to suppress the demonstrations with force, fueling larger and more violent protests in which the deaths of civilians were recorded on cell phones and transmitted around the world on the Internet.

In the early days of the Syrian civil war, President Obama repeatedly issued public protests of the killing of Syrian civilians. On August 18, 2011, after one of Assad's crackdowns, Obama declared that "the time has come for President Assad to step aside." Obama vowed to help the opposition by "pressuring President Assad to get out of the way" and "standing up for the universal rights of the Syrian people along with others in the international community."

Obama refused to take actions that might have changed Assad's mind, such as arming or training Syrian rebels or enforcing a no-fly zone. Obama did have some valid reasons to exercise caution. The United States had little understanding of the rebel factions, in considerable part because the CIA had been so concentrated on surgical strikes in Afghanistan and Pakistan in recent years. Rebel leaders had failed to demonstrate convincingly that they had either the desire or the ability to maintain an effective and just government if Assad left the scene. Some of the rebel groups were led by Sunni extremists of the most abominable sort. The Pentagon warned that if Assad were dethroned, up to 75,000 U.S. troops would be needed to secure the regime's fifty chemical weapons sites and keep the weapons out of extremist hands.[27]

While the threat of an Islamist takeover of Syria existed from the outset, it was not initially the most likely outcome in the event of Assad's downfall. During 2011, most rebel leaders were moderate nationalists. Some Republicans in the U.S. Congress advocated military assistance to the rebels as a means of replacing Assad with moderate leadership, which would not only end the violence but also deprive Iran of its principal Arab ally. In 2012, most of Obama's top national security officials, including Panetta, Clinton, Petraeus, and Dempsey, recommended that the U.S. government arm and train moderate Syrian rebels.[28] The chances of bringing moderate Syrians to power shrank over the course of that year, as Al Qaeda and other international extremist groups sent more fighters to Syria, killed moderate oppositionists, and gained the support of more opposition groups.

Obama repeatedly rejected the recommendations to arm and train rebels. One reason that he offered in public was that the fall of Assad was a foregone conclusion. "The Syrian regime's policy of maintaining power by terrorizing its people only indicates its inherent weakness and inevitable collapse," Obama said at one press conference.[29] He would deal with Syria, he asserted, by working with other nations to unite Syria's opposition and apply economic and political pressure on the Assad regime.[30]

By the middle of 2012, the moderate Syrian opposition had become exasperated by the unwillingness of the West, and particularly the United States, to help them overthrow Assad. Numerous Syrians attested that moderate Syrians were throwing in their lot with extremist rebels after seeing that pro-Western groups were not receiving assistance from the West.[31] In October, a rebel leader told *New York Times* correspondent C. J. Chivers, "We are now at a very critical juncture. We are not only facing Syria, but Iran, Iraq, Russia and China behind it as well. Behind us, we have nothing but the provocative stance and empty promises of the U.S." Chivers commented that "across northern Syria, in areas that rebels have wrested from government control, such sentiments have become an angry and routine element of the public discourse."[32]

During the fall, the United States allowed Qatar and Saudi Arabia to provide small arms to Syrian rebels but prevented them from supplying heavy weapons for fear that they would fall into the hands of extremist groups.[33] The rebels and their Arab supporters heaped scorn on the U.S. policy, complaining that small arms could do no more than maintain a stalemate. "You can give the rebels AKs, but you can't stop the Syrian regime's military with AKs," remarked Khalid al-Attiyah, a Qatari state minister for foreign affairs. Saudi and Qatari officials wanted a rapid rebel victory, according to Robert F. Worth of the *New York Times*, because they "fear that the fighting in Syria is awakening deep sectarian animosities and, barring such intervention, could turn into an uncontrollable popular jihad with consequences far more threatening to Arab governments than the Afghan war of the 1980s."[34]

Fears of rising extremism proved well founded. Fighters and bomb makers from Al Qaeda, the Pakistani Taliban, and other Sunni extremist groups arrived in Syria in increasing numbers during 2013.[35] The two largest Al Qaeda franchises operating in Syria—Al Qaeda in Iraq and the Al Nusra Front—merged in April. In a twenty-one-minute audio clip posted on the AQI website, Al Qaeda in Iraq leader Abu Bakr al-Baghdadi announced that his organization was dedicating half its budget to Syria.[36] Soon thereafter, Al Qaeda took control of areas of Syria where much of the nation's oil was located. To skirt international sanctions, Al Qaeda's logisticians sent the crude to homemade mini-refineries and sold the refined product to finance their activities.[37]

In the summer of 2013, CIA deputy director Michael Morell said publicly that Syria had become the number-one threat to U.S. security in the world. The foremost dangers posed by Syria's extremists, Morell observed, were attacks on the United States and acquisition of the Syrian government's chemical weapons and other advanced weapons. According to Morell, more foreign fighters were entering Syria to fight on the side of Al Qaeda than had been entering Iraq at the peak of the Iraq War.[38] U.S. and European intelligence agencies were aghast at the large number of Muslims with Western passports who were traveling to Syria to fight alongside the rebels and were, in the process, acquiring skills that could be used to carry out terror attacks when they returned to the West.[39]

The CIA informed the White House in the middle of 2013 that the Syrian government had repeatedly employed chemical weapons against civilians during recent months. Obama had previously said that the use of chemical weapons would be a "red line," so he felt compelled to do something, but he remained averse to deeper involvement in the Syrian morass. He therefore settled on a course of action that looked enough like a reprisal to save face but was sufficiently insubstantial to ensure that the United States would not get pulled in further. He would send the Syrian rebels small arms and ammunition, which they had already been receiving for many months from the Sunni Arab countries.

According to Obama's aides, the President did not express any confidence that sending the small arms would alter the outcome, but he hoped that it might "buy time to bring about a negotiated settlement." Obama did not even announce the decision publicly. "His ambivalence about the decision seemed evident even in the way it was announced," the *New York Times* explained. "Mr. Obama left it to a deputy national security adviser, Benjamin J. Rhodes, to declare Thursday evening [June 13] that the president's 'red line' on chemical weapons had been crossed and that support to the opposition would be increased. At the time, Mr. Obama was addressing a gay pride event in the East Room. On Friday, as Mr. Rhodes was again dispatched to defend the move at a briefing, the president was hosting a Father's Day luncheon in the State Dining Room."[40]

On August 21, rockets carrying sarin nerve gas landed in Ghouta, an agricultural area on the outskirts of Damascus. More than one thousand people perished, including several hundred children, their strangely unblemished corpses placed in rows and videotaped for circulation on the Internet. U.S. intelligence agencies concluded that the rockets had been fired from a Syrian government base.

White House aides began dropping hints that Obama was preparing retaliation for this crossing of the "red line." Secretary of State Kerry announced that "President Obama believes there must be accountability for those who would use the world's most heinous weapons against the world's most vulnerable people."[41] In a conference call with House Democrats, Kerry said that the United States faced a "Munich moment," referring to the 1938 Munich conference at which British prime minister Neville Chamberlain had yielded to Hitler's territorial demands in a vain effort to achieve peace. A failure to stand up to the Syrians now, Kerry warned, would embolden Assad, just as Chamberlain's unwillingness to confront Hitler had led the Nazi dictator to further acts of aggression.[42] Secretary of Defense Hagel, who was traveling in Asia, informed Obama of South Korean concerns that the lack of a U.S. response in Syria would convince North Korea that it could get away with using chemical weapons.[43]

Obama himself was much less inclined to take action than his lieutenants were letting on. But he also recognized that inaction would cause further harm to his domestic popularity and international credibility. Although Obama did not believe that he needed congressional approval for air strikes on Syria—he had not gone to Congress before initiating the bombing campaign in Libya—he pondered the option of seeking a congressional resolution, which would allow him to shift blame should the air campaign be ineffective or unpopular. National Security Advisor Susan Rice advised against putting the strike to a congressional vote, cautioning that it would set a precedent that could hamstring him in the future. Senior adviser Dan Pfeiffer warned Obama that there was a strong possibility that a majority in Congress would vote against the use of force. As Pfeiffer and others saw it, Obama ought to at least test the waters with Congress before asking for an official stamp of approval.[44]

Obama disregarded this advice. On August 31, during a speech in the Rose Garden, he called upon Congress to hold a vote on the use of force in Syria. "I have decided that the United States should take military action against Syrian regime targets," the President announced. "This would not be an open-ended intervention. We would not put boots on the ground." The destruction of these targets, he said, would discourage use of chemical weapons in the future.

"I believe I have the authority to carry out this military action without specific congressional authorization," Obama continued. Nevertheless, he would still seek congressional approval for the use of force in Syria, because "I've long believed that our power is rooted not just in our military might, but in our example as a government of the people, by the people, and for the people."

As Pfeiffer had predicted, Congress did not respond enthusiastically. During the first week of September, congressional opinion gaugers concluded that a resolution authorizing force in Syria was likely to fail in the House. Obama now found himself in a deep quandary. If he chose not to act after vowing to take action, he would look indecisive and weak. The empty threat of the "red line" would become the punch line of TV comedians, even the ones who liked him. On the other hand, if he went ahead with the strikes without congressional support, it would undercut Obama's objective of showing the resolve of the entire American people in opposing Syrian use of chemical weapons.

At a press conference in Sweden on September 4, Obama attempted to evade responsibility for the unraveling of his Syria policy. "My credibility is not on the line," he said. "The international community's credibility is on the line. And America and Congress's credibility is on the line, because [otherwise] we give lip service to the notion that these international norms are important." When a reporter asked Obama about the "red line" he had set for Syrian chemical weapons, Obama said, "I did not set a red line, the world set a red line."[45]

As *Washington Post* fact-checker Glenn Kessler noted, Obama had indeed said in August 2012 that "a red line for us is we start seeing a whole bunch of chemical weapons moving around or being utilized." Obama also had authorized a series of statements in April 2013 reiterating the point, including a letter to lawmakers asserting that "the president has made it clear that the use of chemical weapons—or transfer of chemical weapons to terrorist groups—is a red line for the United States of America."[46]

Fortunately for Obama, Russian president Vladimir Putin intervened with a solution that would allow Obama to save some face. Putin said he would convince Assad to relinquish Syria's chemical weapons if Obama refrained from undertaking military action against Syria. Secretary of State Kerry warned Obama that such a deal would not work.[47] Just as Putin's first proposal on the subject had arrived in Washington, in fact, the White House had sent Congress a message stating that Russia could not be trusted on Syria.[48]

Skeptics noted that the Syrian regime had begun dispersing its chemical weapons one year earlier to make it more difficult for its adversaries to locate and destroy them, permitting Assad to claim that he had yielded all of his chemical weapons while still retaining some in secret locations. According to Western intelligence estimates, the weapons had been dispersed to at least fifty sites by September 2013. "We know a lot less than we did six months ago about where the chemical weapons are," a U.S. official told the press.[49]

Obama, nevertheless, saw the Russian deal as the least bad of the options available. Aborting the congressional vote on the use of force, he announced that he had found a diplomatic solution that would prevent Syria from using chemical weapons again. While Obama's acceptance of Putin's deal was met mainly with skepticism in the West, it met with hot rage among Syria's rebels, who viewed it as a capitulation to deceitful Syrian and Russian regimes. U.S. and European diplomats urged rebel leaders not to air their dissatisfaction publicly, but some ignored the pleas. "To hell with America," blurted out Brigadier General Adnan Selou, who had headed one of Assad's chemical warfare programs before his defection to the rebels.[50] Disillusionment with the Russian-brokered deal caused a further shifting of rebel allegiances from moderate to extremist groups.[51]

Obama did authorize the CIA to train some Syrian rebel forces in Jordan in an effort to counter the growing strength of Islamists among the rebels. Greg Miller of the *Washington Post* reported in October that "the CIA program is so minuscule that it is expected to produce only a few hundred trained fighters each month even after it is enlarged, a level that officials said will do little to bolster rebel forces that are being eclipsed by radical Islamists." Miller noted that the White House had limited the CIA's support of the rebels such that it could "provide enough support to help ensure that politically moderate, U.S.-supported militias don't lose, but not enough for them to win." In the White House view, a military stalemate was better than a rebel victory because it would make possible a negotiated settlement of the conflict.[52]

Western fears of Sunni extremism in Syria mounted during the early months of 2014. In January, Director of National Intelligence James Clapper told the Senate Intelligence Committee that U.S. intelligence had obtained evidence of training complexes in Syria that were intended "to train people to go back to their countries and conduct terrorist acts."[53] Clapper added, "Not only are fighters being drawn to Syria, but so are technologies and techniques that pose particular problems to our defenses."[54] In May, U.S. intelligence and counterterrorism officials divulged that at least 100 Americans and 3,000 Europeans had gone to Syria or attempted to go there since the civil war began, and that some of their identities remained unknown, preventing Western countries from putting them on no-fly lists and other terrorist databases.[55]

Assad was allowing the removal of many of his chemical weapons.[56] Syria handed over more than 90 percent of its declared weapons by an April 2014 deadline, but Western officials maintained that Assad had failed to declare some of his chemical weapons, and warned that he retained twelve facilities that Syria had used previously to manufacture chemical weapons. In addition, Syria was reported to be using chlorine gas, a less potent form of chemical weapon that was not included in the original declarations.[57] The United States remained deeply concerned that the Syrian government's chemical weapons could fall into the hands of Sunni terrorists who might use them against Western targets.

· · ·

Prior to February 2014, the Obama administration had one area of the world where it could confidently say there were no major security challenges—Europe. With problems in the Middle East and Africa refusing to go away, Obama needed some place from which he could pivot toward Asia, and Europe seemed to offer it. The Obama administration continued a drawdown of U.S. forces in Europe that had begun after the Cold War, removing several additional brigades. In February 2014, the United States had only 67,000 troops left in Europe, only 15 percent of what it had possessed on the continent in 1989.

The military threat to Europe returned abruptly at the end of February 2014 with the Russian invasion of the Crimean peninsula. Just a few days after the completion of the Winter Olympics at Sochi, Russian special operations forces and pro-Russian separatists seized the Crimean peninsula from the Ukrainian government, which had just been paralyzed by a coup d'état. The swiftness of the Russian advance and the lack of resistance from the Ukrainian government presented the rest of the world with little opportunity to weigh in. The United States and other countries reacted only by expressing indignation at the violation of Ukrainian sovereignty.

In the ensuing weeks, Russia massed forces along its border with Ukraine and gave encouragement to secessionist groups in eastern Ukraine, provoking fears that the Russians would tear into the Ukrainian torso. Ukrainian political figures called upon the Obama administration to live up to the Budapest Memorandum of 1994, in which the United States had pledged to guarantee Ukrainian security in return for the surrender of Ukraine's nuclear weapons. Obama, however, refused to take a hard line, explicitly ruling out the possibility of force. "The American people are not going to war with Russia over Ukraine, full stop," a senior administration official told the *New York Times* in late March.[58] At a speech on March 26, at the Palais des Beaux-Arts in Brussels, Obama said that Russia would not "be dislodged from Crimea or deterred from further escalation by military force."[59] Diplomacy and economic sanctions, he argued, were the proper solution to the problem of Russian expansionism.

At the end of April, the Obama administration imposed economic sanctions on seventeen members of the Russian political and economic elite. The sanctions were much less severe than what Obama had initially threatened, reportedly because of fear of harming the global economy and alienating European nations that were dependent on Russia for oil and gas. One senior administration official conceded, "We don't expect there to be an immediate change in Russia's policy."[60]

General Philip M. Breedlove, the Supreme Allied Commander of NATO, recommended that the United States give the Ukrainians military equipment and information on the location of Russian forces. He also advocated moving U.S. forces closer to Ukrainian territory. Obama rejected the proposals, choosing to limit U.S. assistance to Ukraine to 300,000 MREs, prepackaged American military rations known officially as "Meals, Ready to Eat" and unofficially as "Meals Rejected by Everyone" and "Meals Ready to Excrete."[61]

The Ukrainians were none too pleased by Obama's forswearing of force. In their estimation, fear of American force was the only thing that stood a chance of deterring Putin from further aggression. "The U.S. and [Britain] betrayed Ukraine," former defense minister Anatoliy Gritsenko said. "They encouraged us to give up our nuclear weapons and said they would come to our defense. But instead, they're just 'deeply concerned.'"[62]

The NATO countries in Eastern Europe, fearing they were next, urged the United States to send more forces into their neighborhood to discourage further Russian advances. In April, Polish defense minister Tomasz Siemoniak remarked, "what we would like to see very much in Poland is the development of NATO and American infrastructure and an increasing military presence of both the U.S. and NATO in our country." He emphasized the need for an "American presence in the eastern regions of Poland."[63]

The United States and its miserly NATO allies, however, had few forces to move across the European chessboard, and few of their heads of state had much appetite for actions that might antagonize the Soviets. In August, NATO leaders announced that they would not be sending any additional forces to Eastern Europe, citing as their excuse a 1997 agreement in which they had promised Russia to refrain from "permanent stationing of substantial combat forces" in Eastern Europe. No explanation was given as to why an agreement with a double-dealing Russia was more binding than the one that the United States and Britain had reached with their erstwhile Ukrainian friends to safeguard Ukraine's security.[64]

· · ·

History has revealed in the United States a tendency to slash military spending as wars end, based on mistaken hopes of future peace. In each instance, the budget cutting diminished U.S. influence and left the nation ill-prepared for the next war. The country ignored looming perils until danger stared it in the face. Young Americans lost their lives because they were not properly trained or equipped before they were rushed into World War II, the Korean War, and the Iraq War.

Despite numerous admonitions to avoid repeating this mistake, including several from the standing secretary of defense, Obama decided to slash the defense budget in 2011, and to consent to a budget deal that doubled the cuts. He proclaimed that the nation's enemies were on their deathbeds, and indulged in self-congratulation about the ending of

America's wars. The world has since seen America's enemies gain ground in Africa, the Middle East, Eastern Europe, South Asia, and East Asia. Whether Obama will send American forces into harm's way in new places before his term expires is unclear. He may simply respond to future challenges with rhetoric, diplomacy, or economic sanctions, as he did with Syria, the Scarborough Shoal, and Ukraine. But if the United States continues down the path of military and strategic weakness, the damage to American interests is likely to become so severe that Obama or his successor will have to go to war. If defense spending continues along its current trajectory, then far too many of the troops whom the nation sends to fight the next war will pay the ultimate price.

15

RECLAIMING MILITARY POWER

In its first two years, the Obama administration erred mainly in how it employed the military and other strategic means at its disposal. Beginning in 2011, the errors were compounded by the shrinkage of the U.S. military, which reduced the strategic means and thus constricted the options for their use. Dramatic changes in strategy and resources are imperative if the United States is to reverse the tide of world affairs and rescue itself from danger and decline.

Strategic Ways and Means

The U.S. government needs to articulate a coherent global strategy, something that the Obama administration has done only once, with the *Defense Strategic Guidance* of January 2012. It must actively pursue its strategy, which the Obama administration has never done.

Effective grand strategizing begins with prioritization of the strategic interests and objectives that the national ways and means will serve. For the United States, the most important interests today include safeguarding America and its allies from attack, maintaining the international trade system, preventing the proliferation of weapons of mass destruction, and keeping illicit persons and narcotics out of the United States. Among the most critical objectives are degrading the nuclear programs of Iran and North Korea, depriving terrorist organizations of sanctuaries, ridding the seas of piracy, retaining influence in international trade organizations, and defeating transnational drug traffickers. Republicans and Democrats, conservatives and liberals, are in general agreement on the core interests and objectives, though they differ to some extent in how they prioritize them.

The big disagreements, those that result in the largest differences in strategy, lie in the ways and the means employed in pursuit of the strategic ends. The difference that has garnered the most attention in recent years is America's global leadership role. The Obama administration has frequently maintained that America must assert global leadership, but in practice it has often chosen to lead from behind, or to lead not at all.

While the strategic landscape has experienced frequent change since the end of the Cold War and is likely to continue its metamorphosis, the need for American leadership has remained high. No other nation has consistently demonstrated the ability to initiate action or spur action by others in a manner that safeguards both its own interests and those of the rest of the world. To deter, contain, and defeat enemies, the United States must lead in the years ahead, and it must not be afraid to lead from the front.

Since the end of World War II, the United States has chalked up an extremely impressive list of accomplishments as global leader. It transformed the militaristic nations of Germany and Japan, instigators of the world's most catastrophic war, into peace-loving democracies. During the Korean War and after, it saved South Korea from the tyranny of communism and paved the way for its democratization. American intervention in South Vietnam rescued Indonesia and most other Southeast Asian nations from communism, and could have saved South Vietnam had the American Congress not cut assistance at the end. In the former Yugoslavia, U.S. military force halted religious and ethnic violence. In Latin America, American support for democracy and counternarcotics transformed governance and spurred economic development.

U.S. diplomacy, funding, and security assistance have been essential to multinational peacekeeping missions in Africa, some of which, such as those in Sierra Leone and Liberia, have enjoyed real success in halting atrocities and economic devastation. By training and educating foreign political and military elites, the United States has improved governance and security in much of the third world. America's development of international institutions, its education of foreign businessmen and economists, and its securing of the high seas have sustained a spectacular era of global economic growth, bringing billions of people out of poverty. When national disasters strike, whether in Pakistan or Haiti or the Philippines, U.S. military forces are invariably among the first on the scene to provide relief.

U.S. efforts to rescue or improve the world have at times been impeded by underestimation of the challenges involved, or by the power of countervailing forces. In attempting to stabilize and democratize Afghanistan and Iraq, the administration of George W. Bush wrongly assumed that a small minority of expatriates with democratic leanings could easily overcome authoritarian cultures and religious, tribal, and ethnic divisions. For Bush in Afghanistan and Iraq, for Carter in Nicaragua and Iran, and for Obama in Egypt, Libya, and Yemen, the exertion of U.S. influence to depose dictators was based on the faulty presumption that externally induced democratization would necessarily result in effective national governance. In Somalia, African peacekeeping forces and foreign-trained Somali forces and officials were expected to provide a much higher degree of security and governance than was realistic. The existence of difficulties in the world and the record of American failures in international affairs, however, do not justify giving up. Rather, they are reminders that America's leaders need a deep understanding of the rest of the world and the instruments of influence available to the United States, and in some cases a higher degree of perseverance.

Military power has been and remains essential to effective U.S. leadership. Superpowers have economic, political, and military interests in far-flung regions, and must protect those interests with military assets in order to remain superpowers. They have to play policeman of many of the world's neighborhoods, because the alternative is to have a rival play that role, or to allow chaos to take hold.

The mere presence of forces in one country often influences events next door, as the preceding chapters attest. The U.S. Army divisions in

South Korea have exerted a great restraining influence on North Korea. The U.S. military presence in Afghanistan has played an enormous role in Pakistan's strategic calculus.

A nation cannot, however, maintain superpower status solely by possession of military forces. It must be willing to use forces on occasion if it is to retain the credibility that a superpower requires. When the United States repeatedly withdraws forces or refrains from wielding military power in the face of major challenges, it is no longer feared or respected, which emboldens nations that would threaten international peace. In Iraq, Afghanistan, Pakistan, Yemen, Somalia, Mali, Libya, and Syria, a clear pattern of American retreat and inertia has emerged since 2009. Countries like Iran, North Korea, China, and Russia are taking note. Iran's fears of military attacks on its nuclear program and China's fears of U.S. intervention in the event of a war over Taiwan are eroding daily.

The United States must also stop conveying the impression that it wishes to avoid serious military action at almost any cost. The current administration's stratagem of reacting to every international crisis by announcing it will not use ground troops may play well to segments of the American populace, but it is disastrous as foreign policy. It conveys timidity, and removes a critical deterrent and bargaining tool.

Recent history has shown conclusively that none of the world's other major powers has the will and military capabilities required to exert decisive influence on the geopolitical stage. The European Union has cut its defense spending to the point that it can no longer project military power on a serious scale. It has too few politicians who are willing to wield military force after their expressions of grave disapproval and exhortations for united diplomatic action fail to halt illicit nuclear weapons programs or religious slaughter. During the Balkan crises of the 1990s, the countries of Western Europe had to call in the United States to take charge of military operations against the Serbs. When the armies of Europe deployed to Afghanistan in 2005, they were poorly equipped, and many of the European governments were so averse to military conflict that they forbade their troops from fighting at all. During the 2011 war against Libya, the modesty of Europe's air forces and supply warehouses forced European statesmen to beg on supplicating knee for U.S. assistance.

While the West has been disarming, China has been building up its military and seeking to assert power on a global basis. Its motives are considerably different from those of the United States and, from the point of view of the United States and most of the world's other countries, considerably more troublesome. The United States, as a nation inspired by Christian universalism, is motivated not only by national self-interest but also by the impulse to help other peoples and convert them to its point of view. Presidents of both U.S. parties have conditioned aid to the third world on good governance and respect for human rights, and have prohibited American corporations from bribing foreign officials. Those policies have not always achieved the desired results, but they have in general benefited the nations receiving American aid. The Chinese, by contrast, are inspired by a Confucian tradition that does not aspire to reform other peoples or promote adherence to universal principles. The Chinese government and citizenry do not make a practice of funding schools or health clinics, providing disaster relief, or supporting the training of civil servants in other countries. Untroubled by the thought of supporting the world's most oppressive regimes, the Chinese lavish aid on rapacious dictators without making demands for democracy or good governance, and they have no qualms about bribing foreign officials to secure economic privileges or plunder natural resources.

Because the Chinese do not seek to spread their civilization and because their approach to the world comes at the expense of much of the rest of the planet, China lacks an appeal comparable to that of the United States. The liberal democratic ideals of the United States resonate with a large fraction of the world's political elites, whereas the authoritarianism of China is attractive to a considerably smaller number of national leaders—although it still has appeal in some of the most economically weak countries. China's support for pariah nations like Iran, North Korea, and Sudan generates moral revulsion in many of the world's capitals.

India, the emerging nation that ranks second only to China in anticipated power, is dominated by Hinduism, which like Confucianism does not seek to convert other nations or spread a universal moral code. India's leaders have little interest in how other countries are governed or how they behave except when it bears directly on India's own well-being. They are preoccupied with developing India's vast and impoverished territory, a project that will take many decades.

Russia, which abandoned most of its global pretensions after the collapse of the Soviet Union, has reemerged as a major international actor under the guiding hand of Vladimir Putin. Effectively tapping into Russian nationalism and religiosity, Putin has revived the interest of the Russian people in world affairs, especially when it comes to protecting Russian minorities in neighboring countries and supporting besieged Orthodox Christians in places like the Balkans and Syria. As his offensives against Georgia and Ukraine have demonstrated, Putin is willing and able to use military force to subdue weaker neighbors and acquire territory, while exploiting foreign reliance on Russian natural resources and military sales to discourage European and Asian opposition to his expansionist projects. Russia's alliances with Iran and Syria have proven formidable obstacles to America's pursuit of strategic objectives in the Middle East. But Russia remains hindered by a shrinking population, the low international appeal of its authoritarianism, and competition with China. The chances are therefore low that Russia will be able to rival the United States for global leadership as it did during the Cold War.

If the United States falls off the pedestal of global leadership, it will not be the result of Chinese, Indian, or Russian actions, but of voluntary abdication by America's leaders. That abdication has begun under the Obama administration, but it has not yet been completed. When faced with a choice between the United States and another major power, most nations today are still more likely to side with the United States, as can be seen in the much larger number of countries that have formal alliance agreements with the United States than with China, India, or Russia. Only when the United States retreats into a shell of isolationism or multilateralism for a protracted period will nations feel they have no choice but to follow the lead of someone else. The cases of the Scarborough

Shoal, Libya, Syria, and Ukraine provide foretastes of what will come if the American train reaches the final station on the abdication line.

The Obama administration was correct in noting that multilateral approaches to international problems have become increasingly valuable, and that the United States hurts itself by engaging in braggadocio about American unilateralism, as some officials did in the early years of George W. Bush's presidency. But it was wrong in its belief that multilateralism would work when the United States was not in the driver's seat. Experiences like Kosovo, Afghanistan, Libya, and Somalia have shown that none of the world's other countries has the fortitude and resources to lead a coalition of nations during a major crisis. These events have also shown that no other nation can provide the long-term training and education that are required to confer skills and cultural norms on the governments and security forces of third-world countries.

The receptivity of other nations to U.S. leadership is in part based on perceptions of the benefits accruing from an American-led international system. It is also the result of respect for U.S. military power. When an international coalition assembles for military action, other countries generally allow the United States to have a voice on matters of policy, strategy, and tactics commensurate with the number of troops, aircraft, and bombs Uncle Sam assigns to the mission. When the United States appears to be afraid to deploy or use its military, as it so often has appeared in the Obama era, lesser countries disregard the Americans, out of self-interest, fear, or disdain.

The "light footprint" has been central to the ways and means of the Obama administration's grand strategy. Surgical strikes have become the preferred way of counterterrorism, with the "light footprint" of drones and special operations forces constituting the means. Counterinsurgency has been shelved and conventional warfare has been reserved for unforeseen contingencies, resulting in a dramatic shrinkage of the conventional military forces that are the primary means for both counterinsurgency and conventional war.

Surgical counterterrorism has proven incapable of achieving its stated objectives of degrading terrorist organizations, denying them sanctuary, and preventing them from attacking Americans. The violent extremist organizations in Pakistan, Yemen, Somalia, and elsewhere have continued to organize attacks in the face of extensive punishment from drones and U.S. special operations forces. Although attrition has reduced the leadership quality of extremist organizations in some cases, extremist countermeasures have prevented the United States from eliminating enough of their leaders to render them inoperable.

Since 2009, Al Qaeda has gained new sanctuaries in Syria, Pakistan, Iraq, Yemen, Libya, and Mali. Its sanctuary areas are larger now than they were on September 11, 2001. As the United States withdraws from Afghanistan, Al Qaeda's sanctuaries in Afghanistan and Pakistan are likely to grow, and if the African Union cannot sustain its occupation of Somalia, then large chunks of Somali territory will likely return to the hands of Al Qaeda's Somalian franchise.

On Obama's watch, Al Qaeda and other extremist groups have inspired or carried out several successful terrorist attacks against Americans, some of which occurred while the United States was employing surgical counterterrorism against those very groups. Prior to the inception of large-scale U.S. drone strikes in Yemen, the Yemeni-based AQAP inspired the shootings at Little Rock and Fort Hood and helped organize the underwear bombing plot in 2009. Since the intensification of the drone campaign in Yemen, AQAP has remained one of the most feared terrorist hotbeds. In 2010, it smuggled printer-cartridge bombs aboard two cargo planes that were scheduled to fly over the United States, which were intercepted only after the planes were en route. AQAP's Anwar al-Awlaki also inspired the horrific Boston Marathon bombing of 2013.

Pakistan churned out extremist plots against the United States even at the peak of U.S. drone attacks. Najibullah Zazi, the would-be bomber of the New York subway system, and Faisal Shahzad, whose SUV bomb nearly filled Times Square with death and dismemberment, were trained in the very areas under attack. Pakistani extremist groups have continuously nurtured young leaders and fighters who have kept up the fighting against American forces in Afghanistan.

The successes of drones in a few places during a few periods of time have obscured the limitations of the drone as a weapon of war. The ability to conduct drone strikes depends heavily on the willingness of local authorities to authorize use of airspace and tolerate the presence of foreign intelligence collectors. Because drones move slowly and emit large amounts of noise and heat, even rudimentary air defenses can easily shoot them down. Drone warfare also depends on intelligence collected on the ground to find the one pickup truck in a thousand that is carrying extremist leaders.

In Syria, which has become the world's most dangerous breeding ground for terrorists, and in Libya, where most of the men involved in killing the U.S. ambassador are still at large, the opposition of the government to drone strikes has precluded their use. Where governments are more receptive, they have often placed major limits that impede the effectiveness of drones. From the start, the Pakistani government restricted the strikes in order to protect its favored extremist groups, such as the Afghan Taliban and the Haqqani Network. Perceptions that drone warfare violates national sovereignty and kills innocent civilians made drone warfare highly unpopular in Pakistan and Yemen, generating political opposition that has led to further restrictions on drone strikes. Extremist organizations have capitalized on the unpopularity of drones to recruit new members.

In 2013, international condemnation of drone warfare made the Obama administration more inclined to rely on the other main instrument of light-footprint counterterrorism, the special operations forces raid. The operations in Somalia and Libya on October 5, 2013, laid plain that this instrument too had serious limitations. In Somalia, special operations forces were unable to nab Abdulkadir Mohamed Abdulkadir because of the protection he enjoyed from the local populace. In Libya, the apprehension of Abu Anas al-Libi created such a backlash that the U.S. government aborted a plan to apprehend one of the leaders of the Benghazi attacks.

Nor has surgical war been as cheap as advertised. On the face of it, drones seem to offer large benefits with few costs. Whereas an F-22 fighter jet costs about $150 million and an F-35 costs $90 million, the price tag on the Reaper is $28 million, and the smaller Predator goes for just $5 million. But the savings are eaten up by the salaries of the people required to operate them. For each combat air patrol, a drone requires nineteen surveillance analysts, a maintenance crew, and a host of other specialists. A Predator requires a total of 168 support personnel, and the Reaper requires 180, compared with approximately 100 for a manned F-16 fighter.[1]

The support requirements for drones and special operations forces have necessitated larger footprints in certain countries than was anticipated in the early years of the Obama administration. Camp Lemonnier in Djibouti, a site originally intended to house a few hundred Marines in tents, had by 2013 become the place of duty for 4,000 U.S. military personnel and civilian contractors who supported the U.S. military presence in Africa. The number of U.S. troops in Africa, of which a large percentage were special operators, rose to 5,000.[2]

As CIA director Michael Hayden informed Obama during the first week of Obama's first term, defeating extremist organizations requires that the United States and its allies "change the facts on the ground." Building foreign security forces that can control areas where extremist organizations wish to operate requires many years, and it requires commitment of U.S. military personnel in larger numbers than are generally available to the U.S. Special Operations Command. Establishing security more quickly requires large-scale U.S. participation in counterinsurgency, with tens of thousands, if not hundreds of thousands, of U.S. troops.

It has been argued that the United States will not fight another prolonged counterinsurgency because a war-weary American public is unwilling to support such a war. The American public has indeed soured on protracted counterinsurgency in recent years, but the souring was not simply the result of accumulating casualties in Iraq and Afghanistan or frustration with inept local allies, as is often assumed. Americans still supported counterinsurgency when Obama took office, after more than five trying years in Iraq. It was Obama's own behavior and the events resulting from it that caused most of the disillusionment with COIN. Obama could have avoided a sharp drop in public support had he been willing to sell counterinsurgency to the American people as George Bush had done, and if he had heeded military commanders who wanted to keep U.S. forces in Iraq and Afghanistan long enough to preserve gains.

Although aversion to counterinsurgency has become widespread in the United States, a major attack on the U.S. homeland or some other cataclysmic event could change the national mood overnight. The United States might then plunge, directly or inadvertently, into counterinsurgency in Syria, Iraq, Iran, North Korea, Pakistan, Afghanistan, Yemen, Somalia, Mali, Libya, or some other dangerous land. The likelihood of such a war will increase over time, for the American public has a short memory, and remembrances of the difficulties of counterinsurgency in Iraq and Afghanistan will no longer grip the American psyche in five or ten years' time, just as the remembrance of 9/11 eventually lost its predominant influence on America's national consciousness and global strategy.

The Obama administration's decision to forswear counterinsurgency has actually increased the risk that the United States will be confronted with insurgency. America's enemies are smart enough to understand America's capabilities, and they are likely to attack in ways that the United States is least capable of handling. By initiating a major insurgency, America's foes would compel the United States to choose between committing ill-prepared forces or suffering the consequences of inaction. To extend an ancient dictum, the best way to avoid a type of war is to prepare for it.

Americans should also keep in mind that the United States has a history of entering counterinsurgencies by accident. George W. Bush did not expect that the invasions of Afghanistan and Iraq would lead to insurgencies. He had, in fact, vowed to avoid the "nation building" that became necessary in both countries.

Neither Bush, nor the American military, nor the American public wanted to stay in Iraq after 2003. But they were even more averse to chaos and the proliferation of Islamist extremism in a country that the United States had just liberated. As wind filled the sails of Iraqi insurgency, the Bush administration canceled its initial plans to withdraw troops, and instead poured its most formidable military resources into the country, making it the focal point of the U.S. military for the next five years. The NATO leaders who agreed to take charge of security in Afghanistan in 2005 presumed that it would be a peacekeeping operation. When the Taliban resurgence began, the NATO forces had little choice but to stay, as the withdrawal of military forces at the first sign of trouble would have been a glaring admission of weakness, as well as a breach of alliance commitments. When the Europeans failed to halt the Taliban, the United States felt obliged to wage a major war of counterinsurgency to prevent the launching pad of the 9/11 attacks from becoming a terrorist base again.

The strategic utility of surgical counterterrorism is also limited by the reality that certain strategic challenges can be met only with large conventional forces, on land as well as on the sea and in the air. A few dozen drones or special operations troops will not convince the Indonesians to ally with the United States or discourage the Russians from seizing foreign territory. They cannot secure all the North Korean nuclear sites if North Korea devolves into civil war, nor can they keep the peace in Syria after the end of civil war.

To maintain preparedness for an uncertain future and to deter would-be military adversaries, the United States requires larger conventional forces, including ground forces that are skilled at both counterinsurgency and conventional warfare. As David Petraeus noted in his retirement speech on the parade ground of Fort Myer, "We have relearned since 9/11 the timeless lesson that we don't always get to fight the wars for which we're most prepared or most inclined. Given that reality, we will need to maintain the full-spectrum capability that we have developed over this last decade of conflict in Iraq, Afghanistan and elsewhere."[3]

The United States must stop employing soft power in insecure areas without protecting it with large amounts of hard power. In Afghanistan, Pakistan, Yemen, Mali, and Mexico, among other places, heavy expenditures on the soft power of development and diplomacy have been thwarted by intimidation and violence because of inadequate security.

The United States must also recognize that military organizations are often essential to the defeat of internal scourges, such as terrorism and narco-trafficking, and thus they are deserving of greater U.S. support. Fixing bad military organizations, and fixing bad governments, requires a different approach to foreign assistance, which focuses aid on long-term development of human capital.[4]

Restoring Spending

In order to carry out the proposed grand strategy, defense spending must be returned to 4 percent of GDP. This level of spending is required to undo the downsizing of forces without compromising quality. Services that have shouldered the burdens of two prolonged wars must be refitted and rejuvenated. Functions and programs that were underfunded as a result of the wars in Afghanistan and Iraq are in need of serious help.

In the latter stages of the Afghan war, as many as two-thirds of U.S. vehicles were out of service at any one time because of enemy action or ordinary wear and tear. The Obama administration, like the Clinton administration in the 1990s, has tried to skimp on replacement of aging and depleted equipment in the interest of cutting defense spending. If the United States does not spend more to replace battered Humvees and helicopters, American service members will incur needless casualties in the next war, as occurred in Afghanistan and Iraq during the early 2000s.

Greater funding is also required to redress the wear and tear that American service members have sustained since 2001. Absent a draft, the military has been sending the same people into Iraq and Afghanistan over and over, which has taken a heavy toll on their physical and mental health and put enormous strains on their families. Frequent and unceasing deployments have caused rates of marital infidelity to climb, which in turn has led to sharp increases in divorce, murder, and suicide among service members and their spouses. Since 2012, the number of American troops killed by suicide has exceeded the number killed in combat.[5]

During a visit to Fort Benning in 2012, Major General Robert Scales was struck by the marked differences between the current generation of troops and his generation of Vietnam veterans. All of the senior noncommissioned officers he met had at least three combat tours under their belts, and some had five or more, whereas in Vietnam the larger size of the conscript armed forces meant that a large fraction of veterans served only one combat tour. In comparison with Vietnam veterans, Scales observed, the veterans of 2012 were "more emotionally exhausted and drained, less spontaneous, and humorless." The military had exacerbated the emotional fatigue through regulations that clamped down on traditional release valves for stress, he noted. "My generation of professionals spent a great deal of time on Friday nights at the officer's club, talking over a beer about the Catch-22 nature of Vietnam and many of the stupid and hilarious experiences we endured," Scales said. "None of this at Benning today. No clubs, no public displays of hilarity and certainly no beer. These guys seemed to view their time in combat as endless and repetitive."[6]

In his 2006 memoir, *The Audacity of Hope,* Barack Obama had sympathized with the plight of service members deployed repeatedly into combat, and had pointed to the most important remedy—possessing armed forces in sufficient quantities to permit lengthy periods between combat rotations. "Putting boots on the ground in the ungoverned or hostile regions where terrorists thrive," Obama had written, "requires a smarter balance between what we spend on fancy hardware and what we spend on our men and women in uniform. That should mean growing the size of our armed forces to maintain reasonable rotation schedules, keeping our troops properly equipped, and training them in the skills they'll need to succeed in increasingly complex and difficult missions."[7] Unfortunately, the shrinkage of the Army and Marine Corps that he engineered as president has made a bad problem worse.

Budget cuts have also devastated research and development of new technologies. Under George W. Bush, the demand for new capabilities in Iraq and Afghanistan caused a concentration of resources in specific areas that were highly valuable for American troops in those countries, but were not necessarily critical to other types of conflict. The rest of the research and development budget had thus experienced a downturn well before taking further hits under Obama's tenure. With the onset of sequestration, research and development has been strangled not only by lower spending but also by uncertainty that has discouraged companies from pursuing new projects. "Sequestration for us is horrendous," said Katrina McFarland, Obama's assistant secretary of defense for acquisition, in October 2014. She noted that funding for the Defense Department's design engineering, "the foundation of innovation" as she called it, had fallen nearly 50 percent in the preceding five years.[8] Now is the time to invest more heavily in aircraft, intelligence, communications, missiles, and other advanced military technologies in order to maintain a technological edge over China and other rivals.

Some of the proponents of big defense cuts, especially among the libertarians of the Tea Party, view the cuts as a valuable means of eliminating inefficient and wasteful spending. In their opinion, the government will not purge unnecessary programs and personnel unless it is stripped of funding and compelled to shed what is unimportant. This argument has a certain degree of merit. I, like most other people who worked in the defense community between 2002 and 2011, saw evidence of large-scale waste and inefficiency in the Department of Defense. The large increases in the defense budget arising from Iraq and Afghanistan accounted for much of the problem, as they diminished scrutiny of spending and enlarged demand for goods and services for which the supply was weak. The defense cuts that began in 2011 imposed enough pressure to compel bureaucrats and Congress to eliminate some unnecessary programs and personnel, which counts as the only positive achievement of those cuts.

The 2011 cuts were so deep, however, that flesh and bone had to be cut along with the fat. As we have seen, the cuts have necessitated huge reductions in the size of conventional U.S. ground forces and have eviscerated the capabilities required for future counterinsurgencies. They have reduced the number of ships available for interdicting drug shipments, resulting in a surge in the amount of cocaine entering the United States. They have degraded the ability of U.S. conventional forces to provide support to special operations forces.

In justifying draconian defense cuts, President Obama and others have contended that the savings are badly needed for "nation building at home." They have warned that high levels of military spending weaken nations, invoking as evidence Eisenhower's admonition "to maintain balance in and among national programs," as well as the collapse of the Soviet Union in 1991. It is indeed true that a nation's economy can stagnate or even collapse as the result of very high levels of military spending. Because a certain amount of inefficiency and corruption invariably accompanies government spending, too much government spending will fritter away too much of the national wealth.

The United States, however, is nowhere close to spending enough on defense to jeopardize the nation's economic strength, and it would still not be anywhere close in the event of an increase in defense spending to 4 percent of GDP. When Eisenhower made his comments about the need for balance, U.S. defense spending accounted for 9 percent of GDP. When the Soviet Union collapsed, the Soviet military was consuming more than 20 percent of GDP—and under a communist economic system that lacked the dynamism and resilience of the U.S. economy. The only part of the federal budget that is dangerously high is entitlement spending, which has increased under Obama from roughly 12 percent of GDP to more than 14 percent.[9]

Economists generally believe that moderate levels of military spending do not undermine a nation's economy, and some economists, such as Harvard's Martin Feldstein, contend that moderate military spending can actually bolster the economy. Security considerations require that most military spending goes to domestic firms and that military jobs go to citizens, increasing domestic employment.[10] The data show, in addition, that higher defense spending can boost the economy, as shown by the upsurge of military spending during World War II, which terminated the Great Depression and ushered in an era of prolonged prosperity by conferring new technologies on private industry and new skills on workers. In the twenty-first century, defense spending offers a valuable means of rejuvenating an American manufacturing base that has been devastated by Chinese currency manipulation and low-cost labor in emerging countries.

16

RALLYING THE PUBLIC

A proactive global strategy and the robust defense spending required to sustain it depend upon the consent of the U.S. public and Congress. With public and congressional support for assertive U.S. global leadership and large defense outlays on the wane, the nation's political leaders need to recharge the batteries of internationalism. Proponents of a more modest U.S. role in the world and lower U.S. defense spending have contended that retrenchment is a necessary reaction to declining U.S. public interest, but in reality it is retrenchment that is the cause, and declining interest the effect.

When Obama was elected in 2008, the American public evidenced no strong interest in a retreat from world affairs. In the 2008 campaign, Obama had called for a greater U.S. commitment in Afghanistan because he thought it would play well with voters, and his electoral victory vindicated the decision. Slashing the Defense Department's budget was not part of the 2008 campaign message, and during the 2012 campaign Obama disavowed his involvement in sequestration and assured voters that the sequestration cuts to defense would never happen.

Public support for the war in Afghanistan was strong in 2008 and 2009. Sentiment shifted sharply between late 2009, when 44 percent of Americans surveyed said that the war was not worth fighting, and March 2011, when 64 percent said as much.[1] What caused public opinion to turn during that interval? First, Obama's emphasis on getting out of Afghanistan, and second, his unwillingness to rally the nation with frequent public statements on the war. Franklin Roosevelt and Dwight Eisenhower had sustained public morale with effective messaging during World War II, and George W. Bush had done so during the Iraq War, a war whose origins were far more controversial than those of the war in Afghanistan. As the *Washington Post* editorialized in early 2012, Americans "rarely hear Mr. Obama explain the mission or the stakes," so "it's little wonder that most Americans favor withdrawing troops as quickly as possible. If it's evident that the president won't defend the war, and is focused on 'winding down' rather than winning, why should anyone else support it?"[2] And if the commander in chief didn't want to lead the country in war, it was no surprise that the country also lost interest in national security more generally.

The "war weariness" of the American people is another oft-cited explanation of, and justification for, military retrenchment. Most of the American public, however, cannot really be said to be war weary, since Iraq and Afghanistan touched the lives of only a small minority of American families and neither conflict resulted in higher taxes or lower benefits for Americans. The families that have cause to be weary have been among the most supportive of persistence in Iraq and Afghanistan. Some, indeed, repudiate the notion that "war weariness" demands that the United States retreat from its military bases and commitments.

Few military officers express these sentiments publicly, the result of a military culture that discourages public opining on political matters. But one Marine officer, General John Kelly, has become a vocal and persuasive spokesman. As a four-star general near the end of his career, Kelly has the status and professional security to speak out. As the father of a Marine who was killed in Afghanistan, he is impervious to accusations of insensitivity to war's costs. In the spring of 2014, General Kelly publicly confronted the claim that the military's weariness justified military retrenchment. "Men and women like us never, ever grow weary of serving our nation," he said during a speech in New York. "To all those who for their own reasons dare to so patronizingly speak for us, calling us victims and weary, but have never walked in our shoes, or stood by a flag-draped casket holding someone so precious, you can all go straight to—we'll speak for ourselves."[3]

As the baby boom generation begins to fade, it is giving way to Generation X, roughly defined as those born from the early 1960s to the early 1980s. The Gen Xers lack the strong antimilitary streaks of the boomers, which bodes well for the next few decades. But Generation X could find itself sandwiched between antimilitary generations if its successor, the Millennial generation, continues to receive too much dispiriting news on its smartphones and iPads. The Millennials, now in their teens and early twenties, have begun forming their own worldviews and will finish forming them in the next decade or so. Like any generation, they are more concerned with the present than the past and thus their views will be shaped largely by current events and the leaders who preside over them. The invasion of Iraq in 2003 did not make a good impression on these younger Americans, due to the inaccuracy of intelligence on Iraqi weapons of mass destruction, the unexpectedly long duration of the conflict, and the incessant drumbeat of anti-Bush rhetoric from the media and popular culture. Young Americans did not, however, exhibit strong antiwar sentiment, as demonstrated by the lack of large protests against the Iraq War and widespread youth support for a candidate in 2008 who called for expanding the "good" war in Afghanistan.

The Obama administration's unwillingness to state the case for American involvement in Afghanistan has left younger Americans with little understanding of the need for war. The unraveling of Iraq and Afghanistan with the hasty departure of U.S. troops can and will be portrayed by some as evidence of the futility of American involvement abroad. It is up to leaders and opinion makers to portray those events, more accurately, as evidence of the costs of precipitous American withdrawal from world affairs.

Obama conceivably could make an about-face before his term ends, if America's enemies make further progress or if the U.S. homeland sustains another major terrorist attack. He could undertake a more confrontational strategy and sell Congress and the public on the need for higher levels of military expenditures. Jimmy Carter, who slashed military spending early in his presidency based on hopes that international threats had subsided, reversed course after watching the U.S. position in the world crumble in the face of communist expansionism and Islamist revolution. But even if Obama changes course, one suspects that he, like Carter, will tackle it with reluctance rather than passion, leaving national spirits sagging in January 2017, much as they were in January 1981.

Although the situation in 2017 is likely to be dire, the next American president should still have an opportunity to right the ship, for the demoralization that has occurred during the Obama years has not irretrievably drained the American people of their patriotism, interest in international affairs, or support for a strong military. If the next president seeks to reinvigorate the American people with an enthusiastic vision of a strong America and large increases in defense expenditures, as Ronald Reagan did, then the erosion of the national psyche can be reversed. If, however, succeeding presidents continue down the path recently trod, then the erosion will continue and the national will to project force abroad will be lost permanently, as has occurred already in much of Europe.

It is to be hoped that up-and-coming leaders of the Democratic Party will bring the party back to the national security traditions of the mid-twentieth century, when Democrats like Franklin D. Roosevelt, Henry "Scoop" Jackson, and John F. Kennedy were not afraid to agree with Republicans on fundamental questions of national security. Those Democrats recognized that America's unique position in the world demanded substantial peacetime spending on the military and, at times, forceful military intervention. If the Generation X leaders of the Democratic Party are willing to make a strong push in this direction, they stand a good chance of inspiring Millennials to follow their lead.

Republicans, for their part, need to reject the isolationism that has emerged in the Tea Party and begun to gain momentum with Millennials. Some of the Republican Party's senior statesmen have denounced the Tea Party's foreign policy in public, but the condescension and vitriol of some of these denunciations are ill-suited to changing people's minds and bringing new people into the fold. Generation X Republicans need to keep the party on its traditional track of strong national defense through positive and friendly messaging. They, like their Democratic counterparts, must also combat their party's tendency to oppose any and all initiatives favored by the other party simply because they are favored by the other party.

. . .

Since 2011, the U.S. government has attempted to guard the nation's security on the cheap, with the light footprints of drones and special operations forces supplanting the heavy footprints of conventional military forces. The experiment has gone disastrously wrong. Terrorists have killed American diplomats at the U.S. mission in Benghazi, American engineers at a gas plant in Algeria, American spectators at the Boston Marathon, and American journalists in Syria. The terrorist organizations responsible for the underwear bomber and the Times Square bomber continue to plot acts of violence against the American homeland. Extremist sanctuaries have expanded, and they have lured Americans and Europeans who are acquiring terrorist skills that they may one day bring back to the United States. Russia and China have capitalized on America's perceived weakness to seize territory belonging to other nations.

These shattered beakers in the laboratory of national security have not as yet caused a general conflagration, but they have set fires that are in danger of burning out of control. Because of the sharp decline in American power in the countries where hateful ideologies originate, the contest is shifting from the ten-yard line of the terrorists to the ten-yard line of the United States. The probability that extremists will obtain weapons of mass destruction, whether from the stockpiles of a disintegrating Syria or North Korea or from international criminals, is on the rise. The spread of war imperils America's allies and the global trade that fuels America's prosperity. If the United States wishes to contain the flames and eventually extinguish them, it must bury the idea that military footprints have lost their value. It must put the world on notice that the fire department has a new chief, and that he is willing to set down big footprints wherever he deems necessary.

EPILOGUE

On June 10, 2014, militants overran Mosul, a city of 1.7 million Iraqis on the Tigris River. The speed of the offensive, as well as the numerical disparity between attackers and defenders, caused a dropping of jaws among the Iraqi leadership in Baghdad and military experts around the world. In a single day, a small force belonging to the Islamic State of Iraq and the Levant, numbering perhaps one thousand men, captured a city garrisoned by 52,000 policemen and 12,000 soldiers. Bewildered Americans wondered how Iraqi forces that had received so much American largesse could fold so quickly.

The collapse of the Iraqi National Security Forces in Mosul had begun at the top. During the rebel advance on the city, Iraqi Army officers were seen boarding aircraft and flying away. Thousands of policemen and soldiers offered their weapons to the militants in return for safe passage, while others simply ditched their weapons and uniforms and donned civilian clothes.[1]

A leading factor behind the meltdown of the Iraqi leadership in Mosul was the aversion of Sunni officers to fighting Sunni rebels on behalf of the Shiite-dominated government in Baghdad, which had repeatedly dug its heel into the chest of the Sunni population in the years since the American departure. Some ISIL leaders were themselves former Iraqi Army officers who had defected out of disillusionment with the Baghdad government.[2] Another factor was Prime Minister Nouri al-Maliki's purges of competent officers in favor of regime loyalists. The practice had become routine following the withdrawal of U.S. military advisers, who had previously monitored the situation from the inside and protested dubious appointments.

The militants freed three thousand prisoners from Mosul's jails, many of them fellow holy warriors. They liberated cash reserves from the city's banks, American heavy weapons and armored vehicles from military bases, and ammunition from Iraq's second-largest ammunition storage site, which one expert called a "Walmart of ammunition." Over the city's public buildings, they raised ISIL's Black Standard, a black flag adorned with white Arabic lettering and the Seal of Mohammad.[3]

Just one day later, ISIL captured Tikrit, the hometown of Saddam Hussein, and Samarra, site of a horrific mosque bombing in 2006 that had turned Iraqi hearts black with sectarian hatred. Samarra lay only seventy miles from Baghdad, barely more than an hour's drive for the American Humvees that ISIL had looted from Mosul. News of these victories caused additional Iraqi units to disintegrate. Michael Knights, one of the world's foremost experts on Iraq, reported on June 17 that "around 60 of 243 Iraqi army combat battalions cannot be accounted for, and all of their equipment is lost."[4]

The Iraqi Army divisions near Baghdad had more Shiites than those that had crumbled farther afield, and they were reinforced by Shiite militias that gathered in the capital in anticipation of a climactic ISIL assault. Yet even in the capital, fear was pulsing through the veins of Iraqis, especially Shiites. Some Iraqi soldiers in Baghdad were showing up for work with civilian clothes under their uniforms so that they could peel off the uniforms and quickly melt into the crowds if the Sunni extremists penetrated the city.[5]

Iraqi diplomats who had blown off their American counterparts in recent years now begged them to launch drone strikes against the militants. U.S. officials responded that Iraqi marginalization of the U.S. intelligence community made it impossible to initiate a drone campaign at the present time. "What does it require to have drones come to a country?" one official commented. "It requires a very, very high level of intel capability and expertise. So you can't just send drones on an airplane and have them land and have them work."[6] ISIL relied mainly on human couriers to pass information, minimizing its vulnerability to the interception of electronic communications, the most readily available means of obtaining targeting data for drones, and the United States did not have people on the ground outside Baghdad to collect information from human sources.[7]

At the end of June, ISIL renamed itself the Islamic State of Iraq and Syria (ISIS) and laid claim to the mantle of the caliphate, the global Islamic empire that had been disestablished in 1924 with the breakup of the Ottoman Empire. Avoiding an all-out onslaught on Baghdad for the moment, ISIS expanded its reach into other parts of Iraq and took additional Syrian territory, occupying more than one-third of each country by late August. These conquests gave ISIS new stores of local manpower from which to recruit, and oil from which profits could be taken. Janine Davidson, a former Obama appointee in the Pentagon, lamented that "ISIS now controls a volume of resources and territory unmatched in the history of extremist organizations."[8]

ISIS fanatics added tallies to their ledger of atrocities against the people of Syria and Iraq, and beheaded several foreign journalists, including the Americans James Foley and Steven Sotloff, videotaping the barbarity for the whole world to witness on the Internet. On July 13, Attorney General Eric Holder disclosed that extremists in Syria were collaborating with Yemen's AQAP bomb makers to plot new acts of destruction against the United States. "It's more frightening than anything I think I've seen as attorney general," Holder acknowledged.[9]

After promising that there would be no American "boots on the ground" in Iraq, President Obama decided in June to deploy nearly one thousand American troops to the country for a set of missions that included guarding American facilities, assessing the status of the depleted Iraqi national security forces, and weighing options for rolling the enemy back. To ease the skittishness of antiwar liberals in his own party, Obama announced that American troops "are not going to be fighting in Iraq again."[10] He also said that he would request $500 million from Congress to assist moderate Syrian groups that were combating ISIS in Syria.

To the consternation of both Democrats who feared another war and

Republicans who feared further ISIS gains, the troop deployments were followed by weeks of strategic drift. On July 3, after a closed-door meeting with senior administration officials, Democratic congresswoman Colleen Hanabusa of Hawaii tweeted, "National Security officials are indicating that we are making this up as we go along in Iraq. We have almost 1,000 troops on the ground, armed drones in the air, and squadrons of attack helicopters in Iraq, but no real plan." Senator John McCain, in the wake of a meeting with defense secretary Chuck Hagel and Joint Chiefs Chairman General Martin Dempsey, remarked that the Defense Department's leadership "could not articulate a strategy to counter what our intelligence estimates [say] is a direct threat to the United States of America."[11]

The lack of strategic direction was most pronounced in the case of Syria. In mid-July, White House aides revealed that the administration had not decided how to use the $500 million that Obama had pledged to provide the Syrian rebels. Nour Kholouf, a former Syrian army general serving as acting defense minister of the principal moderate coalition, informed the Western press that he had a plan to defeat ISIS in Syria but had been unable to obtain an audience with the U.S. government. "I need weapons," Kholouf said. "I need money. I need a no-fly zone or anti-aircraft weapons. I need intelligence data." With U.S. support, he said, his fighters could retake 80 percent of Syria in six months.[12]

Obama had some valid doubts about the ability of the rebels to deliver on such promises. The moderate Syrian rebels were much weaker in 2014 than they had been in 2011, or in 2012, when most of Obama's top national security officials had called for arming the rebels in a serious fashion. Obama's prior avoidance of robust military support to the moderate rebels had led large numbers to defect to ISIS and other radical groups, and ISIS and the Assad government had whittled away at the strength of the remainder. Thus the odds were now much higher than two or three years earlier that American-supplied weapons would fall into the hands of ISIS, or the hands of the Syrian government, which along with its Iranian patron still posed a grave danger to the United States.

On the other hand, the option of letting ISIS and the Syrian government bleed each other white while marshaling an international anti-ISIS coalition also had serious disadvantages. The possibility of a successful terrorist attack by ISIS or other Syrian-based extremists on the West grew by the day. The longer that ISIS survived in the face of U.S. opposition, the more credibility and prestige it accrued among Muslims, including many who did not concur with its harsh variant of Islam. A poll taken in France in August revealed widespread sympathy for ISIS among French Muslims; 16 percent of all French citizens expressed support for ISIS, a figure close to the total percentage of Muslims in France.[13] Leaving ISIS and the Syrian government to their druthers also entailed high humanitarian costs, as both were routinely torturing and executing prisoners and civilians.

On August 8, Obama sat down in the White House Map Room for an interview with Thomas Friedman of the *New York Times*. Friedman began by recalling the words of former secretary of state Dean Acheson, who had described himself as "present at the creation" of the post–World War II order. Friedman asked Obama whether he felt "present at the disintegration."

Obama replied, "First of all, I think you can't generalize across the globe because there are a bunch of places where good news keeps coming." The President mentioned Asia and Latin America as examples, though he did not say what good news was coming from those places or how that news compared with the bad news about Chinese expansionism and Latin American drug trafficking. "I do believe," Obama continued, "that what we're seeing in the Middle East and parts of North Africa is an order that dates back to World War I starting to buckle."

With respect to Syria and Iraq, Obama said, "We do have a strategic interest in pushing back ISIS. We're not going to let them create some caliphate through Syria and Iraq, but we can only do that if we know that we've got partners on the ground who are capable of filling the void." The United States could help those partners combat ISIS, but "we cannot do for them what they are unwilling to do for themselves." Friedman did not ask Obama how he would prevent the caliphate from spreading if he could not find partners on the ground who were capable and willing. Obama disputed the claim that large-scale U.S. support of Syrian rebels in 2011 or 2012 could have spared Iraq and Syria from the ravages of ISIS. It was "a fantasy," he scoffed. The Syrian rebels had never stood a chance against the Assad government, according to Obama, because they were "essentially an opposition made up of former doctors, farmers, pharmacists and so forth."[14]

One day later, at a press conference on Iraq, a reporter asked, "Mr. President, do you have any second thoughts about pulling all ground troops out of Iraq?"

Obama replied, "What I just find interesting is the degree to which this issue keeps on coming up, as if this was my decision." In 2011, Obama maintained, he had offered to keep troops in Iraq beyond the end of the year, but the Iraqis had turned him down. "We needed the invitation of the Iraqi government and we needed assurances that our personnel would be immune from prosecution," both of which the Iraqis "declined to provide."[15]

"Thanks a lot, guys," Obama said, ending the press conference before anyone could follow up on his response.

This interpretation of events was strangely incongruous with what Obama had been saying about Iraq for the preceding three years. On innumerable occasions since October 2011, Obama had claimed credit for "ending the war in Iraq," by which he meant ending the U.S. presence there, as major combat had already ended in Iraq before Obama took office. Obama's 2012 presidential campaign had even produced a video titled "Ending the War in Iraq: A Promise Kept." As Rich Lowry of the *National Review* quipped, "It's only after the ensuing disaster that we learn he was an innocent bystander."[16]

The President had, moreover, badly misrepresented the events of 2011. It was Obama, not the Iraqis, who had made an enduring U.S. presence contingent on conditions known to be unattainable. The Iraqi executive branch had invited American troops to stay and was willing to offer immunity, only to be told by Obama that the Iraqi parliament had to sign off as well. The fact that parliamentary approval was not an essential legal or diplomatic prerequisite was reconfirmed in the summer of 2014 when Obama sent U.S. troops back to Iraq without a parliamentary invitation or immunity deal.

In an interview published two days after Friedman's talk with Obama, former secretary of state Clinton contradicted the President's claim that arming the Syrian rebels earlier would have made no difference. She told Jeffrey Goldberg of the *Atlantic* that "the failure to help build up a credible fighting force of the people who were the originators of the protests against Assad—there were Islamists, there were secularists, there was everything in the middle—the failure to do that left a big vacuum, which the jihadists have now filled."

When Goldberg asked Clinton about a recent Obama statement describing his foreign policy doctrine as "Don't do stupid stuff," she responded, "Great nations need organizing principles, and 'Don't do stupid stuff' is not an organizing principle." Clinton drew an unflattering comparison between Obama's foreign policy and that of the Democrats' top whipping boy, George W. Bush, remarking, "When you're down on yourself, and when you are hunkering down and pulling back, you're not going to make any better decisions than when you were aggressively, belligerently putting yourself forward."[17]

Obama's belittling of the Syrian opposition drew a host of rebuttals from other current and former members of his own administration. Several officials informed the press that the rebels had not solely, or even primarily, been "doctors, farmers, pharmacists" as Obama had said. Their leadership had included many professional soldiers who had defected from the Assad regime, and most of the other rebels had possessed some military skills since all Syrian men were required to serve a stint in the military.[18]

· · ·

On August 15, in one of the summer's only promising developments, Nouri al-Maliki agreed to step down as Iraq's prime minister. The Obama administration, having belatedly realized that Maliki's Shiite sectarianism was a leading cause of Iraq's woes, had called for Maliki's departure as a precondition for additional U.S. assistance in combating ISIS. Although the evaporation of Maliki's dreams for perpetual rule appeared to be good news, little was known about the motives of his replacement, Haider al-Abadi, and the fact that he belonged to the same Shiite political party as Maliki was a worrisome sign.

Following Maliki's departure, Obama employed American air strikes in support of Iraqi forces that were assaulting the Mosul Dam. American airpower allowed the Iraqis to retake the critical dam, their first significant combat victory over ISIS. Hoping that this operation foretold greater White House receptivity to action against ISIS, U.S. military commanders urged Obama to ramp up offensive air sorties. But Obama would have none of it. He restricted the use of airpower to obstruction of further ISIS advances.[19]

On August 28, in answering a reporter's question about ISIS, Obama uttered one of the biggest gaffes of his presidency. "We don't have a strategy yet," the President said. The remark precipitated a storm of criticism and ridicule, some of it from experts who pointed out that the intelligence community had brought ISIS to the White House's attention long ago. To contain the damage, White House Press Secretary Josh Earnest went on television and Twitter to say that the President had been talking only about Syria, and that the President did have a strategy for dealing with ISIS in Iraq. Options for military action in Syria, he added, "are still being developed by the Pentagon."[20]

That answer also came under fire for implying that the lack of strategy was the Pentagon's fault. The Pentagon, in fact, had already developed options and was waiting for the White House to request a list of ISIS targets, according to two senior Pentagon officials interviewed by McClatchy. Those officials also accused the White House of "dithering" on Syria.[21]

On September 3, hours after the beheading of American journalist Steven Sotloff, Obama spoke to the press about ISIS again, and once more opened himself up to criticism. "The bottom line is this," Obama said. "Our objective is clear and that is to degrade and destroy ISIL so it is no longer a threat." But when ABC News correspondent Ann Compton asked him for clarification, the President backtracked, asserting that "our objective is to make sure they aren't an ongoing threat to the region." In response to a subsequent question, Obama stepped away still further, saying, "We know that if we are joined by the international community, we can continue to shrink ISIL's sphere of influence, its effectiveness, its military capability to the point where it is a manageable problem."[22]

The Obama administration, having been embarrassed by its unwillingness to enforce the "red line" against the Syrian government and by Obama's disavowal of responsibility for the "red line," now chose a different sort of red line. Secretary of State John Kerry told a gathering of NATO ministries that when it came to combating ISIS, "no boots on the ground" was "a red line for everybody here."[23] A red line that limited one's own actions might not have been the best way to put fear in America's enemies, but it would at least be easier to enforce. It also served as a warning to U.S. military commanders to avoid recommending deployment of U.S. ground troops.

Other senior administration officials began saying that defeating ISIS was a long-term undertaking, likely to outlive Obama's time in the White House. "This, as the President has said, is going to have to be a sustained effort," said Deputy National Security Advisor Tony Blinken. "It's going to take time, and it will probably go beyond even this administration to get to the point of defeat."[24] Secretary of State Kerry remarked, "We're convinced in the days ahead we have the ability to destroy ISIL. It may take a year, it may take two years, it may take three years. But we're determined."[25] It was a thinly disguised way of taking pressure off Obama to show results in Syria, and of punting ultimate responsibility to an as-yet-undetermined successor.

In early September, polls showed that nine out of ten Americans said ISIS posed a serious threat to the United States. Seventy-one percent of Americans said that they supported air strikes in Iraq, and 65 percent supported air strikes in Syria. Obama's approval rating on international affairs fell to 38 percent, while those disapproving increased to 56 percent. His overall approval rating stood at 42 percent, close to the lowest point in his presidency thus far.[26] The polling numbers may have had some influence on Obama, as he soon decided to expand the air campaign into Syria.

On September 10, Obama announced that he had come up with a Syrian strategy. The main "counterweight to extremists like ISIL," he said, would be the moderate Syrian rebels—the same rebels whom he had dismissed a month before as "former doctors, farmers, pharmacists and so forth." Obama added that the efforts in Iraq and Syria "will not involve American combat troops fighting on foreign soil" and "will be waged through a steady, relentless effort to take out ISIL wherever they exist, using our air power and our support for partner forces on the ground."

A bevy of recently retired national security officials publicly criticized Obama for forswearing American participation in ground operations, arguing that it needlessly tipped America's hand and that U.S. ground troops would be essential for defeating ISIS. "There will be boots on the ground if there's to be any hope of success in the strategy," former secretary of defense Robert Gates remarked.[27] General James Conway, the former Marine Corps commandant, said, "I don't think the president's plan has a snowball's chance in hell of succeeding."[28] In congressional testimony, Chairman of the Joint Chiefs of Staff Martin Dempsey acknowledged that General Lloyd Austin, the commander of U.S. Central Command, had recommended employing U.S. ground troops as combat advisers in Iraq, and that he himself might recommend employment of U.S. ground forces if Obama's strategy did not succeed. A concerned Obama traveled to Central Command's headquarters in Tampa the next day to pronounce, "I want to be clear: The American forces that have been deployed to Iraq do not and will not have a combat mission."[29]

Unsurprisingly, ISIS adjusted its tactics to minimize the impact of American airpower, much as kindred extremists had done across the Middle East, North Africa, and South Asia in recent years. They disestablished command-and-control centers, training camps, and other easy targets, and dispersed themselves among women and children. "Two days ago, they left their main headquarters, and they moved to live inside our civilian neighborhoods," one Mosul resident told a British correspondent. Other residents reported that ISIS was holding female captives from the Yazidi sect at key locations as "human shields."[30] ISIS acquired encryption devices that impeded foreign intelligence collectors and software that enabled ISIS operatives to erase their Internet tracks.[31]

In October, administration officials revealed that the United States was not going to support existing Syrian rebel groups, owing to their dubious loyalties and capabilities, but would instead form a new rebel fighting force of 5,000 men, consisting mainly of Syrian refugees recruited in nearby countries. One year would be needed before this new force would be ready. These officials also divulged that the United States would train these forces not to take territory back from ISIS but to defend territory not already held by ISIS or the Syrian government—the amount of which was diminishing by the day. These 5,000 combatants would not be strong enough for offensive purposes because of their modest size and Obama's unwillingness to assign them U.S. combat advisers who could coordinate American air strikes. Critics within the U.S. military noted that limitations on U.S. support to rebel fighters appeared inconsistent with the strategy of defeating ISIS. "We have a big disconnect within our strategy," a senior U.S. official told Rajiv Chandrasekaran of the *Washington Post.* "We need a credible, moderate Syrian force, but we have not been willing to commit what it takes to build that force."[32]

Moderate Syrian rebel groups whom the United States had been trying to cultivate chimed in with criticisms, both in public and in private. The American air strikes on Sunni militants, they complained, were abetting the Assad regime, which in their view was the number-one enemy. They interpreted Obama's unwillingness to assail Assad, either rhetorically or militarily, as proof that the United States no longer sought Assad's removal.[33] During the fall, when rebels who had previously received American support requested air strikes against Assad's forces and extremist Sunni groups, the White House stayed its hand. Major territorial losses ensued for these erstwhile friends.[34]

As criticisms of the U.S. strategy multiplied, administration officials explained that the purpose of the new Syrian rebel force was not to achieve a military victory, but to facilitate a political resolution of the conflict. In the words of John Allen, Obama's point man on anti-ISIS forces, the 5,000 rebels were intended to serve as a "credible force that the Assad government ultimately has to acknowledge and recognize." They would be central to negotiations aimed at achieving a "political outcome that does not include Assad."[35] According to Secretary of State John Kerry, the United States planned to work with Iran and Russia to arrange this political outcome.[36] How exactly the United States would be able to induce cooperation from Iran and Russia—leading adversaries of the United States and the staunchest friends of Assad—was left unexplained.

In Iraq, a combination of Iranian forces, Iranian-backed Iraqi militias, and American airpower prevented ISIS from achieving major gains in the fall of 2014, but efforts to win over Sunni tribes in ISIS-held areas made little headway. Although Iraq's Sunni tribes did not care much for ISIS, they saw ISIS as preferable to the Iraqi central government, which had been unable to shake its reputation as an oppressor of Sunnis and a close ally of Iran, despite Prime Minister Maliki's departure. "The Sunni community has two options," said Zaydan al-Jibouri, one of numerous Sunni tribal leaders who had agreed to join forces with ISIS during 2014. Sunnis could either "fight against ISIS and allow Iran and its militias to rule us, or do the opposite. We chose ISIS for only one reason. ISIS only kills you. The Iraqi government kills you and rapes your women."[37]

The United States had won over Iraq's Sunni tribes during the administration of George W. Bush by establishing security and preventing the Baghdad government from abusing the Sunnis. The United States would have to do so again if it were to attain Obama's objective of defeating ISIS in Iraq. But the Bush administration had put to use tens of thousands of American troops and huge sums of money, and it had possessed a high degree of influence over the Iraqi government. Obama refused to make those assets available now, and he had long since forfeited most of America's influence.

                                    •   •   •

In his September 10 speech on ISIS, Obama had stated that "this strategy of taking out terrorists who threaten us, while supporting partners on the front lines, is one that we have successfully pursued in Yemen and Somalia for years."[38] While some limited progress had been made in Somalia in recent months, Yemen was in deep trouble, and about to get worse. At the time of Obama's speech, U.S. experts were saying that AQAP continued to thrive in Yemen, with some asserting that it posed a greater threat to the U.S. homeland than ISIS or any other terrorist organization.[39]

Ten days after the speech, Iranian-backed Houthi rebels overthrew the fragile Yemeni government, America's main partner in combating AQAP. The coup led to purges within the Yemeni government that debilitated the Yemeni security forces, stoked tensions between Shiites and Sunnis, and heightened hostility to the West. On the streets of the capital, Houthi militiamen were seen cruising in newly acquired military vehicles emblazoned with the words "Death to America, Death to Israel."[40]

Among the early adverse consequences of the coup was the ruination of prolonged American efforts to increase Yemeni security capabilities. AQAP and other extremist groups in Yemen thus found it easier to carry out all their nefarious activities, from plotting attacks to recruiting fighters to taking and holding hostages. The inability of the Yemeni government to impede the extremists led the U.S. government to launch a special operations raid on December 6, 2014, to rescue two hostages—American Luke Somers and South African Pierre Korkie—from the clutches of Al Qaeda in the Arabian Peninsula.

As the American rescue team crept forward that night, a Yemeni guard dog detected their presence and started barking. One of the Yemeni guards decided to shoot the two prisoners before they could be saved. Somers and Korkie were still alive when the special operators reached them, but Korkie died minutes after medics loaded him aboard a V-22 Osprey, and Somers died a short time later in the operating room of the USS *Makin Island*.

Yemen's pro-American president, Abd Rabbuh Mansur Hadi, managed to retain his title and some of his power after September's events, but in January 2015 Houthi thugs forced him to step down and hand over the keys to the palace. The Houthis then completed the purging of Yemeni security personnel who had assisted the Americans, resulting in a loss of targeting data for the surgical strikes that Obama had thought would suffice to hold Yemeni extremists at bay. "The agencies we worked with are really under the thumb of the Houthis," one senior U.S. official commented in late January. "Our ability to work with them is not there." This official added, "The chaos has aided al-Qaeda." The White House told the press that "the political instability in Yemen has not forced us to suspend counterterrorism operations," and that "we also continue to partner with Yemeni security forces in this effort," but when questioned as to whether those forces were still intact and functional, a senior administration official conceded that "it is difficult for me to assess what is a very fluid situation on the ground."[41]

Two weeks later, the Obama administration evacuated the remaining U.S. embassy personnel, many of whom had been engaged in intelligence work, as well as the Marine embassy guards. On the streets of Sana'a, crowds of Houthis jeered the American departure with chants of "Death to America! Death to Israel!" When the Americans arrived at the Sana'a airport, Houthi authorities treated them like the minions of a third-rate vassal, confiscating their vehicles and forbidding them from taking weapons with them on the flight home. The State Department issued a feeble protest that the vehicle seizures were "completely unacceptable," while also directing the Americans on the ground to comply with the Houthi demands. Marines had to remove the bolts from their weapons and destroy them with sledgehammers, while gleeful Houthi militants sped off in the U.S. embassy's fleet of sport-utility vehicles. An American who had been involved in U.S. operations in Yemen called the closure of the embassy compound "extremely damaging" to CIA activities in Yemen.[42]

. . .

During the second half of 2014, Obama also faced a mounting crisis in Eastern Europe. Russian tanks and more than one thousand Russian troops entered the Ukraine in early August to fight alongside separatist forces that enjoyed the Kremlin's covert backing. One separatist leader admitted that Russian soldiers had come into the country, but added that they had come only for vacation. The Ukrainian government appealed to the United States and NATO's European members for military aid and other assistance.

Several of Obama's senior officials publicly and vehemently denounced Russia's late-summer troublemaking. "The mask is coming off," intoned Samantha Power, the U.S. ambassador to the United Nations. "Russia's soldiers, tanks, air defense, and artillery" had joined with "illegal separatists in another sovereign country," she said, in order to "open a new front in a crisis manufactured in and fueled by Russia." An impassioned Power asked her UN colleagues, "What message are we sending to other countries with similarly alarming ambitions around the world, when we let Russia violate these rules without sufficient consequences? In the face of this threat, the cost of inaction is unacceptable."[43]

Prominent Democrats in Congress joined Republicans in urging Obama to send weapons to the Ukrainians. Senator Robert Menendez, the Democratic chairman of the Senate Foreign Relations Committee, said that the United States "should be providing the Ukrainians with the types of defensive weapons that will impose a cost upon Putin for further aggression."[44]

Secretary of Defense Hagel privately urged Obama to stop dithering. He argued that Putin "would interpret U.S. inaction as indifference," according to a senior defense official. In a stinging indictment of Obama and his national security inner circle, the bluntness of which may have contributed to Hagel's firing in November, Hagel warned Obama that "the U.S. wasn't focused enough on Russia, and was lurching from crisis to crisis without direction."[45]

Obama rejected all recommendations to send arms to the Ukrainians. Instead, he countered the Russian offensive with a few halfhearted bits of rhetoric. The latest "incursion into Ukraine will only bring more costs and consequences for Russia," he admonished. The United States, Obama averred, had an "unwavering commitment" to the Ukraine.[46]

On the same day that Samantha Power had declared that "inaction is unacceptable" at the UN, Obama announced, "We are not taking military action to solve the Ukrainian problem. What we're doing is to mobilize the international community to apply pressure on Russia. But I think it is very important to recognize that a military solution to this problem is not going to be forthcoming."[47]

Ukrainian president Petro Poroshenko came to Washington in the middle of September to beg for more assistance. Obama offered to provide the Ukrainians night-vision goggles, blankets, and medical kits, but no weapons. Poroshenko told a joint session of the U.S. Congress that Ukrainian military forces "need more military equipment, both lethal and non-lethal. One cannot win a war with blankets."

Poroshenko then issued a plea for the United States to reclaim the mantle of global leadership. "I urge America to help us," the Ukrainian president said. "I urge America to lead the way."[48]

By December, the U.S. Congress had become so fed up with continued Russian support of Ukrainian separatists that it passed a bill authorizing new economic sanctions against Russia and $350 million in weapons for the Ukrainian armed forces. The fact that the bill passed with strong bipartisan support convinced Obama not to veto it, but as commander in chief he was not required to employ those tools. Within days of signing the bill, he announced that he would not impose new sanctions, at least for the time being. He kept quiet about whether the weapons would be sent. Once more, the sword was to remain sheathed, neither to be swung, nor even brandished to give the enemy pause.

. . .

In his penultimate State of the Union Address, on January 20, 2015, Obama declared, "Tonight, we turn the page." He explained that "for the first time since 9/11, our combat mission in Afghanistan is over. Six years ago, nearly 180,000 American troops served in Iraq and Afghanistan. Today, fewer than 15,000 remain." He neglected to mention that the number was on the rise in Iraq, where a critical mass of persons were staying on the page where they had been for the past six months.

"Instead of Americans patrolling the valleys of Afghanistan, we've trained their security forces, who've now taken the lead," Obama said.

One might have presumed that the handover of the war to the Afghans was proceeding satisfactorily. In reality, the Afghan security forces were now suffering casualties at rates that American military observers deemed "unsustainable," and Afghan president Ashraf Ghani was pleading with the Obama administration to reconsider its plans to withdraw the last American troops.[49]

For Obama, some pages would turn in silence. The address contained no reference to the unraveling crisis in Yemen, where, as Obama was reading from the teleprompter, the government was in its death throes and Al Qaeda's affiliate was claiming credit for terrorist attacks that had just killed sixteen people in Paris. Only the most attentive Americans knew that the pages Obama wanted to turn showed him spurning advice from American generals that Yemen needed more than precision strikes to suppress the country's extremist groups.

Obama spoke not a word on Libya, where ISIS veterans and other extremists were metastasizing and wanton violence was multiplying in the absence of a central government. Earlier on this very day, the State Department had issued a new security advisory on Libya, in which it noted that U.S. government personnel remained absent from the Tripoli embassy. The document also enumerated a multitude of dangers to Americans, and stated, "The Department of State warns U.S. citizens against all travel to Libya and recommends that U.S. citizens currently in Libya depart immediately."[50] Obama and the other veterans of his administration were understandably eager to move beyond pages of history on which Hillary Clinton had envisioned intervention in Libya as a "crucible in which to test the theories of smart power, multilateralism, and democracy promotion," Obama had announced that "the dark shadow of tyranny has been lifted" in the wake of Gaddafi's execution, and the State Department had rejected the U.S. military's offers of forces that could have saved Ambassador Chris Stevens at Benghazi.

Obama did discuss Iraq and Syria in the State of the Union address, asserting that "American leadership" of "a broad coalition" was "stopping ISIL's advance" and would "ultimately destroy this terrorist group." He did not divulge that the "broad coalition" now included the governments of Iran and Syria, which until recently the Obama administration had treated as dangerous enemies of the United States. Neither Iran nor Syria could be said to be following American leadership; both were pursuing their own interests and those of Shiite extremists, which partly overlapped with American interests in Syria and Iraq but conflicted with those interests in numerous other respects.

ISIS had been stopped in Iraq primarily because the Iranian military had inserted itself into the conflict, employing its own combat forces and supporting Iraqi Shiite militias. The Iraqi official in charge of those militias, deputy national security adviser Abu Mahdi al-Muhandis, had previously been convicted in absentia for bombings at the U.S. and French embassies in Kuwait, and since 2009 had been sanctioned by the U.S. Treasury Department for his ties to Iran's Revolutionary Guard Corps. Iraqi and foreign media reported that Shiite militias were torching Sunni villages and murdering Sunni civilians, cementing the perception among Iraq's Sunnis that the militias were vile pawns of Iran. The exacerbation of tensions between Iraq's Shiites and Sunnis made more unlikely the attainment of Obama's stated objective of an inclusive Iraqi national government that could handle the nation's problems on its own.[51]

Obama, moreover, had compromised efforts to reconstitute Iraq's security forces through his selection of a light-footprint approach to training. Because he had kept the number of U.S. trainers low, the duration of training had to be limited to six weeks, much too short to effect any real improvements, and the total throughput had to be capped at 3,000 individuals per year, too few to make much of a difference in the war against ISIS, or to lessen the influence of the 100,000 Iraqi Shiite militiamen whom the Iranians were training.[52] The United States was not providing Iraqi units with equipment or supplies, so Iraqi trainees did not have ammunition for exercises, but instead were reduced to shouting "bang bang" when it was time to fire.[53]

In Syria, neither the United States nor anyone else was stopping ISIL's advance. In the days preceding Obama's speech and the days that followed, journalists, military officials, and think tank analysts all stated that ISIS was continuing to gain ground in Syria despite American and other foreign air strikes. American-backed Syrian rebels were declining in strength.[54]

In the short section of the State of the Union Address on Iran, Obama claimed that his diplomatic initiatives had succeeded in frustrating Iran's nuclear ambitions. "Our diplomacy is at work with respect to Iran, where, for the first time in a decade, we've halted the progress of its nuclear program and reduced its stockpile of nuclear material," the President told the American people. *Washington Post* fact-checker Glenn Kessler gave this assertion a rating of three Pinocchios, citing international experts who said that Iran's nuclear program was continuing to advance and its nuclear stockpiles were continuing to increase.[55] On the day after Obama's speech, Senator Robert Menendez remarked, "The more I hear from the administration, the more it sounds like talking points coming out of Tehran."[56]

Obama had even less to say about the Ukrainians, whose pleas for American arms he continued to disregard. He stated that the United States was "opposing Russian aggression," and had been engaged in the "hard work of imposing sanctions." The United States "stands strong and united with our allies, while Russia is isolated, with its economy in tatters."

At this moment in time, former Obama appointees Ivo Daalder and Michèle Flournoy were applying the finishing touches on a study in which they noted that the sanctions were "not by themselves sufficient" to thwart the Russians. The Russian forces and their separatist allies in Ukraine had intensified their offensive activities in mid-January despite the sanctions. Daalder, Flournoy, and company called for "direct military assistance—in far larger amounts than provided to date and including lethal defensive arms." Concerning the allies who were supposedly "united" with the United States, the authors concluded that "some NATO members did not fully appreciate the threat posed by Russia's more aggressive policies," and hence were too willing to go easy on Russia, while other member nations, including the Baltic States, Poland, and Canada, "might be prepared to provide lethal military assistance to

Ukraine if the United States were to do so," but were "reluctant to go first."[57]

Within a week of the State of the Union Address, Obama's praise for his own national security strategy came under fierce assault from several highly distinguished and recently retired generals. Not since MacArthur's repudiation of Truman during the Korean War had the military's leading lights fired so many salvoes at the President's policies in public. At a Congressional hearing, General James Mattis testified that the United States needed "to come out now from its reactive crouch and to take a firm strategic stance in defense of our values." The nation had "an urgent need to stop reacting to each immediate vexing issue in isolation."[58] General Jack Keane attested, "It is unmistakable that our policies have failed and the unequivocal explanation is U.S. policy has focused on disengaging from the Middle East." Deriding the "very piecemeal effort using drones in Yemen and Pakistan," he called the Obama administration's approach in those countries a "tactic but not a strategy."[59]

At a special-operations symposium in the nation's capital, Lieutenant General Mike Flynn lambasted those in the government who "accept a defensive posture, reasoning that passivity is less likely to provoke our enemies." Drawing on his recent experience as head of the Defense Intelligence Agency, General Flynn warned that "the U.S. is now facing a wide range of expanding threats from both state and non-state actors." As he spoke with the candor of a newly retired officer, one could see the nodding of heads of special operators whose active-duty status prevented them from openly expressing these sentiments themselves. "The dangers to the U.S. do not arise from the arrogance of American power," General Flynn declared to his fellow warriors, "but from unpreparedness or an excessive unwillingness to fight when fighting is necessary."[60]

During the next few months, complaints about Obama's light-footprint strategy arose from active-duty military officers, spurred on by acceleration of the meltdown in Yemen. In February, the United States had to discontinue drone strikes over Yemen because the overthrow of the Yemeni government and the evacuation of the U.S. embassy had choked off the flow of targeting information.[61] Pentagon officials reported in March that the United States had lost its ability to account for $500 million in American-supplied military hardware. Most of the goods were believed to have fallen into the hands of the Houthis or Al Qaeda, the two groups responsible for sacking most of Yemen's military bases in the preceding weeks. The Houthis also got their hands on secret files that named U.S. intelligence sources, imperiling those sources and sending a signal to potential spies in other countries that the United States could not safeguard their identities. In eastern Yemen, Al Qaeda staged a jailbreak that freed three hundred inmates, including a high-ranking Al Qaeda leader.[62]

On March 23, the State Department announced that the United States was evacuating the last U.S. special operations forces from Yemen because of the worsening security environment.[63] Obama refused to dispatch U.S. military assets to retrieve American civilians who were still in Yemen, of whom there remained a considerable number. "We have to make a decision based on the security situation and what is feasible to do," said State Department spokeswoman Marie Harf in explaining why the administration was leaving U.S. citizens to fend for themselves. "Given the situation in Yemen, it's quite dangerous and unpredictable. Doing something like sending in military assets, even for an evacuation, could put U.S. citizen lives at greater risk." No one explained just how Americans in a lawless country overrun with Al Qaeda, the Houthis, and other anti-American zealots were at less risk on their own than with the assistance of U.S. Marines. For the stranded Americans, the State Department limited its assistance to a message containing suggestions on how to reach Djibouti by boat.[64]

Captain Robert A. Newsom, an active-duty Navy SEAL who had commanded the U.S. special operations headquarters in Yemen from 2010 to 2012, blasted the administration's Yemen strategy in an interview with West Point's Center for Combating Terrorism. "The solution that some people champion," said Newsom, "where the main or whole effort is drone strikes and special operations raids, is a fantasy." He recounted how he had lobbied in vain for a broader security effort in

Yemen, based on his belief that "you cannot hold the jungle back with a weed whacker." Surgical strikes alone, said Newsom, could serve as no more than "a delaying action, and everywhere I have been, in Iraq, Afghanistan, Yemen, every military person up and down the chain of command acknowledges this."[65]

Lieutenant General H. R. McMaster, one of the rare breed of military officers to attain stardom as both a warrior and a scholar, published an essay in the March-April issue of *Military Review* warning against several pernicious fallacies embraced by recent American strategists. Like Newsom, he did not name the strategists in question, which would have flouted the military's code of deference to civil authority, but one did not need a doctorate in forensic science to discern the offenders. One of these fallacies he termed the "vampire fallacy," according to which the recent improvements in information technology enabled the United States to destroy enemies with precision strikes. Another was the "*Zero Dark Thirty* fallacy," taking its name from the popular Kathryn Bigelow film on the Bin Laden raid. Subscribers to this fallacy believed that counterterrorism raids were sufficient in themselves to destroy terrorist organizations. Then there was the "*Mutual of Omaha Wild Kingdom* fallacy," in which the United States could outsource all the hazardous work to others, just as *Wild Kingdom* host Marlin Perkins had left the job of standing near dangerous beasts to assistant Jim Fowler. In each of these cases, McMaster observed, military tools had been turned into strategies, and in each case the strategy had failed to yield the anticipated strategic dividends.[66]

· · ·

Obama's failing policies even came under attack from his impending Secretary of Defense, Ashton Carter, who had agreed to take Chuck Hagel's place after the other leading candidates had declined what was clearly a frustrating and thankless job. During his confirmation hearings, Carter said that he was "very much inclined" to provide weapons to the Ukrainians, adding that "we need to support the Ukrainians in defending themselves."[67] It was a loud addition to an ever-growing chorus of administration officials, national security experts, and congressmen exhorting Obama to give the Ukrainians weapons to counteract the covert influx of Russian men and equipment.

On the Ukrainian crisis, as most everything else, the President continued to focus on non-involvement and risk-avoidance. In March, Obama explained that he was not sending the congressionally authorized military aid because "arming the Ukrainians would encourage the notion that they could actually defeat the far more powerful Russians, and so it would potentially draw a more forceful response from Moscow."[68]

Like the straight-A student who never figured out how to deal with the schoolyard bully, Obama had not learned how to restrain international bullies after more than seven years as president. A nation, no less than a boy in the schoolyard, earns ridicule and shame when it responds to the bullying of a friend by running away. No one can blame the Ukrainians for scoffing at an American president who pledged an "unwavering commitment" to their country but then responded to Russian provocations with nothing more than shipments of blankets, modest economic sanctions, and pronouncements that the Ukrainians should not expect to defeat the Russian aggressors. Like teenaged ruffians, the bullies in Moscow and in such other places as Beijing and Pyongyang rub their hands with glee as they see the world's chief of police sipping coffee in the donut shop while windows are smashed, stores are looted, and citizens are murdered in their homes.

For the neighbors of bully nations, the American cowering and the unchecked mayhem in Ukraine—as well as in Syria and Iraq and Yemen and Libya and Somalia—necessitate reconsideration of national security strategies that for decades have been anchored upon American security guarantees. Like middling school boys with no Marty McFly or Harry Potter to lead them, these nations are liable to pander to the bullies, preferring the safety of subservience to the knuckles and knives of the tyrant. On February 6, Germany's Angela Merkel and France's Francois Hollande visited Vladimir Putin without consulting the United States, in order, as they put it, to avert "total war."[69] Desperate for peace because their militaries were too weak for war, Merkel and Hollande pleaded with the Russians to end the conflict. The Russians consented to a cease-fire, which officially took effect on February 15, but it proved to be a sham, as the pro-Russian forces committed three hundred violations within the first week.[70]

In the first months of 2015, Asian leaders poured into Beijing to pander to the Chinese leadership. While visiting China in March, Malaysian prime minister Datuk Seri Najib Razak told his hosts that Malaysia was prepared to conduct joint military exercises with Chinese forces for the first time.[71] The Thai defense minister, traveling to China in April for the second time in sixth months, took the unprecedented step of bringing along all of Thailand's top military commanders to discuss expanded cooperation between the Thai and Chinese militaries.[72] Vietnam's leaders, who had previously talked of collaborating with the United States in thwarting Chinese intrusion into Vietnam's territorial waters, made a pilgrimage to Beijing in April to "mend relations" with the Chinese.[73] During April, moreover, the leaders of nearly all Asian nations, including historic U.S. allies like South Korea, Indonesia, Taiwan, and the Philippines, signed on to the massive new China Development Bank, which the United States had urged every Asian nation to reject, since it was certain to undermine international institutions in which the United States had a large voice.[74]

Treading lightly in the Middle East, abstaining in Europe, and conducting a pivotless pivot in Asia, the United States watches its prestige and credibility wilt like the grass on a California lawn. By the time Obama vacates the White House, he could go down in history as the president who forfeited America's global captaincy and ushered in a long era of global strife and instability. Whether the United States will stand a chance of halting and reversing the downward slide will hinge on whether the American people elect another president who subscribes to the misguided strategic principles that produced the disaster, or whether they instead choose someone committed to rebuilding America's military and reestablishing the United States as the world's preeminent power.

Acknowledgments

Having worked for the Department of Defense for most of the past decade, I have been privileged to speak with a wide variety of people, in a wide variety of places, about the topics covered in this book. Most of them toil tirelessly and anonymously in the service of causes only dimly understood in their homeland. I am most grateful for the time they have spent sharing their knowledge and insights, and regretful that various sensitivities preclude thanking them by name. The views expressed in the book are solely those of the author, and do not represent official positions or policies of the U.S. government.

My agent, Alexander Hoyt, deserves kudos for helping develop the concept for this book. At Threshold Editions, Anthony Ziccardi saw promise in the project and breathed life into it, while Mitch Ivers and Natasha Simons brought it to maturity. The shrewd editorial advice of Kevin Smith did much to strengthen the final product.

To my family I owe the deepest debt of gratitude. As a consequence of my research and career pursuits, they have put up with repeated interstate moves and changes of schools. They have tolerated my absorption in writing during evenings and weekends. The prices they have paid have also increased my awareness of the prices paid by millions of American families who follow fathers or mothers from one military or diplomatic post to the next and go for long periods without their loved ones—sacrifices that seldom receive the thanks from society that they merit. I would therefore also like to express my appreciation for the families of America's national security professionals, as well as the professionals themselves.

Notes

Preface

1. "Views from the Newsroom: Challenges to American Power," Council on Foreign Relations, June 19, 2012, http://www.cfr.org/media-and-foreign-policy/views-newsroom-challenges-american-power/p28590.

2. Michael C. Desch, "Exorcising George McGovern: How the GOP Lost Its Foreign-Policy Advantage," *American Conservative*, July 26, 2012.

3. George Packer, "A Foreign-Policy President," *New Yorker*, June 11, 2012.

4. "President Obama Job Approval—Foreign Policy," realclearpolitics.com; Stephen Losey, "America's Military: A Conservative Institution's Uneasy Cultural Evolution," *Military Times*, December 21, 2014.

1. A Man of Change

1. David Maraniss, *Barack Obama: The Story* (New York: Simon & Schuster, 2012), 460.

2. Ibid., 462.

3. James Mann, *The Obamians: The Struggle Inside the White House to Redefine American Power* (New York: Viking, 2012), 27.

4. Mark Bowden, *The Finish: The Killing of Osama Bin Laden* (New York: Atlantic Monthly Press, 2012), 22.

5. "Transcript: Obama's Speech Against the Iraq War," October 2, 2002, npr.org.

6. "The Ax-Man Cometh," *Economist*, August 21, 2008.

7. Jonathan Alter, *The Promise: President Obama, Year One* (New York: Simon & Schuster, 2010), 225; Vali Nasr, *The Indispensable Nation: American Foreign Policy in Retreat* (New York: Doubleday, 2013), 13–14.

8. "Obama's Speech at Woodrow Wilson Center," August 1, 2007, http://www.cfr.org/elections/obamas-speech-woodrow-wilson-center/p13974.

9.   Anne E. Kornblut and Dan Balz, "Obama Questions Rivals on Iraq," *Washington Post*, February 12, 2007.

10. Philip Elliott, "Obama Gets Warning from Friendly Voter," Associated Press, August 14, 2007.

11. Jeff Zeleny, "The Cancellation of Obama's Troop Visit," *New York Times*, Caucus blog, July 25, 2008, http://thecaucus.blogs.nytimes.com/2008/07/25/obama-skips-visit-with-troops/?_php=true&_type=blogs&_r=0.

12. Domenico Montanaro, "What's Not on Obama's Schedule," NBC News, July 24, 2008, http://firstread.nbcnews.com/_news/2008/07/24/4423882-whats-not-on-obamas-schedule.

13. Zeleny, "A Canceled Obama Visit, and the Story Behind It," *New York Times*, July 29, 2008.

14. Ibid.

15. Michael Hastings, *The Operators: The Wild and Terrifying Inside Story of America's War in Afghanistan* (New York: Blue Rider Press, 2012), 20.

16. Perry Bacon Jr., "Clinton Compares Obama to Bush," *Washington Post*, February 26, 2008.

17. Cate Doty, "Oh, Oh, Tempest in a Teapot," *New York Times*, December 28, 2007.

18. Greg Craig, "Senator Clinton's Claims of Foreign Policy Experience Are Exaggerated," *RealClearPolitics*, March 11, 2008.

19. "McCain and Obama Mix it Up," CBS/AP, September 27, 2008.

2. The Strategy of Team Obama

1.   Robert Gates, *Duty: Memoirs of a Secretary at War* (New York: Knopf, 2014), 298.

2.   Ibid., 298–99.

3.   Mann, *The Obamians*, 55.

4.   Daniel Klaidman, *Kill or Capture: The War on Terror and the Soul of the Obama Presidency* (New York: Houghton Mifflin Harcourt, 2012), 3–4.

5.   David Greenberg, "The Write Stuff? Why Biden's Plagiarism Shouldn't Be Forgotten," *Slate*, August 25, 2008.

6.   John Heilemann and Mark Halperin, *Game Change: Obama and the Clintons, McCain and Palin, and the Race of a Lifetime* (New York: Harper, 2010), 413.

7. "President Elect Obama Unveils National Security Team," CNN, December 1, 2008, http://transcripts.cnn.com/TRANSCRIPTS/0812/01/cnr.02.html.

8. "Clinton: Believing Petraeus and Crocker Requires 'Willing Suspension of Disbelief,'" *Politico*, September 11, 2007.

9. Bob Woodward, *Obama's Wars* (New York: Simon & Schuster, 2010), 38–40.

10. Edward Luce and Daniel Dombey, "US Foreign Policy: Waiting on a Sun King," *Financial Times*, March 30, 2010.

11. Jason Horowitz, "Tom Donilon: Political Wunderkind to Policy Trailblazer," *Washington Post*, December 20, 2010; Josh Gerstein and Abby Phillip, "Tom Donilon's Résumé: Policy, Law and Fannie Mae," *Politico*, October 8, 2010.

12. Peter Baker, "A Manager of Overseas Crises, As Much As the World Permits," *New York Times*, September 24, 2012; Woodward, *Obama's Wars*, 289; Gates, *Duty*, 291–92.

13. Alter, *The Promise*, 212–13.

14. Mann, *The Obamians*, 10.

15. Woodward, *Obama's Wars*, 198.

16. Ibid., 214.

17. Klaidman, *Kill or Capture*, 77.

18. Woodward, *Obama's Wars*, 138.

19. Nasr, *The Indispensable Nation*, 2.

20. Woodward, *Obama's Wars*, 159.

21. Rosa Brooks, "Obama vs. the Generals," *Politico*, November 2013.

22. Amanda Carpenter, "Gen. McChrystal Talked to Obama Once," *Washington Times*, September 28, 2009.

3. The Afghanistan Debate

1. Alter, *The Promise*, 363.

2. Woodward, *Obama's Wars*, 80.

3. Gates, *Duty*, 338.

4. Woodward, *Obama's Wars*, 96–98.

5. White House Office of the Press Secretary, "Press Briefing by Bruce Riedel, Ambassador Richard Holbrooke, and Michelle [*sic*] Flournoy on the New

Strategy for Afghanistan and Pakistan," March 27, 2009; Woodward, *Obama's Wars*, 105–9.

6. Fred Kaplan, *The Insurgents: David Petraeus and the Plot to Change the American Way of War* (New York: Simon & Schuster, 2013), 297; Woodward, *Obama's Wars*, 101–2; Alter, *The Promise*, 368.

7. Woodward, *Obama's Wars*, 104.

8. White House Office of the Press Secretary, "Remarks by the President on a New Strategy for Afghanistan and Pakistan," March 27, 2009.

9. Alter, *The Promise*, 371.

10. Gates, *Duty*, 349.

11. Woodward, *Obama's Wars*, 133–34.

12. "Generation Kill: A Conversation with Stanley McChrystal," *Foreign Affairs*, March/April 2013.

13. Gates, *Duty*, 364.

14. Woodward, *Obama's Wars*, 190.

15. Ibid., 159–60.

16. Gates, *Duty*, 364.

17. Woodward, *Obama's Wars*, 166–67.

18. Alter, *The Promise*, 376.

19. Gates, *Duty*, 378.

20. Ibid., 368–69.

21. Woodward, *Obama's Wars*, 235–36.

22. Ibid., 273–75.

23. Gates, *Duty*, 373–74.

24. Woodward, *Obama's Wars*, 251.

25. Ibid., 301–5.

26. Alter, *The Promise*, 393.

27. Ibid., 390.

28. David E. Sanger, *Confront and Conceal: Obama's Secret Wars and Surprising Use of American Power* (New York: Crown, 2012), 28.

29. Woodward, *Obama's Wars*, 329–30.

30. Ibid., 343–44.

31. Alter, *The Promise*, 373.

32. Gates, *Duty*, 384.

33. White House Office of the Press Secretary, "Remarks by the President in Address to the Nation on the Way Forward in Afghanistan and Pakistan," December 1, 2009.

34. Andrew Malcolm, "Obama's Revealing Afghanistan War Speech," *Los Angeles Times*, December 2, 2008.

35. Ken Dilanian, "Afghanistan Plan Leaves Dems Doubtful, Republicans Critical," *USA Today*, December 2, 2009.

36. Elisabeth Bumiller, "Obama Team Defends Policy on Afghanistan," *New York Times*, December 2, 2009.

37. Chip Reid, "White House: July 2011 Is Locked In for Afghanistan Withdrawal," CBS News, December 3, 2009.

4. Slashing the Budget

1. Mackenzie Eaglen and Diem Nguyen, "Super Committee Failure and Sequestration Put at Risk Ever More Military Plans and Programs," Heritage Foundation, December 5, 2011.

2. James F. Schnabel, *History of the Joint Chiefs of Staff, Volume I: The Joint Chiefs of Staff and National Policy, 1945–1947* (Washington, D.C.: Joint History Office, 1996), 99.

3. Dennis S. Ippolito, *Blunting the Sword: Budget Policy and the Future of Defense* (Washington, D.C.: National Defense University Press, 1994), 10.

4. James Kitfield, "The Risks of Military Drawdowns," *National Journal*, July 28, 2012.

5. Gates, *Duty*, 464.

6. Ibid., 547–48.

7. Thom Shanker, "Gates Warns Against Big Cuts in Military Spending," *New York Times*, May 22, 2011.

8. Fred W. Baker III, "Gates: Defense Cuts Must Be Prioritized, Strategic," American Forces Press Service, May 24, 2011.

9. Kevin Baron, "Gen. Martin Dempsey: The Quiet American," *National Journal*, February 11, 2012.

10.   Bob Woodward, *The Price of Politics* (New York: Simon & Schuster, 2012), 326–48.

11.   David Alexander, "Panetta Spells Out Budget Cut Doomsday Fears," Reuters, November 14, 2011.

12.   House Armed Services Committee, hearing on "The Future of the Military Services and Consequences of Defense Sequestration," November 2, 2011.

13.   David Alexander, "Budget Cuts Take U.S. Military 'to the Edge': Panetta," Reuters, October 13, 2011.

14.   Donna Cassata, "Panetta Details Impact of Deeper Cuts in Military," Associated Press, November 14, 2011; Alexander, "Panetta Spells Out Budget Cut Doomsday Fears."

15.   Jennifer Steinhauer, "Automatic Military Cuts May Stand in Congress," *New York Times*, November 23, 2011.

5. Lightening the Footprints

1.   White House Office of the Press Secretary, "Remarks of John O. Brennan, Assistant to the President for Homeland Security and Counterterrorism, on Ensuring al-Qa'ida's Demise," June 29, 2011.

2.   David Rohde, "The Obama Doctrine," *Foreign Policy*, March 2012.

3.   Jim Garamone, "Winnefeld Discusses Defense Strategy, Budget Link," American Forces Press Service, November 28, 2012.

4.   Bowden, *The Finish*, 262.

5.   Henry A. Crumpton, *The Art of Intelligence: Lessons from a Life in the CIA's Clandestine Service* (New York: Penguin, 2012), 261.

6.   Stephen Biddle, *Afghanistan and the Future of Warfare: Implications for Army and Defense Policy* (Carlisle, PA: Strategic Studies Institute, 2002), 27–28, 34–36, 43–49; Max Boot, *War Made New: Technology, Warfare, and the Course of History: 1500 to Today* (New York: Gotham, 2006), 371–72; Mark Clodfelter, "A Strategy Based on Faith: The Enduring Appeal of Progressive American Airpower," *Joint Force Quarterly* 49 (Spring 2008): 154.

7.   Crumpton, *The Art of Intelligence*, 259–60; Yaniv Barzilai, *102 Days of War: How Osama bin Laden, al Qaeda & the Taliban Survived 2001* (Dulles, VA: Potomac Books, 2013), 90–113.

8.   Barzilai, *102 Days of War*, 100.

9.   Kaplan, *The Insurgents*, 354–56.

10. Micah Zenko, "100% Right 0% of the Time," ForeignPolicy.com, October 16, 2012.

11. Department of Defense, "Sustaining U.S. Global Leadership: Priorities for 21st Century Defense," January 2012.

12. Department of Defense, "Defense Budget Priorities and Choices," January 2012.

13. Department of Defense, "Sustaining U.S. Global Leadership"; Department of Defense, "Defense Budget Priorities and Choices."

14. White House Office of the Press Secretary, "Remarks by the President on the Defense Strategic Review," January 5, 2012.

15. Lolita C. Baldor, "Senators Clash Over Idea of More Pentagon Cuts," Associated Press, February 28, 2012.

16. Adam Entous, "Top Military Officer: U.S. Can Stay Global Power Despite Threatened Cuts," *Wall Street Journal*, March 28, 2012.

17. Walter Pincus, "Ignoring Sequestration Won't Make It Vanish," *Washington Post*, March 12, 2012.

18. Kate Wiltrout, "End Impasse on Defense Cuts," *Norfolk Virginian-Pilot*, August 21, 2012.

19. Leon Panetta, *Worthy Fights: A Memoir of Leadership in War and Peace* (New York: Penguin, 2014), 376, 442.

20. Philip Ewing, "D.C. Caught Off Guard by Obama Sequester Vow," *Politico Pro*, October 23, 2012.

21. Bob Woodward, "Obama's Sequester Deal-Changer," *Washington Post*, February 22, 2013.

22. Zachary A. Goldfarb, "White House Pushing Tax Hikes, Spending Cuts to Avoid Sequester," *Washington Post*, February 22, 2013.

23. White House Office of the Press Secretary, Remarks by the President on the Sequester, February 19, 2013.

24. Jackie Calmes, "Fault-Finding Grows Intense as Cuts Near," *New York Times*, February 24, 2013.

25. Woodward, "Obama's Sequester Deal-Changer."

26. Scott Wilson and Philip Rucker, "Stymied by a GOP House, Obama Looks Ahead to 2014 to Cement His Legacy," *Washington Post*, March 2, 2013.

27. White House Office of the Press Secretary, Statement by the President on the Sequester, March 1, 2013.

28. Karen Parrish, "Pentagon Review Reveals Best, Worst Case, Hagel Says," *American Forces Press Service*, July 31, 2013.

29. Thom Shanker, "General Says 20,000 Troops Should Stay in Afghanistan," *New York Times*, March 6, 2013.

30. "DOD Releases Report on Estimated Sequestration Impacts," *American Forces Press Service*, April 15, 2014.

6.   Military Footprints Matter

1. CBS News, *Face the Nation*, January 14, 2007.

2. "Obama's Speech at Woodrow Wilson Center," August 1, 2007, http://www.cfr .org/elections/obamas-speech-woodrow-wilson-center/p13974.

3. Michael R. Gordon and Bernard E. Trainor, *The Endgame: The Inside Story of the Struggle for Iraq, from George W. Bush to Barack Obama* (New York: Pantheon, 2012), 532–39.

4. Ibid., 542–48.

5. Tim Arango and Michael S. Schmidt, "Despite Difficult Talks, U.S. and Iraq Had Expected Some American Troops to Stay," *New York Times*, October 21, 2011.

6. Martha Raddatz, "Iraq Withdrawal Plan May Prove Difficult," ABC News, July 11, 2008; Gordon and Trainor, *The Endgame*, 560.

7. Gordon and Trainor, *The Endgame*, 567.

8. Ibid., 566.

9. Gates, *Duty*, 325.

10. Alter, *The Promise*, 228–29.

11. Gordon and Trainor, *The Endgame*, 582–84.

12. Ibid., 607; Missy Ryan and Erin Cunningham, "U.S. Seeks to Build Lean Iraqi Force to Fight the Islamic State," *Washington Post*, November 27, 2014.

13. Richard R. Brennan Jr. et al., *Ending the U.S. War in Iraq: The Final Transition, Operational Maneuver, and Disestablishment of United States Forces–Iraq* (Santa Monica, CA: RAND Corporation, 2013), 151–52.

14. "Iraq Election Campaigning Delayed," BBC News, February 4, 2010.

15. Patrick Markey and Suadad al-Salhy, "In Syrian Shadow, Iraq's Maliki Juggles Tehran, Washington," Reuters, September 30, 2012.

16. Gordon and Trainor, *The Endgame*, 615.

17. Michael R. Gordon, "In U.S. Exit from Iraq, Failed Efforts and Challenges," *New York Times*, September 22, 2012.

18. Gordon and Trainor, *The Endgame*, 655–56.

19. Ibid., 656–58.

20. Gates, *Duty*, 553–54; Barry Malone and Peter Apps, "Troops Gone, U.S. Increasingly Sidelined in Iraq," Reuters, December 20, 2012.

21. Gordon and Trainor, *The Endgame*, 662–63.

22. Ibid., 664.

23. Dexter Filkins, "What We Left Behind," *New Yorker*, April 28, 2014; Gordon and Trainor, *Endgame*, 665–66.

24. Josh Rogin, "How the Obama Administration Bungled the Iraq Withdrawal Negotiations," *Cable*, October 21, 2011.

25. Panetta, *Worthy Fights*, 393.

26. Brennan Jr. et al., *Ending the U.S. War in Iraq*, 135; Dave Butler, "Lights Out: ARSOF Reflect on Eight Years in Iraq," *Special Warfare*, January–March 2012, 32.

27. Tim Arango, Duraid Adnan, and Yasir Ghazi, "U.S. Loses Ally as Iraqi General Waits for Trial," *New York Times*, July 27, 2011.

28. Arango and Schmidt, "Despite Difficult Talks, U.S. and Iraq Had Expected Some American Troops to Stay."

29. Dan Lamothe, "Washington Shifts, Accepts Iraqi Promise of Immunity for U.S. Military Advisers," *Washington Post*, June 23, 2014.

30. White House Office of the Press Secretary, Press Briefing by Denis McDonough, Tony Blinken, and Jay Carney, October 21, 2011.

31. Gordon and Trainor, *The Endgame*, 671.

32. CNN/ORC Poll, December 16–18, 2011, http://i2.cdn.turner.com/cnn/2011/images/12/22/rel2od.pdf.

33. Tim Arango and Michael S. Schmidt, "Despite Difficult Talks, U.S. and Iraq Had Expected Some American Troops to Stay."

34. Liz Sly, "U.S. Role Debated as Iraq Churns," *Washington Post*, April 9, 2012.

35. Hannah Allam, "Iraq Unstable, Sectarian, with Signs of Authoritarian Rule," McClatchy Newspapers, April 5, 2012.

36. Sly, "U.S. Role Debated as Iraq Churns."

37. Lara Jakes, "Court Lets Suspect in Deaths of U.S. GIs Go Free," Associated Press, August 3, 2012.

38. Kristina Wong, "Iraq Resists U.S. Prod, Lets Iran Fly Arms to Syria," *Washington Times*, March 16, 2012.

39. Josh Rogin, "U.S. Struggles with Iran for Influence in Iraq," *Cable*, March 23, 2012.

40. Michael R. Gordon, Eric Schmitt, and Tim Arango, "Flow of Arms to Syria Through Iraq Persists, to U.S. Dismay," *New York Times*, December 2, 2012.

41. Brennan Jr. et al., *Ending the War in Iraq*, 228; Office of the Special Inspector General for Iraq Reconstruction, "Iraq Police Development Program: Lack of Iraqi Support and Security Problems Raise Questions About the Continued Viability of the Program," July 31, 2012.

42. Department of Defense Inspector General, "Assessment of the Office of Security Cooperation–Iraq Mission Capabilities," September 18, 2013, 10.

43. Barry Malone and Peter Apps, "Troops Gone, U.S. Increasingly Sidelined in Iraq," Reuters, December 20, 2012.

44. Greg Miller, "CIA Is in Baghdad, Kabul for Long Haul," *Washington Post*, February 8, 2012.

45. Siobhan Gorman and Adam Entous, "CIA Prepares Iraq Pullback," *Wall Street Journal*, June 5, 2012.

46. Ibid.

47. Jack Healy, "Exodus from North Signals Iraqi Christians' Slow Decline," *New York Times*, March 11, 2012.

48. Dan Morse, "Sunnis Who Aided U.S. in Iraq Struggle to Fit In," *Washington Post*, January 29, 2012.

49. Joby Warrick, "Al-Qaeda Branch in Iraq Poses New Threat," *Washington Post*, December 3, 2012.

50. Kamal Naama and Raheem Salman, "Iraqi Sunnis Stage Big Anti-Government Rallies," Reuters, December 28, 2012.

51. Ahmed Maher, "Iraq Sunnis Threaten Army Attacks After Protest Deaths," BBC News, January 25, 2013.

52. Adam Schreck, "U.N.: 1,045 Iraqis Died in Violence Last Month," Associated Press, June 2, 2013.

53. Jabbar Yaseen and Liz Sly, "Iraq Jailbreak Highlights Al-Qaeda Affiliate's Ascendancy," *Washington Post*, July 22, 2013; Kareem Raheem and Ziad al-Sinjary, "Al Qaeda Militants Flee Iraq Jail in Violent Mass Break-Out," Reuters, July 22, 2013.

54. Eileen Sullivan, "Official: Al-Qaida in Iraq Strongest Since 2006," Associated Press, November 14, 2013.

55. ABC News, *This Week*, transcript, May 26, 2013.

56. "Iraqi Air Force Strikes City to Try to Oust al-Qaida," Reuters, January 6, 2014.

57. "Islamist Militants Strengthen Grip on Iraq's Falluja," Reuters, January 18, 2014.

58. Loveday Morris, "Iraqi Army Struggles in Battle Against Islamist Fighters in Anbar Province," *Washington Post*, February 25, 2014.

59. Richard A. Serrano, "Kerry Vows to Help Iraq Fight Militants, Says U.S. Won't Send Troops," *Los Angeles Times*, January 5, 2014.

7. COIN Can Work

1. "Fact Check: Did Obama Say the Iraq Troop 'Surge' Could Not Work?" CNN, September 26, 2008.

2. Mark Moyar, *A Question of Command: Counterinsurgency from the Civil War to Iraq* (New Haven, CT: Yale University Press, 2009).

3. Stanley McChrystal, *My Share of the Task: A Memoir* (New York: Portfolio, 2013), 105–7.

4. Ibid., 149, 161–62.

5. Ibid., 177.

6. Yochi Dreazen, "Joint Special Forces, CIA Hit Teams Are McChrystal's Legacy," *National Journal*, September 1, 2011.

7. McChrystal, *My Share of the Task*, 145.

8. Moyar, *A Question of Command*, 246–58.

9. "Generation Kill: A Conversation with Stanley McChrystal." See also William B. Ostlund, "Irregular Warfare: Counterterrorism Forces in Support of Counterinsurgency Operations," Institute of Land Warfare, Land Warfare Pa-

pers, No. 91, September 2012, http://www.ausa.org/publications/ilw/ilw_pubs /landwarfarepapers/Documents/LWP_91_web.pdf.

10. Linda Robinson, *One Hundred Victories: Special Ops and the Future of American Warfare* (New York: PublicAffairs, 2013), 12–13.

11. U.S. Department of Defense, Office of the Assistant Secretary of Defense (Public Affairs), "DoD Media Roundtable with Gen. McChrystal NATO Headquarters in Brussels," June 10, 2010.

12. Woodward, *Obama's War*, 355.

13. McChrystal, *My Share of the Task*, 363–64.

14. "DoD Media Roundtable with Gen. McChrystal NATO Headquarters in Brussels," transcript, June 10, 2010, http://www.defense.gov/transcripts /transcript.aspx?transcriptid=4640.

15. Carlotta Gall, "Afghans See Sharp Shift in U.S. Tone," *New York Times*, December 4, 2009.

16. Jerome Starkey, "Afghans May Need Western Help Up Until 2029," *Scotsman*, December 9, 2009.

17. Hastings, *The Operators*, 191, 292–93.

18. Karen DeYoung and Rajiv Chandrasekaran, "Gen. McChrystal Allies, Rolling Stone Disagree Over Article's Ground Rules," *Washington Post*, June 26, 2010.

19. Michael S. Child, "Review of Army Inspector General Agency Report of Investigation (Case 10-024)," http://www.dodig.mil/foia/ERR/ROI-508.pdf, 5.

20. "Rolling Stone Fact Checker Sent McChrystal Aide 30 Questions," *Washington Post*, June 25, 2010; http://www.washingtonpost.com/wp-dyn/content/article /2010/06/25/AR2010062504194.html?sid=ST2010062504101.

21. Gates, *Duty*, 488.

22. Ibid., 491.

23. Paula Broadwell, *All In: The Education of General David Petraeus* (New York: Penguin, 2012), 2.

24. Ibid., 54.

25. Douglas Saltmarshe and Abhilash Medhi, "Local Governance in Afghanistan: A View from the Ground," Afghanistan Research and Evaluation Unit, June 2011.

8. Half a COIN Doesn't Work

1. Gates, *Duty*, 500–501.

2. Rajiv Chandrasekaran, *Little America: The War Within the War for Afghanistan* (New York: Knopf, 2012), 326–27.

3. Chandrasekaran, *Little America*, 322.

4. Rajiv Chandrasekaran, "Afghan War Cost to Be Big Factor in Troop Drawdown," *Washington Post*, May 31, 2011.

5. Jonathan S. Landay and Hashim Shukoor, "In Valley Where SEALs Died, U.S. Raids Boost Taliban Support," McClatchy, August 7, 2011.

6. Chandrasekaran, *Little America*, 323–25.

7. Gates, *Duty*, 564.

8. Ibid., 564–65.

9. Chandrasekaran, *Little America*, 327–28.

10. White House Office of the Press Secretary, Remarks by the President on the Way Forward in Afghanistan, June 22, 2011.

11. Maria Abi-Habib, "Ethnic Leaders Forge Alliance Against Karzai," *Wall Street Journal*, June 29, 2011.

12. Rod Nordland and Alissa J. Rubin, "Taliban Captives Dispute U.S. View on Afghanistan War," *New York Times*, February 2, 2012.

13. Graham Bowley, "Afghans Fear Downturn as Foreigners Withdraw," *New York Times*, February 1, 2012.

14. Jeremy Kelly and Jerome Starkey, "Secret NATO Files Reveal Taleban Set for Return," *Times* (London), February 1, 2012.

15. Matthew Green, Geoff Dyer, and James Blitz, "Afghanistan Warns US of Pull-Out Date Fears," *Financial Times*, February 3, 2012.

16. David S. Cloud and Kathleen Hennessey, "Obama's Pakistan Gamble Fails to Pay Off," *Los Angeles Times*, May 22, 2012.

17. Aryn Baker, "On His Own," *Time*, June 11, 2012.

18. Greg Jaffe, "U.S. Promises a Long-Term Commitment to Afghanistan," *Washington Post*, April 19, 2012.

19. Dexter Filkins, "After America," *New Yorker*, July 9, 2012.

20. Kevin Sieff, "Amid Growing Fear, Another Exodus," *Washington Post*, January 31, 2013.

21. Laura King, "A Fond Farewell to Afghanistan," *Los Angeles Times*, October 23, 2012.

22. Filkins, "After America."

23. Carter Malkasian and J. Kael Weston, "How to Accomplish More with Less," *Foreign Affairs*, March 2012.

24. James M. Dubik and Jeffrey Dressler, "10,000 Troops in Afghanistan Is Not Enough," Institute for the Study of War, January 2, 2013, http://www .understandingwar.org/sites/default/files/CommandPerspectives_Developmental SupportForce.pdf.

25. Adam Entous and Julian E. Barnes, "Deeper Troop Cutback Weighed," *Wall Street Journal*, January 5, 2013.

26. Alissa J. Rubin, "In Old Taliban Strongholds, Qualms on What Lies Ahead," *New York Times*, January 9, 2013.

27. Carlotta Gall, *The Wrong Enemy: America in Afghanistan, 2001–2014* (New York: Houghton Mifflin Harcourt, 2014), 280–81.

28. Ronald E. Neumann, "A Numbers Game in Afghanistan," *Washington Post*, January 11, 2013.

29. Dion Nissenbaum and Julian E. Barnes, "Two U.S. Officials Back Higher Afghan Troop Levels," *Wall Street Journal*, March 14, 2013.

30. Thom Shanker, "General Says 20,000 Troops Should Stay in Afghanistan," *New York Times*, March 6, 2013.

31. Rod Nordland, "Study Finds Sharp Rise in Attacks by Taliban," *New York Times*, April 20, 2013.

32. Nathan Hodge and Margherita Stancati, "Afghan Army Deaths Hit Record as U.S. Exits," *Wall Street Journal*, September 21, 2013.

33. Nathan Hodge and Margherita Stancati, "Commander Cautions Against Full Afghan Pullout," *Wall Street Journal*, July 20, 2013.

34. Trudy Rubin, "On Afghan Options, Obama Floats a Big Zero," *Philadelphia Inquirer*, July 14, 2013.

35. David S. Cloud, "Insurgents Could Quickly Bounce Back in Afghanistan, Analysis Warns," *Los Angeles Times*, December 29, 2013.

36. Peter Baker and Matthew Rosenberg, "Old Tensions Resurface in Debate Over U.S. Role in Post-2014 Afghanistan," *New York Times*, February 4, 2014.

37. Ernesto Londoño, Karen DeYoung, and Greg Miller, "Afghanistan Gains Will Be Lost Quickly After Drawdown, U.S. Intelligence Estimate Warns," *Washington Post*, December 28, 2013; Cloud, "Insurgents Could Quickly Bounce Back in Afghanistan."

38. Ernesto Londoño, "U.S. Commander in Afghanistan Warns That Full Withdrawal Will Allow Al-Qaeda to Regroup," *Washington Post*, March 12, 2014.

39. Chris Carroll, "Dunford Pushes for Post-2014 US Presence in Afghanistan," *Stars and Stripes*, March 12, 2014.

40. David E. Sanger and Eric Schmitt, "Afghanistan Exit Is Seen as Peril to C.I.A. Drone Mission," *New York Times*, January 26, 2014.

41. Kimberly Dozier, "Al-Qaeda Plots Comeback in Afghanistan," Associated Press, February 28, 2014.

42. Kimberly Dozier, "CIA Falls Back in Afghanistan," *Daily Beast*, May 4, 2014.

43. David S. Cloud, "CIA's Plan to Retrench in Afghanistan Worries U.S. Military," *Los Angeles Times*, May 8, 2014.

44. Lolita C. Baldor, "U.S. Military Didn't Seek Afghan Pullout in 2017," Associated Press, July 17, 2014.

45. Matthew Rosenberg, "Amid Drawdown, Fears of Taliban Resurgence and Economic Collapse," *New York Times*, May 28, 2014.

9.   Hard Power Crosses Borders

1. Pervez Musharraf, *In the Line of Fire: A Memoir* (New York: Free Press, 2006), 201.

2. Ibid., 204–6.

3. Ibid., 201–3.

4. Daniel S. Markey, *No Exit from Pakistan: America's Tortured Relationship with Islamabad* (New York: Cambridge University Press, 2013), 126.

5. Zahid Hussain, *The Scorpion's Tail: The Relentless Rise of Islamic Militants in Pakistan—and How It Threatens America* (New York: Free Press, 2010), 206–7; Gretchen Peters, "Call the Haqqanis Terrorists," *Washington Post*, September 7, 2012; Stephen Tankel, *Storming the World Stage: The Story of Lashkar-e-Taiba* (New York: Columbia University Press, 2011).

6. Alissa J. Rubin, "Taliban Bet on Fear Over Brawn as Tactic," *New York Times*, February 27, 2011.

7. National Intelligence Estimate, "The Terrorist Threat to the U.S. Homeland," July 2007, www.c-span.org/pdf/nie_071707.pdf.

8. Crumpton, *The Art of Intelligence*, 156–60.

9. Jane Mayer, "The Predator War," *New Yorker*, October 26, 2009.

10. Nic Robertson and Greg Botelho, "Ex-Pakistani President Musharraf Admits Secret Deal with U.S. on Drone Strikes," CNN, April 12, 2013.

11. Eric Schmitt and Thom Shanker, *Counterstrike: The Untold Story of America's Secret Campaign Against Al Qaeda* (New York: Times Books, 2011), 99–103; Nasr, *Indispensable Nation*, 70.

12. Hussain, *The Scorpion's Tail*, 147.

13. Schmitt and Shanker, *Counterstrike*, 123–24.

14. Mark Tran, "Pakistan Orders Troops to Fire on US Cross-Border Raids," *Guardian*, September 16, 2008.

15. Woodward, *Obama's Wars*, 10–11.

16. Husain Haqqani, *Magnificent Delusions: Pakistan, the United States, and an Epic History of Misunderstanding* (New York: PublicAffairs, 2013), 338 –39.

17. Woodward, *Obama's Wars*, 93.

18. Klaidman, *Kill or Capture*, 122.

19. Ibid.

20. Woodward, *Obama's Wars*, 1–11.

21. Matthew M. Aid, *Intel Wars: The Secret History of the Fight Against Terror* (New York: Bloomsbury, 2012), 120–22.

22. Hussain, *The Scorpion's Tail*, 161–62.

23. Ibid., 174–80.

24. Greg Miller, "Broader Drone Tactics Sought," *Washington Post*, April 19, 2012.

25. Adam Entous, Siobhan Gorman, and Julian E. Barnes, "U.S. Tightens Drone Rules," *Wall Street Journal*, November 4, 2011.

26. Schmitt and Shanker, *Counterstrike*, 242.

27. Jane Mayer, "The Predator War," *New Yorker*, October 26, 2009.

28. David Rohde and Kristen Mulvihill, *A Rope and a Prayer: A Kidnapping from Two Sides* (New York: Viking, 2010), 326.

29. Markey, *No Exit from Pakistan*, 164.

30. Ibid., 165.

31. Adam Entous, "Drones Kill Low-Level Militants, Few Civilians," Reuters, May 3, 2010.

32. Peter Bergen and Katherine Tiedemann, "Washington's Phantom War: The Effects of the U.S. Drone Program in Pakistan," *Foreign Affairs* 90, no. 4 (July/August 2011), 12.

33. Paul Cruickshank, "The Militant Pipeline Between the Afghanistan–Pakistan Border Region and the West," New America Foundation, July 2011.

34. Declan Walsh, "Mysterious 'Chip' Is CIA's Latest Weapon Against Al-Qaida Targets Hiding in Pakistan's Tribal Belt," *Guardian*, May 31, 2009.

35. Declan Walsh, "Drone War Spurs Militants to Deadly Reprisals," *New York Times*, December 30, 2012.

36. Ibid.

37. Craig Whitlock and Barton Gellman, "U.S. Documents Detail Al-Qaeda's Efforts to Fight Back Against Drones," *Washington Post*, September 3, 2013.

38. Schmitt and Shanker, *Counterstrike*, 121; Pir Zubair Shah and Carlotta Gall, "For Pakistan, Deep Ties to Militant Network May Trump U.S. Pressure," *New York Times*, November 1, 2011.

39. Declan Walsh and Eric Schmitt, "Militant Group Poses Risk to U.S.-Pakistan Relations," *New York Times*, July 31, 2012.

40. "Taliban Chief Hides in Pakistan," *Washington Times*, November 20, 2009.

41. Zia Ur Rehman, "The Pakistani Taliban's Karachi Network," *CTC Sentinel* 6, no. 5 (May 2013), 1–5.

42. Zia Ur Rehman, "Taliban Recruiting and Fundraising in Karachi," *CTC Sentinel* 5, no. 7 (July 2012), 9–11.

43. Tom Hussain, "U.S. Pullback in Lahore Another Sign of Growing Al Qaida Violence in Pakistan," McClatchy, August 9, 2013.

44. Declan Walsh, "Pakistani Militant, Price On Head, Lives in Open," *New York Times*, February 7, 2013; Riedel, *Avoiding Armageddon*, 175–76.

45. Woodward, *Obama's Wars*, 284–87.

46. Peter Bergen and Katherine Tiedemann, "Washington's Phantom War: The Effects of the U.S. Drone Program in Pakistan," *Foreign Affairs* 90, no. 4 (July/August 2011), 12–18.

47. Woodward, *Obama's Wars*, 363–66.

48. Haqqani, *Magnificent Delusions*, 341–43.

49. Woodward, *Obama's Wars*, 367.

50. Julian E. Barnes and Adam Entous, "U.S. Seeks Wider CIA Role," *Wall Street Journal*, October 23, 2010.

51. Declan Walsh, "In Hiding, Bin Laden Had Four Children and Five Houses," *New York Times*, March 29, 2012.

52. Gall, *The Wrong Enemy*, 250.

53. Haqqani, *Magnificent Delusions*, 318–19; Gall, *The Wrong Enemy*, 251.

54. M. Ilyas Khan, "Bin Laden Neighbours Describe Abbottabad Compound," BBC News, May 2, 2011; Sam Greenhill, David Williams, and Imtiaz Hussain, "How a 40-Minute Raid Ended Ten Years of Defiance," *Daily Mail*, May 3, 2011; "What Was Life Like in the Bin Laden Compound?" BBC News, May 9, 2011.

55. Bowden, *The Finish*, 112–16, 248–49.

56. Ibid., 152, 165–66.

57. Peter L. Bergen, *Manhunt: The Ten-Year Search for Bin Laden from 9/11 to Abbottabad* (New York: Crown, 2012), 166–67.

58. Ibid., 175–77.

59. Klaidman, *Kill or Capture*, 235.

60. Bergen, *Manhunt*, 199.

61. Bowden, *The Finish*, 204.

62. Ibid., 164.

63. Nicholas Schmidle, "Getting Bin Laden," *New Yorker*, August 8, 2011.

64. "Osama Bin Laden Dead," May 2, 2011, http://www.whitehouse.gov/blog/2011/05/02/osama-bin-laden-dead.

65. John Hudson, "More Revisions to the Official Bin Laden Raid Story," The AtlanticWire.com, April 12, 2012.

66. Klaidman, *Kill or Capture*, 43–44; Sanger, *Confront and Conceal*, 73–74.

67. Bergen, *Manhunt*, 116.

68. Mark Landler and Helene Cooper, "Qaeda Woes Fuel Talk of Speeding Afghan Pullback," *New York Times*, June 19, 2011.

69. Mann, *The Obamians*, 314.

70. Julie Ray and Rajesh Srinivisan, "Pakistanis Criticize U.S. Action That Killed Osama Bin Laden," Gallup World, May 18, 2011.

71. Markey, *No Exit from Pakistan*, 65.

72. Chris Brummitt and Zarar Khan, "1 Year on from OBL Raid, No Answers from Pakistan," Associated Press, May 1, 2013.

73. Government Accountability Office, "Foreign Police Assistance: Defined Roles and Improved Information Sharing Could Enhance Interagency Collaboration," May 2012, 14.

74. Bergen, *Manhunt*, 248.

75. Bruce Riedel, *Avoiding Armageddon: America, India, and Pakistan to the Brink and Back* (Washington, DC: Brookings Institution Press, 2013), 169.

76. Missy Ryan and Mark Hosenball, "US Pushed Ahead with Drone Strikes Despite Pakistani Resistance," Reuters, February 22, 2012.

77. Jeffrey Goldberg and Marc Ambinder, "The Ally from Hell," *Atlantic*, December 2011.

78. Nasr, *The Dispensable Nation*, 78.

79. Jo Becker and Scott Shane, "Secret 'Kill List' Proves a Test of Obama's Principles and Will," *New York Times*, May 29, 2012.

80. Justin Elliott, "Obama Administration's Drone Death Figures Don't Add Up," *ProPublica*, June 19, 2012.

81. Adam Entous, Siobhan Gorman, and Julian E. Barnes, "U.S. Tightens Drone Rules," *Wall Street Journal*, November 4, 2011.

82. "US Incursion into Waziristan Unlikely: Pakistan," Agence France-Presse, October 19, 2011.

83. Eric Schmitt and David E. Sanger, "U.S. Seeks Aid from Pakistan in Peace Effort," *New York Times*, October 31, 2011.

84. Eric Schmitt, "U.S. Report Faults NATO Delays on Pakistan Strike," *New York Times*, December 27, 2011.

85. "Costs Soar for New Afghanistan Supply Routes," Associated Press, January 20, 2012.

86. Helene Cooper and Matthew Rosenberg, "Supply Lines Cast Shadow at NATO Meeting on Afghan War," *New York Times*, May 21, 2012.

87. Eric Schmitt, "Clinton's 'Sorry' to Pakistan Ends Barrier to NATO," *New York Times*, July 4, 2012.

88. Greg Jaffe and Greg Miller, "Cable: Pakistan Havens a Threat," *Washington Post*, February 25, 2012.

89. Bill Roggio and Alexander Mayer, "Charting the Data for US Airstrikes in Pakistan, 2004–2013," http://www.longwarjournal.org/pakistan-strikes.php.

90. "UN Expert Says Drone Use, Deadly Attacks Down in Pakistan, on the Rise in Afghanistan, Yemen," Associated Press, March 12, 2014.

91. Greg Miller, Craig Whitlock, and Barton Gellman, "Secret Files Show Rising U.S. Doubts About Pakistan," *Washington Post*, September 3, 2013.

92. Robinson, *One Hundred Victories*, 238; Craig Whitlock and Greg Miller, "Paramilitary Force Is Key for CIA," *Washington Post*, September 23, 2010.

93. Bruce Riedel, "Al Qaeda Is Back," *Daily Beast*, July 26, 2013; Kathy Gannon, "In Pakistan's Punjab Area, Militants Plan for Next Afghanistan War After Foreign Troops Leave," Associated Press, September 7, 2013.

94. Ellen Nakashima and Anne Gearan, "Al-Qaeda Leader Zawahiri Is Said to Have Ordered Terrorist Attack," *Washington Post*, August 5, 2013.

95. Ken Dilanian, "CIA Drone Strike Program in Pakistan Winding Down," Associated Press, May 29, 2014.

96. Shaukat Khattak, "Taliban Cut Hair and Beards to Flee Pakistan Army Assault," Agence France-Presse, July 6, 2014.

97. Ismail Khan and Declan Walsh, "Pakistan Claims Win Against Militants Along Afghan Border, but Enemy Slips Away," *New York Times*, July 10, 2014.

98. Bruce Riedel, "Al Qaeda's Next Comeback Could Be Afghanistan and Pakistan," *Daily Beast*, January 13, 2014.

99. Ibid.

10. Drones Are Not Enough

1. Kristina Goetz, "Muslim Who Shot Soldier in Arkansas Says He Wanted to Cause More Death," *Knoxville News Sentinel*, November 13, 2010.

2. Paul Cruickshank, "Revelations from the Underwear Bomber Trial," CNN .com, October 14, 2011.

3. Bryan Bender, "Some Radicals Make Heroes of Tsarnaev Brothers," *Boston Globe*, July 14, 2013.

4. Daniel Klaidman, "The Awlaki/Tsarnaev Connection," *Daily Beast*, April 26, 2013.

5. "Napolitano Warns Against Anti-Muslim Backlash," Associated Press, November 8, 2009.

6. Mark Mazzetti, *The Way of the Knife: The CIA, a Secret Army, and a War at the Ends of the Earth* (New York: Penguin, 2013), 232–33.

7. Ibid., 305.

8. Gregory D. Johnsen, *The Last Refuge: Yemen, Al-Qaeda, and America's War in Arabia* (New York: Norton, 2013), 264–65.

9. Greg Miller, "Increase in Drone Strikes in Yemen Raises Questions," *Washington Post*, June 3, 2012.

10. Mazzetti, *The Way of the Knife*, 307–8.

11. "The Al-Qaida Papers—Drones," http://hosted.ap.org/specials/interactives /_international/_pdfs/al-qaida-papers-drones.pdf.

12. Jose A. Rodriguez, *Hard Measures: How Aggressive CIA Actions After 9/11 Saved American Lives* (New York: Threshold Editions, 2012), 248.

13. Ibid., 252.

14. Ibid., 255–56.

15. Klaidman, *Kill or Capture*, 124–26.

16. Ibid., 127–28.

17. Ibid., 249–60.

18. Jo Becker and Scott Shane, "Secret 'Kill List' Proves a Test of Obama's Principles and Will," *New York Times*, May 29, 2012.

19. Klaidman, *Kill or Capture*, 261–63.

20. David G. Savage, "Bush Critic Is Now in Cross Hairs," *Los Angeles Times*, January 6, 2013.

21. Klaidman, *Kill or Capture*, 215–18.

22. Charlie Savage, "Secret U.S. Memo Made Legal Case to Kill a Citizen," *New York Times*, October 8, 2011; Jonathan S. Landay, "Leaked US Justification for

Drone Killings Assailed as Rewriting Definition of 'Imminent Threat,'" Mc-Clatchy, February 5, 2013; Timothy M. Phelps and David Lauter, "Secret 2010 Memo Justified US Drone Strike Killings of Americans," *Stars and Stripes*, June 23, 2014.

23. Mark Mazzetti, Charlie Savage, and Scott Shane, "How a U.S. Citizen Came to Be in America's Cross Hairs," *New York Times*, March 10, 2013.

24. Jimmy Carter, "A Cruel and Unusual Record," *New York Times*, June 25, 2012.

25. David Rohde, "The Obama Doctrine," *Foreign Policy*, March 2012.

26. Doyle McManus, "Who Reviews the U.S. 'Kill List'?" *Los Angeles Times*, February 5, 2012.

27. Ibid.

28. Mazzetti, Savage, and Shane, "How a U.S. Citizen Came to Be in America's Cross Hairs."

29. Edmund J. Hull, *High-Value Target: Countering Al Qaeda in Yemen* (Dulles, VA: Potomac Books, 2011).

30. Rukmini Callimachi, "Yemen Terror Boss Left Blueprint for Waging Jihad," Associated Press, August 9, 2013.

31. Christopher Swift, "Arc of Convergence: AQAP, Ansar al-Shari`a and the Struggle for Yemen," *CTC Sentinel* 5, no. 6 (June 2012), 4–5.

32. Callimachi, "Yemen Terror Boss Left Blueprint for Waging Jihad."

33. Johnsen, *The Last Refuge*, 276–80.

34. Klaidman, *Kill or Capture*, 253–54.

35. Ibid., 253–56.

36. Ibid., 256.

37. Mohammed Mukhashaf, "Besieged South Yemen Brigade Appeals for Help," Reuters, July 3, 2011.

38. Johnsen, *The Last Refuge*, 281–82.

39. Sudarsan Raghavan, "Militants Create Haven in Southern Yemen," *Washington Post*, December 31, 2011.

40. Kevin Baron, "Pentagon Says Yemen Not 'Outgunned' by Al-Qaida," *National Journal*, June 1, 2012.

41. Adam Entous, Siobhan Gorman, and Julian E. Barnes, "U.S. Relaxes Drone Rules," *Wall Street Journal*, April 26, 2012.

42. Greg Miller and Karen DeYoung, "Al-Qaeda Airline Bomb Plot Disrupted, U.S. Says," *Washington Post*, May 7, 2012.

43. Entous, Gorman, and Barnes, "U.S. Relaxes Drone Rules."

44. Greg Miller, "Increase in Drone Strikes in Yemen Raises Questions," *Washington Post*, June 3, 2012; Anna Mulrine, "US Sends Troops to Yemen as Al Qaeda Gains Ground," *Christian Science Monitor*, May 11, 2012.

45. Ken Dilanian and David S. Cloud, "A Deepening Role for the U.S. in Yemen," *Los Angeles Times*, May 17, 2012.

46. Miller, "Increase in Drone Strikes in Yemen Raises Questions."

47. Ibid.

48. Sudarsan Raghavan, "Drone Strikes Spur Backlash in Yemen," *Washington Post*, May 30, 2012.

49. Hull, *High-Value Target;* Johnsen, *The Last Refuge*, 264.

50. Raghavan, "Drone Strikes Spur Backlash in Yemen."

51. Ahmed Al-Haj and Aya Batrawy, "As U.S. Drone Strikes Escalate in Yemen, So Does Anger, Fear," Associated Press, May 3, 2013.

52. Sudarsan Raghavan, "Yemen Tries to Cover Up Drone Hits," *Washington Post*, December 25, 2012.

53. Adam Baron, "Family, Neighbors of Yemeni Killed by U.S. Drone Wonder Why He Wasn't Taken Alive," McClatchy, November 28, 2012.

54. Adam Baron, "U.S. Drone Strikes Increase," McClatchy, December 28, 2012.

55. Johnsen, *The Last Refuge*, 264.

56. Oren Dorell, "Is Africa Al-Qaeda's New Launch Pad?" *USA Today*, January 23, 2013.

57. Adam Baron, "Yemenis Call U.S. Drone Strikes an Overreaction to Al Qaida Threat," McClatchy, August 9, 2013.

58. Greg Miller, Anne Gearan, and Sudarsan Raghavan, "U.S. Authorized Series of Drone Strikes in Yemen," *Washington Post*, August 7, 2013.

59. Greg Miller, "Yemeni Victims of U.S. Military Drone Strike Get More than $1 Million in Compensation," *Washington Post*, August 18, 2014.

11.   Allies Are Unreliable

1.   Robert M. Perito, *Where Is the Lone Ranger When We Need Him? America's Search for a Postconflict Stability Force* (Washington, DC: U.S. Institute of Peace, 2004), 127.

2.   Julius Cavendish, "Afghan Taliban Hone Hit-and-Run Tactics, Assassination Campaign," *Christian Science Monitor*, June 10, 2010.

3.   UK MOD Afghanistan Briefing, February 16, 2010, http://www.blogs.mod.uk/afghanistan/2010/02/uk-mod-afghanistan-briefing-16-february-2010.html.

4.   Adam Entous and Julian E. Barnes, "Training Shortfall Persists," *Wall Street Journal*, December 7, 2010.

5.   Rajiv Chandrasekaran, "NATO Cites Progress in Afghanistan," *Washington Post*, March 12, 2011.

6.   Ethan Chorin, *Exit the Colonel: The Hidden History of the Libyan Revolution* (New York: PublicAffairs, 2012), 194–97.

7.   Ibid., 207–8.

8.   Jonathan Allen and Amie Parnes, *HRC: State Secrets and the Rebirth of Hillary Clinton* (New York: Crown, 2014), 216–17.

9.   Josh Rogin, "How Obama Turned on a Dime Toward War," *Foreign Policy*, March 18, 2011.

10.   Mann, *The Obamians*, 293–94.

11.   Ryan Lizza, "The Consequentialist: How the Arab Spring Remade Obama's Foreign Policy," *New Yorker*, May 2, 2011.

12.   Mann, *The Obamians*, 296.

13.   Chorin, *Exit the Colonel*, 228.

14.   Mann *The Obamians*, 297–98.

15.   Robert J. Lieber, *Power and Willpower in the American Future: Why the United States Is Not Destined to Decline* (New York: Cambridge University Press, 2012), 142.

16.   Sebastian Moffett, "NATO Underplayed Civilian Deaths in Libya: HRW," *Reuters*, May 14, 2012.

17.   Robert Gates, "The Security and Defense Agenda (Future of NATO)," June 10, 2011.

18. James Blitz, Carola Hoyos, Kathrin Hille, and Geoff Dyer, "Asia Set to Spend More on Defence than Europe, Says Top Think-Tank," *Financial Times*, March 8, 2012.

19. Anders Fogh Rasmussen, "To Keep the West Safe, We Must Join Forces," *Times* (London), May 17, 2012.

20. James Kitfield, "NATO's 'Window Dressing,'" *National Journal*, May 18, 2012.

21. J. Peter Pham, *State Collapse, Insurgency, and Counterinsurgency: Lessons from Somalia* (Carlisle, PA: Strategic Studies Institute, 2013), 14–15.

22. Sean Naylor, "The Secret War: Tense Ties Plagued Africa Ops," *Army Times*, November 28, 2011.

23. Jonathan Masters, "Al-Shabab," Council on Foreign Relations, September 23, 2013, http://www.cfr.org/somalia/al-shabab/p18650.

24. Claudia Parsons, "U.N. Peacekeeping Force for Somalia Not Viable: Ban," Reuters, November 8, 2007.

25. Secretary-General to the President of the Security Council, December 19, 2008, UN S/2008/709; Bronwyn E. Bruton and Paul D. Williams, *Counterinsurgency in Somalia: Lessons Learned from the African Union Mission in Somalia, 2007–2013* (Tampa, FL: Joint Special Operations University Press, 2014), 50.

26. UN Security Council, "Report of the Monitoring Group on Somalia Pursuant to Security Council Resolution 1853 (2008)," S/2010/91, March 10, 2010.

27. Paul D. Williams, "The African Union Mission in Somalia and Civilian Protection Challenges," *Stability: International Journal of Security & Development* 2, no. 3 (2013), 1–17.

28. James Fergusson, *The World's Most Dangerous Place: Inside the Outlaw State of Somalia* (Boston: Da Capo, 2013), 102–4.

29. Josh Kron, "American Identified as Bomber in Attack on African Union in Somalia," *New York Times*, October 30, 2011.

30. Richard Norton-Taylor, "MI5 Chief Warns of Terror Threat from Britons Trained in Somalia," *Guardian*, September 16, 2010.

31. Alexander Meleagrou-Hitchens, "Al-Shabab's Western Recruitment Strategy," *CTC Sentinel* 5, no. 1 (January 2012), 18–22.

32. Naylor, "The Secret War."

33. Jeffrey Gettleman and Eric Schmitt, "U.S. Kills Top Qaeda Militant in Southern Somalia," *New York Times*, September 14, 2009; Daniel Klaidman, "Navy SEALs: Obama's Secret Army," *Newsweek*, February 27, 2012.

34. Chris Reinolds Kozelle, "American Killed in Uganda Was Dedicated to Service," CNN, July 14, 2010.

35. Fergusson, *The World's Most Dangerous Place*, 14–15; Ken Menkhaus, "Al Shabab's Capabilities Post-Westgate," *CTC Sentinel* 7, no. 2 (February 2014), 5.

36. Jessica Hatcher, "Somalia's Young Army Recruits Face Uphill Battle for Credibility," *Guardian*, April 19, 2013.

37. Ibid.

38. Gabe Joselow, "UN Urges More Military Force to Confront al-Shabab in Somalia," Voice of America, October 7, 2013.

39. "Aid Agencies 'Paid Somalia's al-Shabab' During Famine," BBC, December 9, 2013.

40. Nicholas Kulish, Mark Mazzetti, and Eric Schmitt, "Carnage in Mall Shows Resilience of Terror Group," *New York Times*, September 23, 2013.

41. Rukmini Callimachi, "Terrorists Used New Tactic to Spare Some Muslims in Mall Attack," Associated Press, September 29, 2013.

42. Nima Elbagir, "Kenya Mall Attack: Four Accused of Having Role in Bloody Siege," CNN, November 4, 2013.

43. James Kitfield, "America's War with Shabab," *National Journal*, September 28, 2013.

44. Joselow, "UN Urges More Military Force to Confront al-Shabab in Somalia."

45. Michelle Nichols, "U.N. Security Council Approves Boost to Somalia Peacekeepers," Reuters, November 12, 2013; Peter Clottey, "Troop Surge Could End Al-Shabab Insurgency, Says AU Official," Voice of America, November 14, 2013.

46. Ken Dilanian and David S. Cloud, "U.S. Raids on Al Qaeda Operatives Show Shift Away from Drone Strikes," *Los Angeles Times*, October 6, 2013.

47. Ernesto Londoño and Scott Wilson, "U.S. Strikes Al-Shabab in Somalia and Captures Bombing Suspect in Libya," *Washington Post*, October 5, 2013; Karen DeYoung, "Heeding New Counterterror Guidelines, U.S. Forces Backed Off in Somalia Raid," *Washington Post*, October 7, 2013; Abdalle Ahmed, Spencer Ackerman, and David Smith, "How the US Raid on Al-Shabaab in Somalia Went Wrong," *Guardian*, October 9, 2013.

48. Eric Schmitt, "U.S. Advisers Sent to Help Somalia Fight the Shabab," *New York Times*, January 10, 2014.

49. ABC News, *This Week*, transcript, May 11, 2014.

12. Bigger Is Better

1. Chorin, *Exit the Colonel*, 54–55.

2. Department of State, "Accountability Review Board Report," http://www.state.gov/documents/organization/202446.pdf.

3. James Risen, Mark Mazzetti, and Michael S. Schmidt, "U.S.-Approved Arms for Libya Rebels Fell into Jihadis' Hands," *New York Times*, December 6, 2012.

4. Marwa Awad and Dina Zayed, "Gaddafi Calls On Libyans to March on Tripoli," Reuters, August 25, 2011.

5. Chorin, *Exit the Colonel*, 256–58.

6. White House Office of the Press Secretary, "Remarks by the President on the Death of Muammar Qaddafi," October 20, 2011.

7. David Rohde, "The Obama Doctrine," *Foreign Policy*, March 2012.

8. Joby Warrick, "Clinton Credited with Key Role in Success of NATO Airstrikes, Libyan Rebels," *Washington Post*, October 30, 2011.

9. "We Came, We Saw, He Died: What Hillary Clinton Told News Reporter Moments After Hearing of Gaddafi's Death," *Daily Mail*, October 21, 2011.

10. Allen and Parnes, *HRC*, 254.

11. "UN Experts Say Libyan Arms Are Fueling Conflicts," Associated Press, March 12, 2014.

12. "Libyans Not Keen on Democracy, Suggests Survey," BBC, February 15, 2012.

13. Abigail Hauslohner, "Islamists Hold Sway in Eastern Libyan City," *Washington Post*, October 27, 2012.

14. Senate Select Committee on Intelligence, "Review of the Terrorist Attacks on U.S. Facilities in Benghazi, Libya, September 11–12, 2012," January 15, 2014, http://www.intelligence.senate.gov/benghazi2014/benghazi.pdf.

15. Susan Cornwell and Mark Hosenball, "U.S. Officer Got No Reply to Requests for More Security in Benghazi," Reuters, October 9, 2012; Michael R. Gordon, "Official Tells Panel a Request for Libya Was Denied," *New York Times*, October 11, 2012.

16. Nancy A. Youssef, "Ambassador Stevens Twice Said No to Military Offers of More Security, U.S. Officials Say," McClatchy Newspapers, May 15, 2013.

17. Cornwell and Hosenball, "U.S. Officer Got No Reply to Requests for More Security in Benghazi"; Gordon, "Official Tells Panel a Request for Libya Was Denied."

18. Mark Hosenball, "New Details Emerge of Second U.S. Facility in Violent Benghazi," Reuters, October 10, 2012.

19. Department of State, "Remarks with Mexican Secretary of Foreign Relations Patricia Espinosa After Their Meeting," September 18, 2012, http://m.state.gov /md197914.htm.

20. Eric Schmitt, "Obama Vows to Fix Flaws Discovered in Benghazi Inquiry," *New York Times*, December 31, 2012.

21. Department of State, "Accountability Review Board Report," http://www.state .gov/documents/organization/202446.pdf.

22. Maggie Michael and Paul Schemm, "Libyan Witnesses Recount Organized Benghazi Attack," Associated Press, October 27, 2012.

23. Fred Burton and Samuel M. Katz, *Under Fire: The Untold Story of the Attack in Benghazi* (New York: St. Martin's Press, 2013), 102.

24. Senate Select Committee on Intelligence, "Review of the Terrorist Attacks on U.S. Facilities in Benghazi."

25. Burton and Katz, *Under Fire*, 112–13; Mitchell Zuckoff, *Thirteen Hours: The Inside Account of What Really Happened in Benghazi* (New York: Twelve, 2014), 86–87.

26. Anne Gearan, "Benghazi Attack May Cloud Clinton's Legacy," *Washington Post*, October 9, 2012; Michael R. Gordon, "Official Tells Panel a Request for Libya Was Denied," *New York Times*, October 11, 2012; Jamie Dettmer, Christopher Dickey, and Eli Lake, "The Truth Behind the Benghazi Attack," *Newsweek*, October 29, 2012; Jamie Dettmer, "Was Benghazi Attack on U.S. Consulate an Inside Job?" *Newsweek*, November 5, 2012; Department of State, "Accountability Review Board Report," http://www.state.gov/documents/organization/202446.pdf.

27. Greg Miller and Julie Tate, "CIA's Global Response Staff Emerging from Shadows After Incidents in Libya and Pakistan," *Washington Post*, December 26, 2012.

28. Zuckoff, *Thirteen Hours*, 97–99.

29. Ibid., 110–11.

30. Kimberly Dozier, "CIA Benghazi Team Clash Led to 'Stand Down' Report," Associated Press, December 14, 2013; Zuckoff, *Thirteen Hours*, 111.

31. Zuckoff, *Thirteen Hours*, 292.

32. Senate Select Committee on Intelligence, "Review of the Terrorist Attacks on U.S. Facilities in Benghazi."

33. Hosenball, "New Details Emerge of Second U.S. Facility in Violent Benghazi"; Dettmer, Dickey, and Lake, "The Truth Behind the Benghazi Attack"; Greg Miller, "CIA Rushed to Save Diplomats as Libya Attack Was Underway," *Washington Post*, November 1, 2012; David Ignatius, "In Benghazi Timeline, CIA Errors but No Evidence of Conspiracy," *Washington Post*, November 1, 2012; Burton and Katz, *Under Fire*, 185–201.

34. Burton and Katz, *Under Fire*, 218.

35. David D. Kirkpatrick, "A Deadly Mix in Benghazi," *New York Times*, December 28, 2013.

36. Dettmer, Dickey, and Lake, "The Truth Behind the Benghazi Attack"; Burton and Katz, *Under Fire*, 233–37; Department of State, "Accountability Review Board Report," http://www.state.gov/documents/organization/202446.pdf.

37. Miller, "CIA Rushed to Save Diplomats as Libya Attack was Underway"; Ignatius, "In Benghazi Timeline, CIA Errors but No Evidence of Conspiracy"; Senate Select Committee on Intelligence, "Review of the Terrorist Attacks on U.S. Facilities in Benghazi"; Burton and Katz, *Under Fire*, 243–45.

38. Zuckoff, *Thirteen Hours8* 269.

39. Elisabeth Bumiller, "Panetta Says Risk Impeded Deployment to Benghazi," *New York Times*, October 26, 2012; Ernesto Londoño, "Pentagon Releases Benghazi Timeline," *Washington Post*, November 10, 2012; Senate Select Committee on Intelligence, "Review of the Terrorist Attacks on U.S. Facilities in Benghazi."

40. Oren Dorell, "Benghazi: So Many Questions Remain," *USA Today*, February 8, 2013.

41. Donna Cassata and Richard Lardner, "Military Looks to Place Quick Reaction Forces After Libya Attack," Associated Press, February 7, 2013.

42. Headquarters Marine Corps, "Marines Rescue Downed Pilot After Fighter Jet Crashes in Libya," March 22, 2011, http://www.hqmc.marines.mil/News/NewsArticleDisplay/tabid/3488/Article/78878/marines-rescue-downed-pilot-after-fighter-jet-crashes-in-libya.aspx; United States Air Force Aircraft

Accident Investigation Board Report, F-15e Strike Eagle, T/N 91-000304, http://usaf.aib.law.af.mil/ExecSum2011/F-15E_Libya_21%20Mar%2011.pdf.

43. Mark Helprin, "Benghazi's Portent and the Decline of U.S. Military Strength," *Wall Street Journal*, April 10, 2013.

44. White House Office of the Press Secretary, Remarks by the President at the Democratic National Convention, September 7, 2012.

45. Mark Hosenball and Tabassum Zakaria, "U.S. Had Early Indications Libya Attack Tied to Organized Militants," Reuters, October 2, 2012; Adam Entous, Carol E. Lee, Siobhan Gorman, and Evan Perez, "Discord Skewed Benghazi Response," *Wall Street Journal*, October 6, 2012; Guy Taylor, "They Knew: Ex-CIA Official Gives Stunning Account on Benghazi," *Washington Times*, April 2, 2014.

46. Siobhan Gorman and Adam Entous, "Bureaucratic Battle Blunted Libya Attack 'Talking Points,'" *Wall Street Journal*, December 4, 2012.

47. Glenn Thrush, "Why Hillary Clinton Didn't Do Sunday Shows After Benghazi," *Politico*, May 13, 2013.

48. "Officials Removed Terror Reference from Benghazi Memo—Report," BBC, May 10, 2013.

49. Scott Wilson and Karen DeYoung, "Petraeus at Heart of Benghazi Dispute," *Washington Post*, May 22, 2013.

50. Allen and Parnes, *HRC*, 305.

51. http://www.judicialwatch.org/wp-content/uploads/2014/04/1919_production -4-17-14.pdf.

52. House Select Committee on Intelligence, "Investigative Report on the Terrorist Attacks on U.S. Facilities in Benghazi, Libya, September 11–12, 2012," November 21, 2014, http://intelligence.house.gov/sites/intelligence.house.gov /files/documents/Benghazi%20Report.pdf, 26.

53. Oren Dorell, "Sen. Graham: CIA Deputy Misled On Benghazi Memo," *USA Today*, February 27, 2014; Stephen F. Hayes, "Lawmakers: CIA #2 Lied to Us About Benghazi," *Weekly Standard*, February 20, 2014; Michael Morell, Written Statement for the Record, House Permanent Select Committee on Intelligence, April 2014, http://intelligence.house.gov/sites/intelligence.house.gov /files/documents/MorellSFR04022014.pdf, 13–21.

54. David Martosko, "Former Deputy CIA Director Denies Being Part of Politically Driven Benghazi Cover-Up as His Ties to Hillary Clinton Are Revealed," *Daily Mail*, April 2, 2014.

55. David Ignatius, "The CIA's Talking Points on Benghazi," *Washington Post*, October 20, 2012.

56. Chris Wallace, "Amb. Susan Rice, Rep. Mike Rogers Discuss Violence Against Americans in the Middle East," foxnews.com, September 16, 2012.

57. Greg Miller, "Attack on U.S. Consulate in Libya Determined to Be Terrorism Tied to Al-Qaeda," *Washington Post*, September 28, 2012; David D. Kirkpatrick, "A Deadly Mix in Benghazi," *New York Times*, December 28, 2013.

58. Senate Select Committee on Intelligence, "Review of the Terrorist Attacks on U.S. Facilities in Benghazi." The Jamal Network was run by a former lieutenant of Ayman al-Zawahiri, the current Al Qaeda chief. Eli Lake, "Yes, There IS Evidence Linking al Qaeda to Benghazi," *Daily Beast*, December 29, 2013.

59. Eric Schmitt, Helene Cooper, and Michael S. Schmidt, "Deadly Attack on Libya Was Major Blow to C.I.A. Efforts," *New York Times*, September 24, 2012.

60. Kimberly Dozier, "U.S. Focuses on Five Men in Libya Assault," Associated Press, May 22, 2013.

61. Michael Birnbaum and Anne Gearan, "Libyans Say Few Questions Being Asked About Attack," *Washington Post*, October 2, 2012; Michael Birnbaum, "Sensitive Documents Left Behind at American Mission in Libya," *Washington Post*, October 3, 2012.

62. Elisabeth Bumiller and Michael S. Schmidt, "F.B.I. Agents Scour Ruins of Attacked U.S. Diplomatic Compound in Libya," *New York Times*, October 5, 2012.

63. David D. Kirkpatrick, "Suspect in Libya Attack, in Plain Sight, Scoffs at U.S.," *New York Times*, October 19, 2012.

64. Michael Birnbaum and Craig Whitlock, "Attack on U.S. Mission in Libya Presents Legal, Policy Dilemma for Obama Administration," *Washington Post*, October 8, 2012.

65. Abigail Hauslohner, "Islamists Hold Sway in Eastern Libyan City," *Washington Post*, October 27, 2012.

66. Kimberly Dozier, "U.S. Focuses on Five Men in Libya Assault," Associated Press, May 22, 2013.

67. Michael S. Schmidt and Eric Schmitt, "Libya Thwarts Arrests in Benghazi Attack," *New York Times*, September 10, 2013.

68. Carlotta Gall and David D. Kirkpatrick, "Libya Condemns U.S. for Seizing Terror Suspect," *New York Times*, October 6, 2013; Michael S. Schmidt and Eric Schmitt, "U.S. Officials Say Libya Approved Commando Raids," *New York*

Times, October 9, 2013; Adam Goldman and Sari Horwitz, "U.S. Efforts Stall in Capturing Suspects in 2012 Benghazi Attacks, Officials Say," *Washington Post*, December 5, 2013.

69. Patrick Cockburn, "Special Report: We All Thought Libya Had Moved On," *Independent*, September 3, 2013.

70. Missy Ryan and Arshad Mohammed, "As Libya Teeters Near Chaos, U.S. Keeps Hands-Off Policy," Reuters, June 24, 2014; John Vandiver, "AF-RICOM Postpones Training Libyan Troops," *Stars and Stripes*, August 28, 2014.

71. Eli Lake, "So Many Jihadists Are Flocking to Libya, It's Becoming 'Scumbag Woodstock,'" *Daily Beast*, May 6, 2014.

72. Eli Lake, "Jihadists Now Control Secretive U.S. Base in Libya," *Daily Beast*, April 23, 2014.

73. State Department Daily Press Briefing, August 26, 2014.

74. Christopher S. Chivvis, Keith Crane, Peter Mandaville, and Jeffrey Martini, "Libya's Post-Qaddafi Transition: The Nation-Building Challenge," RAND Corporation, October 22, 2012.

13. Not So Smart Power

1. Micah Zenko and Michael A. Cohen, "Clear and Present Safety," *Foreign Affairs*, March/April 2012.

2. "Compelled Iraq Duty Angers U.S. Envoys," Associated Press, November 1, 2007.

3. Paul Richter, "Diplomats Won't Be Forced to Go to Iraq, for Now," *Los Angeles Times*, November 14, 2007.

4. Chandrasekaran, *Little America*, 108.

5. Committee on Foreign Relations, United States Senate, "Evaluating U.S. Foreign Assistance to Afghanistan," S. Prt. 112–21, 112th Congress, First Session, June 8, 2011, 6–8.

6. Chandrasekaran, *Little America*, 308.

7. Haqqani, *Magnificent Delusions*, 343.

8. Hassan Abbas and Shehzad H. Qazi, "Rebellion, Development and Security in Pakistan's Tribal Areas," *CTC Sentinel* 6, no. 6 (June 2013), 23–26.

9. Joint Prepared Statement of Ambassador Jeffrey D. Feltman, Assistant Secretary of State for Near Eastern Affairs, and Ambassador Daniel Benjamin, Coordi-

nator for Counterterrorism, Department of State, February 3, 2010, http://www .gpo.gov/fdsys/pkg/CHRG-111shrg62357/html/CHRG-111shrg62357.htm.

10. Karen DeYoung, "Yemen Airstrikes Part of Broad Strategy to Curb Al-Qaeda, Obama Adviser Says," *Washington Post*, August 8, 2012.

11. Government Accountability Office, "Uncertain Political and Security Situation Challenges U.S. Efforts to Implement a Comprehensive Strategy in Yemen," February 2012, 4.

12. Johnnie Carson, "Opening Remarks for Hearing on Counterterrorism in Africa (Sahel Region)," Testimony Before the Senate Committee on Foreign Relations, Subcommittee on Africa, November 17, 2009, http://www.state.gov/p/af /rls/rm/2009/132062.htm.

13. Mali Fiscal Year 2011 Disbursements, foreignassistance.gov, http://foreign assistance.gov/OU.aspx?OUID=209&FY=2011&AgencyID=0&budTab=tab _Bud_Spent&tabID=tab_sct_Peace_Disbs; U.S. Department of State, "International Military Education and Training Account Summary," http://www.state .gov/t/pm/ppa/sat/c14562.htm; U.S. Department of State, Foreign Military Financing Account Summary, http://www.state.gov/t/pm/ppa/sat/c14560.htm; Millennium Challenge Corporation, "Quarterly Status Report, Mali Compact," March 2012, http://www.mcc.gov/documents/reports/qsr-2012002103102 -mali.pdf.

14. USAID, Mali Overview, http://www1.usaid.gov/locations/sub-saharan_africa /countries/mali/.

15. Earl Gast, "Mali: Current Threats to Development Gains and the Way Forward," Testimony Before the Senate Committee on Foreign Relations Subcommittee on African Affairs, December 5, 2012, http://www.state.gov/r/pa/usaid /201589.htm.

16. Modibo Goita, "West Africa's Growing Terrorist Threat: Confronting AQIM's Sahelian Strategy," Africa Center for Strategic Studies, February 2011; "Mali Report Claims CFA 112 Billion Lost to Mismanagement in 2009," African Press Agency, August 4, 2010.

17. David Pugliese, "African Special Forces Improve but Lack Gear," *Defense News*, March 14, 2011, 22. See also United Nations Security Council Report S /2012/894, "Report of the Secretary-General on the Situation in Mali," November 29, 2012, 4.

18. U.S. Senate Committee on Foreign Relations, Subcommittee on African Affairs, "Assessing Developments in Mali: Restoring Democracy and Reclaiming the North," December 5, 2012, http://www.foreign.senate.gov/hearings

/assessing-developments-in-mali-restoring-democracy-and-reclaiming-the
-north.

19. Stew Magnuson, "Mali Crisis Officer Lessons for Special Operations Command," *National Defense*, May 2013.

20. Simon J. Powelson, "Enduring Engagement Yes, Episodic Engagement No: Lessons for SOF from Mali," Master's Thesis, Naval Postgraduate School, December 2013, 29–30.

21. Ahmed Mohamed, "Christopher Leggett Death: Al Qaida Says It Killed American in Mauritania For Proselytizing," Associated Press, June 25, 2009.

22. Alexis Arieff and Kelly Johnson, "Crisis in Mali," Congressional Research Service, August 16, 2012, 15.

23. Rukmini Callimachi, "Does Al-Qaeda Have Feared Weapon?" Associated Press, June 11, 2013.

24. Testimony of Ambassador Johnnie Carson, "The Tuareg Revolt and the Mali Coup," House Foreign Affairs Committee Subcommittee on African Affairs, June 29, 2012.

25. Andrew Lebovich, "The Local Face of Jihadism in Northern Mali," *CTC Sentinel* 6, no. 6 (June 2013), 4–10; International Crisis Group, "Mali: Security, Dialogue and Meaningful Reform," April 11, 2013, 22–23.

26. Steven Lee Myers, "Clinton Suggests Link to Qaeda Offshoot in Deadly Libya Attack," *New York Times*, September 26, 2012.

27. Nina Munk, *The Idealist: Jeffrey Sachs and the Quest to End Poverty* (New York: Doubleday, 2013), 225.

28. Eric Schmitt, "American Commander Details Al Qaeda's Strength in Mali," *New York Times*, December 4, 2012; Bruce Crumley, "Mali's Crisis: Is the Plan for Western Intervention 'Crap'?" *Time*, December 18, 2012; "Insight: Islamist Inroads in Mali May Undo French War on Al Qaeda," Reuters, March 13, 2013.

29. Alexis Arieff, "Crisis in Mali," Congressional Research Service, January 14, 2013, 2.

30. "Official: Mali Islamists Closer to Gov't Areas," Associated Press, January 7, 2013; United Nations Security Council Report S/2013/189, "Report of the Secretary-General on the Situation in Mali," March 26, 2013, 1.

31. Mark Hosenball and Tabassum Zakaria, "French Urgency, U.S. Caution Collide in Mali Operation," Reuters, January 26, 2013; Edward Cody, "France's Hollande Intervenes in Mali," *Washington Post*, January 12, 2013.

32. Anne Applebaum, "A New Cop on the Beat?" *Washington Post*, January 25, 2013; "Why France Can't Fight," *Wall Street Journal*, January 28, 2013.

33. Anne Gearan, Karen DeYoung, and Craig Whitlock, "U.S. Weighs Military Aid for France in Mali," *Washington Post*, January 16, 2013; Applebaum, "A New Cop on the Beat?"; Adam Entous, "U.S. Agrees to Support French in Mali with Plane Refueling," *Wall Street Journal*, January 27, 2013.

34. Adam Entous and Julian E. Barnes, "Mali Exposes Flaws in West's Security Plans," *Wall Street Journal*, January 24, 2013.

35. Elisabeth Bumiller, "Leon Panetta Says U.S. Has Pledged to Help France in Mali," *New York Times*, January 14, 2013.

36. Entous and Barnes, "Mali Exposes Flaws in West's Security Plans."

37. David S. Cloud, Shashank Bengali, and Ken Dilanian, "Mali Conflict Exposes White House–Pentagon Split," *Los Angeles Times*, January 19, 2013.

38. International Crisis Group, "Mali: Security, Dialogue and Meaningful Reform," April 11, 2013, 6–7.

39. Jim Michaels, "USA Should Do More to Help France in Mali, Says House Chairman," *USA Today*, January 15, 2013.

40. Joby Warrick, "Al-Qaeda Branch's Image Soars After Hostage Drama in Algeria," January 20, 2013; Adam Nossiter and Eric Schmitt, "Algeria Defends Tough Response to Hostage Crisis as Toll Rises," *New York Times*, January 22, 2013.

41. Adam Nossiter and Alan Cowell, "Hostages Dead in Bloody Climax to Siege in Algeria," *New York Times*, January 20, 2013.

42. Michael Birnbaum and Anthony Faiola, "Algerian Leader Ties 2 Canadians to Hostage Crisis," *Washington Post*, January 22, 2013.

43. Hearing, Committee on Foreign Affairs, House of Representatives, "The Crisis in Mali: U.S. Interests and the International Response," 113th Cong., 1st Sess., February 14, 2013.

44. Hosenball and Zakaria, "French Urgency, U.S. Caution Collide in Mali Operation."

45. "U.S., Africa Say Mali Action Counters Growing Islamist Threat," Reuters, January 23, 2013.

46. United Nations Security Council Report S/2013/189, "Report of the Secretary-General on the Situation in Mali," March 26, 2013, 8.

47. Joseph Bamat, "US Slams African Force as French Begin Mali Pullout," Agence France-Presse, April 9, 2013.

48.　"Mali Dismisses Candidates for Fraud in Elections," Reuters, January 1, 2014.

49.　Afua Hirsch, "Mali's Fight with Militants Is Far from Over in Gao," *Guardian*, October 17, 2013.

50.　http://www.justice.gov/dea/programs/money.htm.

51.　"Remarks by President Obama and President Chinchilla of Costa Rica in a Joint Press Conference," May 3, 2013, http://www.whitehouse.gov/photos -and-video/video/2013/05/03/president-obama-holds-press-conference -president-chinchilla#transcript.

52.　Robert D. Ramsey III, *From El Billar to Operations Fenix and Jaque: The Colombian Security Force Experience*, 1998–2008 (Fort Leavenworth, KS: Combat Studies Institute Press, 2009), 47–48.

53.　Daniel Sabiet, "Police Reform in Mexico: Advances and Persistent Obstacles," in Eric L. Olson, David A. Shirk, and Andrew Selee, eds., *Shared Responsibility: U.S.-Mexico Policy Options for Confronting Organized Crime* (Washington, DC: Woodrow Wilson Center, 2010), 254; Marcos Pablo Moloeznik, "The Militarization of Public Security and the Role of the Military in Mexico," in Robert A. Donnelly and David A. Shirk, eds., *Police and Public Security in Mexico* (San Diego: University Readers, 2010), 80.

54.　Sylvia Longmire, *Cartel: The Coming Invasion of Mexico's Drug Wars* (New York: Palgrave Macmillan, 2011), 179.

55.　Richard Wike, "Mexicans Continue Support for Drug War," Pew Global Attitudes Project, August 12, 2010.

56.　Roderic Ai Camp, "Armed Forces and Drugs: Public Perceptions and Institutional Challenges," in Olson et al., eds., *Shared Responsibility*, 306.

57.　"Peace Corps Reviews Operations in Honduras," December 21, 2011, http:// www.peacecorps.gov/index.cfm?shell=resources.media.press.view&news_id =1932.

58.　Evan Munsing and Christopher J. Lamb, *Joint Interagency Task Force–South: The Best Known, Least Understood Interagency Success* (Washington, DC: National Defense University Press, 2011), 87.

59.　Dianna Cahn, "Budget Cuts Force Navy out of Anti-Drug Operation," *Norfolk Virginian-Pilot*, March 6, 2013.

60.　Kristina Wong, "Commanders Say Defense Cuts Have Helped Drug Trafficking," *Hill*, February 26, 2014; Munsing and Lamb, *Joint Interagency Task Force–South*, 3.

61. Ernesto Londoño, "Head of Southern Command Says He Lacks Resources to Fight Drug Trafficking," *Washington Post*, March 13, 2014; Lolita C. Baldor, "Military: 80 Percent of Colombian Drugs Gets to US," Associated Press, March 13, 2014.

14. Dangerous Nations

1. Greg Jaffe, "Hauling Out the 'Goofy Meat Ax,'" *Washington Post*, February 23, 2012; Zenko and Cohen, "Clear and Present Safety."

2. Micah Zenko, "100% Right 0% of the Time," ForeignPolicy.com, October 16, 2012.

3. Jim Zanotti et al., "Israel: Possible Military Strike Against Iran's Nuclear Facilities," Congressional Research Service, September 28, 2012, 17.

4. Joe Sterling, "Obama Says He's Not Bluffing on Iran Nukes," CNN, March 3, 2012.

5. Michael O'Hanlon, "Deterrence," in Jon B. Alterman, ed., *Gulf Kaleidoscope: Reflections on the Iranian Challenge* (Washington, DC: Center for Strategic and International Studies, 2012), 32–45; Thomas Donnelly, Danielle Pletka, and Maseh Zarif, "Containing and Deterring a Nuclear Iran: Questions for Strategy, Requirements for Military Forces," American Enterprise Institute, May 2011.

6. Joby Warrick, "Obama's Record: Confronting Iran's Nuclear Advance," *Washington Post*, September 25, 2012.

7. Jeremy Page, "For Xi, a 'China Dream' of Military Power," *Wall Street Journal*, March 13, 2013.

8. Shannon Tiezzi, "Chinese Strategists Reflect on the First Sino-Japanese War," *Huffington Post*, April 21, 2014.

9. Page, "For Xi, a 'China Dream' of Military Power."

10. "China Defence Budget to Double Over 5 Years: IHS," Agence France-Presse, February 14, 2012.

11. Stuart Grudgings, "As Obama's Asia 'Pivot' Falters, China Steps into the Gap," Reuters, October 6, 2013.

12. Quadrennial Defense Review Independent Panel, "The QDR in Perspective: Meeting America's National Security Needs in the 21st Century," U.S. Institute of Peace, 2010, http://www.usip.org/sites/default/files/qdr/qdrreport.pdf.

13. Craig Whitlock, "Asia Plans Give Navy Key Role, Fewer Ships," *Washington Post*, February 16, 2012.

14. Statement of Admiral Jonathan Greenert, U.S. Navy, Chief of Naval Operations, Before the Senate Armed Services Committee on the Impact of Sequestration on the National Defense, November 7, 2013, http://www.armed-services .senate.gov/imo/media/doc/Greenert_11-07-13.pdf.

15. Yuka Hayashi and Patrick Barta, "Pentagon Cuts Feared Tripping Up Pivot to Asia," *Wall Street Journal*, May 4, 2013.

16. Richard Sisk, "Official Backpedals on Pacific Pivot 'Can't Happen,'" *DoD Buzz*, March 4, 2014.

17. Doug Cameron, "Pentagon Insists Pacific 'Pivot' Plan Intact," *Wall Street Journal*, March 4, 2014.

18. Grudgings, "As Obama's Asia 'Pivot' Falters, China Steps into the Gap."

19. David S. Cloud and Mark Magnier, "India Not Sold on Closer Military Ties with U.S.," *Los Angeles Times*, June 7, 2012.

20. Ely Ratner, "Learning the Lessons of Scarborough Reef," *National Interest*, November 21, 2013.

21. Otto Kreisher, "China's Carrier Killer: Threat and Theatrics," *Air Force Magazine* 96, no. 12 (December 2013).

22. Michael O'Hanlon, *The Wounded Giant: America's Armed Forces in an Age of Austerity* (New York: Penguin, 2011), 177–78.

23. Lizzie Parry, "Now Kim Jong-Un Executes His Late Uncle's Entire Family to Prevent 'Mutiny,'" *Daily Mail*, January 26, 2014.

24. Bruce E. Bechtol Jr., "Planning for the Future: Conditions of Combined ROK-U.S. Military Intervention in Potential DPRK Contingencies," *Korean Journal of Defense Analysis* 24, no. 4 (December 2012), 489–502.

25. Chris Carroll, "Experts: If N. Korea Falls, US Must Be Prepared to Fill Void," *Stars and Stripes*, October 20, 2013; Bruce W. Bennett, *Preparing for the Possibility of a North Korean Collapse* (Santa Monica, CA: RAND Corporation, 2013).

26. Sanger and Schmitt, "Afghanistan Exit Is Seen as Peril to C.I.A. Drone Mission."

27. Barbara Starr, "Military: Thousands of Troops Needed to Secure Syrian Chemical Sites," CNN, February 22, 2012.

28. Craig Whitlock, "Pentagon Leaders Favored Arming Syrian Opposition," *Washington Post*, February 8, 2013.

29. White House Office of the Press Secretary, Statement by the President on Syria, February 4, 2012.

30. Karen DeYoung, "Assad's Forces Have 'Momentum,' U.S. General Says," *Washington Post*, March 7, 2012.

31. Neil MacFarquhar and Hwaida Saad, "As Syrian War Drags On, Jihadists Take Bigger Role," *New York Times*, July 30, 2012.

32. C. J. Chivers, "Syrian Rebels Say Inaction May Cost West an Ally," *International Herald Tribune*, October 5, 2012.

33. David E. Sanger, "Rebel Arms Flow Is Said to Benefit Jihadists In Syria," *New York Times*, October 15, 2012.

34. Robert F. Worth, "Citing U.S. Fears, Arab Allies Limit Syrian Rebel Aid," *New York Times*, October 7, 2012.

35. Adam Entous, Siobhan Gorman, and Nour Malas, "CIA Expands Role in Syria Fight," *Wall Street Journal*, March 23, 2013; Ahmed Wali Mujeeb, "Pakistan Taliban 'Sets Up a Base in Syria,'" BBC, July 12, 2013; Zarar Khan and Sebastian Abbot, "Islamic Militants Leave Pakistan to Fight in Syria," Associated Press, July 14, 2013.

36. Nour Malas, "Al Qaeda Declares Stake in Syrian Rebellion," *Wall Street Journal*, April 10, 2013.

37. Richard Spencer, "Al-Qaeda Seizes Syrian Oilfields," *Sunday Telegraph* (London), May 19, 2013.

38. Siobhan Gorman, "CIA Official Warns Syria Is Top Threat to U.S. Security," *Wall Street Journal*, August 7, 2013.

39. Eric Schmitt, "Worries Mount as Syria Lures West's Muslims," *New York Times*, July 28, 2013.

40. Peter Baker, "Heavy Pressure Led to Decision by Obama on Syrian Arms," *New York Times*, June 15, 2013.

41. Tim Lister, "What Justifies Intervening If Syria Uses Chemical Weapons?" CNN, August 28, 2013.

42. John Bresnahan, Seung Min Kim, and Jonathan Allen, "John Kerry to Democrats: 'Munich Moment,'" *Politico*, September 2, 2013.

43. Adam Entous, Janet Hook, and Carol E. Lee, "Inside White House, a Reversal on Syrian Arms," *Wall Street Journal*, September 16, 2013.

44. Ibid.

45. Steve Holland and Matt Spetalnick, "Obama: U.S. Credibility on the Line in Syria Response," Reuters, September 4, 2013.

46. Glenn Kessler, "President Obama and the 'Red Line' on Syria's Chemical Weapons," *Washington Post*, September 6, 2013.

47. Peter Baker and Steven Lee Myers, "As Obama Pauses Action, Putin Takes Center Stage," *New York Times*, September 12, 2013.

48. Entous, Hook, and Lee, "Inside White House, a Reversal on Syrian Arms."

49. Adam Entous, Julian E. Barnes, and Nour Malas, "Elite Syrian Unit Scatters Chemical Arms Stockpile," *Wall Street Journal*, September 13, 2013.

50. Entous, Hook, and Lee, "Inside White House, a Reversal on Syrian Arms."

51. Ben Hubbard and Michael R. Gordon, "Syrian Rebels Will Abandon Exile Leaders," *New York Times*, September 26, 2013.

52. Greg Miller, "CIA Ramping Up Covert Training Program for Moderate Syrian Rebels," *Washington Post*, October 2, 2013.

53. Spencer Ackerman, "Al-Qaida Faction in Syria Contemplating US Attack, Intelligence Officials Warn," *Guardian*, January 29, 2014.

54. Ken Dilanian, "Syria-Trained U.S. Militants Pose Threat, Officials Say," *Los Angeles Times*, February 4, 2014.

55. Eli Lake, "Al Qaeda's American Fighters Are Coming Home—and U.S. Intelligence Can't Find Them," *Daily Beast*, May 20, 2014.

56. Jamie Crawford, "Syria, al Qaeda: U.S. Officials Offer Grim Assessment," CNN, February 11, 2014.

57. Louis Charbonneau, "Suspicions of Possible Undeclared Syrian Chemical Agents Voiced at U.N.," Reuters, May 1, 2014.

58. Helene Cooper and Steven Erlanger, "Military Cuts Render NATO Less Formidable as Deterrent to Russia," *New York Times*, March 26, 2014.

59. White House Office of the Press Secretary, "Remarks by the President in Address to European Youth," March 26, 2014.

60. "Obama's Half-Measures Give Vladimir Putin Little to Fear," *Washington Post*, April 28, 2014.

61. Eli Lake, "Key General Splits with Obama Over Ukraine," *Daily Beast*, April 11, 2014.

62. Karen DeYoung and Michael Birnbaum, "U.S. Imposes New Sanctions on Russia," *Washington Post*, April 28, 2014.

63. Marcus Weisgerber, "Poland Wants Larger U.S., NATO Troop Presence," *Defense News*, April 16, 2014.

64. James G. Neuger and Patrick Donahue, "NATO to Shun Substantial Eastern Footprint in Nod to Russia," Bloomberg News, August 19, 2014.

15. Reclaiming Military Power

1. "Unmanned Vehicles: Liberating or Enslaving?" *National Defense*, February 14, 2012; Micah Zenko, "Ten Things You Didn't Know About Drones," *Foreign Policy*, March/April 2012, 62.

2. Andrew Tilghman, "DOD Quietly Expanding AFRICOM Missions," *Air Force Times*, April 16, 2014. Smaller bases sprouted in Kenya, Uganda, and Burkina Faso. Shashank Bengali, "U.S. Military Investing Heavily in Africa," *Los Angeles Times*, October 20, 2013.

3. Elisabeth Bumiller, "In His Military Farewell, Petraeus Issues a Warning on Looming Budget Cuts," *New York Times*, September 1, 2011. See also Francis G. Hoffman, "What the QDR Ought to Say About Landpower," *Parameters* 43, no. 4 (Winter 2013–14), 7–14.

4. More information on these subjects is contained in a forthcoming book by the author.

5. Warren Strobel, "U.S. Special Forces Struggle with Record Suicides," Reuters, April 17, 2014.

6. Robert H. Scales, "Too Many Wars, Too Few U.S. Soldiers," *Washington Post*, March 13, 2012.

7. Barack Obama, *The Audacity of Hope: Thoughts on Reclaiming the American Dream* (New York: Crown, 2006), 307.

8. Sydney J. Freedberg Jr., "How DoD Is Trying to Save Innovation," *Breaking Defense*, October 28, 2014.

9. Office and Management and Budget, Historical Tables, http://www.whitehouse.gov/omb/budget/Historicals/.

10. Martin Feldstein, "Defense Spending Would Be Great Stimulus," *Wall Street Journal*, December 24, 2008.

16. Rallying the Public

1. Scott Wilson and Jon Cohen, "Afghan War Isn't Worth Fighting, Most in U.S. Say," *Washington Post*, March 15, 2011.

2. "Fighting a War Half-Heartedly," *Washington Post*, March 14, 2012.

3. Andrew deGrandpre, "Gen. John Kelly's Mission to Defend Marines," *Marine Corps Times*, May 25, 2014.

Epilogue

1. Loveday Morris and Liz Sly, "Insurgents in Northern Iraq Seize Key Cities, Advance Toward Baghdad," *Washington Post*, June 12, 2014.

2. Hamza Hendawi and Bassem Mroue, "Fear, Sectarianism Behind Iraq Army Collapse," Associated Press, June 12, 2014.

3. Suadad Al-Salhy and Tim Arango, "Sunni Militants Drive Iraqi Army Out of Mosul," *New York Times*, June 10, 2014; Alissa J. Rubin and Michael R. Gordon, "Iraq's Military Seen as Unlikely to Turn the Tide," *New York Times*, June 22, 2014; Michael Knights, "ISIL's Political-Military Power in Iraq," *CTC Sentinel* 7, no. 8 (August 2014), 1–7.

4. Michael Knights, "Iraq's Dire Situation," Washington Institute, June 17, 2014, http://www.washingtoninstitute.org/policy-analysis/view/iraqs-dire-situation.

5. Eric Schmitt and Michael R. Gordon, "The Iraqi Army Was Crumbling Long Before Its Collapse, U.S. Officials Say," *New York Times*, June 12, 2014.

6. "U.S. Focus Is on Boosting Iraqi Forces, Not Air Strikes," Reuters, June 11, 2014.

7. Ken Dilanian and Julie Pace, "CIA Facing Gaps in Iraq as It Hunts for Militants," Associated Press, June 18, 2014.

8. Janine Davidson, "ISIS Hasn't Gone Anywhere—and It's Getting Stronger," Council on Foreign Relations, July 24, 2014, http://blogs.cfr.org/davidson/2014/07/24/isis-hasnt-gone-anywhere-and-its-getting-stronger/.

9. Dana Ford, "Eric Holder: 'We Are at a Dangerous Time,'" CNN, July 14, 2014.

10. Leo Shane III, "Obama to Send up to 300 Military Advisers to Iraq," *Hill*, June 19, 2014.

11. John T. Bennett, "McCain, House Democrat Warn US Has 'No Plan' for Iraq, ISIL," *Defense News*, July 8, 2014.

12. Roy Gutman, "Syrian Opposition Seeks US Support for Battle Plans," McClatchy, July 13, 2014.

13. Madeline Grant, "16% of French Citizens Support ISIS, Poll Finds," *Newsweek*, August 26, 2014.

14. Thomas L. Friedman, "Obama on the World," *New York Times*, August 8, 2014.

15. White House Office of the Press Secretary, "Statement by the President on Iraq," August 9, 2014.

16. Rich Lowry, "The Abandoned War," *National Review*, August 12, 2014.

17. Jeffrey Goldberg, "Hillary Clinton: 'Failure' to Help Syrian Rebels Led to the Rise of ISIS," *Atlantic*, August 10, 2014.

18. Gayle Tzemach Lemmon, "Obama Insiders Frustrated Over Reluctance to Attack Syria and Iraq," *Defense One*, August 22, 2014.

19. Tom Vanden Brook, "Officials: Commanders Want More Iraq Airstrike Power," *USA Today*, August 20, 2014.

20. Lucy McCalmont, "Josh Earnest Clarifies Barack Obama ISIL Answer," *Politico*, August 28, 2014.

21. Nancy A. Youssef, Jonathan S. Landay, and Lesley Clark, "US Weighs Risks of Attacking Jihadists in Syria," McClatchy, August 27, 2014.

22. Jonathan Karl, "Obama Suggests ISIS Must Be Destroyed (or Maybe Not)," ABC News, September 3, 2014.

23. "Obama Says Key Allies Ready to Join U.S. Action In Iraq," Reuters, September 5, 2014.

24. "Defeat of ISIS Called Unlikely on Obama Watch," CNN, September 3, 2014.

25. Phil Stewart and Julien Ponthus, "U.S. Says Forms 'Core Coalition' to Counter Iraq Militants," Reuters, September 5, 2014.

26. Dan Balz and Peyton M. Craighill, "Poll: Public Supports Strikes in Iraq, Syria; Obama's Ratings Hover Near His All-Time Lows," *Washington Post*, September 9, 2014.

27. Craig Whitlock, "Rift Widens Between Obama, U.S. Military over Strategy to Fight Islamic State," *Washington Post*, September 18, 2014.

28. James Weinstein, "Retired Head of Marine Corps: Obama's ISIS Strategy Doesn't Have 'a Snowball's Chance in Hell of Succeeding,'" *Daily Caller*, September 19, 2014.

29. Travis Tritten, "Political Promises Against Ground Troops Clash with Military Realities," *Stars and Stripes*, September 19, 2014.

30. Magdy Samaan and Richard Spencer, "ISIL Fighters Disperse Within Syrian and Iraqi Cities to Evade US Air Attacks," *Telegraph*, September 21, 2014.

31. Shane Harris and Noah Schachtman, "ISIS Keeps Getting Better at Dodging U.S. Spies," *Daily Beast*, November 14, 2014.

32. Rajiv Chandrasekaran, "Syrians to be Trained to Defend Territory, Not Take Ground from Jihadists, Officials Say," *Washington Post*, October 22, 2014.

33. Anne Barnard, "Opposition in Syria Is Skeptical of U.S. Airstrikes on ISIS," *New York Times*, September 29, 2014.

34. Jamie Dettmer, "The Battle for Aleppo: A Decisive Fight for ISIS, Assad, and the USA," *Daily Beast*, October 24, 2014; Mousab Alhamadee and Roy Gutman, "US-Backed Forces in Syria Suffer Big Setback," McClatchy, November 1, 2014; Roy Gutman and Mousab Alhamadee, "Moderate Syrian Rebels Say U.S. Airstrikes Helped Extremists Seize Province," McClatchy, November 13, 2014.

35. "U.S. Sees Syria Rebels in Political, Not Military Solution: Asharq Al-Awsat Newspaper," *Reuters*, October 27, 2014.

36. Josh Rogin and Eli Lake, "Military Hates White House 'Micromanagement' of ISIS War," *Daily Beast*, October 31, 2014.

37. David Ignatius, "Iraq and the U.S. Are Losing Ground to the Islamic State," *Washington Post*, October 23, 2014.

38. White House Office of the Press Secretary, "Statement by the President on ISIL," September 10, 2014.

39. Spencer Ackerman, "Only 20 to 30 Americans Fighting for Jihadist Groups in Syria, US Official Says," *Guardian*, September 22, 2014.

40. Yara Bayoumy and Mohammed Ghobari, "How Yemen's Houthis Control Sanaa and Alarm the West," Reuters, December 10, 2014.

41. Greg Miller and Craig Whitlock, "Yemen Crisis Disrupts U.S. Counterterrorism Operations, Officials Say," *Washington Post*, January 23, 2015.

42. Greg Miller and Hugh Naylor, "CIA Scales Back Presence and Operations in Yemen, Home of Potent Al-Qaeda Affiliate," *Washington Post*, February 11, 2015; Kim Hjelmgaard and Jane Onyanga-Omara, "Yemen Rebels Seize U.S. Embassy Vehicles as Diplomats Flee," *USA Today*, February 11, 2015; Rod Nordland, "In Yemen, Militants Are Increasingly Isolated," *New York Times*, February 11, 2015; Hope Hodge Seck, "Marines Provide New Details About Yemen Evacuation," *Marine Corps Times*, February 13, 2015.

43. "Remarks by Ambassador Samantha Power, U.S. Permanent Representative to the United Nations, at a Security Council Session on Ukraine," August 28, 2014, http://www.washingtonpost.com/world/full-transcript

-remarks-by-ambassador-samantha-power-us-permanent-representative
-to-the-united-nations-at-a-security-council-session-on-ukraine/2014/08
/28/b3f579b2-2ee8-11e4-bb9b-997ae96fad33_story.html.

44. Michael Flaherty and Andrea Shalal, "U.S. Lawmakers Call For Arming Ukraine Government," Reuters, August 31, 2014.

45. Adam Entous, Julian E. Barnes, and Carol E. Lee, "Resignation Capped Tense Year for Defense Secretary Hagel," *Wall Street Journal*, November 25, 2014.

46. Paul Richter, "Obama Rules Out Military Response to Russian Moves in Ukraine," *Los Angeles Times*, August 28, 2014.

47. Ben Watson, "Obama Says Still No Ukraine Intervention as More Russians Cross Border," *Defense One*, August 28, 2014.

48. Martin Matishak, "Levin: Arming Ukraine up to Obama," *Hill*, September 18, 2014.

49. Kay Johnson, "Smaller NATO Mission Has Big Job to Train Afghan Army in Time," Reuters, January 7, 2015.

50. U.S. Department of State, Libya Travel Warning, January 20, 2015, http://travel.state.gov/content/passports/english/alertswarnings/libya-travel-warning.html

51. Patrick Cockburn, "War on ISIS: Flood of Jihadi Volunteers to Syria 'Unstoppable,' Warns Turkish Prime Minister," *The Independent*, January 21, 2015; Joseph V. Micallef, "The Enemy of My Enemy: Islamic State and the Internationalization of the Syrian and Iraqi Civil Wars," *Huffington Post*, January 25, 2015; Eli Lake, "Iran's Militias Are Taking Over Iraq's Army," *Bloomberg*, February 3, 2015; Liz Sly, "Iraq's Pro-Iranian Shiite Militias Lead the War Against the Islamic State," *Washington Post*, February 15, 2015.

52. Nancy A. Youssef, "Pentagon Insider on New Plan to Fight ISIS: 'Of Course It's Not Enough,'" *Daily Beast*, January 6, 2015.

53. Loveday Morris, "The U.S. Military Is Back Training Troops in Iraq, But It's a Little Different This Time," *Washington Post*, January 8, 2015.

54. Dion Nissenbaum, "Months of Airstrikes Fail to Slow Islamic State in Syria," *Wall Street Journal*, January 14, 2015; Tim Mak and Nancy A. Youssef, "ISIS Gaining Ground in Syria, Despite U.S. Strikes," *Daily Beast*, January 15, 2015; Adam Entous, "Covert CIA Mission to Arm Syrian Rebels Goes Awry," *Wall Street Journal*, January 26, 2015.

55. Glenn Kessler, "Obama's Claim That Iran's Nuclear Program Has Been 'Halted' and Its Nuclear Stockpile 'Reduced,'" *Washington Post*, January 22, 2015.

56. "Dem Sen. Menendez: Obama Statements on Iran 'Sound Like Talking Points Straight Out of Tehran,'" *Real Clear Politics*, January 21, 2015.

57. Ivo Daalder et al., "Preserving Ukraine's Independence, Resisting Russian Aggression: What the United States and NATO Must Do," Atlantic Council, February 2015.

58. Statement of James N. Mattis before the Senate Armed Services Committee, January 27, 2015, http://www.armed-services.senate.gov/imo/media/doc/Mattis_01-27-15.pdf.

59. Testimony by General John M. Keane (Ret), USA on Global Challenges and U.S. National Security Strategy, United States Senate Committee on Armed Services, 27 January 2015.

60. Thomas E. Ricks, "The Text of General Flynn's Speech," *Foreign Policy*, January 27, 2015.

61. Greg Miller, "Al-Qaeda Franchise in Yemen Exploits Chaos to Rebuild, Officials Say," *Washington Post*, April 5, 2015.

62. Brian Bennett and Zaid Al-Alayaa, "Iran-Backed Rebels in Yemen Loot Secret Files About US Spy Operations," Tribune Content Agency, March 25, 2015.

63. Greg Botelho and Hakim Almasmari, "State Department: U.S. Pulls Remaining Forces out of Yemen," CNN, March 23, 2015.

64. Victoria Macchi, "Americans Struggle to Get Families Out Amid Yemen Conflict," Voice of America, April 6, 2015.

65. Brian Dodwell and Marielle Ness, "A View from the CT Foxhole: An Interview with Captain Robert A. Newson," *CTC Sentinel*, vol. 8, no. 2 (February 2015), 1–4.

66. H. R. McMaster, "Continuity and Change: The Army Operating Concept and Clear Thinking About Future War," *Military Review*, vol. 95, no. 2 (March–April 2015), 6–20.

67. Luis Martinez, "Defense Secretary Nominee Supports Arming Ukrainian Military," ABC News, February 4, 2015.

68. Peter Baker, "Obama Said to Resist Growing Pressure From All Sides to Arm Ukraine," *New York Times*, March 10, 2015; Molly O'Toole, "One Year Later, Obama Administration Still 'Reviewing' Lethal Aid to Ukraine," *Defense One*, March 10, 2015.

69. Colin Freeman, Ben Farmer, and Tom Parfitt, "Merkel and Hollande on Mission to Avert 'Total War,'" *Telegraph*, February 5, 2015.

70. Frances Coppola, "The Minsk Ceasefire Has Failed," *Forbes*, February 22, 2015.

71. Muzli Mohd Zin, "China Prioritises Malaysia Ties," *New Straits Times*, March 28, 2015.

72. Wyatt Olson, "China Lurks as US Ties With Thailand Splinter, Military Experts Say," *Stars and Stripes*, April 11, 2015.

73. Tran Van Minh, "Vietnam Officials Visit China to Mend Ties After Rig Spat," *Associated Press*, April 7, 2015.

74. Jane Perlez, "Stampede to Join China's Development Bank Stuns Even Its Founder," *New York Times*, April 2, 2015.

Index

Abadi, Haider al-, 300
Abbott, James, 142
Abbottabad, 142–47, 152
ABC, ABC News, 94, 194, 213, 300–301
Abdulkadir, Abdulkadir Mohamed,
    192–93, 279
Abdullah, Abdullah, 125
Abdulmutallab, Umar Farouk, 156–57, 168
Abu Bakr Tantoush, Ibrahim Ali, 219
Abu Ghraib prison, 94
Abu Khattala, Ahmed, 217–18
Abu Risha, Sheikh Ahmed, 94
Achakzai tribesmen, 121
Acheson, Dean, 297
Adams, Gordon, 247
Aden, 166
Afghanistan, Afghanistan War, 31–49, 55,
    60–65, 94, 101–30, 154, 235, 261
  Bin Laden and, 63–65, 114–15, 144,
    146–47
  casualties in, 9, 102, 104, 107, 112,
    115–16, 122–23, 149, 163, 179, 226,
    280, 283, 288
  CIA and, 40, 64–65, 113–14, 116,
    124–25, 130, 151, 260
  civilian surge in, 224–26
  COIN and, 32–34, 36–37, 39, 41–42,
    44–45, 47, 61, 97, 102–5, 107, 110–16,
    120–21, 125–26, 134, 178–79, 227,
    282
  counterterrorism and, 36, 39–42, 47,
    60–61, 75, 104, 113–15, 121–25, 130,
    151
  debates on, 32–48, 60, 83, 113–14
  defense budgets and, 20, 48, 120, 283–85
  drones and, 34, 36, 113, 124, 138–39,
    146, 148
  economy and, 37, 117, 125, 178
  exodus of Afghans from, 119
  fear of civil war in, 117, 119
  human capital in, 106, 126
  lawlessness and violence in, 122–23, 130,
    140–41, 149
  leader development in, 106–7

light-footprint approach and, 36, 39,
    43, 47, 61, 64–65, 68–69, 102, 107,
    113–14, 120, 122, 124–25, 150, 220
McChrystal and, 37–43, 60, 103–10,
    112, 177
National Intelligence Estimates on,
    124
nation building and, 36, 42–45, 220,
    223, 281
9/11 terrorist attacks and, 7, 63, 124, 128,
    248, 250, 282, 308
Obama and, 6–9, 12–13, 16, 24, 29,
    31–38, 40, 42–49, 60–61, 68–69, 75,
    77, 97, 103, 106–11, 113, 115–18,
    120, 122–26, 133–35, 137–38, 144,
    146, 150, 152–53, 177–79, 224, 281,
    287–89, 308–9
Operation Moshtarak and, 105
Pakistan and, 101–2, 104, 112, 115,
    118–19, 123, 128–30, 133–34,
    137–39, 144, 148, 150–53, 175, 228,
    274, 278–79
police in, 106–8, 112, 115, 121, 179, 224,
    226–27
politics and governance of, 36, 38, 104–7,
    112, 117, 120–22, 125, 179–80,
    225–27, 309
public opinion on, 107, 287–89
restrictions on use of force in, 111–12
security forces of, 34, 43, 45, 102, 105–8,
    112, 115, 117, 119–24, 179, 308–9
smart power and, 223–27
and strategic ways and means, 273–74,
    277–82
terrorism and, 34, 36–37, 39–42, 47,
    60, 77, 141, 161, 163, 179, 228, 282,
    289
U.S. allies' military contributions in,
    177–80
U.S. residual force in, 108, 119–20,
    122–26
U.S. troop surge in, 43–44, 46–49,
    106–8, 112, 114–17, 133–34, 137,
    152–53, 178

Afghanistan, Afghanistan War (*cont.*)
U.S. troop withdrawal from, 46–47,
107–8, 112, 115–18, 121, 123–25,
137–38, 150–53, 278, 287–88, 309
Afghanistan NGO Safety Office, 122
African-led International Support Mission
in Mali (AFISMA), 235, 239
Africans, Africa, 5, 69, 200, 270, 272, 280
attacks on U.S. embassies in, 218–19
military contributions of, 184–93, 235,
239, 273, 278
Obama and, 12, 184–85, 188, 191–93,
267
African Union:
Mali and, 233, 239
Somalia and, 186–93, 278
Air Force, U.S., 19, 58
Asia and, 251–52, 257
drones and, 130–31
Algeria, 231, 237–38, 291
Ali, Abdisalan Hussein, 187–88
Allam, Hannah, 89
Allawi, Ayad, 82
Allen, John:
Afghanistan and, 55, 94, 120–22
COIN and, 120–21
Iraq and, 94
ISIS and, 303–4
Allen, Jonathan, 181, 199, 213–14
Al Qaeda, 190, 228
Afghanistan and, 34–37, 40, 45–46,
64–65, 101, 114, 124–25, 129–30,
146–47, 154, 278
alleged decline of, 61, 68–69
Awlaki and, 155
Benghazi and, 211–13, 216–17
COIN and, 114
drones and, 34–35, 124, 132, 137–39,
146
Iraq and, 13, 77, 81, 83, 92–96, 262, 278
and killing of Bin Laden, 140, 143,
145–47
Libya and, 195–96, 200, 211–13,
216–21, 278
light–footprint approach and, 64–65
Mali and, 231, 278
National Intelligence Estimates on, 130
Obama and, 13, 35, 37, 45–46, 68–69,
77, 81, 83, 92
Pakistan and, 35–37, 45–46, 64, 77, 101,
118, 124, 128–33, 135, 137–40, 143,
145–47, 151–54, 278
Somalia and, 154, 162, 185–87, 259, 278
Syria and, 260–62, 278
Yemen and, 151, 229, 259, 278, 313
see also Islamic State of Iraq and the
Levant

Al Qaeda in Eastern Libya, 195–96
Al Qaeda in Iraq (AQI), 77, 83, 92–96, 262
Al Qaeda in the Arabian Peninsula
(AQAP), 156–59
and Awlaki, 156–57, 162–63, 165
and drones, 158–59, 165, 169–72
governance of, 165–66
and Libya, 216, 219
publicity campaigns of, 170–71
territorial expansion of, 165–69, 172
and underwear bomb plot, 157
and Yemen, 154, 158–59, 162, 165–73,
278, 295, 305, 309
Al Qaeda in the Islamic Maghreb (AQIM):
Libya and, 216, 219
Mali and, 229, 231, 234–37
Al Shabaab:
in Mogadishu, 187, 189
Navy SEAL raid and, 192–93
Somalia and, 166, 186–92
Uganda and, 188–89
Westgate Mall assault of, 190–91
Alter, Jonathan, 32, 43–44
Aly Ahly Benghazi soccer club, Al, 195
American Conservative, ix
Amman, 93
Anbar province, 94–95
Ankunda, Paddy, 190
Ansar al-Dine, 231, 235
Ansar al-Shariah, 202, 208, 213, 216–17
Apps, Peter, 91
Arabian Sea, 152
Arabs:
Afghanistan and, 261
Awlaki and, 155
Iraq and, 81–82
Pakistan and, 130
Syria and, 259, 261–62
Arab Spring, 180, 218, 259
Arango, Tim, 89
Armitage, Richard, 128
Arms Race Alternatives, 3–4
Army, U.S., 155–56, 205, 273–74
Afghanistan and, 64, 102–3, 114
defense budgets and, 48, 52, 74–75, 284
drones and, 131
Field Manuals of, 33, 160
Iraq and, 76, 199
light-footprint approach and, 68, 75
North Korea and, 258
Army Marine Corps Counterinsurgency
Field Manual, 33
Asadi, Khaled al–, 89
Asians, Asia, 5, 184, 251–57, 263, 276
defense budgets and, 254–55
Obama and, 251–53, 255, 257, 267, 291
pivot to, 251–55, 267

Asia-Pacific region, 62, 68, 254
Asiri, Ibrahim al-, 156
Aspen Institute, 20, 23, 26, 28, 53, 95
Assad, Bashar al-, 90, 259–61, 263, 265,
   267, 296, 298–99, 303–4
Associated Press, 124, 223
Atlantic, 299
Attiyah, Khalid al-, 261
attrition math, 103–4
Audacity of Hope, The (Obama), 284
Austin, Lloyd, 83–84, 302
Australia, 119, 253–54
auto company bailouts, 15
Awlaki, Abdulrahman al-, 164–65
Awlaki, Anwar al-:
   AQAP and, 156–57, 162–63, 165
   education and, 154–55
   killing of, 162–65, 188
   terrorism and, 154–57, 162, 278
   Yemen and, 154–56, 162–63, 165
Axelrod, David, 6–7, 26, 29

Baathists, Baath Party, 67, 78
baby boomers, 289
Baghdad, 65–66, 86, 91–92, 304
   COIN and, 100
   ISIL and, 293–95
Baghdadi, Abu Bakr al-, 262
Bagram, 39–40, 115, 125
Baguma, Michael, 190
Baker, Aryn, 118
Baker, Peter, 23
Balkans, 274, 276
Baltic States, 311–12
Baluchistan, 135, 148
Bamako, 230, 232, 235–37
Ban Ki-moon, 186
banks, 15, 240, 294
Banna, Ibrahim al-, 164
Bannu, 151
Baraawe, 192–93
Barnes, Julian E., 120
Barnett, Bruce, 259
Baron, Adam, 171
Barzilai, Yaniv, 65
Bates, Eric, 110
Beacon Global Strategies, 215
Bechtol, Bruce E., Jr., 259
Becker, Jo, 162
Belmokhtar, Mokhtar, 237–38
Benghazi:
   administration talking points on, 213–15
   annex in, 205–9, 215
   attacks on U.S. citizens in, x, 195,
      202–18, 220–21, 234, 279, 291, 309
   casualties in, 195, 205, 208–9, 211, 216
   criminal investigations in, 216–18

   fighting in, 180–82
   light-footprint approach and, 202,
      216–17, 220
   Obama and, x, 214–16, 218, 221
   rebel counteroffensive in, 195–97
   security for U.S. civilians in, 201–9,
      211–12, 216, 220
Bergen, Peter, 146
Berman, Howard, 227
Berntsen, Gary, 64
Biden, Joe:
   Afghanistan and, 34–36, 38–42, 60–61,
      75, 104, 116, 144
   Al Qaeda and, 36, 40
   COIN and, 34, 61, 104, 110, 116
   comparisons between Obama and,
      20–21
   counterterrorism and, 36, 39–41, 60–61,
      67, 75, 110
   defense budgets and, 56
   Donilon's relationship with, 25–26, 60
   drones and, 144
   foreign policy and, 20, 22
   Iraq and, 80, 82–84, 86, 90, 95
   and killing of Bin Laden, 144, 147
   light-footprint approach and, 95
   military and, 34, 40–42, 61
   national security and, 22–23, 60–61, 95
   Obama's relationship with, 22–23
   Pakistan and, 144, 147
   presidential campaigns of, xi, 21–22, 25
   senatorial career of, 20–21, 38
   Syria and, 90
Bigelow, Mark, 4
bin Ali Jaber, Sheikh Salem Ahmed, 170
Bin Laden, Osama, 77, 154–55, 238
   Abbottabad compound of, 142–47, 152
   Afghanistan and, 63–65, 114–15, 144,
      146–47
   AQAP and, 167
   Awlaki and, 155
   killing of, 61, 69, 114–15, 140, 142–48,
      152, 163, 211
   Pakistan and, 65, 127, 130
   Somalia and, 185, 187
Blinken, Tony, 144, 301
   Iraq and, 86–88
   national security and, 61
Boehner, John, 55–57
Bosnian war, 177
Boston Marathon bombing, 157, 278, 291
Bourei, 235
Boxer, USS, 161
Breedlove, Philip M., 268
Brennan, John:
   Afghanistan and, 116, 125
   Al Qaeda and, 61

Brennan, John (*cont.*)
  COIN and, 167
  and killing of Bin Laden, 144, 146
  Yemen and, 166–67, 228
Brookings Institution, 90, 184, 257
Brooks, Rosa, 29
Brown, Tina, 28
Brussels, 179–80, 268
Budapest Memorandum, 268
Budget Control Act, 57
budget deficits, 48–49, 58
Bundy, McGeorge, 25, 29–30
Bush, George W., 11, 14, 33, 62, 299
  Afghanistan and, 43, 63, 130, 177–78,
    223, 273, 281, 284
  Africa and, 184–85
  Bin Laden and, 63, 130, 143–44, 146
  capturing terrorists and, 159, 161–64
  COIN and, 281
  counterterrorism and, 67
  drones and, 130, 132, 134–36
  enhanced interrogation techniques and,
    160, 164
  hard power and, 17
  Iran and, 250–51
  Iraq and, 7, 16, 24, 46, 76, 78–79, 81, 98,
    130, 174–75, 223, 273, 281–82, 284,
    288–89, 304
  Latin America and, 242–43
  military and, 45–46, 304
  national security and, 16, 67, 132
  9/11 terrorist attacks and, 5
  Pakistan and, 128, 130, 132–33
  and relations with foreign governments,
    174–75, 177–78
  and strategic ways and means, 273, 277,
    281–82
  terrorism and, 130–31, 136
  and whole-of-government approach,
    223, 228
  Yemen and, 154, 228

Cairo, 215–16
Calderón, Felipe, 243
Caldwell, William, 106–7
Cameron, David, 182
Campbell, Kurt, 33
Camp Lemonnier, 280
Canadians, Canada, 237, 311–12
  Afghanistan and, 102, 129
Carney, Jay, 58, 123
  Benghazi and, 212–13
  Iraq and, 87
Carson, Johnnie, 229, 234
Carter, Ashton, 69, 314
Carter, Jimmy, x, 15, 19–20, 25, 164, 273
  defense budgets and, 19, 51–52, 289–90

Carter, Nick, 178–79
Cartwright, James E. "Hoss," 41–42, 86, 161
Casey, George W., Jr., 98–99
CBS News, 70
Center for a New American Security, 33, 97
Central Command, U.S. (CENTCOM),
    29, 33, 65, 82, 122, 158, 248, 302
Central Intelligence Agency (CIA), 35,
    55, 280
  Afghanistan and, 40, 64–65, 113–14,
    116, 124–25, 130, 151, 260
  Al Qaeda and, 40, 92
  Awlaki and, 162, 164
  Benghazi and, 205–8, 212–15, 221
  Bin Laden and, 130
  black sites of, 159–60
  COIN and, 100
  counterterrorism and, 20, 151, 160
  drones and, 61, 124, 130–32, 136, 139,
    141, 148, 151
  Global Response Staff of, 205–7
  Iraq and, 92, 100
  and killing of Bin Laden, 142–43,
    145–46
  Libya and, 199–200, 205–8, 212–15, 221
  National Clandestine Service of, 160
  Pakistan and, 129–32, 134–36, 139–40,
    142–43, 145–46, 148, 150–51, 260
  Syria and, 262, 266
  underwear bomb plot and, 168
  Yemen and, 306
Chamberlain, Neville, 263
Chamberlin, Wendy, 128
Chandrasekaran, Rajiv, 114, 303
Chechens, 130, 157
Cheonan, 257
Chicago, Ill., 118, 226
  Obama's Federal Plaza speech in, 5–6
  poverty in, 4–5
Chicago Tribune, 6
China, 175, 182, 291
  containment policy for, 255–56
  defense budgets and, 53, 253, 285–86
  North Korea and, 275
  Obama and, 12, 252–53, 257, 297
  politics and governance of, 252–53, 256,
    275
  Russia and, 276
  and strategic ways and means, 274–76
  Syria and, 261
  threat of, 251–53, 255–58
Chivers, C. J., 261
Christians, Christianity, 189, 231, 275–76
  Iraq and, 92–93
  Somalia and, 186
Churchill, Winston, 55
Clapper, James, 144, 266

Clinton, Bill, 12, 15, 33
  Afghanistan and, 130
  defense budgets and, 20, 52, 283
  Latin America and, 241–42
  military and, 19–20, 29, 283
  presidential campaigns of, 8
  U.S. allies' military contributions and,
    176–77
Clinton, Hillary:
  Afghanistan and, 47, 113, 116, 178,
    224
  Benghazi and, 202, 212, 215
  foreign policy and, 12, 23
  Iraq and, 11, 24, 80, 83–84, 91
  and killing of Bin Laden, 144
  Libya and, 181–82, 199, 202, 212, 215,
    234, 309
  Mali and, 233
  military and, 11, 29
  national security and, 11–12, 23–24, 26,
    28, 260
  Obama's relationship with, 28
  Pakistan and, 150, 227
  presidential campaign of, xi, 7–8, 11–12,
    21–24, 181
  smart power and, 222–23, 309
  speeches of, 11–12
  State Department appointment of, 23
  Syria and, 91, 260, 299
Cloud, David S., 125, 256
CNN/ORC polls, 88–89
Coast Guard, U.S., 245, 256
Cohen, Michael A., 222
Cold War, 19, 63, 267, 272, 276
Colombia, 240–44
Columbia University, 2–4
Combined Joint Special Operations Task
    Force–Afghanistan, 102
Committee for the Promotion of Virtue
    and Prevention of Vice, 95
communists, communism, 175, 272, 286
  Afghanistan and, 107
  China and, 252–53
  defense budgets and, 50–52, 290
  Korean War and, 50
Compton, Ann, 300–301
Confucianism, 275–76
Congress, U.S., x, 2, 11, 15–16, 25, 27, 272,
    312
  Afghanistan and, 38, 41, 107, 122
  Benghazi and, 202, 209, 213–15
  budget deficits and, 49
  COIN and, 41
  defense budgets and, 48, 52, 54, 56–60,
    69–71, 73–75, 285, 287, 289
  Iraq and, 24, 79–80
  Libya and, 182, 184, 264

Mali and, 233, 238
Pakistan and, 227
Syria and, 260, 263–66, 295, 302
trying terrorists and, 161
Ukraine and, 307–8
see also House of Representatives, U.S.;
    Senate, U.S.
conservatives, 272
  Afghanistan and, 46–47
  Benghazi and, 214
  trying terrorists and, 161
  university radicalism and, 2
Constitution, U.S., 162–64
Conway, James, 302
Council of Islamic Courts (CIC), 185,
    187–88
Council on Foreign Relations, 137, 222
counterinsurgency (COIN), 67–68
  Afghanistan and, 32–34, 36–37, 39,
    41–42, 44–45, 47, 61, 97, 102–5,
    107, 110–16, 120–21, 125–26, 134,
    178–79, 227, 282
  defense budgets and, 285
  enemy-centric, 99, 101, 103–4
  Iraq and, 32–34, 37, 61, 93, 97–100,
    102–4, 106, 111, 250, 280–81
  Latin America and, 242
  Nagl and, 33, 97–99
  nonmilitary aspects of, 33
  North Korea and, 258
  Obama and, 33–34, 41–42, 44–45, 68,
    97, 105, 110–11, 116, 125–26, 134,
    228, 280–81
  Operation Moshtarak and, 105
  Pakistan and, 36–37, 102, 104, 134,
    136–37, 148
  population-centric, 33, 97, 99, 101, 103,
    111
  public opinion on, 280–81
  Somalia and, 193
  and strategic ways and means, 277,
    280–82
  Task Force 714 and, 99–101
  Yemen and, 167–69, 228
counterproliferation, 124
counterterrorism, 20, 36–37, 160, 228
  Afghanistan and, 36, 39–42, 47, 60–61,
    75, 104, 113–15, 121–25, 130, 151
  Al Shabaab's Westgate Mall assault and,
    191
  AQI and, 83
  Benghazi and, 218
  drones and, 61, 67, 69, 138, 151
  Iraq and, 78, 86, 91
  and killing of Awlaki, 162–63
  and killing of Bin Laden, 146
  Libya and, 218–19

counterterrorism (*cont.*)
  light-footprint, 36, 47, 61–62, 67–68,
    110, 113–14, 120, 146, 217, 279
  Obama and, 67–68, 75, 123, 162–63,
    279
  Pakistan and, 124, 130, 138, 141–42,
    146, 151–52, 154
  and strategic ways and means, 277–78,
    282
  Syria and, 266
  Yemen and, 158–59, 168–69, 306
counterterrorism plus, 36, 39, 41–42, 60,
    75
Craig, Greg, 12
Crimea, 267–68
Croatia, 177
Crocker, Ryan:
  Afghanistan and, 123, 150
  Iraq and, 24, 77, 79–80
  Pakistan and, 150
Croddy, Jack, 223
Cunningham, James, 122

Daalder, Ivo, 311
Dahl, Kenneth, 225
Daily Beast, 28
Daley, Bill, 53
Daqduq, Ali Mussa, 90
Darna, 201
Davidson, Janine, 295
Dawa Party, 81–82, 89
defense budgets:
  Afghanistan and, 48, 120, 283–85
  Asia and, 254–55
  Carter and, 19, 51–52, 289–90
  China and, 53, 253, 285–86
  cutting of, xi–xii, 48–60, 69–75, 245,
    247, 251, 255, 269–70, 274, 283–88
  domestic policy and, 48, 54–58, 69, 286
  federal budget ceiling and, 55
  increasing spending on, 283–87, 290
  inefficiencies in, 52–53
  Latin America and, 245
  light-footprint approach and, 69–71,
    74–75
  military preparedness and, 48, 51–52
  national security and, 19, 49, 52–54,
    57–58, 60, 68, 70, 73–75, 254
  Obama and, xi, 48–50, 52–60, 69–75,
    253–54, 269–70, 283–87, 289–90
  in peacetime, 19–20, 50, 290
  as percentage of GDP, 50, 52, 56–57, 70,
    283, 286
  public opinion on, 290–91
  research and development in, 284–85
  sequestration and, 56–60, 69–75, 247,
    254, 285, 287

Defense Department, U.S. (DoD), 23, 27,
    29, 33, 61, 295
  Afghanistan and, 34, 37, 44, 113, 179–80
  Asia and, 254–55
  Benghazi and, 209–10, 220
  China and, 255
  counterterrorism and, 67
  defense budgets and, 50, 52–53, 56, 58,
    60, 69, 74–75, 254, 269, 285, 287
  drones and, 131–32
  Gates's appointment to, 16, 24
  Iraq and, 65, 85, 91, 296, 300
  ISIS and, 302
  and killing of Awlaki, 162
  Latin America and, 244
  light-footprint approach and, 69, 220
  Mali and, 230, 238
  on 9/11, 157
  Pacific and, 253
  Pakistan and, 128, 131–32
  Russia and, 307
  smart power and, 222
  Syria and, 260, 263, 290
  trying terrorists and, 161
Defense Intelligence Agency, 312
Defense Strategic Guidance, 68–69, 74, 271
democracy:
  Afghanistan and, 273
  China and, 275
  Iran and, 249–50
  Iraq and, 96, 273
  Libya and, 181, 197, 200–201, 273, 309
  Mali and, 233–34
  Obama's commitment to, 17–18
  and strategic ways and means, 272–73
  Syria and, 259
  Yemen and, 168, 273
Democrats, Democratic Party, x, 15–16,
    20–24, 33, 47, 62, 72, 176, 181–82,
    211, 272, 275
  Afghanistan and, 38
  Benghazi and, 202
  Biden's presidential campaign and, 21
  budget deficits and, 49
  counterterrorism and, 67
  defense budgets and, 48–49, 52, 55,
    57–59, 71, 73, 290
  Iraq and, 7–8, 80, 295–96
  Libya and, 182
  national security and, ix, xi, 290–91
  Obama's presidential campaigns and, 7,
    11, 20, 24
  Syria and, 263
  Ukraine and, 307–8
Dempsey, Martin, 55
  Benghazi and, 209–10
  defense budgets and, 69, 254

Iraq and, 296
Syria and, 260, 302
Desch, Michael, ix
Des Moines Register, 8–9
Diabaly, 237
Din, Miraj, 117
Directorate for Interservices Intelligence
    (ISI), 140, 152
    Afghanistan and, 129
    and campaign in North Waziristan, 149
    drones and, 132, 148
    in sharing intelligence with U.S., 141–42
    Talban and, 136
Directorate of National Intelligence, 211–12
Doherty, Glen, 208–9
domestic policy:
    Afghanistan and, 38, 46
    defense budgets and, 48, 54–58, 69, 286
    Obama and, 15–16, 20, 28, 43, 48–49,
        53, 167, 255, 286
Donilon, Tom:
    Afghanistan and, 45, 83, 104
    Biden's relationship with, 25–26, 60
    COIN and, 104, 110
    counterterrorism and, 61, 110
    Goldstein's book and, 30
    Iraq and, 45, 83–84
    and killing of Bin Laden, 144
    Libya and, 181
    military and, 83–84
    national security and, 25–28, 46, 55, 60–61
Don't Ask, Don't Tell, 16
Dory, Amanda, 230, 238
Doyle, Patty Solis, 22
Dozier, Kimberly, 124
drones:
    Afghanistan and, 34, 36, 113, 124,
        138–39, 146, 148
    Benghazi and, 217–18
    Bin Laden and, 130
    civilian casualties from, 148–49, 164–65,
        169–72, 279
    COIN and, 100
    counterterrorism and, 61, 67, 69, 138, 151
    enemy countermeasures and, 132,
        138–39, 158–59
    Iraq and, 100, 294–96
    and killing of Awlaki, 163
    Libya and, 198, 217–18, 220
    light–footprint approach and, 61, 220,
        277, 291
    limitations of, 136, 140–41
    Obama and, 62, 67, 134–37, 140, 148–51,
        153, 160, 162–65, 168–69, 312
    Pakistan and, 35–36, 131–32, 134–36,
        138–40, 142, 144, 146, 148–52, 159,
        172, 278–79, 312

public opinion on, 169, 172–73
    signature strikes of, 136
    Somalia and, 191, 278
    and strategic ways and means, 277–80,
        282
    support requirements of, 280
    Yemen and, 158–59, 163–65, 168–72,
        228, 278–79, 312
drugs, xi, 231
    defense budgets and, 285
    Latin America and, xi, 239–45, 272,
        297
    and strategic ways and means, 271–72,
        283
    Taliban and, 105
Dubik, James M., 120
Dukakis, Michael, 21
Dunford, Joseph, 122–25

Earnest, Josh, 300
East China Sea, 252, 257
Eastern Europe, 5, 269–70, 306
Economic Community of West African
    States (ECOWAS), 233, 235
economics, economy, xii, 228
    Afghanistan and, 37, 117, 125, 178
    budget deficits and, 48–49, 58
    China and, 175, 252–53, 275
    COIN and, 98
    crises in, 5, 12, 286
    defense budgets and, 73–74, 286
    federal debt ceiling and, 55–56
    Iran and, 248, 251
    Latin America and, 240
    Mali and, 229, 234
    national security and, 68
    Obama and, ix, 5, 12, 14, 49, 175, 270
    Pakistan and, 128
    Russia and, 268, 308, 311
    and strategic ways and means, 272–73,
        279–80
    Syria and, 261, 270
    see also poverty
Economist, 1, 6
education, 6, 14, 73–74, 245–46
    Afghanistan and, 119, 121, 126,
        226–27
    Awlaki and, 154–55
    China and, 275
    Iraq and, 106
    Mali and, 229–30
    smart power and, 222, 228
    and strategic ways and means, 272–73,
        277
    university radicalism and, 2–4
    Yemen and, 166, 228
Egypt, 6, 164, 212, 215–16, 273

Eikenberry, Karl, 224–25
Eisenhower, Dwight D., 175, 288
  defense budgets and, 19, 286
  national security and, 18–19
El Billar, 241
Emanuel, Rahm, 20
  national security and, 25–28
  Pakistan and, 134–35
employment, 15, 86, 91–92, 223, 225
  defense budgets and, 73–74, 286
  Mali and, 229
Endgame, The (Gordon and Trainor), 79–80
"Ending the War in Iraq," 298
"Enduring Engagement Yes, Episodic
    Engagement No" (Powelson), 230
enhanced interrogation techniques, 160,
    164
entitlements, 54–58, 286
  defense budgets and, 49, 54–55, 57–58,
    69
Entous, Adam, 92, 120
Escobar, Pablo, 241
Ethiopians, Ethiopia, 185–90
Europeans, Europe, 175, 290–91
  Afghanistan and, 102–3, 105, 108, 119,
    122, 129, 177–80, 274, 282
  Al Qaeda and, 35
  Benghazi and, 210
  Libya and, 180–84, 196, 198–201, 210,
    274–75
  Mali and, 231, 233–39
  military contributions of, 176–85,
    193–94, 236–39
  Russia and, 267–69
  Somalia and, 185
  and strategic ways and means, 274–76,
    282
  Syria and, 262, 266
  terrorist plots in, 141
  Ukraine and, 307
Evans, Jonathan, 188
Ezeagwula, Quinton, 155–56

Fallujah, 93–95, 206
Fannie Mae, 25–26
Federal Bureau of Investigation (FBI), 140,
    142, 155, 157
  Benghazi and, 216–18
  Somalian terrorists and, 187
  Warsame case and, 187
Feinstein, Dianne, 202
Feldstein, Martin, 286
Feltman, Jeffrey, 228
Filkins, Dexter, 119
Flournoy, Michèle, 33, 144, 311
  Iraq and, 83–84
Flynn, Mike, 312

foreign policy, 222, 274, 290
  Biden and, 20, 22
  domestic vs., 15
  Libya and, 199
  Obama and, ix–xi, 1, 8, 11–12, 15–18,
    22–23, 25–26, 28–29, 54, 71, 174–78,
    194, 299
  proactive, xii, 18, 20
Foreign Policy, 85
Foreign Service, U.S., 223–24, 226
Forrestal, James V., 50, 52
Fort Benning, 283–84
Fort Hood shootings, 156–57, 278
Fort Myer, 282
Fox News Sunday, 215
France, 66, 297, 310
  Afghanistan and, 105, 179
  Bosnia and, 177
  Libya and, 181–82, 198, 200
  McChrystal scandal and, 108–9
  Mali and, 233–39
Franks, Tommy, 65
Friedman, Thomas, 297–99

Gaddafi, Muammar, 205
  Benghazi and, 182, 195–97
  death of, 198–200
  and Libyan lawlessness and violence,
    200–201
  overthrow of, 61, 180, 183, 198, 219–20
  rebel counteroffensive and, 195–98
Gaddafi, Mu'tassim, 198
Gaddafi, Saadi, 195
Gall, Carlotta, 121
Gates, Robert:
  Afghanistan and, 16, 24, 37–40, 42–44,
    46–47, 60, 107, 110, 113, 116, 144,
    179–80
  COIN and, 32, 36, 41–42, 110, 116
  defense budgets and, 52–55
  Iraq and, 16, 24, 32–33, 47, 79–80,
    83–84
  ISIS and, 302
  and killing of Bin Laden, 144, 147
  Libya and, 181, 183–84
  McChrystal scandal and, 110
  national security and, 26, 28, 46, 53–55
  trying terrorists and, 161
Generation X, 289–91
Gentile, Gian, 99
George Washington University, 11
Georgia, 13, 257, 276
Gergen, David, 47
Germany, 9, 182, 272
  Bosnia and, 177
  Iraq and, 81
  Nazi, 247, 249, 263

Ghani, Ashraf, 125, 309
Ghouta, 263
Gibbs, Robert, 9–10, 26, 47
Goldberg, Jeffrey, 299
Goldstein, Gordon M., 29–30
Gordon, Michael, 79–80, 88
Gorman, Siobhan, 92
Government Accountability Office (GAO), 148, 228
Graham, Lindsey, 58, 71, 84
Gration, Scott, 10
Great Depression, 5, 286
Greenert, Jonathan, 254
Gritsenko, Anatoliy, 268
Guantanamo Bay detention facility, 159–61
Guatemala, 243–44
Guindo, Mamadou, 235
Gulf Cartel, 242
Gulf War, 19, 52, 62–63, 65–66

Haddar, Khaled al-, 203
Hadi, Abd Rabbuh Mansur, 168, 305
Hadley, Stephen, 254
Hagel, Chuck, 194, 314
    Asia and, 255, 263
    defense budgets and, 74
    Iraq and, 77, 296
    Russia and, 307
Ham, Carter, 201
Hammami, Omar, 188
Hanabusa, Colleen, 296
Haqqani Network, 40, 279
    Afghanistan and, 122, 130, 149–50
    Pakistan and, 129–30, 133, 137, 139, 149–52
hard power, 17, 54, 134, 233, 245, 282
    Latin America and, 240, 244
Harf, Marie, 313
Hasan, Nidal Malik, 156
Hashimi, Tariq al-, 89
Hastings, Michael, 10–11
    McChrystal scandal and, 108–11
Hayden, Michael, 134, 164, 280
health, health care, 56, 73, 240, 275
    Afghanistan and, 226, 283
    Mali and, 234
    Obama and, ix, 9–10, 15
Hellfire missiles, 131–32, 135, 139–40, 160, 172
Helmand province, 112, 121, 178, 225–26
Helprin, Mark, 211
Henderson, Alec, 203
Henn, Nate, 189
Hezbollah, 90, 248
Hill, Christopher, 80, 82, 85
Hinduism, 275–76
Hitler, Adolf, 249, 263

Holbrooke, Richard, 109, 224
Holder, Eric, 160, 163, 295
Hollande, François, 235–37, 239, 315
Honduras, 175, 240, 243–44
Hosenball, Mark, 202, 238
House of Representatives, U.S., 55, 72, 215
    and Afghanistan, 38, 47
    and budget deficits, 49
    and counterterrorism, 162
    and defense budgets, 56–58, 69, 71, 73
    and Iraq, 80
    and Mali, 238
    and Pakistan, 227
    and Syria, 263–64
    see also Congress, U.S.
Houthis, 305–6, 313
HRC (Allen and Parnes), 199, 213–14
Hull, Edmund J., 169
human rights, humanitarianism, 231, 275, 297
    Afghanistan and, 37
    and killing of Awlaki, 164
    Libya and, 180–81
    Mali and, 239
    North Korea and, 258–59
    Obama's commitment to, 17–18
    smart power and, 222, 228
    Somalia and, 186
    Yemen and, 228
Hussein, Saddam, 66–67, 78, 82, 96, 99, 294
Hyde Park Herald, 4–5

IHS Global Insight, 253
improvised explosive devices (IEDs), 104, 108, 123
India, 21, 175, 182, 275–76
    Afghanistan and, 129, 133–34, 137–38, 140
    China and, 255–56
    Pakistan and, 35, 128–30, 133–34, 137–38, 140, 142, 153
Indonesia, 272, 282
Indyk, Martin, 131
International Security Assistance Force (ISAF), 178
Invisible Children, 189
Iowa State University, 8
Iran, 273
    Afghanistan and, 119
    China and, 275
    defense budgets and, 53–54
    hostage crisis in, 20, 152
    Iraq and, 82–83, 86, 90–91, 93, 96, 304, 310
    nuclear weapons and, 248–51, 271–72, 274, 311
    Obama and, 249–51, 310–11

Iran (*cont.*)
  politics and governance of, 249–50
  Russia and, 276
  security forces of, 250, 310
  and strategic ways and means, 271–72,
    274, 276, 281
  Syria and, 90–91, 96, 260–61, 296
Iraq, Iraq War, 20, 47, 65–69, 76–106,
    129–30, 149, 206, 248, 259, 269
  air strikes on, 300–301, 304
  Bush and, 7, 16, 24, 46, 76, 78–79, 81,
    98, 130, 174–75, 223, 273, 281–82,
    284, 288–89, 304
  casualties and injuries in, 8–9, 13, 52, 66,
    90, 93–96, 100–101, 280, 283
  civil war in, 76–78, 88
  Clinton and, 11, 24, 80, 83–84, 91
  COIN and, 32–34, 37, 61, 97–100,
    102–4, 106, 111, 250, 280–81
  defense budgets and, 52, 283–85
  Donilon and, 45, 83–84
  end of U.S. combat mission in, 79–80
  Gulf War and, 52, 65
  ISIS and, 96, 295–98, 300–304, 309–10
  lawlessness and violence in, 66–67, 94,
    96, 98
  light–footprint approach and, 61, 66–69,
    86, 95, 220, 310
  nation building in, 220, 223, 281
  Obama and, 7–14, 16, 24, 62, 68–69,
    76–90, 92, 94–98, 125, 196, 281, 295,
    297–300, 302, 304, 308–10
  police in, 81, 93, 95, 99, 101, 224, 293
  politics and governance of, 77–78,
    80–83, 85, 88–89, 92, 98, 101, 105–6,
    199, 293, 298–300, 304, 310
  public opinion on, 88–89, 288–89, 301
  security forces of, 66–67, 78, 81, 86, 88,
    93, 95, 120, 199, 293–95, 310
  and strategic ways and means, 273–74,
    278, 280–82
  Syria and, 90–91, 96, 261–62
  U.S. civilians in, 86–87, 91, 199, 224
  U.S. residual force in, 78–79, 82–88, 91
  U.S. Status of Forces Agreement
    (SOFA) with, 82
  and U.S. troops' immunity from
    prosecution, 87, 298–99
  U.S. troop surge in, 13, 24, 46, 76, 98
  U.S. troop withdrawal from, 13, 24,
    76–81, 83, 86–94, 96, 293–94, 298
  and weapons of mass destruction, 96,
    289
Iraqiya Party, 81–82
Iraq War De-Escalation Act, 76
Iryani, Abdulghani al-, 171
Islamabad, 136, 139, 141

Islamic Courts Union, 185, 187–88
Islamic Movement of Uzbekistan, 140–41
Islamic State of Iraq and Syria (ISIS):
  France and, 297
  Iraq and, 96, 293–98, 300–304, 309–10
  Obama and, x, 295–98, 300–305, 309–10
  public opinion on, 297, 301
  Syria and, 96, 295–98, 301–4, 309–11
Islamic State of Iraq and the Levant
    (ISIL), 300–302, 309–10
  Iraq and, 94–95, 293–95, 300, 304
Islamists, Islam, 190, 237
  Afghanistan and, 63–64, 101, 141
  AQAP and, 165–67, 171
  Awlaki and, 154–55, 188
  Benghazi and, 201–2, 211–12, 214–17
  counterterrorism and, 68
  defense budgets and, 290
  drones and, 217
  drug trade and, 240
  Fort Hood shooting and, 156–57
  France and, 297
  Iraq and, 95–96, 281, 295
  Israel and, 249
  Libya and, 182, 195, 197, 201, 211–12,
    214–17
  light-footprint approach and, 69
  Mali and, 231–33, 235, 239
  Pakistan and, 130, 140–41, 150, 227, 259
  Somalia and, 185–87, 189, 191
  Syria and, 260, 262, 266, 299
  video critical of, 211–12, 214–15
Israel, 195, 305–6
  Iran and, 248–50
  nuclear weapons and, 249–50
  Palestinian extremists and, 131
Issawi, Rafie al-, 93

Jaar, 165
Jalalabad, 64, 115, 145
Jang Song Thaek, 258
Japan, 132, 175, 252–54, 272
Jawad, Numan Dakhil, 86
Jeffrey, James, 84–85
Jews, 249
Jibouri, Zaydan al-, 304
Johnsen, Gregory D., 169
Johnson, Lyndon, 15, 30–31
Joint Chiefs of Staff, 55
  Afghanistan and, 37, 39, 41
  Benghazi and, 201
  defense budgets and, 58, 74
  Iraq and, 83–84, 296
  light-footprint approach and, 68
  McChrystal and, 40
  Pakistan and, 132
  Syria and, 302

Joint Interagency Task Force South
  (JIATF–South), 245
Joint Special Operations Command, U.S.
  (JSOC), 37, 143
Jones, James L.:
  Afghanistan and, 38, 60
  Donilon's relationship with, 26
  foreign policy and, 28
  McChrystal scandal and, 109
  national security and, 24–28, 38, 55,
    109
  Pakistan and, 141
Jones, Terry, 212
Jordan, 93, 266
Judicial Watch, 214
Justice Department, U.S., 162–63

Kabul, 107, 149, 225
  U.S. troop withdrawal and, 115, 117,
    124–25
Kahn, Rob, 3
Kampala, 189
Kandahar, 39–40, 112, 121, 225
Kappes, Stephen, 132
Karachi, 139, 147
Karzai, Hamid, 106, 118, 129
  U.S. troop withdrawal and, 117, 123
Kay, Nick, 191
Kayani, Ashfaq Parvez, 141–42, 149
Keane, Jack, 312
Kearsarge, USS, 210–11
Kelly, John F., 245, 288–89
Kennedy, John F., 15, 290
Kennedy, Robert, 21
Kenya, 190–91
Kerry, John:
  Iraq and, 95
  ISIS and, 301
  Pakistan and, 148, 227
  Syria and, 263, 265, 304
Kerry-Lugar-Berman aid, 227
Kessler, Glenn, 265, 311
Khamenei, Ali, 249
Khan, Zafarullah, 152
Khanaqin, 78
Kholouf, Nour, 296
Kibler, Brenda, 189
Kilcullen, David, 33
Kim Chol, 258
Kim Jong Un, 257–59
King, Laura, 119
Kinnock, Neil, 21
Kirkpatrick, David D., 217
Klaidman, Daniel, ix, 27–28, 134
Knights, Michael, 294
Koh, Harold, 162–63
Konna, 235

Korea, North, 50–51
  nuclear weapons and, 80, 248, 257, 259,
    271–72, 282, 291
  and strategic ways and means, 271–72,
    274–75, 281–82
  threat of, 257–59, 263
Korea, South, 257–58, 263, 272, 274
Korean War, 19, 248, 269, 272, 312
  defense budgets and, 50–52
Korkie, Pierre, 305
Kosovo, 183, 277
Kunar province, 118
Kurds, 78, 81, 89, 304
Kuwait, 65, 89, 310

Lahore, 139–40, 147
Lamb, Charlene, 202
Landstuhl military hospital, 9–10
Lashkar-e-Taiba, 130, 133, 139–40, 151
Latin America, 5
  drug trade and, xi, 239–45, 272, 297
  Obama and, 240, 243–44, 297
  politics and governance of, 241–44
Lee Hsien Loong, 255
Leggett, Chris, 231
Lessons in Disaster (Goldstein), 29–30
Lew, Jack, 53, 55–56, 71
liberals, 17, 24, 29, 46, 272
  and capturing and trying prisoners, 161
  defense budgets and, 58, 247
  Iraq and, 7, 80, 295
  and killing of Awlaki, 163–64
  and relations with foreign governments,
    175–76
libertarians, 49, 56–57, 285
Libi, Abu Anas al-, 218, 279
Libya, 195–221, 259
  air campaign against, 61, 181–83,
    196–98, 210–11, 221, 247, 264
  atrocities in, 180–83
  casualties in, 180, 182–83, 195, 205,
    208–9, 211, 216, 279
  civil war in, 180–83, 195–201, 219–20
  defense budgets and, 53
  ISIS and, 309
  lawlessness and violence in, 200–221
  light-footprint approach and, 198–200,
    202, 206, 216–17, 219–20
  Mali and, 197, 200, 234
  nuclear weapons and, 247–48
  Obama and, 180–83, 196, 198–200,
    214–16, 218–21, 264, 273, 309–10
  police in, 200–201
  politics and governance of, 196–200,
    216–20, 309
  public opinion and, 200–201, 217–18,
    221

Libya (*cont.*)
  security forces of, 180, 200, 216–20
  and strategic ways and means, 274–75,
    277–79, 281
  U.S. allies' military contributions in,
    180–84
  U.S. civilians in, 195–96, 199–218,
    220–21, 309
  see also Benghazi
light-footprint approach, 228
  Afghanistan and, 36, 39, 43, 47, 61,
    64–65, 68–69, 102, 107, 113–14, 120,
    122, 124–25, 150, 220
  counterterrorism and, 36, 47, 61–62,
    67–68, 110, 113–14, 120, 146, 217, 279
  defense budgets and, 69–71, 74–75
  Iraq and, 61, 66–69, 86, 95, 220, 310
  Libya and, 198–200, 202, 206, 216–17,
    219–20
  national security and, 69, 95, 291
  and strategic ways and means, 277, 279
  Yemen and, 312
Lippert, Mark, 26–28
Little Rock shootings, 155–56, 278
littoral combat ships (LCS), 253
Liu Yazhou, 252–53
Lizza, Ryan, 182
London, Obama's speech in, 174
Long, William A., 155–56
Los Angeles Times, 164, 256
  Afghanistan and, 119, 125
Lowry, Rich, 298
Lugar, Richard, 227

MacArthur, Douglas, 312
McCain, John:
  defense budgets and, 58
  Iraq and, 12–14, 84, 296
  presidential campaign of, 1, 9–10, 12–14
McChrystal, Stanley A., 29
  Afghanistan and, 37–43, 60, 103–10,
    112, 177
  on attrition math, 103–4
  COIN and, 37, 39, 41, 99–101, 103–5,
    110
  firing of, 111
  Iraq and, 37, 99–101, 103–4
  Operation Moshtarak and, 105
  scandal of, 108–11
  Task Force 714 and, 99–101
McClatchy, 89, 171, 300
McClellan, John, 38
McDonough, Denis, 144, 181
  Iraq and, 86–88
  national security and, 26–28, 61
McFarland, Katrina, 254–55, 285
McGovern, George, ix, 33

McGurk, Brett, 85
McKeon, Buck, 71
McKiernan, David, 34, 36–37
McMaster, H. R., 314
McManus, Doyle, 164
McNamara, Robert S., 30
McRaven, William, 75
  and killing of Bin Laden, 143–45
  Mali and, 230
Magnier, Mark, 256
Mahmoud, Muhammmad, 93
Mali, 259
  corruption in, 229–30, 232
  Libya and, 197, 200, 234
  military coup in, 232–33
  Obama and, 229–30, 233, 235–37
  politics and governance of, 229, 232–34
  rebellion in, 230–39
  security forces of, 230–33, 235, 237
  smart power and, 229–39
  and strategic ways and means, 274, 278,
    281–82
Maliki, Nouri al-, 81–87, 96, 293
  Al Qaeda and, 92, 95
  COIN and, 101
  elections and, 81
  Obama's videoconference with, 84–85
  protests against, 93–94
  stepping down of, 299–300, 304
  Sunni arrests and, 89, 93
  Syria and, 90
  U.S. residual force and, 78, 82, 84–87
  U.S. troop withdrawal and, 89–90
Malkasian, Carter, 119–20, 225–26
Malone, Barry, 91
Mann, James, 4, 17
Maraniss, David, 3
Marine Corps, U.S., 24, 33, 41, 205
  Afghanistan and, 65, 103, 105, 114,
    178–79, 225, 288
  Benghazi and, 201, 210–11
  defense budgets and, 71, 75, 284
  Iraq and, 66, 199
  light-footprint approach and, 68, 75
  North Korea and, 258
  Syria and, 302
  Yemen and, 306, 313
Marjah, 105, 179
Markey, Daniel, 137–38
Marshall, George, 50, 52
Masked Brigade, 219, 237
Mattis, James, 248, 312
  Afghanistan and, 64–65, 122
  Iraq and, 82
  Yemen and, 166–67
Mauritania, 231
Mayo, Anssaf Ali, 169

media, 1–5, 20, 223, 231
  Afghanistan and, 32, 41, 43–44, 106, 107,
    108–10, 114, 116–25, 178–79, 288
  Asia and, 253, 255
  Benghazi and, 202, 209, 211–15, 217–18
  Biden's presidential campaign and, 21
  China and, 256
  Clinton's State Department
    appointment and, 23
  COIN and, 33, 97
  counterterrorism and, 122
  defense budgets and, 73–74
  drones and, 124, 134, 146, 149
  enhanced interrogation techniques and,
    160
  Iran and, 311
  Iraq and, 8–9, 83, 87–89, 91, 94–95, 97,
    289, 298, 310
  ISIS and, 295, 300–301
  and killing of Awlaki, 164
  and killing of Bin Laden, 144, 146–47
  Libya and, 182, 197–202, 209, 211–15,
    217–19
  McCain's presidential campaign and, 14
  McChrystal scandal and, 108–11
  Mali and, 229, 236–38
  as misleading, x–xi
  national security and, ix, 25, 27–29
  Obama's foreign policy choices and, 194
  and Obama's interview with Friedman,
    297–98
  Obama's Prague speech and, 1–2
  Obama's presidential campaigns and,
    8–10, 12
  Pakistan and, 135, 140, 144, 146–49, 152
  Petraeus and, 33
  Russia and, 268
  Syria and, 261, 263, 265–66, 291, 296,
    299, 303, 310–11
  Vietnam War and, 108
  Yemen and, 169, 171, 306
Medicaid, Medicare, 54–55
Mediterranean, 210–11
Mehsud, Baitullah, 135, 137
Memphis, Tenn., 155–56
Menendez, Robert, 307, 311
Merida Initiative, 243
Merkel, Angela, 315
Mexico, 242–44, 282
Middle East, 5–6, 61–62, 69, 151, 172, 200,
    237, 267, 270, 276, 297, 302, 312
  defense budgets and, 254
  foreign policy and, 29
  U.S. military presence in, 250–51
military, militarism, 16–20, 33, 246, 248
  Afghanistan and, 9, 13, 16, 29, 34–36,
    40–45, 47, 62–64, 83, 102–8, 111–26,

    129, 133–34, 137, 149–50, 152–53,
    177–80, 224–27, 283–84, 308–9
  Asia and, 251–55
  Benghazi and, 201, 203, 205–6, 209–11,
    216, 218, 220
  Bosnia and, 177
  Bush and, 45–46, 304
  China and, 252–53, 255–58
  COIN and, 61, 67, 98–101, 103–5, 111,
    120–22, 126
  Columbia protests and, 3–4
  counterterrorism and, 67–68, 110
  defense budgets and, 19–20, 48, 50–54,
    58, 70–71, 73–74, 247, 251, 254, 274,
    283–86
  drones and, 149
  economy and, 175
  Iran and, 250–51
  Iraq and, 8–11, 13, 24, 46, 62, 65–66,
    76–104, 199, 224, 250, 283–84,
    293–96, 298–300, 302, 304, 308, 310
  ISIS and, 301, 310
  and killing of Bin Laden, 115
  Latin America and, 240–45
  Libya and, 180–82, 195–98, 200–206,
    209–11, 216, 218–21
  light-footprint approach and, 61, 67–71,
    75, 95, 277, 291
  McChrystal scandal and, 110–11
  Mali and, 230–33, 235–39
  network-centric warfare and, 62–63
  North Korea and, 257–59
  Obama and, 2–4, 8–11, 22–24, 29–31,
    40–41, 44–45, 47, 62, 76–90, 92,
    94–96, 106–7, 111, 115–18, 120,
    122–25, 133–34, 137–38, 152–53,
    175–85, 188, 191–94, 196, 198, 200,
    218–20, 236, 240, 255, 268, 270–72,
    276–81, 283–85, 287–88, 290,
    295–96, 298–302, 308–9, 312
  Pakistan and, 35, 128–29, 132–33,
    136–39, 142, 147–53, 228, 259, 273
  power across borders of, 127, 153
  public opinion on, xii
  and relations with foreign governments,
    175–77
  Russia and, 267–69
  Somalia and, 185–93, 273
  and strategic ways and means, 271–83
  suicides in, 283
  Syria and, 260, 262, 264–66, 296, 299,
    302–3, 310–11
  trying terrorists and, 161
  Ukraine and, 306–8, 311–12
  U.S. allies' contributions to, 176–94,
    235–39, 273, 278
  of U.S. in Middle East, 250–51

military, militarism (*cont.*)
  Vietnam War and, 30–31
  war weariness and, 288
  Yemen and, 158, 165–69, 305–6, 309
Millennials, 289–90
Millennium Challenge Corporation, 240
Millennium Villages Project, 234
Miller, Greg, 266
Miram Shah, 152
Misrata, 197–98
Mississippi, University of, 12
Mitú, 241
Mogadishu, 185–87, 206
  Islamist control of, 187, 189 191
Mogadishu, Battle of, 185
Mohammad, 190, 294
Mohammad, Sultan, 121
Mohammed, Sultan Ahmed, 171
Mohammed Jamal Network, 216
Mopti, 235–38
Morell, Michael:
  Benghazi and, 213–15
  Syria and, 262
Mortenson, Greg, 222
Moshtarak, Operation, 105
Mosul, 293–94, 302–3
Mosul Dam, 81, 300
Movement for Unity and Jihad in West
    Africa (MUJAO), 231, 235
MSNBC, 110
Muhammad, Abdulhakim Mujahid (Carlos
    Leon Bledsoe), 155–56
Muhandis, Abu Mahdi al-, 310
mujahideen, 107, 121
Mullen, Mike, 55
  Afghanistan and, 37, 39, 41, 44, 60, 116
  Iraq and, 83–84
  and killing of Bin Laden, 144
  light-footprint approach and, 68
  Pakistan and, 132, 144, 149
  Yemen and, 166
multilateralism, 17, 175–76, 193–94,
    309
  Libya and, 180–82
  and strategic ways and means, 276–77
Mumbai attacks, 139
Munich conferences, 34, 263
Musharraf, Pervez, 128–29, 131
Mutual of Omaha *Wild Kingdom* fallacy,
    314
Mwencha, Erastus, 191

Nabors, Rob, 56
Nagl, John, 33, 97–99
Napolitano, Janet, 157
Nashir, Nizamuddin, 119
Nasr, Vali, 29

National Intelligence Estimates:
  on Afghanistan, 124
  on Al Qaeda, 130
National Review, 298
national security, 18–19, 290–91
  Afghanistan and, 32–34, 36, 42–44,
    46–47, 113–14
  Biden and, 22–23, 60–61, 95
  counterterrorism and, 162
  defense budgets and, 19, 49, 52–55,
    57–58, 60, 68, 70, 73–75, 254
  domestic policy and, 15
  drones and, 135, 137
  Emanuel and, 25–28
  Iraq and, 89, 95, 199, 295–96, 310
  and killing of Bin Laden, 143–44, 146
  Libya and, 200
  light-footprint approach and, 69, 95, 291
  North Korea and, 258
  Obama and, ix–xii, 4, 7–8, 11–14, 16–17,
    20, 22–34, 36, 43–44, 47, 49, 52–53,
    60, 62, 67–73, 89, 95, 113, 133–35,
    137, 143–44, 146, 211, 260, 263, 267,
    296, 302, 307, 312
  Pakistan and, 132, 134, 143–44, 146, 259
  politicizing of, 28–29
  public opinion on, 288
  Russia and, 307
  smart power and, 222
  Syria and, 260, 262–63, 296, 302
  trying terrorists and, 161
  Vietnam War and, 30
National Security Agency (NSA), 100
National Security Council (NSC), 12, 24
  Afghanistan and, 34, 113–14
  Benghazi and, 213
  Obama's appointments to, 26–27
  Yemen and, 168–69
Navy, U.S., 27
  Asia and, 251–53, 257
  defense budgets and, 19, 48, 70–71, 245,
    254
  Pacific and, 253–54
Navy SEALs, U.S., 115, 208–9
  and killing of Bin Laden, 145
  Pakistan and, 132–33
  Somali raid of, 192–93
Neller, Robert, 201, 210
Netherlands, 186, 189
network-centric warfare, 62–63
Neumann, Ronald E., 122
New America Foundation, 149
Newsom, Robert A., 313–14
Newsweek, ix, 134
New York City, 20, 288
  terrorist plots in, 140–41, 291
New Yorker, 182

New York Times:
  Afghanistan and, 121, 125
  Benghazi and, 217–18
  capturing terrorists and, 162
  Clinton's State Department
    appointment and, 23
  COIN and, 97
  drones and, 146, 149
  Iraq and, 88–89, 97
  and killing of Awlaki, 164
  and killing of Bin Laden, 146
  Obama's foreign policy choices and, 194
  and Obama's interview with Friedman,
    297–98
  Obama's presidential campaigns and, 10
  Pakistan and, 146, 149, 152
  Russia and, 268
  Syria and, 261, 263
Niang, Amadou, 234
Nicaragua, 175, 273
Niger river, 235, 238
9/11 terrorist attacks, 155–57, 278, 281–82
  Afghanistan and, 7, 63, 124, 128, 248,
    250, 282, 308
  Awlaki and, 155
  Axelrod and, 6
  Iraq and, 248
  Libya and, 196
  Obama and, 4–6
  Pakistan and, 128–29, 131
  Somalia and, 185
Nixon, Richard, 15, 18, 175
nongovernmental organizations (NGOs),
  122, 227, 231
Nordstrom, Eric, 201–2
North Africa, 151, 172, 229, 237, 254, 297,
  302
North Atlantic Treaty Organization
  (NATO), 194
  Afghanistan and, 43, 102, 106, 112,
    117–20, 122–23, 129, 177–80, 282
  ISIS and, 301
  Libya and, 61, 182–84, 195, 197–99,
    201, 247
  Pakistan and, 150
  Russia and, 268–69, 311
  Smart Defense policy and, 184
  Ukraine and, 307, 311–12
Northern Alliance, 63–65, 117
North Waziristan, xi, 137–39, 149, 151–52
Northwest Airlines Flight 253, 156–57
Norwegians, 237–38
Notre Dame, University of, 54
NPR, 33
nuclear weapons, 127
  China and, 256–57
  Columbia protests and, 3–4

  disarmament and, 2, 247
  Iran and, 248–51, 271–72, 274, 311
  North Korea and, 80, 248, 257, 259,
    271–72, 282, 291
  Obama and, 1–4, 247–48, 268, 311
  Pakistan and, 35, 128–29, 147, 150, 153,
    248, 259
  and strategic ways and means, 271–72,
    274, 282
  Ukraine and, 268
Nuland, Victoria, 213
Nusra Front, Al, 262
Nye, Joseph S., Jr., 17

Obama, Barack:
  Afghanistan and, 6–9, 12–13, 16, 24,
    29, 31–38, 40, 42–49, 60–61, 68–69,
    75, 77, 97, 103, 106–11, 113, 115–18,
    120, 122–26, 133–35, 137–38, 144,
    146, 150, 152–53, 177–79, 224, 281,
    287–89, 308–9
  Africa and, 12, 184–85, 188, 191–93, 267
  Al Qaeda and, 13, 35, 37, 45–46, 68–69,
    77, 81, 83, 92
  Al Shabaab's Westgate Mall assault and,
    191
  AQAP and, 157
  Asia and, 251–53, 255, 257, 267, 297
  Awlaki and, 157, 162–64
  Benghazi and, x, 214–16, 218, 221
  Biden's relationship with, 22–23
  Biden's vice presidential campaign and,
    22
  black site closures and, 159–60
  China and, 12, 252–53, 257, 297
  Clinton's State Department
    appointment and, 23
  COIN and, 33–34, 41–42, 44–45, 68, 97,
    105, 110–11, 116, 125–26, 134, 228,
    280–81
  Columbia radicalism and, 2–4
  comparisons between Biden and, 20–21
  counterterrorism and, 67–68, 75, 123,
    162–63, 279
  defense budgets and, xi, 48–50, 52–60,
    69–75, 253–54, 269–70, 283–87,
    289–90
  domestic policy and, 15–16, 20, 28, 43,
    48–49, 53, 167, 255, 286
  drones and, 62, 67, 134–37, 140, 148–51,
    153, 160, 162–65, 168–69, 312
  economics and, ix, 5, 12, 14, 49, 175, 270
  enhanced interrogation techniques and,
    160
  foreign policy and, ix–xi, 1, 8, 11–12,
    15–18, 22–23, 25–26, 28–29, 54, 71,
    174–78, 194, 299

Obama, Barack (*cont.*)
  Friedman's interview with, 297–99
  Goldstein's book and, 30
  Guantanamo and, 159–61
  health care and, ix, 9–10, 15
  idealism of, 17, 37
  Iran and, 249–51, 310–11
  Iraq and, 7–14, 16, 24, 62, 68–69,
    76–90, 92, 94–98, 125, 196, 281, 295,
    297–300, 302, 304, 308–10
  ISIS and, x, 295–98, 300–305, 309–10
  and killing of Awlaki, 162
  and killing of Bin Laden, 69, 142–46,
    211
  Latin America and, 240, 243–44, 297
  Libya and, 180–83, 196, 198–200,
    214–16, 218–21, 264, 273, 309–10
  light-footprint approach and, 43, 47, 62,
    67–71, 95, 277, 279, 310
  McChrystal scandal and, 109–11
  Mali and, 229–30, 233, 235–37
  military and, 2–4, 8–11, 22–24, 29–31,
    40–41, 44–45, 47, 62, 76–90, 92,
    94–96, 106–7, 111, 115–18, 120,
    122–25, 133–34, 137–38, 152–53,
    175–85, 188, 191–94, 196, 198, 200,
    218–20, 236, 240, 255, 268, 270–72,
    276–81, 283–85, 287–88, 290,
    295–96, 298–302, 308–9, 312
  national security and, ix–xii, 4, 7–8,
    11–14, 16–17, 20, 22–34, 36, 43–44,
    47, 49, 52–53, 60, 62, 67–73, 89, 95,
    113, 133–35, 137, 143–44, 146, 211,
    260, 263, 267, 296, 302, 307, 312
  9/11 terrorist attacks and, 4–6
  nuclear weapons and, 1–4, 247–48, 268,
    311
  Pakistan and, 8, 34–35, 46, 109, 133–38,
    140–53, 227
  popularity of, ix–x, 20, 28, 40, 60, 134,
    176, 194, 263, 280–81, 301–2
  poverty and, 5, 8, 222–23
  pragmatism of, 18
  presidential campaigns of, ix, xi, 1, 4,
    7–14, 20–24, 26–27, 35, 43–44, 48–49,
    70–72, 78–81, 143–44, 159, 177, 211,
    216, 249–50, 287, 289, 298
  Russia and, 268, 307–8, 311
  smart power and, 17, 222–23, 227–30,
    233, 235–37, 240, 244–45
  Somalia and, 188, 190–91, 305
  speeches of, 1–2, 5–6, 8–9, 37, 46–47,
    53, 69, 76–77, 107, 116–17, 145–46,
    157, 174, 198, 264, 268, 304–5,
    308–12
  state senatorial career of, 5
  Syria and, 260–66, 270, 295–303, 309–10

  terrorism and, 4–6, 8, 18, 62, 69, 77,
    134, 141, 153, 157–65, 168, 184, 199,
    222–23, 245, 278, 284, 289, 304–5, 309
  Ukraine and, x, 268, 270
  U.S. senatorial campaign of, 6–7
  U.S. senatorial career of, 7–8, 10, 76–77,
    98
  writings of, 2–5, 133, 284
  Yemen and, 163–65, 167–69, 228, 273,
    305–6, 309
Obama, Michelle, 1
Obama doctrine, 17
Odierno, Ray, 74–75, 79–80
O'Donnell, Clara Marina, 184
Office of Management and Budget, 53
Office of the Coordinator for
  Reconstruction and Stabilization
  (S/CRS), 224
O'Hanlon, Michael, 257
oil, 73
  ISIS and, 295
  Russia and, 268
  Syria and, 262
Olsen, Matt, 94
Operators, The (Hastings), 108–10
Orszag, Peter, 43
Ottoman Empire, 295

Pace, Peter, 79
Pacific, 62, 68, 243, 245, 251–54
Packer, George, ix
Pakistan, 64–65, 109, 127–54, 224, 235
  Afghanistan and, 101–2, 104, 112,
    115, 118–19, 123, 128–30, 133–34,
    137–39, 144, 148, 150–53, 175, 228,
    274, 278–79
  Al Qaeda and, 35–37, 45–46, 64, 77,
    101, 118, 124, 128–33, 135, 137–40,
    143, 145–47, 151–54, 278
  Bin Laden and, 65, 127, 130
  casualties in, 132–33, 136, 138–40, 142,
    145, 148–50
  COIN and, 36–37, 102, 104, 134,
    136–37, 148
  counterterrorism and, 124, 130, 138,
    141–42, 146, 151–52, 154
  drones and, 35–36, 131–32, 134–36,
    138–40, 142, 144, 146, 148–52, 159,
    172, 278–79, 312
  Federally Administered Tribal Areas
    (FATA) of, 129–30, 132, 139–42, 148,
    151
  and killing of Bin Laden, 115, 142–48,
    152, 163
  lawlessness and violence in, 138–40
  North Waziristan campaign in, 137–39,
    149, 151–52

nuclear weapons and, 35, 128–29, 147, 150, 153, 248, 259
Obama and, 8, 34–35, 46, 109, 133–38, 140–53, 227
politics and governance of, 8, 128–29, 132–33, 150–51, 172, 227, 259, 279
Riedel and, 34–36, 133, 152
security forces of, 141, 147–49, 151, 228
smart power and, 227–28
South Waziristan campaign in, 136–37
strategic reviews on, 34–36
and strategic ways and means, 273–74, 278–79, 281–82
Swat Valley campaign in, 135–37, 139, 159
Taliban and, 40, 101–2, 118, 128–29, 135–40, 150, 261, 279
terrorism and, 8, 35–36, 128, 132, 134, 136, 140–41, 153, 188, 228, 259
threat of, 259–62
U.S. access to territory and airspace of, 128, 139, 144, 147, 150, 152
U.S. aid to, 133, 150
U.S. alliance with, 133–34
Yemen and, 159
Palestinians, 131, 156
Palin, Sarah, 14, 21
Panetta, Leon:
  Afghanistan and, 113, 116, 118
  Benghazi and, 209–10
  China and, 255
  defense budgets and, 55, 58, 70, 74, 254
  drones and, 61, 142
  Iraq and, 83, 86
  and killing of Bin Laden, 142, 144–46
  Mali and, 236–37
  national security and, 58, 260
  Pacific and, 253
  Pakistan and, 140, 142, 144–46
  Syria and, 260
Panjwayi district, 121
Paris, 66, 108–9, 309
Parnes, Amie, 181, 199, 213–14
Paronto, Kris, 205–6
Pashtuns:
  Afghanistan and, 102, 117, 119, 141
  Pakistan and, 130, 139
Peace Corps, U.S., 80, 244
Pelosi, Nancy, 80
Pérez Molina, Otto, 244
Perry, William, 254
Petraeus, David:
  Afghanistan and, 34, 39, 41–42, 44, 55, 60, 111–16, 282
  Al Qaeda and, 77
  Benghazi and, 213
  COIN and, 33–34, 39, 42, 98–99, 101, 111–13, 115–16

counterterrorism and, 41, 158
Iraq and, 24, 33–34, 76–77, 79, 98–99, 101, 111, 282
national security and, 29
Syria and, 260
Yemen and, 158
Pfeiffer, Dan, 264
Philadelphia Inquirer, 123
Philippines, 256, 273
Pillar, Paul, 92
platform-centric warfare, 62, 224
Poland, 269, 311–12
Police, N.Y.C., 3, 85
Politico, 212
Pollack, Ken, 90
Poroshenko, Petro, 308
poverty, 4–6, 273
  Mali and, 229
  Obama and, 5, 8, 222–23
  smart power and, 222–23, 228
  terrorism and, 5–6
  Yemen and, 228
Powell, Colin, 25, 128
Powelson, Simon J., 230
Power, Samantha, 180–81, 307–8
Prague, Obama's speech in, 1–2
Predators, 130–31, 142, 163, 280
Price of Politics, The (Woodward), 73
Problem from Hell, A (Power), 181
Psaki, Jen, 219
Putin, Vladimir:
  Syria and, 265–66, 276
  Ukraine and, 268, 276, 307, 315

Qadhi, Adnan al-, 171
Qaeda, Al, *see* Al Qaeda
Qalat, 226
Qatar:
  Libya and, 196–97
  Syria and, 261
Qiushi, 253
Quetta, 135

Rabbani, Burhanuddin, 118
Radda, 170–71
Raddatz, Martha, 94, 194
Rafsanjani, Akbar Hashemi, 249
Raghavan, Sudarsan, 169
Ramadi, 93–95
RAND Corporation, 219–20, 259
Rasmussen, Anders Fogh, 184
Rawalpindi, 139
Reagan, Ronald, 175, 241
  defense budgets and, 19, 52, 290
  national security and, 18–19
Reapers, 163, 280
Reed, Jack, 77

Reeder, Edward, 102
Regional Command South, U.S., 178
Reid, Harry, 56
Reines, Philippe I., 215
Republicans, Republican Party, 272, 275
  Asia and, 255
  Benghazi and, 210, 213, 215–16
  Biden's vice presidential campaigns and, 22
  budget deficits and, 49
  defense budgets and, 47, 55–59, 69–73
  foreign policy and, 29
  Iraq and, 16, 296
  Libya and, 182
  McCain's presidential campaign and, 9, 14
  national security and, ix, 4, 290–91
  Obama's college writings and, 4
  Obama's presidential campaigns and, 8
  Syria and, 260
  Ukraine and, 307–8
responsibility to protect (R2P) doctrine, 181
Reuters, 91, 202, 238
Revolutionary Armed Forces of Colombia (FARC), 241–42
Revolution in Military Affairs (RMA), 62, 64, 66
Rhodes, Benjamin J., 144
  Al Shabaab's Westgate Mall assault and, 191
  Libya and, 198–99, 213–14
  national security and, 26–28, 61, 263
Rice, Susan:
  Benghazi and, 212–15
  Libya and, 181–82
  Syria and, 264
Riedel, Bruce:
  Afghanistan and, 34–36, 38, 152
  and killing of Bin Laden, 152
  Pakistan and, 34–36, 133, 152
Rodriguez, Jose, 160
Rogin, Josh, 85
Rohde, David, 164
Rolling Stone, 108–10
Romney, Mitt, ix, 70–72, 216
Roosevelt, Franklin D., 18, 132, 288, 290
Roosevelt, Theodore, 18–19
Rosenberg, Matthew, 125
Rubin, Alissa J., 121
Rubin, Trudy, 123
Rucker, Philip, 73
Rumsfeld, Donald:
  Afghanistan and, 24, 63–65
  Iraq and, 24, 66–67
  network-centric warfare and, 62–63
"Runaway General, The" (Hastings), 110–11

Russia, 175, 182, 291
  Georgia and, 13, 276
  North Korea and, 258
  Obama and, 268, 307–8, 311
  politics and governance of, 265–68, 276
  and strategic ways and means, 274, 276, 282
  Syria and, 261, 265–66, 276, 304
  threat of, 267–70, 311–12
  Ukraine and, x, 247, 267–69, 276, 306–8, 311–12

Saeed, Hafiz Muhammad, 139–40
Saleh, Abdul Mohamed, 168
Saleh, Ali Abdullah, 158, 167
Samarra, 294
Sana'a, 155, 158, 171, 306
Sanger, David, 44
Sanogo, Amadou Haya, 232
Sarkozy, Nicolas, 182
Saudi Arabia, 6, 167, 173, 261
Scales, Robert, 283–84
Scarborough Shoal, xi, 256, 270, 276–77
Schieffer, Bob, 70–71
Schmidt, Michael S., 89, 218
Schmitt, Eric, 218
Search Bloc, 241
Sediqqi, Sediq, 118
Selou, Adnan, 266
Senate, U.S., 23, 26
  Afghanistan and, 38, 47, 122, 124
  Armed Services Committee of, 47, 122, 124, 245, 248
  Benghazi and, 202, 210
  Biden's career in, 20–21, 38
  budget deficits and, 49
  defense budgets and, 56, 71–72
  Foreign Relations Committee of, 20, 227, 229, 307
  Foreign Relations Subcommittee on European Affairs of, 7
  Intelligence Committee of, 202, 266
  Iran and, 311
  Iraq and, 76–77, 84, 94, 296
  Mali and, 229–30
  Obama's campaign for, 6–7
  Obama's career in, 7–8, 10, 76–77, 98
  Pakistan and, 227
  Syria and, 266
  Ukraine and, 307
  see also Congress, U.S.
Serbs, 177, 274
17 February Martyrs Brigade, 205–6
Shabaab, Al, *see* Al Shabaab
Shabwa, 164
Shah, Ejaz, 142
Shahzad, Faisal, 140–41, 278

Shamsi Air Base, 148
Shane, Scott, 162
sharia courts, 135, 165–66
Sheehan, Michael, 236, 239
Shiites:
  Al Qaeda and, 92–93
  Iraq and, 78, 81–82, 85–86, 89, 92–93,
    293–94, 299–300, 304, 310
  Syria and, 310
  Yemen and, 305
Shlmani, Saad el-, 217
Siemoniak, Tomasz, 269
Silva, Jack, 209
Sinaloa Cartel, 242
Sirte, 197–98
Sixth Fleet, U.S., 211
Sly, Liz, 89
Smart Defense policy, 184
smart power, 17, 54, 222–46
  Afghanistan and, 223–27
  Latin America and, 239–45
  Libya and, 181, 309
  Mali and, 229–39
  Pakistan and, 227–28
  Yemen and, 228–29
smart wars, 97
Smedinghoff, Anne, 226
Smith, Charles B., 51
Smith, Sean, 204–5, 209
soft power, 17, 240, 245, 282
Somalia, xi, 185–93, 206
  Al Qaeda and, 154, 162, 185–87, 259, 278
  capturing prisoners and, 161–62
  guerrilla war in, 185–87, 189, 191
  Navy SEAL raid in, 192–93
  Obama and, 188, 190–91, 305
  politics and governance of, 185–87,
    189, 192–93, 273
  security forces of, 185–87, 189–90,
    193
  and strategic ways and means, 273–74,
    277–79, 281
  Yemen and, 166
Somers, Luke, 305
Sons of Iraq, 93–94
Sotloff, Steven, 295, 300
South Asia, 69, 133, 137, 152, 270, 302
  Riedel and, 34–35
South China Sea, 252, 257
Southeast Asia, 252, 272
Southern Command, U.S. (SOUTH-
  COM), 245
South Waziristan, 136–37
Soviet Union, 170, 175, 247, 249, 269
  Afghanistan and, 64
  collapse of, 276, 286
  expansionism of, 19–20

Spain, 189, 210
Special Forces, U.S., 42, 62, 99, 102,
  250
special operations, 39–40, 312
  Afghanistan and, 64, 102–5, 113–15,
    123–24
  COIN and, 99–105
  counterterrorism and, 104
  defense budgets and, 75, 285
  Iran and, 250
  Iraq and, 37, 78, 80–81, 99–102, 206
  and killing of Bin Laden, 61, 115,
    143–44, 163
  Latin America and, 241
  Libya and, 208, 210, 218–21
  light-footprint approach and, 61–62, 69,
    220, 277, 291
  Mali and, 230, 237
  Pakistan and, 36, 143–44, 147, 278
  Russia and, 267
  Somalia and, 185–86, 188, 191, 206,
    278–79
  and strategic ways and means, 277–80,
    282
  Yemen and, 158, 168, 278, 305
Special Operations Command, U.S.
  (SOCOM), 37, 75, 230, 280
State Department, U.S., 29
  Afghanistan and, 113, 178, 223–26
  Al Qaeda and, 95, 228
  Clinton's appointment to, 23
  defense budgets and, 50
  drones and, 132, 149
  Iraq and, 10, 80, 84, 91, 95, 223
  ISIS and, 301
  and killing of Awlaki, 162
  Libya and, 181, 199–202, 206, 210,
    212–13, 215, 219, 309
  Mali and, 229, 233–34, 238
  Pakistan and, 128, 132, 150, 227
  Policy Planning Staff of, 137
  Syria and, 91, 263, 265, 304
  and whole-of-government approach,
    223
  Yemen and, 168, 306, 313
State of the Union Addresses, 308–12
Stevens, J. Christopher:
  and attack on U.S. Benghazi mission,
    204–8, 309
  death of, x, 208–9, 211, 279, 291
  Libyan civil war and, 196
  and security for U.S. civilians in
    Benghazi, 201–2, 204, 211, 220
Stieta, Ebtisam, 217
Students Against Militarism, 3–4
Sundial, 2–4
Sunni Awakening, 94, 101

Sunnis:
    Al Qaeda and, 92–93, 95
    arrests of, 89, 93
    COIN and, 101
    Iraq and, 78, 81–82, 86, 89, 92–96, 101,
        293–94, 304, 310
    Syria and, 260–62, 266–67, 303
    Yemen and, 305
Swat Valley, 135–37, 139, 159
Syria:
    air campaign in, 302–3, 311
    chemical weapons of, 260, 262–67, 291
    civil war in, 90–91, 260–62, 266, 282,
        290, 296, 298–99, 302–4, 311
    demonstrations in, 259–60
    Iraq and, 90–91, 96, 261–62
    ISIL and, 94
    ISIS and, 96, 295–98, 301–4, 309–11
    Libya and, 197
    Obama and, 260–66, 270, 295–303,
        309–10
    politics and governance of, 259–63, 265,
        267, 296–99, 303–4
    and strategic ways and means, 274,
        276–79, 281
    threat of, 259–67

Taiwan, 252, 257, 274
Tajiks, 117, 119
Taliban:
    Afghanistan and, 36–38, 40, 45–46,
        63–64, 101–2, 104–5, 108, 114–18,
        121–23, 125, 133, 135, 138, 150–51,
        227, 279, 282
    COIN and, 104, 114
    drones and, 135–37
    education and, 222
    light-footprint approach and, 64–65
    Northern Alliance vs., 63–64
    Obama's term sheet and, 45
    Operation Moshtarak and, 105
    Pakistan and, 40, 101–2, 118, 128–29,
        135–40, 150, 261, 279
    in Panjwayi, 121
    Syria and, 261–62
Tammany Hall, 20, 25–26, 28–29
Tangi Valley, 115
Task Force 714, 99–101
taxes, 15, 48, 55, 150, 177, 241, 288
    defense budgets and, 57–58, 70, 72–73
Tea Party, 55, 285, 290
    defense budgets and, 49, 57–58
terrorists, terrorism, 54, 130–32, 237
    Afghanistan and, 34, 36–37, 39–42, 47,
        60, 77, 141, 161, 163, 179, 228, 282,
        289
    alleged decline of, 61–62

Al Shabaab's Westgate Mall assault and,
        190–91
    Awlaki and, 154–57, 162, 278
    Axelrod and, 6
    Benghazi and, 203, 212, 291
    capturing of, 159–64
    defense budgets and, 284
    drones and, 134, 140–41
    drug trade and, 240
    interrogation of, 160–64
    Iran and, 250
    Iraq and, 77, 81, 89, 92, 98, 259
    killing of, 162–65
    and killing of Bin Laden, 144
    Libya and, 199, 212, 259
    Mali and, 239, 259
    Obama and, 4–6, 8, 18, 20, 62, 69, 77,
        134, 141, 153, 157–65, 168, 184, 199,
        222–23, 245, 278, 284, 289, 304–5, 309
    Pakistan and, 8, 35–36, 128, 132, 134,
        136, 140–41, 153, 188, 228, 259
    smart power and, 222–23
    Somalia and, 185, 187–88, 259
    and strategic ways and means, 271–72,
        277–79, 282–83
    Syria and, 265–67, 279, 291
    trying of, 161–62
    war on, 67, 77
    Yemen and, 154, 158, 162–65, 168–69,
        172–73, 228, 259, 278
    see also counterterrorism; 9/11 terrorist
        attacks
This Week, 94
Three Cups of Tea (Mortenson), 222
Tiegen, John, 205
Tikrit, 294
Time, 118
Times Square terrorist plot, 140–41, 278,
        291
Tora Bora, 64–65, 127, 144–45
torture, 160, 180, 191
Touré, Amadou Toumani, 232–33
Toya, 234
trade, 17, 19, 176, 256, 291
    Pakistan and, 133
    and strategic ways and means, 271–72
Trainor, Bernard, 79–80
Transformation plan, 63
Trans-Sahara Counterterrorism
        Partnership, 229
Traoré, Dioncounda, 235
Treasury Department, U.S., 310
Tripoli, 180, 218, 309
    Benghazi attacks and, 203, 208, 210,
        216–17
    rebel counteroffensive in, 196–97
    security for U.S. civilians in, 201–2

Truman, Harry, 19, 50, 312
Tsarnaev, Tamerlan and Dzhokhar, 157
Tuareg separatists, 230–32

Uganda, 186, 188–90
Ukraine, 257, 270, 277
    Russia and, x, 247, 267–69, 276, 306–8,
        311–12, 315
underwear bomb plot, 156–58, 168, 173,
    278, 291
United Arab Emirates, 179, 196
United Kingdom, 21, 142, 237, 263
    Afghanistan and, 105, 178
    ISIS and, 302
    Libya and, 181–82, 200–201
    Russia and, 268–69
    Somalia and, 188
United Nations, 30, 140, 175
    Afghanistan and, 119
    Al Shabaab's Westgate Mall assault and,
        191
    Bosnia and, 177
    Libya and, 181–83
    Mali and, 235
    Russia and, 307–8
    Security Council of, 182, 186, 191, 194,
        235
    Somalia and, 186–87, 191
United States Commission on
        International Religious Freedom, 93
Uribe, Alvaro, 242
U.S Agency for International Development
    (USAID), 224–25, 227, 229, 242
Uzbeks, 117, 130, 151

Vampire fallacy, 314
Vietnam War, 13, 33, 97, 108, 272, 284
    civilians vs. military on, 30–31
    defense budgets and, 19, 49, 51
    Donilon and, 45
    Goldstein's book on, 29–30
    opposition to, 2–3
Vietor, Tommy, 168–69

Wahishi, Nasser al–, 166
Wall Street Journal, 92, 120
Wardak, Roshanak, 115
War Powers Act, 182
Warsame, Ahmed, 161–63
war weariness, 280, 288–89
Washington Post:
    Afghanistan and, 114, 288
    defense budgets and, 73
    Iran and, 311
    Iraq and, 89
    Libya and, 199

Syria and, 265–66, 303
Yemen and, 169
weapons of mass destruction, 271, 291
    and Iraq, 96, 289
welfare programs, welfare states, 15, 176–77
Westgate Mall assault, 190–91
Westmoreland, William, 30
Weston, J. Kael, 120
West Point, 46–47, 107
whole-of-government approaches, 222–23,
    228
Wickland, Scott, 204–5
Williams, Aaron S., 244
Wilson, Scott, 73
Wilson, Woodrow, 15, 19
Woods, Tyrone, 208–9
Woodward, Bob, 27, 40, 73
World War I, 19, 50, 297
World War II, 19, 249, 269, 272, 286, 288,
    297
    defense budgets and, 50–51
Worth, Robert F., 261

Xi Jinping, 252

Yayi, Thomas Boni, 239
Yemen, 154–59, 161–73, 259
    AQAP and, 154, 158–59, 162, 165–73,
        278, 295, 305, 309
    capturing prisoners and, 161–62
    casualties in, 158, 162–65, 169–72, 305
    civil war in, 305–6
    closure of U.S. embassy in, 151, 306
    drones and, 158–59, 163–65, 168–72,
        228, 278–79, 312
    Obama and, 163–65, 167–69, 228, 273,
        305–6, 309
    police in, 155, 171
    politics and governance of, 158, 165–72,
        228, 305–6
    security forces of, 158, 165–72, 305–6
    smart power and, 228–29
    and strategic ways and means, 273–74,
        278, 281–82
    Zanjubar campaign in, 165–68
Yugoslavia, 63, 177, 183, 272

Zakaria, Tabassum, 238
Zanjubar, 165–68
Zardari, Asif Ali, 133, 141
Zawahiri, Ayman al-, 151
Zazi, Najibullah, 140, 278
Zeleny, Jeff, 10
Zenko, Micah, 222
Zero Dark Thirty fallacy, 314
Zubeyr, Sheikh Moktar Ali, 187